THE DESTRUCTION OF BRAZILIAN SLAVERY

1850–1888

"The Fortnightly Slave-Muster at the Casa Grande, Morro Velho"

Robert Conrad

The
Destruction of
Brazilian Slavery
1850-1888

UNIVERSITY OF CALIFORNIA PRESS

BERKELEY · LOS ANGELES · LONDON

SOURCES OF THE ILLUSTRATIONS

Frontispiece: Richard F. Burton, *Explorations of the Highlands of the Brazil* (London, 1869), Vol. I; numbers 1 through 12: J. B. Debret, *Voyage Pittoresque et historique au Brésil* (3 vols., Paris, 1834, 1835, 1839); number 13: Charles Edmond Akers, *A History of South America* (E. P. Dutton & Co., New York, 1904); number 14: William Hadfield, *Brazil and the River Plate* (London, 1877); numbers 15, 16, and 25: Biblioteca Nacional, Rio de Janeiro; numbers 17 through 19, 22, and 24: Arquivo do Museu Imperial, Petrópolis; number 20: André Rebouças, *Diário e notas autobiográficas* (Livraria José Olympio Editôra, Rio de Janeiro, 1938); number 21: *Revista Illustrada* (1884); number 23: Brazil. Ministerio da Educação, *Floriano, Memórias e Documentos* (Rio de Janeiro, 1939), Vol. II; number 26: Reginald Lloyd, ed., *Twentieth Century Impressions of Brazil* (London, 1913).

University of California Press
Berkeley and Los Angeles, California
University of California Press, Ltd.
London, England
Copyright © 1972, by
The Regents of the University of California
ISBN 0–520–02139–8 (Cloth)
      0–520–02371–4 (Paper)
Library of Congress Catalog Card Number: 74–174457
Printed in the United States of America
Designed by W. H. Snyder

To Ursula

CONTENTS

Part One: 1850–1879

Part Two: 1879–1888

ILLUSTRATIONS

TABLES

PREFACE

From its beginnings in the sixteenth century until its final decades, slavery was an extraordinarily vital and deeply rooted institution in most of the settled parts of Brazil. As a result of its great importance, during the first sixty-five years of the nineteenth century Brazil, in contrast to the United States, failed to develop a vigorous anti-slavery movement. Even during the 1860's and the following decade, opposition to the institution was weak, sporadic, emancipationist (as opposed to abolitionist), and generally inspired from abroad. Why, then, did a true abolitionist movement finally appear in 1880 to emerge triumphantly from the struggle against slavery only eight years later?

This study, covering the period from 1850 to 1888, provides a narrative of the events leading to the downfall of Brazilian slavery and an analysis of the socio-political, economic, and abolitionist forces involved in that process. Extensive research on the period after the suppression of the African slave trade in 1852 has shown that, although the work of the abolitionists was important in the destruction of slavery, economic and demographic developments in various regions of the country also worked strongly against the survival of the institution.

Without powerful opposition from abroad and the moral example of other countries, felt in the highest circles of Brazilian government, Brazil would hardly have acted to deprive herself of her two sources of slaves. The suppression of the African slave trade in the early 1850's and the freeing of the newborn children of slave women in 1871 were decisions which effectively condemned the slave system to extinction, despite its enormous importance to the Brazilian economy and society. The abolition of the slave trade, accomplished after more than forty years of titanic British pressure, by itself condemned Brazilian slavery to eventual extinction. Slaves in Brazil were not capable of maintaining their numbers through natural reproduction; the system was dependent for its replenishment upon a permanent source of new African workers. The decision of 1871 to free the newborn (made palatable by then by the decline of slavery in much of the country) hastened the conversion to a free-labor system. Yet it was not until the beginning of the 1880's that this conversion had proceeded to the point that a powerful, popular, and widespread abolitionist movement could at last appear.

The reasons for this lack of opposition to slavery are not difficult to find. They are related to the survival long after independence of an essentially colonial society. In Brazil slavery was still regarded as necessary to the functioning of the most respected and profitable segment of the economy, even when this was no longer true. A planter class dominated the land and the very lives of a large part of the active population, both slave and free. That same class controlled political institutions and most economic opportunities, including those of merchants, magistrates, bureaucrats, and a small and dependent intelligentsia, the very groups who might have been expected to oppose slavery most strongly.

A comparison of the situation in the United States with that of Brazil reveals the Brazilian situation in bold relief. Unlike the United States, Brazil lacked a large and politicized middle class. Effective popular education was never instituted in Brazil during the period of the Empire (1822–1889), and as late as the 1870's more than eighty-six percent of the population, including slaves, were classified as illiterate. Most of these unschooled people were undoubtedly without any political voice or influence, and therefore made poor candidates for the ranks of an effective protest movement. Protest, when it came, was almost always the individual act of the slave, which took the form of flight, rebellion, or personal assault upon the visible representatives of the system, the overseer or the master.

Until slavery was almost defeated, Brazil, unlike the United States, provided no havens where slaves could find refuge on free soil or where abolitionism could flourish unhampered by local economic interests. Until the appearance of Castro Alves, the poet of the slaves, in the mid-1860's, there was no developed Brazilian school of abolitionist writers, only individual voices expressing personal sentiments. Before 1880 even the press seldom took advantage of its unfettered state under the benign rule of Emperor Pedro II to attack the nation's dominant economic institution, except for brief periods when the issues of the slave trade and free birth were under debate. In the United States Protestant clergymen were among the most fearless and persistent leaders of abolitionism, but in Brazil, where the Catholic Church was the supreme moral and spiritual force, organized religion never developed an anti-slavery mission, and individual clergymen who opposed the institution were exceptional.

In the United States a literate and independent public reacted strongly against slavery a hundred years before this occurred in Brazil, and opponents of slavery in the United States continued to harass the system until they helped to bring on a major war. Again, by contrast, widespread and prolonged violence were avoided in Brazil during the final conversion to a free-labor system. In the United States slavery was struck down in its prime by that section of the country which had given it up, while in Brazil the institution collapsed in a late stage of disintegration. When slavery at last came under attack during the 1880's, most of Brazil had advanced far toward a free-labor system. Nevertheless, a small but powerful group of planters and their representatives defended their "legal" rights until the end, fully aware that slavery could no longer be sustained for a long period of time but determined to derive profit from their remaining workers until the processes of aging and death reduced their economic importance to insignificance.

Sectional differences on the slavery issue were not as clear-cut in Brazil as in the United States, but they were important. As stressed throughout this study, a significant factor in the abolitionist process was the differing degree of commitment to slavery in the various regions of the country. Though Brazilian slavery was subjected to little organized opposition until its last years, regional cracks in the façade of the national pro-slavery consensus were apparent in the 1860's and 1870's, and they rapidly widened during the 1880's to threaten the stability of the entire structure. The most avid supporters of the institution, certainly during the last thirty years of its existence, were concentrated in the coffee-producing provinces—Rio de Janeiro, Minas Gerais, and São Paulo—while in the northeastern sugar and cotton regions and in other less prosperous sections, the interest in slavery was rapidly dissipated during the same period as a result of relative poverty and the consequential shift of tens of thousands of slaves into the coffee zones.

A large body of evidence derived from a study of Brazil as a whole and not merely the coffee provinces, where slavery was strongest and its collapse most dramatic, negates the theory that, as a group, the coffee planters of western and northern São Paulo were in the vanguard of opposition to slavery. Although the planters of that part of Brazil showed signs of a greater willingness than planters elsewhere to adopt modern solutions to their economic problems, in part as a result of their greater affluence, few of them displayed much of a tendency to adopt a free-labor system until only months before the abolition of slavery. The coffee planters of São Paulo, in fact, were one of the most powerful and adamant pro-slavery groups in Brazil until the second half of 1887, when a rapidly changing local and national situation forced them to accomplish at once that conversion to a free-labor system which had been under way for decades in other parts of the country. The elucidation of the role of São Paulo in the process of abolition is a major aim of this work, for it was indeed an important one. As the leading abolitionist, Joaquim Nabuco, put it years after the slaves had been freed, "the last of the apostles can become the first, like St. Paul (São Paulo), in services and proselytism."

Throughout this study I have been concerned with the attitudes of the slaveholding planter class and their opinions regarding labor, slavery, class relationships, and economic and social organization. Convinced that traditionalism is a factor contributing even today to the underdevelopment of Latin America, I have given much attention to the variety of fascinating if not always logical arguments which the slaveholding class employed in the defense of slavery during this period of extraordinary challenge to their economic and social privileges. I have shown, I believe, the general disregard of many members of this class for law, international obligations, and even the ethics of their own society when these were out of harmony with their interests.

The aims of the abolitionists have also been the object of some analysis. These varied greatly, from ardent and consistent commitment to justice and social change to late and reluctant surrender to the unavoidable. As the struggle neared its culmination in 1887 and 1888, most informed Brazilians probably felt a strong desire to rid their country of an unjust and humiliating institution, but far fewer persons were conscious of a need for collateral reforms, which the leaders of the movement had been urging for years: the establishment of a system of popular education, broader political representation, and alterations in the landholding system. Abolitionism, however, meant more than liberation, as Joaquim Nabuco and other prominent leaders claimed. Abolition, they hoped, was to be the first of a series of national reforms intended to end the domination of the traditional slaveholding class over the nation's institutions. The tragic aftermath of slavery is not one of the subjects of this book, but the work would be incomplete if it did not reveal that the reformers of the era envisioned not only freedom for the slaves but the transformation of Brazil into a social and political democracy in which ex-slaves and the impoverished rural population would be prepared to participate more fully in national life.

The book is divided into two parts. The first, topical as well as chronological, deals with the period between the suppression of the African slave trade at mid-century and the beginning of the abolitionist movement thirty years later. It contains a study of the inter-provincial slave trade and its effects upon the equilibrium of slavery in the nation as a whole, as well as an analysis of the national debate over the liberation of the newborn and the consequences of that vital reform. The main purpose of the first part is to reveal both the importance of slavery to Brazilian society during the period from 1850 to 1880 and the causes of that institution's rapid decline during those thirty years. It is intended to set the stage for the second part of the work, which deals with the phenomenon of abolitionism in the various regions of the country.

The current dispute over the character of Latin American slavery (as compared with that of the United States) is not a major concern of this work, and therefore allusions to the crueler aspects of Brazilian slavery have normally been made only when they seemed relevant to the central theme of slavery's decline. The author, however, is now preparing a book in which he hopes to reveal the character of Brazilian slavery more completely

ACKNOWLEDGMENTS

Many persons and organizations have helped to make this study possible or have contributed their time and knowledge toward its improvement. First of all I am thankful to my wife, Ursula, who has read the manuscript several times and offered many valuable suggestions.

I am grateful to the staffs of the various archives and libraries where I have worked, including the Biblioteca Nacional and ministerial archives and libraries in Rio de Janeiro, the Instituto Histórico e Geográfico Brasileiro, the Arquivo Nacional, the public archives of Bahia, Pará, São Paulo, Sergipe, Guanabara and the state of Rio de Janeiro, the British Museum and Public Record Office in London, the Library of Congress, the New York Public Library, the Newberry Library, the libraries of the University of Illinois and the University of Chicago, and the library system at Columbia University. I am particularly indebted to Dona Constança Wright and the staff of the archive and library at the Brazilian Ministry of Foreign Affairs, Professor Manoel Cardozo and the staff of the Oliveira Lima Library at the Catholic University of America in Washington, D.C., Professor Thalita de Oliveira of the Public Library of the state of Rio de Janeiro in Niterói, Professors José Luiz Werneck da Silva and Ondemar Ferreira Dias of the Divisão do Patrimonio Histórico e Artístico of the state of Guanabara, Francisco Marques dos Santos and the staff of the Imperial Museum in Petrópolis, and Lourenço Lacombe, director of the Divisão de Documentação Histórica of the same institution. The distinguished Brazilian scholars, Caio Prado, Jr., Sergio Buarque de Holanda, and Octavio Ianni also graciously granted me their valuable time and assistance.

I am thankful too to Professors Marvin Harris, Dwight C. Miner, Raymond S. Sayers, and Ronald Schneider, who helped me at an early stage in the development of this study. I owe much as well to Professors David Brion Davis, Robert William Fogel, Peter d'A. Jones, Franklin W. Knight, Robert M. Levine, John V. Lombardi, Joseph L. Love, Peter McKeon, Gilbert Osofsky, Max Savelle, and Stanley J. Stein, and to James Gottreich, Barry L. Smith, and Mark Cramer, who have read part or all of the manuscript and offered useful advice.

Financial aid came from several sources. An NDFL-Fulbright-Hays Fellowship enabled me to travel to Brazil in the spring of 1965 and to remain there for some fifteen months. A graduate research assistantship from the Institute of Latin American Studies at Columbia University, arranged by Professor Charles Wagley, made possible the rapid completion of a preliminary study of the abolition of the Brazilian slave trade, which gave me insights into the broader problem of the decline of the Brazilian slave system. Grants received from the American Philosophical Society and the University of Illinois at Chicago Circle also helped to finance research in Brazil during the summer of 1969.

Finally, I am particularly grateful to Professor Lewis Hanke, whose advice, assistance, and encouragement over an extended period of time made this study possible. I am of course responsible for all of the opinions expressed, and any mistakes of fact or judgment are mine alone.

R. C.

ABBREVIATIONS
USED IN FOOTNOTES

AESP Arquivo do Estado de São Paulo, São Paulo
AHI Arquivo Histórico do Itamarati, Rio de Janeiro
AMIP Arquivo de Museu Imperial, Petrópolis
AN Arquivo Nacional, Rio de Janeiro
APS Arquivo Público do Estado de Sergipe, Aracaju
BFSP *British and Foreign State Papers*
BNSM Biblioteca Nacional, Seção de Manuscritos, Rio de Janeiro
DPHAG Divisão do Patrimonio Histórico e Artístico, Estado da Guanabara
HAHR *Hispanic American Historical Review*
IHGB Instituto Histórico e Geográfico Brasileiro, Rio de Janeiro
PRO Public Record Office, London
SECRJ Secretaria de Educação e Cultura, Departamento de Difusão Cultural, Biblioteca Pública do Estado, Niterói

THE BRAZILIAN EMPIRE

SUGAR and COFFEE
PRODUCTION

Sugar
Coffee

Part One : 1850–1879

The late resolution
of the Quakers in Pennsylvania
to set at liberty all their negro slaves,
may satisfy us that their number
cannot be very great.

ADAM SMITH,
The Wealth of Nations

1

INTRODUCTION:
THE FOUNDATIONS OF BRAZILIAN SLAVERY

SLAVERY AND THE BRAZILIAN ECONOMY

In the years following the American and French Revolutions slavery came under strong pressure in areas of the world under the direct influence of Western European opinion, and after the fall of Napoleon, European liberalism, backed by the power of Great Britain, condemned both slavery and the African slave trade. The ability of a particular New World slave society to withstand this attack upon slavery was in approximate proportion to the importance of the institution to its economy. If geographic conditions favored the production of crops or minerals with good markets, if a large slave population was already on hand and an alternative labor force was unavailable, slavery persisted well into the nineteenth century, or even gained a new importance in response to new circumstances and opportunities.[1] In such societies, slavery was deemed

---

1. An obvious example in Latin America, aside from coffee-producing regions of Brazil, is Cuba, where slavery was stimulated during the nineteenth century by the growth of the sugar and tobacco industries. See Franklin W. Knight, *Slave Society in Cuba* (Madison, Wisconsin, 1970), pp. 3–46.

essential, and the anti-slavery philosophy was repelled. In some countries—notably Cuba and Brazil—where slaves could not maintain their
numbers through natural reproduction, the African slave trade remained
almost as sacrosanct as slavery itself.[2]

Of all the countries of Latin America, Brazil was the one where
economic, geographic, and social conditions most favored a rejection of
the anti-slavery crusade, for not even Cuba possessed the same pervasive
attachment to slavery until the nineteenth century. Rich in minerals and
almost entirely tropical, Brazil could produce precious stones and metals,
sugar, coffee, cotton, tobacco, and other valuable products, and early in
the colonial era her economy had been geared to the production of such
exports. The large-scale plantation system established along the Brazilian
littoral in the sixteenth and seventeenth centuries had required inexpensive, docile workers, and little effort had been made to engage
European peasants to work under plantation conditions. Indians at first,
and then Africans, the latter more expensive but hardier workers, were
found and utilized. Unlike Europeans, these darker peoples with their
"barbaric" customs and religions could be enslaved without prohibitive
strains on European morality and tradition, and their enslavement could
be justified by the opportunity to be found in the New World environment for conversion to Christianity and a more civilized way of life.[3]
More important, these new peoples were near at hand. Indians in the
Brazilian hinterland could be herded together by raiding parties or otherwise enticed into a servile state,[4] and on the coast of Africa, a short
voyage away, there was an apparently inexhaustible supply of black
human beings. It was this labor force that produced most of Brazil's
tropical and mineral exports for some three hundred years.

As the colonial period neared its end, slavery was the institution most
characteristic of Brazilian society, and, as independence approached, the
emergence of coffee cultivation strengthened slavery's grip upon the
economy.[5] Planted in Maranhão in the Brazilian north during the first
half of the eighteenth century, coffee was brought to Rio de Janeiro in
the 1770's, and in the years immediately following the establishment of
the Portuguese royal government in Rio (1808), coffee became the most
important crop of the nearby mountainous hinterland. From 1817 to
1820 Brazilian coffee exportation averaged about 5,500 metric tons per

2. For causes of the decline of the Brazilian slave population, see Rollie E.
Poppino, *Brazil, The Land and People* (New York, 1968), p. 168.
3. *Ibid.,* p. 162.
4. See Alexander Marchant, *From Barter to Slavery* (Baltimore, 1942); Richard
M. Morse, *The Bandeirantes* (New York, 1965); Poppino, *Brazil,* pp. 57–60, 78–
83.
5. Caio Prado, Jr., *The Colonial Background of Modern Brazil* (Berkeley and
Los Angeles, 1967), pp. 313, 325; Celso Furtado, *The Economic Growth of
Brazil* (Berkeley and Los Angeles, 1968), p. 123; Emilia Viotti da Costa, *Da
senzala à colônia* (São Paulo, 1966), p. 19 ff.

year, and from 1826 to 1829 the average annual exportation reached nearly 25,000 tons, a gain of nearly four hundred percent.[6] During the next twenty years coffee production continued to grow, and the crop became a powerful bulwark of the slave system, providing the means to import slaves despite the illegality of the slave trade after 1831. Once the African traffic was finally suppressed in mid-century, coffee production continued to absorb a major part of the slave population, drawing slaves from less prosperous regions of the country into the coffee-producing areas. Thus, coffee planters developed the greatest personal interest in the survival of the slave system, an interest which lasted in limited areas until the last days of slavery.

Even without coffee, however, slavery would have survived longer in Brazil than in most of the rest of Latin America, for it was of extraordinary economic and social importance even in non-coffee areas. An important characteristic of Brazilian slavery during much of the nineteenth century was its omnipresence. As late as the 1870's all of the Empire's 643 *municípios* for which statistics were available contained slaves, ranging from the 48,939 in the Município Neutro (the district of the capital) to the three bondsmen registered in the Bahian município of Villa Verde.[7] Slaves were not only an almost universal element in the population, but were also employed in nearly every kind of labor (see Table 19 in Appendix I). Aside from the major products, slaves also produced a large variety of minor exports in almost every region of the country. A Brazilian writer defended the continuation of the African slave trade in 1826 with an enumeration of average annual exports from Brazil for the years 1815 through 1821. These included respectable amounts of sugar, coffee, cotton, tobacco, ox hides, brazilwood, rice, cacao, sarsaparilla, cinnamon, oil of copaiba (an indigenous stimulant), curcuma (a yellow dye root), vanilla, anil, gold, diamonds, and various woods for dyes, construction, and cabinet making—all allegedly produced by slave labor.[8]

6. Sebastião Ferreira Soares, *Notas estatisticas sobre a producção agrícola e carestia dos generos alimenticios no Imperio do Brazil* (Rio de Janeiro, 1860), p. 209. For the quantity and value of Brazilian coffee production from 1850 to 1890, see Table 26 in Appendix I. For more complete data on coffee production, see Affonso de E. Taunay, *Pequena historia do café no Brasil, 1727–1937* (Rio de Janeiro, 1945), pp. 547–549.
7. Directoria Geral da Estatistica, *Recenseamento da população no Imperio do Brazil a que se procedeu no dia 1º de Agosto de 1872* (21 vols.; Rio de Janeiro, 1873–1876), III, 508–511; XXI, 58–59.
8. José Eloy Pessoa da Silva, *Memoria sobre a escravatura e projecto de colonisação dos europeus, e pretos da Africa no Imperio do Brasil* (Rio de Janeiro, 1826), p. 15. For another list of Brazilian products drawn up a few years earlier, see John Mawe, *Travels in the Interior of Brazil* (London, 1812), pp. 467–471. See also Luis Amaral, *Historia geral da agricultura brasileira* (2 vols.; São Paulo, 1958), I, 291–407; II, 3–354.

Population statistics for the early nineteenth century are of questionable accuracy, but any of those available may be used to show that the slaves of Brazil represented an immense investment. As reliable perhaps as any before the 1872 census are the statistics on slave and free populations which Perdigão Malheiro gave for the years 1798, 1817–18, and 1864 (see Table 1). These statistics show that in the earlier years more than half of the inhabitants of Brazil (excluding Indians, who were largely outside the national life) were slaves, and only a small percentage of non-whites were free after nearly three centuries of slavery in Brazil.[9] By 1864 slaves made up less than a fifth of the Brazilian population, due to a rapid increase of the free population that had no parallel among the slaves. Yet the number of slaves had hardly decreased since the earlier years, and they still constituted a huge capital investment.[10]

In certain parts of the country slaves were nearly always more numerous than free persons.[11] A military chart of 1821 placed the slave and free populations of the province of Rio de Janeiro at 173,775 and 159,271 respectively, with proportionally larger percentages of slaves in rural areas, and by 1840 the total population of the same province, where the coffee industry was then largely concentrated, had risen to nearly 400,000, including nearly 225,000 slaves.[12] By the 1870's the free population of Rio de Janeiro province exceeded the slave population by nearly 200,000, but the slaves of four coffee-producing municípios (São Fidelis, Vassouras, Valença, and Piraí) still outnumbered the free population by more than 10,000 (71,954 slaves and 61,205 free persons). In neighboring São Paulo the coffee município of Campinas contained 13,685 slaves and only 6,887 free persons about 1872, while in nearby Bananal 8,281 slaves lived among 7,325 free persons.[13]

Slaves were also abundant in major towns, particularly during the first half of the nineteenth century when the African traffic kept them comparatively inexpensive. In 1849, just before the importation of Africans ended, the population of the largely urban Município Neutro, the city

9. Poppino, *Brazil*, p. 170. For the significance of this latter fact, as it relates to the alleged mildness of Brazilian slavery, see Marvin Harris, *Patterns of Race in the Americas* (New York, 1964), pp. 85–86.
10. For other population statistics, see Stanley J. Stein, *Vassouras: A Brazilian Coffee County, 1850–1890* (New York, 1970), pp. 294–296, and Tables 2 through 6 in Appendix I.
11. Stanley J. Stein and Barbara H. Stein place the Brazilian slave population of 1820 at about two million, or two-thirds of the total population. See *The Colonial Heritage of Latin America* (New York, 1970), p. 148.
12. Mappa dos fogos, pessoas livres e escravos comprehendidos nas freguezias da cidade e provincia do Rio de Janeiro, AN, I G 1-428; *Relatorio do presidente da provincia do Rio de Janeiro . . . para o anno de 1840 a 1841* (2nd ed.; Niterói, 1851).
13. *Recenseamento da população*, XV, 352–354, XIX, 427–430.

of Rio de Janeiro and environs, included about 156,000 free persons and 110,000 slaves, and twenty-three years later the 48,939 slaves of the same município still represented nearly eighteen percent of the population.[14] In 1872 one out of every ten slaves (153,815 persons) resided in the municípios containing the city of Rio de Janeiro and the twenty provincial capitals.[15]

Until the end of the slave trade, and even after in some parts of Brazil, slaves rather than animals were used to transport most heavy burdens and even people through the streets of the major cities. "The Negroes who are employed as hired porters to carry burthens," wrote Lieutenant Chamberlain early in the century, "are always to be found in considerable numbers, in the wide part of the Rua Direita, near the Custom House, with ponderous poles and strong ropes for carrying, or with low badly contrived trucks for dragging merchandize from place to place." [16] The first slaves which the British pastor, Robert Walsh, saw in Rio in 1828 were ragged carriers, some "yoked to drays," others moving burdens while "chained by neck and legs . . . ." [17] Thirty-two years later the slave porters of Bahia, who were hired out by their masters to carry produce up the steep slopes between the lower and upper districts of the city, were similarly described as dressed in tattered bits of cotton and burdened with immense loads carried on poles balanced on their backs, to which labor these "black animals" were subjected as long as strength remained to them.[18] A Bahian, writing in 1887, revealed that before 1850 wagons or carts were almost never used in his city to carry loads. Weights were carried on the heads of slaves or "by means of the most barbaric and anti-economic instrument imaginable—the pole and line," with which eight or even twelve men were sometimes employed in carrying a single burden. Wealthy persons were transported about Brazilian cities or even through the countryside in sedan chairs, palanquins, or hammocks with a similar lavish use of personnel, two men as bearers with at times one or two pairs of substitutes and one or two *mucamas* or female servants occupied in keeping the curtains of the palanquin discreetly closed if the passenger was a lady. Yet these typical slave scenes, with their ostentatious use of manpower, grew rare in the cities of Brazil during the last decades of

14. *Correio Mercantil,* Rio de Janeiro, January 7, 1851; *Recenseamento da população,* XXI, 58–59.
15. *Ibid.*
16. Sir Henry Chamberlain, *Vistas e Costumes da Cidade e arredores do Rio de Janeiro em 1819–1820* (Rio de Janeiro, n.d.), p. 199.
17. Robert Walsh, *Notices of Brazil in 1828 and 1829* (2 vols.; London, 1830), I, 134–135.
18. Maximilian I, *Recollections of My Life* (3 vols.; London, 1868), III, 163–164.

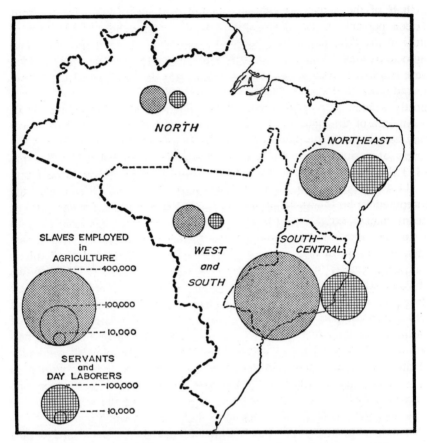

FIGURE 1. Slaves Employed in Agriculture and as Servants and Day Laborers, 1872, by Region.

Source: *Recenseamento da população*

slavery, as captive workers, in short supply, were shifted into rural areas to perform the practical productive labor for which they had always been primarily intended. By 1887, the sedan chair had almost disappeared from Bahian streets, free men were performing most of the mechanical services in the city, and most of the slaves employed there were household servants.[19]

A large percentage of persons regarded as having occupations were slaves. Of some 46,000 persons credited with occupations in a 1799 report from Maranhão, nearly 40,000 were captives.[20] At about the same time the slaves of the town of Curitiba in the Brazilian south made

19. L. Anselmo da Fonseca, *A escravidão, o clero e o abolicionismo* (Bahia, 1887), pp. 182–184. Bahian slave institutions were, however, durable. A few sedan chairs remained on the streets of Bahia even after the abolition of slavery. See Raimundo Nina Rodrigues, *Os africanos no Brasil* (São Paulo, 1935), p. 173.
20. BNSM, I-17, 12, 4, No. 22.

up half of the active population, though they constituted only about sixteen percent of the inhabitants.[21] In the 1872 census nearly four-fifths of the slave population, including children, were classified as having occupations. More than 800,000 were agricultural workers, 270,000 were employed as servants or day laborers, and another twenty thousand in trades and crafts, or as fishermen, miners, and sailors. Nearly 54,000, mostly women, were seamstresses and textile workers (see Table 19).

An idea of the value of slaves compared with other plantation assets may be glimpsed from figures on capital invested in the agricultural industry at various times and places during the nineteenth century. In 1833 the 48,240 slaves on 603 Bahian sugar plantations were valued at 14,472 contos (14,472:000$000)[22] compared to 17,823 contos computed to be the value of the land, buildings, horses, oxen, forests, steam engines, irrigation systems, and all other assets of the plantation, a sum not much greater than the value of the slaves.[23] The value of captive workers in relation to other assets undoubtedly declined in the following decades in Bahia, but in coffee regions a similarly high ratio of slave values to plantation values lasted into the 1880's. In 1882, 230 slaves on a coffee plantation in Rio de Janeiro province were valued at 280 contos compared to a value of 354 contos on all the other assets of the property, including the coffee trees and the land. Over a thirty-year period after mid-century, slaves accounted for more than half of the plantation assets of the coffee-producing município of Vassouras, and in 1857/58 slave values comprised 73 percent of that community's fazenda wealth.[24]

Almost any threat to the slave system or to the importation of Africans upon which the system depended was an occasion for a remonstrance from persons arguing the importance of slaves to the economy. Countless documents attest to this. When early in the nineteenth century João VI imposed an eight-day quarantine on Africans arriving at

---

21. Octavio Ianni, *As metamorfoses do escravo* (São Paulo, 1962), p. 90.

22. Brazilian currency units used in the nineteenth century were the *conto, milréis,* and the *real* (plural: *réis*). One thousand milréis was a conto, written 1:000$000. In 1825 a conto was worth $1,050 (U.S.), $580 in 1850, and $550 in 1875. See Stein, *Vassouras*, p. 293.

23. Amaral, *Agricultura brasileira*, I, 341. In the sixteenth century, the value of slaves was also high in relation to other assets. See *Documentos para a história do açucar* (3 vols.; Rio de Janeiro, 1954, 1956, 1963), III, 84–105.

24. *The South American Journal and Brazil and River Plate Mail*, London, July 20, 1882; Stein, *Vassouras*, pp. 225–226. The nine coffee plantations of the Viscount Nova Friburgo in Rio de Janeiro province were evaluated in 1883 at 2,570 contos. The total value of the land, buildings, machinery, and livestock was put at 943 contos; the 1,627 slaves were thought to be worth 1,627 contos. See C. F. van Delden Laërne, *Brazil and Java. Report on Coffee Culture* (London and The Hague, 1885), pp. 332–333, 339–342.

Rio de Janeiro, a petition from forty-two slave merchants of that city called the measure unwise and harmful to commerce, arguing that slaves were almost the only workers employed or employable in agriculture. If their importation were reduced by as much as one-third, they warned, incalculable harm would result, both for agriculture and public finances, since the annual income to the treasury from taxes on the importation of some thirty to forty thousand slaves was two million cruzados.[25]

When British naval vessels began seizing Portuguese slave ships off the coast of Africa about 1812, protests resulted. A petition from the merchants of Bahia to João, who had just recently established his government at Rio de Janeiro, warned that the injury caused by the seizures of slave vessels was "common to the whole nation, whose prosperity and maintenance in Brazil is derived, in great measure, from the resources which this very traffic affords it, for the cultivation of the produce of the country, and for its consumption and exportation." It was not possible "that the general order of things, which have received the stamp of ages, should thus be modified or changed, without running the risk of greater inconvenience." British seizures of ships on the coast of Africa had already resulted in the loss of fortunes, in a paralysis of African commerce, a decline in shipping, and a decay of agriculture due to a lack of workers, as well as a decrease of royal revenues.[26]

In 1818 a high Portuguese official stressed the importance of the slave trade in an advisory message to King João VI. "A very great quantity of workers" was needed to labor in the mines, he wrote, and many more to provide the sustenance of the miners. The sugar mills required hands (*braços*) for the harvest, the planting, "and the other tasks of a great factory." He compared the Brazilian sugar plantation with a town or village where there was need of a chaplain, a surgeon, an infirmary, carpentry and blacksmith shops, herds of animals, gardens, a flour mill, and other equipment. Tobacco cultivation required many workers "occupied in a continuous tillage, in a very careful curing process lasting many days." Domestic service and urban public works required slaves, "because there are no laboring men as in Europe, nor white men who want to be servants or pages." [27]

A German mining engineer used similar arguments to justify slavery and the slave trade. The slave, wrote Wilhelm von Eschwege, who was

25. Representação dos negociantes de escravos, BNSM, II, 34, 27, 15.
26. *Representation of the Brazilian Merchants Against the Insults Offered to the Portuguese Flag, and Against the Violent and Oppressive Capture of Several of Their Vessels by Some Officers Belonging to the English Navy* (London, 1813), pp. 4–7.
27. Sôbre a questão da escravatura (Por Thomaz Antônio da Villanova Portugal) BNSM, I-32, 14, 22.

well acquainted with Brazil, had always been the "tiller of the soil, the maker of sugar and brandy, the pack animal, the breaker and pulverizer of stones, the cook, the footman, groom, shoemaker, tailor, courier and carrier." The slave was the only property of the free man. Without his help the free man could consider himself poor even with an abundance of money. Without slaves mining and agriculture would cease to exist. The slave provided the sustenance of the master, who would otherwise emigrate or live in misery. The newly freed person avoided all labor and every master, working only to avoid starvation. Under these conditions, Eschwege believed, Brazilian landowners had no choice but to rent or buy slaves.[28]

The possession of slaves, however, was not restricted to a small master class. Although wealthy landholders always owned a majority of Brazilian slaves, particularly during the final years, many poorer people lived from the labor of one or more captives. For many persons slaves were the sole source of income. The free Brazilian, wrote Eschwege, normally owned a single slave who provided his support. Even when poor, "he does not move a straw, for even in idleness he finds a living." [29] A British traveler, John Mawe, noted that Africans were among the first possessions acquired by persons amassing new wealth.[30] Another Britisher observed in 1828 that a large part of Rio's wealth was "vested in this property, and slaves form the income and support of a vast number of individuals, who hire them out as people in Europe do horses and mules." Slavery prevented the adoption of labor-saving machinery, "as so many persons have an interest in its being performed by slaves alone." This was true in the customhouse of Rio de Janeiro, where an English crane capable of permitting two slaves to do the work of twenty was introduced, "but this was violently opposed and effectively resisted, as every person in the establishment possessed a number of negroes, even down to the lowest clerks, who had five or six each, for whose labour they were paid." [31]

Similarly, the slaves belonging to officials at the diamond mines in Minas Gerais were guaranteed employment in the mines in their masters' contracts. The hiring of blacks to the diamond works in the city of Tejuco was "the favorite occupation of all ranks. . . , rich and poor . . . . Numbers of persons," wrote Mawe, "are thus induced to reside in Tejuco under various pretexts, but with no other view than to get their negroes into the service, and to live idly on their wages, and on

28. W. L. von Eschwege, *Pluto Brasiliensis* (2 vols.; São Paulo, 1944), II, 445–447.
29. *Ibid.*
30. Mawe, *Travels,* p. 362.
31. Walsh, *Notices,* II, 361–362.

what they can conceal or pick up." [32] Much the same was true of the typical slaveowner in the mining town of Ouro Preto:

His negroes constitute his principal property [wrote Mawe], and them he manages so ill, that the profits of their labor hardly defray the expenses of their maintenance. . . . every trade is occupied either by mulattoes or negroes, both of which classes seem superior in intellect to their masters, because they make a better use of it.[33]

In Bahia early in the nineteenth century, slaves working as porters or in trades were the sole support of many idle families.[34] Labor, in fact, was looked upon by free persons as dishonorable and worthy only of chattels.

Slavery was so ingrained in the mores of Brazil as to reduce the importance of race as a criterion of slave or free status. Legally and customarily, the condition of the newborn child was determined before 1871 not by the color of his skin but by the status of his mother. "The regulating principle," wrote the lawyer and student of slavery, Perdigão Malheiro, in the 1860's, "is that—*partus sequitur ventrem*—as Roman law resolved." The child of the female slave came into the world in legal bondage, "little mattering whether his father was slave or free." [35]

Observance of this legal principle resulted in the existence of white slaves in Brazil, as attested to in 1827 by a member of the national Chamber of Deputies.[36] "It is a taint in the blood," as Walsh put it with Anglo-Saxon incredulity, "which no length of time, no change in relationship, no alteration of colour can obliterate." Slaves could be found of every shade, this same writer attested, "from jet black to pure white," while Henry Koster observed that "no line is drawn at which the near approach to the colour and blood of the whites entitles the child, whose mother is a slave, to freedom." [37] One of the few Brazilian opponents of the abolition of the importation of African slaves provided an explanation:

In many combinations of diverse bloods, the African origin has disappeared, and the slaves came to be of the same species as the masters . . . . A slave master almost never frees the children he has with his slave women, and

32. Mawe, *Travels*, pp. 358–359.
33. *Ibid.*, pp. 251–252.
34. Oficio do Conde da Ponte ao Visconde d'Anandia, IHGB, Copias extrahidas do Archivo do Conselho Ultramarino, XX, 304.
35. Agostinho Marques Perdigão Malheiro, *A escravidão no Brasil* (2 vols.; 2nd ed.; São Paulo, 1944), I, 50.
36. *Annaes do Parlamento Brasileiro. Câmara dos Senhores Deputados* (hereafter *Annaes da Câmara*) (1827), III, 41.
37. Walsh, *Notices*, II, 352; Henry Koster, *Travels in Brazil* (2 vols.; 2nd ed.; London, 1817), II, 190–191.

he demands of them all the labor and submission he requires of the others: he sells them, trades them, or transmits them to his heirs. If one of his legitimate sons receives them as an inheritance, he makes no distinction between them and his other slaves; thus a brother can become the owner of his brothers; over them he exercises the same tyranny and satiates the same desires.

As late as September 1886 Princess Isabel, the heiress to the Brazilian throne, officiated at the liberation of two young "properly dressed" white men in a ceremony in Rio de Janeiro.[38]

If whites or near whites were sometimes kept in a state of slavery, mulattoes or blacks (sometimes slaves themselves) also owned slaves.[39] On an estate of the wealthy Benedictine monks, the British traveler, Henry Koster, met a mulatto slave who managed the property and owned two slaves of his own, but was "himself obliged to attend to the business of the plantations and to see that the work of his masters is properly executed."[40]

In Brazil, slavery was much more than an economic institution, for the possession of slaves was not only profitable, but elevated the status of the owner in the eyes of others. There was a personal kind of satisfaction to be derived from the ownership of slaves which was frankly described about 1855 by the scion of a rich planter family of Rio de Janeiro province:

The slave is not only an agent of labor and of production. One must be ignorant of the human heart to think so. The slave is an object of luxury, a means of satisfying certain vanities and certain vices of the nature of man. Just as landed property has certain attractions, so also the slave offers to the master a certain pleasure of command and authority, which exists in the human heart, we know not whether for good or evil.[41]

Years later another Brazilian revealed the fondness of slave masters and their women for collecting about them a class of female slaves known as mucamas, "seeing that it is a dominant idea among us, particularly on our estates, that it is a signal of nobility and wealth to have at the orders of our ladies a large number of those slave women generally

38. Frederico L. C. Burlamaque, *Analytica acerca do commercio d'escravos e acerca dos malles da escravidão domestica* (Rio de Janeiro, 1837), p. 31; *South American Journal*, October 16, 1886.
39. Eschwege, *Pluto Brasiliensis*, II, 445–447.
40. Koster, *Travels*, II, 221.
41. Luiz Peixoto de Lacerda Werneck, *Idéas sobre colonisação precedidas de uma succinta exposição dos principios geraes que regem a população* (Rio de Janeiro, 1855), p. 47.

occupied in thousands of useless futilities." [42] In 1858 a Brazilian confessed that planters were accustomed to being served by slaves and to rule over them with absolute power. The relationship between masters and slaves was so "comfortable" that masters would not abandon that relationship unless forced to do so.[43]

Even Englishmen owned slaves in Brazil, despite official British opposition and the Brougham Law of 1843, which prohibited the purchase or sale of slaves by British subjects in foreign countries.[44] Probably the largest single British slaveholding organization in Brazil was the São João d'El Rei Mining Company of Minas Gerais, which in mid-century employed some 800 of its own slaves and hired a thousand more, and still possessed 200 slaves as late as 1879.[45] Departing from the usual British opposition to slavery, a company report of 1842 recommended kindness and goodwill toward its charges in Minas Gerais, "from the conviction that, although the colour of their skin be different from ours, they are the creatures of the Almighty Creator, and entitled to the utmost forbearance at our hands by reason of the inferior position in which it has pleased Providence to permit them to be placed." [46] Even a British diplomat could succumb to the reality of the Brazilian environment. Robert Hesketh, British Consul in Rio de Janeiro and long a critic of Brazilian slavery,[47] admitted to his government in 1840 that he employed three slaves as domestic servants, though promising to dismiss them with the reservation "that in this country of slave labour, no provisions can be had, no articles of dress made, no dwellings repaired, nor any hired conveyance, or porterage made use of, without employing slaves." [48]

42. Veloso de Albuquerque Lins, Ensaio sôbre a emancipação do elemento servil, AMIP, 148–7179.
43. Viotti da Costa, Da senzala à colônia, p. 120.
44. Richard F. Burton, Explorations of the Highlands of the Brazil (2 vols.; London, 1869), I, 272. In 1882 the Brougham Law was "practically . . . a dead letter." South American Journal, March 16, 1882.
45. Daniel P. Kidder and J. C. Fletcher, Brazil and the Brazilians (Philadelphia, 1857), p. 137; The Rio News, Rio de Janeiro, October 15, 1879; Annaes da Câmara (1879), V, 256–257.
46. Bernard Hollowood, The Story of Morro Velho (London, 1955), p. 35. The author is grateful to Professor Robert W. Randall for a gift of this study of the British mining company. For a detailed account of conditions at Morro Velho in the late 1860's, see Burton, Explorations, I, 236–278.
47. See Robert Hesketh, "A British Consular Report on Slavery in Northern Brazil," in Lewis Hanke (ed.), History of Latin American Civilization (Boston, 1967), II, 174–180.
48. Hesketh to Palmerston, Rio de Janeiro, December 12, 1840, Class B. Correspondence with Spain, Portugal, Brazil, the Netherlands and Sweden Relative to the Slave Trade. From May 11 to December 31, 1840, inclusive (London, 1841), p. 731. (Henceforth Class A. or Class B., with dates.)

Slavery pervaded Brazilian life, finding its way into the press in a day-to-day manner in the form of advertisements for the sale and rental of slaves or for the capture of runaways. The slave was the servant in the home and in the street, the wet nurse of the master's legal children and often the mother of his illegitimate ones. The system created professions: the slave merchant, the importer, the evaluator, the *capitão-do-mato* or bush captain—the local hireling who captured runaways.[49] All classes and types of persons could own slaves legally: priests and friars, the Emperor and his family, the rich and the poor, blacks and whites, the foreigner and the native. The Brazilian government itself possessed them and used their labor. One hundred seventy "slaves of the nation" were employed in 1845 in the Marine Arsenal in Rio de Janeiro. Two hundred forty-four slaves were at work at the various palaces and rural estates of the Imperial Family in 1831.[50]

The slave in Brazil [asserted a writer in 1870] occupies a very important place in all the conditions of the existence of the country; he represents labor, the origin of all wealth; he represents capital through his value and through his production; he represents small industry, because, aside from agricultural and domestic labor, he is employed in all the crafts. Finally, the slave is an integral part of the Brazilian society, which has thus been organized over the long span of three centuries.[51]

SLAVERY AND BRAZILIAN SOCIETY

Brazilian reluctance to abandon the slave system was not solely a consequence of the institution's great social and economic importance. The maintenance of slavery was also intimately related to the survival of traditional attitudes which sheltered and protected most of the customs and institutions that Brazil had inherited from the colonial past. Not only slavery remained vigorous during the first two-thirds of the nineteenth century, but most other characteristics of the era of Portuguese rule also survived with remarkably little alteration. The population was still largely rural, and the cities consequently small and dependent.

49. For documents relating to these professions, see Avaliadores de escravos, 1777–1819, DPHAG, 6-1-10; Capitão do mato, Freguesia de N. Sra. da Guia de Pacopaiba, 1823, DPHAG, 40-3-74.
50. *Relatorio do Ministerio da Marinha de 1845,* Chart No. 6; Relação das despesas com os escravos das quintas da Bôa Vista e Cajú, até Julho de 1831, BNSM, I-35, 32, 20.
51. Peixoto de Brito, *Considerações geraes sôbre a emancipação dos escravos no Imperio do Brazil e indicação dos meios para realisa-la* (Lisbon, 1870), p. 3.

Agriculture and commerce dominated the economy at the expense of industry (practically non-existent before 1850), but farming remained wasteful and primitive, and foreigners still controlled much of the lucrative overseas commerce. Interior transportation was difficult, expensive, and dangerous, and movement between the provinces was largely confined to coastal shipping, including the movement of large numbers of slaves from region to region. Social classes were stratified, as they had been under the Portuguese, and the individual's class origins nearly always determined the place he was to occupy in society. Education was elitist, unscientific, impractical, and reserved for the few. Most Brazilians, therefore, remained illiterate, although a small minority acquired an education which granted prestige and power to the individual and a ruling class, but granted small returns to the multitude. As late as 1872 less than one-fifth of all free Brazilians were classified as literate in a national census, and not one slave in a thousand could read and write (see Table 17).[52] Government displayed a certain grandeur in the apparatus of a constitutional monarchy, including an impressive Emperor and a bicameral legislature, but much of the real power in the provinces was in the hands of the slaveholding landlord class.[53]

In the years after 1850 the slow pace of Brazilian change was somewhat quickened, but life styles were altered primarily in the cities and among the elite, while the average Brazilian on the land and in the isolated interior towns witnessed little that was new. Changes, moreover, were more cultural than social and economic, and many of the structural improvements were intended to advance traditional economic sectors. Despite the introduction of modern equipment and methods in the second half of the nineteenth century, Brazil remained "an essentially agricultural country," as politicians and landlords would reiterate in defense of slavery. Cities were refurbished after 1850, tramlines built, and gas lamps installed. Railroads were constructed to connect rich plantation districts with coastal ports, industrialization was started, and

52. *Recenseamento da população,* XIX, 1–2. In contrast, in the United States, where the value of literacy was better understood, and the printed word more available, a larger percentage of slaves learned to read and write despite legal prohibitions. See Richard C. Wade, *Slavery in the Cities: The South 1820–1860* (New York, 1964), pp. 90–91, 173–176. For the eagerness of ex-slaves for education after the Civil War, see Gilbert Osofsky, *Puttin' on Ole Massa* (New York, 1969), pp. 42–43.

53. Richard Graham, *Britain and the Onset of Modernization in Brazil, 1850–1914* (Cambridge, England, 1968), pp. 10–22; Stanley J. Stein, *The Brazilian Cotton Manufacture* (Cambridge, Massachusetts, 1957), pp. 2–7; Gilberto Freyre, *The Mansions and the Shanties* (New York, 1963), pp. xxiii, 22–23, 37–39; T. Lynn Smith, *Brazil. People and Institutions* (Baton Rouge, Louisiana, 1963), pp. 323–329; André Rebouças, *Agricultura Nacional* (Rio de Janeiro, 1883).

an increasingly informed public, influenced by foreign ideas and philosophies, began to question the validity of some traditional concepts. Yet all these symptoms of progress were stunted and jeopardized by the survival of deeply ingrained economic, social, and cultural institutions, conditions, and values: slavery, mono culture, the large, underutilized agricultural estate, the export-oriented economy, a limited internal market, traditional master-man relationships even among the free, prejudice against manual labor, racial and class barriers to opportunity, and antiquated aristocratic attitudes toward education.[54] As Richard Graham has pointed out, the changes occurring in Brazil in the decades after 1850 were not always easily recognized, and as late as 1914 Brazil had only begun to modernize.[55]

THE PRO-SLAVERY CONSENSUS

Under these circumstances, the anti-slavery attitudes which became commonplace in London and Boston and even in Mexico and Chile during the first half of the nineteenth century reverberated dully upon the immense South American Empire of Brazil. Confronted with the need to react to ideas well suited to Western Europe and to British economic needs but out of step with Brazilian institutions, Portuguese and Brazilian leaders and governments sometimes seemed to sympathize with foreign views on the slavery issue, but were compelled by the economic and political structure of their society and the demands of their leading citizens to carry out policies that would best assure the continued importation of hundreds of thousands of black men and women. Given the nature of the slave system, the single-minded opposition of the British, and the prestige and influence of foreign ideas, some Brazilian opposition to the slave trade and even slavery itself was inevitable, though opponents of slavery remained a small minority until the 1880's. In 1823, under pressure from Great Britain to end the African slave trade in exchange for diplomatic recognition, a liberal minority among the members of the Brazilian Constituent Assembly tried to set in motion a process leading toward the establishment of a free-labor system, and prominent Liberals continued to oppose the slave trade when op-

---

54. Brazil was not alone. For informed statements on colonial survivals in Latin America, see Woodrow Borah, Charles Gibson, and Robert A. Potash, "Colonial Institutions and Contemporary Latin America," in Lewis Hanke (ed.), *Readings in Latin American History* (2 vols.; New York, 1966), II, 18–37.
55. Graham, *Britain and the Onset*, pp. xi, 23, 47–48.

portunities arose during the next twenty-five years.[56] A few books or pamphlets written by Brazilians during the first half of the nineteenth century contained anti-slavery messages,[57] and for a brief time beginning in 1848 a few organs of the Brazilian press, some subsidized by the British government, carried on a campaign against the slave trade.[58] In the Brazilian General Assembly, furthermore, anti-slavery statements were heard from time to time before 1865,[59] though most members of that body were either silent on the issue or were quick to defend slavery when it came under attack from abroad. There were almost always a few persons, however, who opposed slavery on moral, religious, or even economic grounds, but opposition had little effect and often went unheard. Until 1880, for example, the now famous anti-slavery appeal of José Bonifacio de Andrada e Silva, Brazil's first Prime Minister, published in London in 1826, was almost totally unknown in Brazil.[60] So uncommon were anti-slavery writings in Brazil before 1865 that historians and later opponents of slavery sometimes professed to find opposition where it hardly existed. These misinterpretations were perhaps the re-

56. See Robert Conrad, "The Struggle for the Abolition of the Brazilian Slave Trade" (unpublished Ph.D. dissertation, Columbia University, 1967), pp. 151–152; *Annaes do Parlamento Brasileiro. Assembléa Constituinte. 1823* (6 vols.; Rio de Janeiro, 1876–1884), V, 12–24; Walsh, *Notices,* I, 234–235.

57. See, for example, Americus, *Cartas politicas extrahidas do Padre Amaro* (2 vols.; London, 1825–1826); José Bonifacio de Andrada e Silva, *Memoir Addressed to the General Constituent and Legislative Assembly of Brazil on Slavery* (London, 1826); Burlamaque, *Analytica;* Henrique Jorge Rebello, "Memoria e considerações sôbre a população do Brasil," RIHGB, Vol. XXX (1867), pp. 5–42.

58. The major anti-slave-trade papers in Rio were *O Monarchista, O Grito Nacional* (both founded in 1848), and *O Philantropo,* first published in April 1849. In 1850 the British Minister in Rio, James Hudson, implied that Britain had given financial aid to the Brazilian anti-traffic press as early as 1848. See Hudson to Palmerston, Rio de Janeiro, July 27, 1850, *Class B., From April 1, 1850, to March 31, 1851,* p. 228. For more evidence, see Leslie Bethell, *The Abolition of the Brazilian Slave Trade* (Cambridge, England, 1970), p. 313; Pierre Verger, *Flux et reflux de la traite des nègres entre le golfe de Bénin et Bahia de Todos os Santos* (Paris, 1968), pp. 385–386.

59. See the statements and proposals of Antônio Ferreira França in the Chamber of Deputies, *Annaes da Câmara* (1827), I, 85; V, 84; *ibid.* (1830), I, 169; II, 211; and those of Pedro Pereira da Silva Guimaraes, reprinted in "Pedro Pereira da Silva Guimaraes (Documentos historicos)," *Revista Trimensal do Instituto do Ceará* (Vol. XX). See also Raimundo Girão, *A abolição no Ceará* (Fortaleza, 1956), pp. 17–27.

60. See A. C. Tavares Bastos, *Cartas do Solitario* (3rd ed.; São Paulo, 1938), p. 456; Miguel Lemos, *O Positivismo e a escravidão moderna* (2nd ed.; Rio de Janeiro, 1934), p. 10. For a modern edition of José Bonifacio's remarkable plea intended for the Brazilian Constitutional Assembly, see "Representação à Assembléa Geral Constituinte e Legislativa do Império do Brasil sobre a Escravatura," in Octavio Tarquinio de Sousa, *O pensamento vivo de José Bonifacio* (São Paulo, 1944), pp. 39–66.

sult of the common Brazilian practice of prefacing pro-slavery arguments with brief denunciations of an institution which even in Brazil was condemned in principle if not at all in practice.[61]

61. In *A escravidão no Brasil* (Rio de Janeiro, 1939), p. 142, João Dornas Filho included writers among the precursors of Brazilian abolitionism whose sentiments regarding slavery were less than liberal. These included Padre M. Ribeiro da Rocha, "the patriarch of the abolitionists of Brazil," author of *Ethiope resgatado, empenhado, sustentado, corrigido, instruido e libertado* (Lisbon, 1758); João Severiano Maciel da Costa, author of *Memoria sobre a necessidade de abolir a introducção dos escravos africanos no Brasil* (Coimbra, 1821); Domingo Alves Branco Moniz Barreto, whose *Memoria sobre a abolição do commercio da escravatura* (Rio de Janeiro, 1837), strongly opposed abolition of the slave trade; and José Eloy Pessoa da Silva, whose *Memoria sobre a escravatura e projecto de colonisação dos europeus, e pretos da Africa no Imperio do Brazil* advocated substitution of a black "colonist" traffic for the slave trade. For some of their proposals, see Perdigão Malheiro, *A escravidão*, II, 235–399.

When Brazil is judged
a million witnesses will rise up against us:
from the backlands of Africa, from the depths of the ocean,
from the baracoons of the beaches,
from the cemeteries of the plantations,
and this mute evidence will be
a thousand times more valid
than all the protestations
of generosity and nobility
of the nation's soul.

JOAQUIM NABUCO
O Abolicionismo

2

THE ABOLITION OF
THE AFRICAN SLAVE TRADE
AND THE ONSET
OF DECLINE

THE SUPPRESSION OF THE AFRICAN SLAVE TRADE

Entrenched as slavery was, it received its first serious blow when its source of replenishment was cut off in 1851 and 1852 by the suppression of the African traffic. This first achievement, however, was not accomplished by Brazilian abolitionists but was primarily the result of outside pressure. In the opening years of the nineteenth century, Britishers were already righteous about their duty to interfere in the affairs of Portugal, Brazil, and practically any other country if by so doing they could hope to eliminate the international slave trade, and this British effort eventually played the predominant role in ending the slave traffic to Brazil.[1]

In pursuit of her forty-year crusade against the Brazilian slave trade, Britain negotiated a series of treaties with Portuguese and Brazilian governments between 1810 and 1826, all of which were entered into with great reluctance by the rulers of Brazil, who were always conscious of

1. For accounts of Britain's role in suppressing the Brazilian slave trade, see Bethell, *The Abolition*; Conrad, "The Struggle"; Verger, *Flux et reflux*, pp. 287–319, 373–397; and Alan K. Manchester, *British Preëminence in Brazil* (Chapel Hill, North Carolina, 1933).

the bitter opposition of most of their powerful citizens to any concessions on the slavery issue. In 1810, with the Portuguese government in
Rio virtually under British protection, Prince Regent João agreed in a
treaty of alliance to cooperate with the British monarch in the gradual
abolition of the slave trade and to outlaw the traffic immediately in
non-Portuguese territories in Africa. The agreement provided the British
government with a feeble justification for its first naval campaign against
Portuguese slave ships, arousing the ire of Portuguese and Brazilian
importers and planters. In 1815, again under coercion, João's government agreed to prohibit the trade north of the equator, and in 1817
the same ruler committed his regime to measures intended to enforce
the partial ban on the slave trade. The latter concessions at last legalized
British boarding of Portuguese merchant ships suspected of transporting
illegally acquired slaves and created international courts or mixed commissions in Rio de Janeiro and Sierra Leone, where ships were to be
delivered for trial. The same British-Portuguese agreement also provided that vessels condemned by the mixed commissions were to be
sold for the profit of the two nations, and that slaves found aboard such
ships were to be freed and placed under the protection of the Portuguese
or British government.[2] The result of these agreements was not a reduction or limitation of the slave trade, but a sudden surge in its volume
and the appearance of a contraband slave trade which grew into immense proportions.[3]

In 1826 Britain got yet another anti-slave-trade commitment from
the government in Rio de Janeiro after four years of difficult negotiations in London and Rio following Brazilian independence. This treaty,
all but forced upon the new Brazilian government, made Brazilian participation in the international slave trade entirely illegal beginning three
years from the date of the treaty's ratification, such trading in slaves
to be "deemed and treated as piracy." [4] As a result of this agreement,[5]
which incorporated the provisions contained in the Portuguese-British
treaties of 1815 and 1817, the legal slave trade ended for Brazilian sub-

2. Bethell, *The Abolition,* pp. 8–19; *A Complete Collection of the Treaties and
Conventions and Reciprocal Regulations, at Present Subsisting between Great
Britain & Foreign Powers . . . so far as they relate to Commerce and Navigation,
to the Repression and Abolition of the Slave Trade . . .* (3 vols.; London, 1827),
II, 73–107.
3. Conrad, "The Struggle," pp. 122–126, 189–206.
4. *A Complete Collection of the Treaties and Conventions,* III, 33–35; Leslie
Bethell, "The Independence of Brazil and the Abolition of the Brazilian Slave
Trade: Anglo-Brazilian Relations, 1822–1826," *Journal of Latin American Studies,* Vol. I, Part 2 (November 1969), pp. 115–147; Bethell, *The Abolition,* pp.
27–61; Conrad, "The Struggle," pp. 133–170.
5. For the intense opposition to it, see Conrad, "The Struggle," pp. 170–185;
Bethell, *The Abolition,* pp. 62–66.

jects on March 13, 1830, and on November 7 of the following year a new Liberal government in Rio confirmed this decision with legislation that declared the freedom of all slaves entering Brazil from that day forward.[6]

Despite the threat of stiff penalties for both importers and purchasers of contraband slaves, the traffic continued. Between 1831 and 1837 and again in 1840 and 1848 Liberal Brazilian governments took some steps to enforce the ban on the trade, but during the two decades after 1831 the African traffic was carried on with almost complete freedom and the full knowledge and approval of most Brazilian regimes.[7] The government itself was "a slave trading Govt against its own laws and treaties," wrote the American Minister to Rio in 1846. "The Ministers & Councillors of State & Senators and Delegates in the Chambers are, undoubtedly, engaged in this bold as well as horrid traffic . . . ."[8] British estimates conservatively place the number of slaves illegally imported into the Empire during those years at nearly half a million.[9] All were legally free, as the Brazilian law of 1831 clearly stated in its first article, but few achieved de facto liberation, and even their offspring were held illegally in slavery.

The ban on the traffic was effective, however, in the extreme southern provinces and on the long northern coast between Cape São Roque and the Amazon, but this partial cessation of the slave trade was not the result of conscientious officials or of a law-abiding population. Rather, it occurred because of the higher cost of slaves brought on by the British policing efforts. As a northerner wrote in the 1850's in reference to the province of Maranhão alone, the slave trade had ended there "because the fall in the price of cotton had impoverished and broken the spirit of our farmers, to the point of not being able to pay for Negroes imported illegally [which were] made more and more expensive by the persecution of the English cruisers." [10] The cotton and sugar growers

6. *Colecção das leis do Imperio* (1832), pp. 100–101; Bethell, *The Abolition*, pp. 69–70; Conrad, "The Struggle," pp. 218–221, 228–229.
7. Robert Conrad, "The Contraband Slave Trade to Brazil, 1831–1845," *HAHR,* Vol. XLIX (1969), pp. 618–638; Conrad, "The Struggle," pp. 224–303; Bethell, *The Abolition, passim.*
8. Henry A. Wise to James Buchanan, Rio de Janeiro, December 9, 1846, in William R. Manning (ed.), *Diplomatic Correspondence of the United States. Inter-American Affairs, 1831–1860* (Washington, 1932), II, 370; same to same, Rio de Janeiro, April 12, 1847, *ibid.,* II, 380.
9. Bethell, *The Abolition,* p. 390; Poppino, *Brazil,* p. 171.
10. Fabio Alexandrino de Carvalho Reis, *Breves considerações sobre a nossa lavoura* (São Luiz de Maranhão, 1856), p. 3. In *The Atlantic Slave Trade, a Census* (Madison, Wisconsin, 1969), pp. 240–241, Philip D. Curtin shows that about eighty percent of African slaves entering Brazil between 1817 and 1843 landed in the coffee provinces, and that another thirteen percent disembarked in northeastern provinces, principally Bahia.

of the north could not compete for slaves with the coffee growers of the south, and therefore planters north of Bahia all but ceased to bid for workers in the international slave market. The coffee industry in the province of Rio de Janeiro and neighboring areas of Minas Gerais and São Paulo, on the other hand, was expanding and prospering in the years of the greatest British involvement against the slave trade, and the high income of the coffee planters enabled them to pay for the slaves they needed, despite British warships, the high cost of bribes, and other expenses caused by the unlawful nature of the trade. Thus, in that part of Brazil the traffic maintained its vitality, and slave traders carried on their business with nearly complete disregard for law.

In 1849 and 1850, however, the British government took drastic action against the slave merchants in Brazilian territorial waters in complete disregard of Brazilian sovereignty, with the intention of wresting a commitment from the Brazilian government to pass an effective anti-slave-trade law and see to its enforcement.[11] Thoroughly humiliated by British incursions into the harbors of the Empire and their seizure and destruction of Brazilian slave ships even within Brazilian territorial waters, faced with threats to the legal shipping of the Empire, with military conflict, and even a blockade of Brazilian ports, the government of the Empire was compelled in July 1850 to accede to British demands in exchange for a promise to suspend the naval attacks.[12] Even then, however, the Brazilian government was reluctant to act against the slave trade, and one more threat, delivered in January 1851, to send British naval vessels rampaging into Brazilian ports was necessary to activate the long-delayed Brazilian suppression of the traffic in Africans. Once it had begun, however, the Brazilian anti-traffic campaign was effective and serious.[13]

---

11. Bethell, *The Abolition*, pp. 327–363; Conrad, "The Struggle," pp. 304–349.

12. See "Annexo B. Relações entre o Brasil e a Grã-Bretanha. Questão do trafico," *Relatorio da repartição dos negocios estrangeiros apresentado á Assembléa Geral Legislativa na terceira sessão da oitava legislatura pelo respectivo Ministro e Secretario de Estado Paulino José Soares de Souza* (Rio de Janeiro, 1851), pp. 23–24; "Memorandum of an Interview between Senhor Paulino de Souza and Mr. Hudson, on the 13th of July, 1850," *Class B., From April 1, 1850, to March 31, 1851*, pp. 233–235.

13. Recent scholarship has questioned the claim of the Brazilian Justice Minister, Eusébio de Queiroz, that the slave trade ended because of an independent Brazilian decision. For this version, see Perdigão Malheiro, *A escravidão*, II, 262–287. In *A History of Brazil* (New York, 1963), pp. 190–191, João Pandiá Calógeras claims that the measures adopted by Brazil to end the traffic owed nothing to Britain, but Leslie Bethell writes more accurately: "At the very least, British naval action could be said to have greatly accelerated, if it did not alone precipitate, Brazil's own, ultimately successful, efforts to suppress the slave trade." See *The Abolition*, pp. 327–363.

"A NATURALLY DECREASING SLAVE POPULATION"

With the traffic all but ended by 1852, British pressure was relaxed. Yet a decisive blow had been delivered to Brazilian bondage, since the slave population of that country, in the words of Philip D. Curtin, was "a naturally decreasing slave population," [14] dependent upon the African traffic for its permanent existence. A variety of conditions and policies contributed to the excess of deaths over births among slaves in Brazil and their consequent inability to maintain their numbers through natural reproduction. These included a low ratio of females to males, a paucity of marriages and family life (see Table 18 for slave-marriage statistics), a customary disregard for slave progeny, the frequent employment of harsh physical punishment, immoderate labor for females as well as males, inadequate clothing, poor and unsanitary food and housing combined with poor medical care, epidemics, and (for newly imported Africans) a new disease environment.[15]

All these conditions and the resulting excess of deaths over births among slaves were often attested to during the nineteenth century. In 1823 José Bonifacio de Andrada e Silva claimed that 40,000 slaves had entered the country during the previous five or six years with no significant increase in the slave population, most of them dying "either of misery or of desperation . . . ." [16] A British surgeon who lived in Rio during the 1840's claimed that the Brazilian slave population was "found to dwindle away, and would shrink into insignificance, except for the shoals of doomed Africans who are annually drawn from the opposite shore to supply the defects." Brazilians, he believed, were unwilling "to submit to all the expenses and risks attendant upon infancy

14. *The Atlantic Slave Trade*, p. 29.
15. Several authors, including Gilberto Freyre, Frank Tannenbaum, Stanley Elkins, and Herbert S. Klein (see bibliography), have popularized the belief that Latin American slavery was comparatively humane, but recent statements on Brazilian slavery seem incompatible with this view. See, for example, Stein, *Vassouras*, pp. 132–195; Roger Bastide and Florestan Fernandes, *Brancos e negros em São Paulo* (2nd ed.; São Paulo, 1959), pp. 1–68; Ianni, *As metamorfoses do escravo*, pp. 131–183; Fernando Henrique Cardoso, *Capitalismo e escravidão no Brasil meridional* (São Paulo, 1962), pp. 133–167; C. R. Boxer, *The Golden Age of Brazil, 1695–1750* (Berkeley and Los Angeles, 1964), pp. 170–178; Harris, *Patterns of Race*, pp. 65–78; Viotti da Costa, *Da senzala à colônia*, pp. 227–299; Carl N. Degler, *Neither Black Nor White* (New York, 1971), pp. 3–93.
16. Andrada e Silva, "Representação," pp. 48–49. According to Roberto Simonsen, the average length of life of slaves in Brazil was seven years. See "Aspectos da história econômica do café," *Anais do Terceiro Congresso de História Nacional* (Rio de Janeiro, 1941), IV, 262.

and childhood, when . . . they can step into the neighboring street, and provide themselves with whatever age or sex they require." [17] Senator Cristiano Otoni told the Brazilian upper chamber in 1883 that while the slave trade had lasted slaveowners had been "careless as to the duration of the life of their slaves." The masters believed that the "proceeds of the first year's labor of a slave were at least enough to cover his cost; that the second and following years were clear profit. Why then, said they, should we bother ourselves about them, when we can so easily get fresh ones at such a low price?" [18] In 1849 a British subject, testifying before a committee of the House of Lords, declared: "In Brazil the slaves are continually brought in and die off. The mortality rate in the first two or three years after importation for some reason or another is immense." Those entering Brazil "do little more than fill up the generations that pass away." [19]

Despite improved conditions after mid-century,[20] the slaves of Brazil were unable even during the last decades of bondage to maintain their numbers through natural means. As late as 1868 Richard Burton, British explorer, Orientalist, and consul at the port of Santos, contended that the excess of deaths over births among Brazilian slaves would be the most important factor in the extinction of Brazilian slavery.[21] In 1870, in an era when the treatment of slaves had definitely improved and lives were being lengthened, the future abolitionist, Joaquim Nabuco wrote: "the Negro population, we confess, does not reproduce like the white; a long series of causes depresses it, debases it, suffocates it too much for it to increase through its descendants." [22] And in 1871 a national deputy from Bahia asserted that an estimated five percent annual decrease of the Brazilian slave population was an abnormal condition, with its roots in the precarious social and hygienic conditions of the slave population. Observing that the free black population was expanding through natural means, he denied that the decline of the slave popu-

17. Thomas Nelson, *Remarks on the Slavery and Slave Trade of the Brazils* (London, 1846), pp. 29–32.
18. Quoted by *Rio News,* June 24, 1884.
19. *Report from the Select Committee of the House of Lords. Appointed to Consider the Best Means which Great Britain can adopt for the final Extinction of the African Slave Trade, Session 1849* (London, 1849), pp. 22–23.
20. See Joaquim Floriano de Godoy, *O elemento servil e as câmaras municipaes da provincia de São Paulo* (Rio de Janeiro, 1887), p. 500; Perdigão Malheiro, *A escravidão,* II, 65; Antonio Joaquim Macedo Soares, *Campanha jurídica pela libertação dos escravos (1867–1888)* (Rio de Janeiro, 1938), pp. 40–41.
21. "The Extinction of Slavery in Brazil, From a Practical Point of View," *The Anthropological Review* (London, 1868), VI, 56; Burton, *Explorations,* I, 277.
22. Joaquim Nabuco, "A escravidão," *RIHGB,* Vol. 204 (July–September, 1949), p. 105.

lation was a consequence of race, ascribing it instead to slavery itself.[23]

Statistics on Brazilian slavery support the abundant contemporary reports of the inability of Brazilian slaves to increase their numbers through natural means during the nineteenth century. The number of slaves in Brazil in 1798 is said to have been about 1,582,000 (see Table 1). Between 1800 and 1850 probably about 1,600,000 were imported into that country.[24] If, therefore, the population had been maintained through natural reproduction (which of course was difficult owing to a low ratio of females to males), the slaves of Brazil should have numbered close to three million in 1871, the year of the Rio Branco Law, which liberated all children born from that time forward. Yet only 1,540,829 slaves were registered under the provisions of that legislation (see Table 2).

In contrast, the slave population of the United States, also afflicted by a high, though less shocking, mortality rate, grew from about 700,000 to nearly four million between 1790 and 1860, while the free colored population of the United States also expanded during the same period from sixty thousand to nearly half a million.[25] These statistics are even more revealing if we compare estimated total slave imports for the two countries. The total importation of slaves into British North America has been estimated at 399,000 (between 1701 and 1870), while the number said to have been transported to Brazil is 3,646,800.[26] In other words, Brazil received perhaps ten times as many slaves as British North America over a much longer period of time, and, nevertheless, during its entire history Brazil never had as many slaves as the United States had in 1860. To put it another way, the largest number of slaves ever existing in Brazil was perhaps not much more than half of the total imported over three centuries. In contrast, the four million slaves existing in the United States in 1860 constituted perhaps ten times the number imported. In the United States the black population, both slave and free, grew almost as fast as the white before the Civil War, even without a large influx from abroad,[27] whereas in Brazil the slave population could hardly maintain existing levels even with a large importa-

23. *Discussão da reforma do estado servil na Câmara dos Deputados e no Senado* (2 vols.; Rio de Janeiro, 1871), II, 193–194.

24. Perdigão Malheiro, *A escravidão*, II, 26; Affonso d'Escragnolle Taunay, "Subsidios para a história do tráfico africano no Brasil," *Anais do Museu Paulista* (São Paulo, 1941), X, 305. Curtin estimates an importation of 1,145,400 between 1811 and 1860. See *The Atlantic Slave Trade*, p. 234.

25. Joseph C. G. Kennedy, *Preliminary Report on the Eighth Census, 1860* (Washington, 1862), p. 7.

26. Curtin, *The Atlantic Slave Trade*, p. 268.

27. Alfred H. Conrad and John R. Meyer, "The Economics of Slavery in the Ante-Bellum South," in Robert William Fogel and Stanley L. Engerman, *The Reinterpretation of American Economic History* (New York, 1971), pp. 353–354.

tion, and only the free colored population grew at a rate comparable to that of the white population (see Table 1). Although the character of Brazilian slavery is not an issue here, it is worth noting that Philip D. Curtin, Carl N. Degler, and David Brion Davis have all recognized the significance of such facts as they relate to the current controversy over the character of slavery in the American countries. Curtin has reasoned that "one measure of well-being is the ability to survive and multiply." For Degler, the inability of Brazilian slavery to survive through reproduction alone is persuasive proof of "a harsher slavery." To David Brion Davis, it "seems probable that planters in Brazil . . . , who were totally dependent on fresh supplies of labor from Africa, were less sensitive than North Americans to the value of human life." [28]

SLAVERY RETAINS ITS IMPORTANCE

The closing of the slave trade to Brazil, at any rate, had a greater effect upon the Brazilian economy and the Brazilian slave system than had the virtual ending of the traffic upon North American institutions nearly half a century earlier. In the United States slavery could expand after the near elimination of the traffic, but the Brazilian slave population declined rapidly after 1850 (see Tables 3, 10, 11). With perhaps two million slaves on hand, however, for another fifteen years, slavery was able to maintain its dominant place in the economic and social life of the Empire almost totally unchallenged. When the African trade ended, a complacent society adjusted to the new reality with a large and spontaneous increase in the movement of slaves internally, the consequence of continuing demands for more slaves in the coffee region and unchanged attitudes regarding the institution of slavery itself.[29]

After the voluntary disbanding in 1852 of the two-year-old Anti-Slave-Trade Society (Sociedade contra o Tráfico de Africanos e Promotora da Colonisação dos Indigenas) and the simultaneous demise of its short-lived propaganda organ, *O Philantropo,* no anti-slavery organization of any stature or popularity existed in Brazil until the 1860's, and no Brazilian newspaper consistently advocated an end to slavery. Brazilians were convinced, wrote a British observer in Pernambuco in

28. Curtin, *The Atlantic Slave Trade,* p. 92; Degler, *Neither Black Nor White,* pp. 67–69; Davis, *The Problem of Slavery in Western Culture* (Ithaca, New York, 1966), pp. 232–233.
29. As Percy Alvin Martin has written, "The same men who inveighed most bitterly against the iniquities of the traffic in slaves found nothing reprehensible in holding several millions of Africans in bondage." See "Slavery and Abolition in Brazil," *HAHR,* Vol. XIII (1933), p. 162. His statement is essentially correct, but the number of Africans overstated. See also Poppino, *Brazil,* pp. 171–172.

1852, of the need to maintain slavery. Some were opposed to the African slave trade, now that it had been effectively abolished, but "none" were against slavery. Brazilians defended their labor system, wrote the same observer, "not only upon political grounds, but . . . upon those of religion and morality." In both the United States and Brazil, he predicted, slavery would one day be destroyed, but in both countries only by force of arms.[30]

In mid-century, then, the Brazilian slave system was in no immediate danger, though it was doomed to eventual extinction owing to the loss of its principal source of renewal. For the life span of another generation its importance seemed assured. Fortunes were invested in slaves, and values had increased. Complex social and economic arrangements continued to be based upon the system, and the legitimacy of slavery in the United States and the desire there to preserve the institution wherever it existed provided a bulwark behind which Brazilian slaveholders could repose secure and virtuous. In the early 1840's, in fact, as Britain threatened slavery in Texas as well as Brazil, an "informal alliance" had been thought to exist between the United States and the South American Empire, and this community of interest was probably protracted until the eve of the American Civil War.[31] Custom, convenience, a persistent labor shortage, even necessity, along with the tacit support of a powerful northern neighbor—all dictated the preservation of the institution in Brazil.

As late as May 1862, just weeks before the Battle of Shiloh in the War between the States, the British Minister in Rio could find no signs in Brazil of a "disposition to prepare for the abolition of slavery, or to mitigate its evils." Educated Brazilians were pleased that the African slave trade was over, but there was a general unwillingness to consider the problem of slavery itself, owing to fears of a labor shortage and concern for the sanctity of private property.[32] Yet important changes

30. British Consul to the Earl of Malmesbury, Pernambuco, May 6, 1852, *Class B., From April 1, 1852, to March 31, 1853,* p. 280. For similar opinions, see *Class B., From April 1, 1857, to March 31, 1858,* pp. 126–128; *British and Foreign State Papers* (hereafter *BFSP*) (1853–1854), XLIV, 1243–1244.
31. Secretary of State Upshur to United States Minister to Brazil, Washington, August 1, 1843, Manning, *Diplomatic Correspondence,* II, 125; United States Minister to Brazil to Daniel Webster, Rio de Janeiro, November 8, 1842, *ibid.,* II, 251. The Brazilian government learned officially in 1844 that it was American policy to resist the interference of any other country in Brazilian affairs, "especially in reference to the important relation between the European and African races as it exists with her and in the southern portion of our union." United States Minister to Brazil to Brazilian Foreign Minister, Rio de Janeiro, September 24, 1844, *ibid.,* II, 256–257.
32. William Christie to Earl Russell, Rio de Janeiro, May 3, 1862, *BFSP* (1862–1863), LIII, 1311–1312.

were occurring that were decisively weakening the grip of slavery upon the nation. The slave population was declining, and surviving slaves were being concentrated into limited parts of the country like sand in an hourglass. These facts, along with the unacceptability of permanent slavery, acknowledged in theory even in Brazil, fostered a slow rejection of the traditional labor system in the thirty years after 1850, while many complementary institutions inherited from the era of Portuguese domination, institutions less vulnerable to foreign criticism, continued to survive almost completely unchallenged and unchanged.

I always heard it said
that the salary rate is the principal factor
in the profits of any industry; the salaries make up a portion
of production expenses, and, the lower these are,
the greater will be the profits. If the salary is low,
you will see the profits increased;
and by the same principle, when the salary is high,
you will see the profit diminished
and even disappear and carry with it
the ruin of the industrious.

DEPUTY JOÃO MAURICIO WANDERLEY
(later the Baron of Cotegipe) in
the Chamber of Deputies, 1854.

If one talks with the large planters,
one must suppose that they support immigration
in the exclusive interest of coffee and sugar-cane planting,
that they only want colonists to work their land
in place of the slaves. They do not want colonists,
but labourers—instrumento(s) de trabalho—
for the benefit of their enterprises.

C. F. VAN DELDEN LAËRNE
Brazil and Java (London, 1885).

3

THE CRISIS OF LABOR

THE LABOR SHORTAGE

The years following the end of the African trade were not a period of unlimited prosperity for the Brazilian planter class. A constant concern of the government for the planters was caused in part by the serious problems which agriculture faced. One of the most troublesome of these was a constant labor shortage. This scarcity of workers was a characteristic of Brazilian society as long as slavery existed, for slave labor repelled free labor, both native and foreign, creating almost constant demands from planters for the aid of government in the acquisition of new and inexpensive workers. Plantation proprietors of the rich coffee regions who had bought Africans when they were still abundant probably did not feel this shortage as quickly as northern planters. Their rural establishments were among the better stocked, and an internal slave trade helped to meet their continuing needs. Planters with an abundance of slaves on hand found their investments expanding in value with the rise in slave prices caused by the ending of the African trade. Along with an increase in the value of their property, there was a gratifying expansion of the ability of coffee planters to command credit.[1] For other planters, however, particularly those in northern provinces, the end of the slave trade aggravated the labor shortage as it increased prices and started a southward movement of slaves over which they had little control. In nearly every important agricultural region of Brazil, nevertheless, even in the rich coffee-producing Paraíba Valley, the shortage of field hands was a constant complaint after 1850.[2]

As the labor problem intensified, Brazilians began to consider various solutions, including the systematic "breeding" of slaves. As long as planters had been assured of a regular supply of Africans, there had been little interest in natural reproduction.[3] Some two-thirds or more of the slaves transported to Brazil had been males, and males continued to outnumber females significantly in the south-central coffee provinces, particularly in coffee-producing municípios, until the end of slavery.[4] After 1850, nonetheless, Brazilians wistfully looked to the successful "breeding" of slaves in the United States and dared to hope that Brazil might follow the example. Deputy Silveira da Mota of São Paulo claimed in 1854 that the "slave-breeding industry" in the United States had still not developed in Brazil.[5] The following year a planter of Rio de Janeiro province observed that the ease of acquiring slaves from Africa had "constituted an impediment to the propagation of the African race among us." Yet the success of North American slave "breeding" offered hope that Brazil too might increase its existing slave population if planters rendered "more solicitude to pregnancy, more zeal and care to infants and small children." The planters, he thought, should promote the increase of slaves by every means compatible with morality and religion. Better clothing, improved housing and nutrition, more care for the sick, "and other measures which are generally scorned among us"

1. Stein, *Vassouras*, p. 29.
2. *Ibid.*, p. 47. Even in the small industrial sector of the Brazilian economy, which developed after 1850, there was a scarcity of labor in the 1870's and 1880's, probably owing to the "comparatively" low wages paid to Brazilian workers, to unfavorable working conditions, and to a distaste for regular labor generated by the slave system. See Stein, *The Brazilian Cotton Manufacture*, pp. 55–56.
3. Perdigão Malheiro, *A escravidão*, II, 65.
4. See Tables 4, 16, 18. During the 1820's 77 percent of the slaves on plantations in one coffee município of Rio de Janeiro province were males, in the late 1880's 56 percent. See Stein, *Vassouras*, pp. 76–77.
5. *Annaes da Câmara* (1854), IV, 246.

would result in the saving of many lives "which today are sacrificed by indifference and carelessness. . . ." [6]

A deputy from Maranhão, whose brief treatise on the agriculture of his native province was published in 1856, doubted that Maranhão could succeed in following Virginia's example, a role expected of it:

Just as previously our every hope lay in the freeing of the traffic through the discouragement of England, today we set all our hopes on the marvels of reproduction of our slave women. And we do not lack those who cite the edifying example of the human stud houses (*caudelarias humanas*) of the United States of America.

After describing the "breeding farms" of Virginia, this writer questioned the ability of Brazilians to achieve the same results:

Can we hope for [such success] here, however? Will the propagation of such ideas, the imitation of such an example, be legal, honest and beneficial to our province? Will our farmers even be disposed to employ all that diligence, all that care which is given there to the nourishment, the clothing, and to the habitations of the Negroes, to the care of the young, and to *communication* between the two sexes? We do not believe it, and we should not aspire to it. [7]

The writer's pessimism was justified; since there is no evidence that systematic and efficient breeding of slaves was ever common in the exporting provinces, or even that masters generally gave much care to the children whom providence granted them. What occurred was the spontaneous disposal of slaves on hand, including unplanned offspring. Unlike the efficient slave-exporting regions of the United States, Brazilian exporting provinces, failing to organize a potentially profitable industry, increased the slave populations of most importing provinces only marginally, the notable exception being São Paulo, and failed entirely to replenish their own captive work forces (see Table 3). [8]

If Brazilian slaveowners were "conscious" slave breeders only rarely, statistics on marriage suggest that, as a practical matter, they often anticipated slave sales long in advance. In a country where nearly all weddings were Church weddings and slave marriages were theoretically as sacred as those of free people, masters envisioning future sales might well have discouraged permanent unions, particularly after 1869, when

---

6. Lacerda Werneck, *Idéas sobre colonisação*, pp. 22–27.

7. Carvalho Reis, *Breves considerações*, p. 6. Italics in original.

8. In a brilliant essay, Alfred H. Conrad and John R. Meyer show that a "specialized breeding operation" in the American border states was important in the development of the slave populations in both exporting and receiving states, helping to increase the slave populations in the Gulf states by an average annual rate of 18 percent from 1790 to 1850. See "The Economics of Slavery in the Ante-Bellum South," pp. 351–355.

the separation of married slaves by sale became illegal. In fact, statistics published by the Ministry of Agriculture (see Table 18) show that slave marriages were infrequent in some northern, north-eastern, western, and southern provinces and even in the city of Rio de Janeiro, but were comparatively common in São Paulo and Minas Gerais, where masters acquiring slaves for long-term possession would have been less inclined to discourage permanent unions. This hypothesis may be supported by the fact that, although males considerably outnumbered females in São Paulo and Minas Gerais, marriages were more common there than in provinces where the ratio between the sexes was more natural.[9]

A possible solution to the labor problem which received more attention than planned reproduction was the promotion of Chinese, European, and African immigration. Chinese workers were never taken to Brazil in large numbers, but their introduction was often proposed and sometimes attempted. As early as 1807 a Bahian economist had suggested that Brazilians import Chinese and East Indian workers,[10] and soon afterward the Portuguese Foreign Minister at Rio considered the importation of two million Chinese into Brazil.[11] No really serious efforts were made, however, to ship Chinese workers to Brazil as long as the traditional source of field hands remained; but after mid-century, a new interest in the importation of Chinese workers developed.[12]

Though little was accomplished in the 1850's and 1860's, the importation of Chinese workers was again seriously debated with the

---

9. Another probable cause of the infrequency of slave marriages was the high cost of the ceremony. After abolition, many former slaves were restrained from church marriages by the fees, allegedly equal to sixteen shillings per couple even in cases of multiple marriages performed in a single ceremony. In late 1888 a Brazilian senator complained that ex-slaves attempting to marry were paying as much as five pounds sterling, and even more in rural districts where fees were higher because of the distances priests were made to travel. See Foreign Office, *Diplomatic and Consular Reports on Trade and Commerce. Brazil. Report for the Years 1887–1888 on the Finances, Commerce, and Agriculture of the Empire of Brazil* (London, 1889), p. 40.

10. João Rodriques de Brito, *Cartas econômico-políticas sôbre a agricultura e commercio da Bahia* (Bahia, 1924), p. 58.

11. Eschwege, *Pluto Brasiliensis*, II, 452.

12. Viotti da Costa, *Da senzala à colônia*, p. 140; José Honório Rodrigues, "Brasil e extremo oriente," *Politica Externa Independente*, Ano 1, No. 2 (August, 1965), pp. 65–69; Memoria sôbre a emigração chineza, 1855, AN, Cod. 807, Vol. 16, pp. 565–592; Carvalho Reis, *Breves considerações*, p. 22; Lacerda Werneck, *Idéas sobre colonisação*, pp. 75–80. Werneck, like later opponents of Chinese immigration, had accepted current racialist doctrine. The Chinese were "condemned to disappear from the face of the earth . . . upon mere contact with the Germanic and neo-Latin nations." The Chinese were "stationary, of doubtful civilization, inert in progress. . . ." They were not even human; but a "species of monster, in both body and spirit, . . . mud, . . . dust, , , , nothing."

decline of the slave population and the threat of abolition in the 1870's and 1880's. "To find new workers to be substitutes for slaves," wrote Salvador de Mendonça in his *Trabalhadores asiaticos* in 1879, "equally cheap but more skillful and intelligent, in order that they may cultivate our coffee . . . is the only way to throw off the crisis through which we are passing. . . . Throughout Brazil it is a recognized fact that the first necessity is cheap labor." [13] With Europeans still unwilling to enter Brazil in large numbers, Chinese workers were believed to have several advantages. They were reputedly cheaper and more manageable than Europeans. Immigrants from China would be without the dangerous political pretensions of Europeans. Always longing for their place of birth, promoters argued, the Chinese would not attach themselves permanently to the Brazilian soil to "mongrelize" the population. The "coolie" would come and go, "a temporary producing agent," leaving behind the products of his strong arm—the cheap, docile, slave-like catalytic instrument of labor who would help to bridge the chasm between slavery and freedom, revive the lagging Brazilian economy, and prepare the way for the European, who would be the true populator of Brazilian soil.[14] The several efforts to find a Chinese solution to the labor problem were also frustrated, however, in part by the fearsome racist arguments of the opponents of Chinese immigration.

European immigration, as Emilia Viotti da Costa has shown, was closely related to the question of emancipation and the labor problem. From the moment that the African slave trade appeared threatened by the British diplomatic offensive following the Napoleonic Wars, Brazilians looked to European workers to replace black slaves, and as the labor problem grew more severe after 1850, interest in European immigration grew. The planters of Brazil, those of São Paulo in particular,

13. Salvador de Mendonça, *Trabalhadores asiaticos* (New York, 1879), pp. 17–19.

14. For ideas like these see *ibid.*, pp. 9–26; Quintino Bocayuva, *A crise da lavoura* (Rio de Janeiro, 1868); *Congresso Agrícola, Colecção de documentos* (Rio de Janeiro, 1878); *Demonstração das conveniencias e vantagens á lavoura no Brasil pela introducção dos trabalhadores asiaticos (Da China)* (Rio de Janeiro, 1877); the 1879 debate on the Chinese question in the Chamber, especially the speech of Martin Francisco Ribeiro de Andrada, *Annaes da Câmara* (1879), V, 32. In 1870 the Brazilian government granted a concession for the importation of Chinese workers, but by 1875 the concessionaires had despaired of success without a Brazilian-Chinese commercial treaty. See *Colecção das leis do Imperio* (1870), II, 382–386; *The British and American Mail,* Rio de Janeiro, March 9, 1878. The Brazilian government tried again in 1879 and 1880 to establish a regular traffic in Asians, but warnings from Brazilian Positivists, abolitionists, and the British and Foreign Anti-Slavery Society of their probable de facto enslavement dampened Chinese interest. See *Annaes da Câmara* (1879), III, 295–299; *Rio News,* September 24, 1879; January 25, 1880; Miguel Lemos, *Immigração Chineza* (Rio de Janeiro, 1881), pp. 5–15.

desired to stimulate immigration from Europe primarily as a means of acquiring European peasants to replace the occupants of their slave huts. The Imperial Government, on the other hand, periodically advanced a policy intended to create nuclei of European settlers, "centers of attraction," through the granting or selling of small plots of land in rich, healthful regions with access to transportation.[15] The primary aim of this policy was the enrichment and civilization of the Empire through the creation of independent communities with access to land and markets, but the economic and social organization of Brazil, notably the landholding system, precluded the robust development of such European settlements.[16] Until just prior to the abolition of slavery, in fact, European immigration failed to develop sufficiently, either to settle many farmers on the land or to satisfy plantation labor needs.[17] Even during the last decade of slavery, when the abolitionist movement and the decline of the slave population caused unusual anxiety regarding labor needs, only the planters of São Paulo were able to organize a mass movement of Europeans onto their fazendas. Yet even this did not occur until the slave system had almost completely broken down in that province.[18] Europeans did not generally find Brazil an attractive place in which to settle. Disappointed by the contrast between the Brazilian reality and the promises of Brazilian promoters, they quickly discovered that in Brazil they were unable to compete with slave labor or to acquire land near transportation and markets.[19] Colonies were created through government action, particularly in the southernmost provinces, but with some exceptions even these did not serve as irresistible centers of attraction for Europeans. Nor did immigration provide a solution to

15. Viotti da Costa, *Da senzala à colônia*, pp. 65, 69; Memorandum em que são expostas as vistas do Governo Imperial a respeito da colonisação e immigração para o Brasil, AN, Cod. 817, Vol. 19, pp. 1–4.
16. Fernando Henrique Cardoso reveals the two conflicting aims of immigration in his study of Rio Grande do Sul. Pro-immigrationists in that province desired an influx of independent foreigners to establish "new forms of property and new types of production relationships . . . ." Planters, when advocating immigration at all, tended to prefer workers for their estates, committed to labor by contracts. See *Capitalismo e escravidão*, pp. 214–218. For causes of the immigration lag, see Smith, *Brazil*, pp. 119–120, 398–408.
17. On the failure of Paulista immigration schemes, see Paula Beiguelman, *A formação do povo no complexo cafeeiro: aspectos politicos* (São Paulo, 1968), pp. 77–89; Richard M. Morse, *From Community to Metropolis* (Gainesville, Florida, 1958), pp. 71, 114–115, 139–140; Smith, *Brazil*, pp. 120–122.
18. Alfredo Ellis, Jr., *A evolução da economia paulista e suas causas* (Sâo Paulo, 1937), pp. 180–181.
19. Viotti da Costa, *Da senzala à colônia*, pp. 66–67. See the *Anglo-Brazilian Times*, October 1, 1881, for a statement on the failure of immigration, "partially repelled by the existence of slavery, by the defects of the land system, and by the sanitary perils of our maritime cities . . . ."

the labor problem until the crisis of the 1880's forced planters to take emergency measures to swell the flow of Europeans to coffee fazendas. The importation of African "colonists" was also frequently recommended, both before and after the abolition of the African slave trade. As early as 1826, the year the Brazilian government agreed to end the traffic, a proposal to establish a monopolistic company for trading in "black colonists" was well received by the Chamber of Deputies, but action on the project was discouraged by the British government and made unnecessary by the advent of the illegal trade.[20]

As the British threat to the African traffic grew more serious in the late 1840's, however, there were new proposals to import African "colonists." [21] At the height of the crisis of 1850, while British officers and men were being assaulted in the Brazilian capital in retaliation for naval attacks on Brazilian ports and shipping, one Antônio Pedro de Carvalho was drafting a proposal to legalize the importation of African "colonists" into Brazil. Carvalho's project, which may well have reached the Emperor himself, was an emergency measure intended to supply sufficient manpower for construction work and heavy agricultural labor three leagues or more outside towns and cities. According to him, the Brazilian government should negotiate treaties with nations interested in the abolition of the slave trade (presumably Britain) to allow the licensing of Brazilian ships for the importation of all the black African "colonists" needed.[22]

In 1855 a Brazilian newspaper contained the following comments and suggestions under the heading "Agriculture and the Shortage of Workers":

Since the attacks of the English cruisers compelled our government to take measures for the repression of the traffic in Africans, the overriding thought of the administrators of the country should have been that of providing substitutes for the hands (*braços*) which agriculture would lack as a result of that repression. Just as England has colonists from Africa and subjects them to a special code, to a regimen of slavery while retaining for them the title of free men, Brazilians might also receive as free workers for the cultivation of their fields those Africans who might come to the [African] coasts as objects of purchase and sale. That the blacks are the best colonists for

20. Pessoa da Silva, *Memoria*, pp. 20–23; *Annaes da Câmara* (1826), IV, 139; Heatherly to Bidwell, Rio de Janeiro, January 26, 1829, *Class B., 1829*, p. 81; Aston to Aberdeen, Rio de Janeiro, March 27, 1830, *Class B., 1830*, p. 39.
21. *O Monarchista*, September 29, October 10, 1848; *Recordações da vida parlamentar do advogado Antonio Pereira Rebouças* (2 vols.; Rio de Janeiro, 1870), II, 237–238.
22. Antônio Pedro de Carvalho, *Projecto de lei para regular a escravidão no Brasil*, AMIP, 113–5634.

Brazilian agriculture, and that for many years at least our planters cannot dispense with them in their agricultural endeavors is a truth which does not suffer debate.

Sea captains formerly involved in the slave trade, the same writer believed, could return to the importation of "those commodities of prime necessity . . . ." [23] In a work sent to the Emperor in 1858, another writer stressed the importance of Negroes "in agriculture and other rugged work in our country which only they can withstand," and advised their admission as free colonists. The Brazilian Empire, he asserted, required a great inflow of colonists, "whatever be their condition —black, yellow, white . . . ." [24]

A series of contract-labor (*locação de serviços*) laws, passed in 1830, 1837, and 1879, probably contributed little to solving the labor problem, but reveal nevertheless the abiding desire of Brazilian planters to maintain control over their labor force through legal obligation rather than through the granting of incentives. The first of these laws, passed by the General Assembly just months after the slave trade became illegal, authorized planters to contract foreigners for agricultural labor for unspecified periods of time. Workers so employed could sever their contracts only by restoring unearned salaries and paying their employer half the income which they would have earned if they had completed their contracts. Employees failing to fulfill their contracts were subject to jail terms or even penal servitude until such time as their debts were paid. The contracting of "barbarous Africans" under these terms was illegal, "with the exception of those now in Brazil." [25]

Seven years later a second contract-labor bill was passed. This law, which permitted individuals or colonization societies to conclude contracts with Brazilian or foreign workers, gave a decided advantage to the users of labor. Employers could dismiss workers on various grounds, but employees discharged were still obligated to pay the debts which they had contracted in the process of their employment and shipment to Brazil. Hired persons failing to meet their obligations could be condemned to penal servitude. Workers who abandoned their employers without good cause before completing their contracts could be arrested and held until they had paid their masters twice the sum of their debts

23. *O Popular,* Porto das Caixas, March 17, 1855.
24. F. L. da C. Pimentel, *Estatutos da Companhia Libertadora ou Reparadora dos direitos da humanidade* (Rio de Janeiro, 1858), p. vii. As late as the 1860's many planters and even a few statesmen still believed that Brazilian prosperity was dependent upon the importation of slaves from Africa. See Ferreira Soares, *Notas estatisticas,* p. 6.
25. *Colecção das leis do Imperio* (1830), I, 32–33.

or had worked twice the length of their contracts. Persons aiding run-away colonists were also subject to imprisonment or the payment of twice the outstanding debt of the fugitives. Workers who completed their contracts were to receive certificates of release, and the lack of such a document was to be legal evidence of a hired man's breach of contract.[26]

In 1879, on the eve of the abolitionist struggle, a third contract-labor law was passed to provide for a system of sharecropping enforced by long-term contracts. According to this law, workers failing to fulfill their obligations were to be subject to imprisonment and obligated to return to their work upon completion of their sentences.[27] The enforcement of such laws was probably difficult, but they further damaged Brazil's poor reputation among prospective immigrants. In 1884 Alfredo d'Escra-gnolle Taunay, noted writer and abolitionist, told the Chamber of Deputies that the accusation so often heard in Europe that Brazil was trying to transform Europeans into serfs, if not slaves, was based largely upon the contract-labor laws of 1830, 1837, and 1879, all of which contained penal sections that gravely affected human liberty.[28]

BRAZILIAN PARIAHS

Considering the intensity of the outcry for workers and the severity of the labor shortage, it is remarkable that so little interest was shown in the hundreds of thousands of indigent Brazilians who subsisted on the fringes of the dominant economy or eked out a living through begging, vice, and crime. For this great social problem, in fact, slavery was also responsible, for, as long as slave labor was available, landholders were little inclined to hire free men and women, and poor Brazilians, many of them former slaves, were themselves reluctant to accept the hardships and even degradation associated with plantation life.

In much of Brazil, in fact, but particularly in areas where slaves were most abundant, planters hesitated to hire poor native Brazilians because experience showed that they were often unwilling to bend to the rigors of plantation life in exchange for the dubious rewards that planters were willing or able to pay. There was no shortage of workers on Brazilian soil, but, to labor-hungry planters, putting the native Brazilian to work on a permanent basis under prevailing conditions seemed

---

26. *Ibid.* (1837), I, 99.
27. *Ibid.* (1879), Part I, Vol. XXVI, pp. 11–18.
28. *Annaes da Câmara* (1884), II, 210–211. About these same laws a Rio abolitionist paper, *Gazeta da Tarde,* stated on July 8, 1884: "Agriculture wanted workers, many workers, and cheap ones, so cheap that they would appear gratis."

to present obstacles greater than those involved in acquiring new slaves from other parts of Brazil or even Chinese workers, who were reputedly more ambitious than marginal Brazilians.[29] Millions were idle, reported a planter delegation to the Agricultural Congress of 1878 at a time when declining slavery had sparked a new interest in the indigent and unemployed Brazilian. Millions lived in partial or complete barbarity, rarely working because they were accustomed to deprivation and misery.[30] "Six million persons," wrote an inquiring French defender of Brazilian slavery about 1881, "are born, vegetate, and die without having served their country."[31] The backlanders were completely unemployed, said another foreigner in 1883 with a touch of scorn, "beyond being possessors of redlined 'ponchos' and guns to slaughter little birds with." The home of the backlander was "a simple roof of rushes, with a little space beneath, walled off by a partition made of poles and laths bound together by dried creeper stems. . . ."[32] The population of Brazil, a writer testified in 1878, "is poor in blood, does not eat, does not know what hygiene is, does not know what civilization is."[33]

In a society where labor was drudgery, poorly paid, and identified with servitude, the Brazilian pariah often preferred this precarious rural existence to regular plantation employment. The countryside was infested with vagabonds—idle not because they were lazy, but because, as Joaquim Nabuco put it, "they did not find about them the incentive which awakens in the poor man a vision of well-being acquired through labor . . . ."[34] The principal causes of this dilemma, as Nabuco and other abolitionists were to claim during the last years of bondage, were slavery and the plantation system. The planters with their large properties, they believed, monopolized the economic life of the country, preventing the growth of markets and small farms. Unpaid for their labor, workers vanished.[35]

That slavery was a major cause of this underemployment of free

29. Beiguelman, *A formação do povo*, pp. 122–124.
30. *Congresso Agrícola. Colecção de documentos*, p. 58.
31. Louis Couty, *L'esclavage au Brésil* (Paris, 1881), p. 87.
32. *Rio News*, April 15, 1883.
33. *Congresso Agrícola. Colecção de documentos*, p. 189. For a discussion of Brazil's huge "socially undefined element" as it existed at the end of the eighteenth century, see Prado, *The Colonial Background*, pp. 328–333.
34. Joaquim Nabuco, *O Abolicionismo* (London, 1883), pp. 165–166. Convinced that the labor shortage was a myth, the mulatto abolitionist, André Rebouças, argued that what Brazil lacked was not people, but the morality, charity, education, industry, and communications needed to advance the welfare of the population it already had. See *Agricultura nacional*, pp. 50, 383.
35. Joaquim Nabuco, *Conferencia a 22 de Junho de 1884 no Theatro Polytheama* (Rio de Janeiro, 1884), p. 21; Nabuco, *O Abolicionismo*, pp. 165–166; *Manifesto da Confederação Abolicionista do Rio de Janeiro* (Rio de Janeiro, 1883), p. 18.

Brazilians became ever more obvious as slavery declined and more of the indigent country people and even ex-slaves were attracted to agriculture as paid hands, tenant farmers, or sharecroppers. Such solutions were particularly common in the northeast, where slavery declined faster than in the coffee provinces in the three decades after 1850. Even in the south-central region, however, planters who had doubted their ability to attract free workers, native or foreign, discovered in 1887 and 1888, as slavery collapsed, that every kind of worker was available to planters who were willing to pay them, though in São Paulo, at least, the Brazilian workers were still reputed the least desirable class of laborers.[36] Nevertheless, until they were really needed by the plantation system, the free Brazilian poor played only a marginal role in the dominant economy, and coffee planters continued to doubt that they would ever provide a satisfactory substitute for slaves until the eve of abolition.[37]

THE HAPLESS BLACK MAN

In the 1850's, in fact, the "solution" to the labor problem remained the slave in most parts of the country. To keep him subject to his master, tolerant national regimes were forced to set aside or ignore statutory inconveniences. In that decade, in fact, slaveholders had reasons to believe that they were particularly favored by the state. Little or no evidence existed to suggest, for example, that the Imperial Government or any ministry would ever take steps to liberate the hundreds of thousands of Africans (and their offspring) brought into Brazil after November 7, 1831, all of whom were legally free according to the first article of the anti-traffic law of that date. The Brazilian government, in fact, never took action to restore these illegally enslaved to freedom. The number of persons held illegally as slaves was nearly half a million, the British Minister to Brazil estimated in 1862, but he warned his government that the Brazilian regime "for reasons similar to those which restrain them from endeavouring to deal with the general question of slavery, would probably receive any representation of Her Majesty's Government with strong repugnance and opposition." [38] Slaves were not required to be registered in Brazil before 1872, and slaveowners lacked bills of sale for slaves illegally imported. Yet the ownership of such persons was rarely questioned, even when their ages and African origins were convincing

36. Beiguelman, *A formação do povo,* pp. 121–132.
37. Godoy, *O elemento servil,* pp. 76, 100, 117.
38. Christie to Earl Russell, Rio de Janeiro, May 3, 1862, *BFSP* (1862–1863), LIII, 1312.

proof of their right to freedom.[39] On such shaky legality as this the Brazilian slave system was based during almost the last half century of its existence. Yet during most of that time Brazilian governments, courts, the Emperor, and most of the press ignored the fate of these hundreds of thousands. The 1831 law was never revoked or rejected by the courts, and in fact its validity was upheld by the Council of State in 1856.[40] In the 1870's and 1880's a few abolitionist lawyers, notably Luiz Gama and Antônio Joaquim Macedo Soares, freed many slaves on the basis of this old law, "supposedly revoked by disuse." [41] Yet most judges and courts overlooked this legal inconvenience, and only a small minority of illegally imported Africans or their descendants could ever have benefited from its major provisions. As late as 1883 a Brazilian court reversed a judge's decision to free Africans presumably imported after 1831 not on the grounds that the law was invalid but because the court was "not satisfied with the evidence produced in proof of age and nationality." [42] The failure to enforce the law had a simple cause: to do so would have meant the liberation of a large part of the slave population, almost the practical equivalent of abolition, which until the final months of slavery could hardly have been accomplished with the toleration of the Brazilian landed elite. Indicative of the slaveholders' faith in the goodwill of the authorities toward them were the advertisements which masters placed in newspapers for the return of runaway Africans too young to have entered Brazil before 1831 and therefore patently free if the law had been respected.[43]

The governments of Brazil were on the whole careless of the right of black men to their freedom. A particularly scandalous example of neglect involved a category of Africans known as *emancipados* who, during the first half of the nineteenth century, had been removed from slave ships, freed by the British-Brazilian mixed commission in Rio de Janeiro, and placed in the custody of the Imperial Government. In the treaties of 1817 and 1826 with Great Britain, Brazil had committed her-

39. In 1862 it was estimated that if all masters were made to prove the ownership of the persons they held in bondage, three-fourths of Brazilian slaves would be found to be free. British Consul to Christie, Bahia, June 14, 1862, *Class B., 1862,* p. 122.
40. Macedo Soares, *Campanha jurídica,* p. 83.
41. "A lei de 7 de Novembro de 1831 está em vigor," in *ibid.,* pp. 29–72; Evaristo de Moraes, *A campanha abolicionista (1879–1888)* (Rio de Janeiro, 1924), pp. 176–186; *Gazeta da Tarde,* December 15, 1880, March 15, 1884; *Rio News,* April 24, 1883.
42. *South American Journal,* August 16, 1883.
43. For such advertisements, see *O Cruzeiro,* Rio de Janeiro, April 13, 1878; *Gazeta de Noticias,* Rio de Janeiro, April 14, 1880. For protests against the practice, see *Gazeta da Tarde,* October 5, 1882; *Rio News,* December 24, 1882.

self to assuring the liberty of such free Africans while they were being employed as servants and free workers, but for nearly half a century Brazilian officials and governments were dismally neglectful of these commitments.[44]

As early as 1826 British judges in Rio de Janeiro reported that records of the emancipados were in such a state of confusion and neglect that "those whose freedom is guaranteed by the government are lost sight of." [45] In 1832 the Brazilian Justice Minister, Father Feijó, revealed the precariousness of the freedom of emancipados. The owners of slave ships, he told the General Assembly, were often able to regain their seized slaves through the issuance of bogus death certificates during the period their vessels awaited adjudication by the mixed commission court. The treatment of free blacks rented to private persons, said Feijó, "burdening them perhaps with excessive labor, or denying them the support strictly necessary for the preservation of life, could excessively shorten their existence and make their condition more precarious and pitiful than that of the slaves themselves." [46]

According to Perdigão Malheiro, free Africans were treated worse than slaves. Whether distributed to private entrepreneurs or to government establishments, they were misused and denied the moral and religious education and protection guaranteed by law.[47] Various writers testified that great difficulties were placed in the way of the true emancipation of "free Africans." The British Minister in Rio, James Hudson, described the freedmen placed in the custody of the Brazilian government as "most wretched, . . . ill-used, ill-fed, beaten without mercy and without reason, sold, false certificates given of their death, and, in short, every man's hand seems to be raised against them; they have no chance of real freedom in Brazil." [48] An informant told William Christie in 1861 that the difficulties encountered by free Africans in obtaining their final certificates of emancipation were "so great that they cannot possibly, through their own exertions alone, obtain those letters." [49] The Brazilian writer, Tavares Bastos, outlined twenty bureaucratic hurdles placed in the path of free Africans who petitioned for their final emancipation, concluding that those who enjoyed the services of a freedman "do not commit the folly of facilitating his emancipation . . . ." [50]

44. See Bethell, *The Abolition,* pp. 380–383; Graham, *Britain and the Onset,* pp. 168–169; Conrad, "The Struggle," pp. 120–122, 199–200, 257.

45. His Majesty's Commissioners to Canning, Rio de Janeiro, November 20, 1826, *Class A., 1827,* p. 153.

46. *Relatorio de Exmo. Ministro da Justiça* (Rio de Janeiro, 1832), p. 3.

47. Perdigão Malheiro, *A escravidão,* II, 70–72.

48. Hudson to Palmerston, Rio de Janeiro, November 11, 1850, *Class B., From April 1, 1850, to March 31, 1851,* p. 319.

49. *Class B., 1861,* p. 46; *Class B., 1862,* p. 94.

50. Tavares Bastos, *Cartas do Solitario,* pp. 461–462.

British diplomatic pressure was apparently decisive on the various occasions when Brazilian governments acted to liberate "emancipados." The British-Brazilian dispute over the state of the free Africans simmered for decades, contributing finally to a major crisis in British-Brazilian relations, the Christie Affair.[51] William Christie first raised the question of the African freedmen in May 1862, and some months later received a dispatch from London virtually ordering him to demand the liberation of all free Africans still held in servitude by the Brazilian government or private persons.[52] In March 1863 Christie was still remonstrating with the Brazilian government concerning free Africans and even the liberation of all slaves imported after 1830, when Brazil broke off relations with Great Britain as a result of British "reprisals" against Brazilian shipping and a six-day naval blockade of Rio de Janeiro.[53]

In *Notes on Brazilian Questions* Christie observed that one effect of the suspension of relations in 1863, for which his own undiplomatic procedures were evidently responsible, was the hastening of the emancipation of free Africans. Christie claimed that the Brazilian government had followed policies of delay when dealing with the question of free Africans which could be compared with their former policies on the slave trade question. "Left to themselves," the Brazilian government "did nothing." For a long time it neglected British notes on the subject. "When obliged to reply, it protested that its dignity did not allow it to act when pressed by a foreign Government . . . ." Brazilian regimes resented foreign interference, and demanded to be left free to execute Brazilian laws. "At last," concluded Christie, "after force had been used, and the English government was known to be serious and there seemed no help for it, [the Brazilian government] has done what it ought to have done long before; and it is now contended that this has been done spontaneously, and that all reproaches are unjust." [54]

While relations were severed, in fact, the Brazilian government at last granted final liberation to all free Africans by a decree of September 24, 1864,[55] but as late as March 1865 a British official reported that

51. According to Richard Graham, the issues involved in the crisis were the status of Africans imported after November 7, 1831, the freedmen, and Brazilian slavery itself. See *Britain and the Onset*, p. 169.

52. Christie to Earl Russell, Rio de Janeiro, May 3, 1862, *BFSP* (1862–1863), LIII, 1312; Earl Russell to Christie, Foreign Office, November 8, 1862, *ibid.*, p. 1319.

53. Graham, *Britain and the Onset*, pp. 167–171; Bethell, *The Abolition*, pp. 382–383; Mary Wilhelmine Williams, *Dom Pedro the Magnanimous* (Chapel Hill, North Carolina), pp. 104–107.

54. William Dougal Christie, *Notes on Brazilian Questions* (London, 1865), pp. xxxiv–xxxv.

55. For a copy of the decree, see Luiz Francisco da Veiga, *Livro do estado servil e respectiva libertação* (Rio de Janeiro, 1876), pp. 15–16.

emancipados "employed in the Public Departments under the eyes of the Supreme Authorities of the State" remained in bondage. "It appears to be clear," the same official added, "that unless some further pressure be brought to bear on the officers charged with the execution of the Decree, that the majority of these Emancipados and their offspring will die in slavery." [56]

The "emancipated Africans" were not the only persons whose claim to freedom was not fully respected. Indian slavery was outlawed in 1831, but reports of their enslavement were not unusual in later years.[57] In the Amazonian province of Pará, Indians, *mestiços,* and blacks were pressed into provincial labor corps as early as 1835 on the basis of their "perpetual intellectual minority." In 1858 the president of that province reported that many of the inhabitants of the province's *quilombos* (runaway slave settlements) were free men who had fled into the forests to avoid forced labor.[58] In Ceará government authorities forced free persons to work gratuitously on cotton and sugar plantations. In some provinces legislative assemblies trying to alleviate the labor problem had "prescribed more or less rigorous rules" with the aim of forcing the idle population to work.[59] Just after the abolition of the African slave trade, Brazilian raiding parties from the southern province of Rio Grande do Sul often crossed into neighboring Uruguay to kidnap persons of color for delivery to Brazilian slave markets. Whole Uruguayan families, according to the British Consul, were seized, separated, and sold in Brazil with an ease which was strong evidence of the ineffectiveness of Brazilian law as a protector of personal freedom. In contrast, less than three years later the Brazilian government gave proof of its concern for the property of slaveholders when it concluded a treaty with the Argentine Confederation providing for the forced return of runaway slaves who found refuge in that neighboring country.[60]

---

56. Hunt to Earl Russell, Rio de Janeiro, March 10, 1865, FO 84/1244, PRO. For documentation on one emancipado who served as an apprentice for 26 years, see Documentos sôbre a repressão ao tráfico de africanos no litoral fluminense, SECRJ, loose documents dated July 26, 1838, and December 12, 1864.
57. Daniel P. Kidder, *Sketches of Residence and Travels in Brazil* (2 vols.; Philadelphia, 1845), II, 267–268; Thomas Ewbank, *Life in Brazil* (New York, 1856), pp. 278–279 and 323; *Rio News,* November 15, 1880; Charles Wagley, *Amazon Town* (New York, 1953), p. 129.
58. *Discurso da abertura da sessão extraordinaria da Assembléa Provincial do Pará. Em 7 de Abril de 1858 pelo Presidente Dr. João da Silva Carrão* (Belém, Pará, 1858), pp. 32–34.
59. *Falla dirigida a Assembléa Legislativa da provincia das Alagôas . . . em o 1º de Março de 1855* (Recife, 1855), p. 55; *Annaes da Câmara* (1866), II, 41.
60. British Consul to Earl of Clarendon, Rio Grande do Sul, June 30, 1855, *Class B., From April 1, 1855, to March 31, 1856; BFSP* (1858–1859), XLIX, 1337–1339.

During the years when the labor shortage was most severe the mere possession of a black skin accompanied by uncertain legal standing could be grounds for the presumption of slave status. An Imperial decree of 1859 regulated the disposal of a class of unclaimed "property" known as *bens do evento* (contingency goods), which were defined as "slaves, cattle or beasts found without knowledge as to their masters." Such men and animals, said the decree, were to be evaluated and auctioned off if their "owners" did not respond to public announcements. This decree, unlike similar regulations for bens do evento in Pernambuco, gave human contingency goods the privilege of purchasing their own freedom if they offered an amount of money equal to their official evaluations, even if other bidders offered more, but nothing was said about their right to prove that they were free men.[61]

As these facts suggest, the attitudes of Brazilian governments toward the enslaved and the enslavable were not always favorable to freedom during the twelve to fifteen years after the termination of the African slave trade. Belonging as they often did to the planter class, Brazilian politicians and statesmen were little motivated toward reform or the enforcement of laws intended to protect the slave population or to secure the freedom of the illegally enslaved. A few men holding elective office during those years spoke out in defense of slaves or even advocated abolition, but their proposals were badly received. In 1850 Pedro Pereira da Silva Guimaraes of Ceará proposed the liberation of the newborn children of slave women, compulsory liberation of slaves offering their price, and a ban on the separation of married couples, but his measures were judged unsuitable for discussion. In 1853, when the same deputy proposed a similar bill, four northern colleagues were willing to debate the project, but a majority disapproved, some with indignant outcries and interruptions.[62] During the decade after the abolition of the African traffic, others occasionally proposed measures to ameliorate the difficult conditions of slaves or to shift them from urban to rural areas to ease the labor shortage, but the legislators and the nation were not yet in a mood to alter the status quo.[63]

While the General Assembly did nothing, the executive branch of government consistently reached decisions adverse to change. In 1852 the government strongly opposed alteration of the status of Africans imported after November 7, 1831, though their slave status was illegal. In the same year the Council of State, the Emperor's advisory body,

61. *Colecção das leis do Imperio* (1859), pp. 452–453; *Pernambuco. Leis, decretos, etc.* (Pernambuco, 1855); Perdigão Malheiro, *A escravidão*, I, 73–74.
62. "Pedro Pereira da Silva Guimaraes (Documentos historicos)," *Revista Trimensal do Instituto do Ceará*, Vol. XX; Girão, *A abolição no Ceará*, pp. 17–27.
63. Osorio Duque-Estrada, *A abolição (esboço historico)* (Rio de Janeiro, 1918), pp. 42–43; Dornas Filho, *A escravidão*, pp. 143–144.

opposed legislation to permit an abused slave to demand his sale to another master. It was preferable, thought the members of that body, to avoid discussion in the General Assembly of any measure concerning the slave population, "since all had been done which could or should be done in the effective repression of the slave trade." Similarly, in 1855, the Council of State decided that a slave could not legally compel his master to release him from servitude through an offer of his appraised value, since the Imperial Constitution guaranteed the right of property and no exception had been made in the case of the slave who offered his value in exchange for his freedom. In 1857, in reply to a British suggestion, the same body opposed the taking of a slave census on the grounds that such a head count would serve no useful purpose and would only encourage further British demands.[64]

The planter class, protected by the government's lack of concern for the welfare of plantation slaves, in fact expected and received direct aid from the authorities. Governments, for example, were much concerned with efforts to foment European immigration, to foster the construction of telegraph lines and railroads for the easy exportation of coffee and other products, to stabilize the national currency, to reform the banking system, to provide a favorable environment for agriculture and commerce, "those two perennial sources of national wealth." [65] Brazilian regimes of the 1850's were little disposed, however, to act on behalf of slaves or to rescue the hundreds of thousands held illegally. Brazil was an agricultural country governed by a slaveholding class whose interests could not then be much advanced by a change of policy on the slavery question. The abolition of the African traffic was therefore followed by more than a decade of near silence on the slavery question. Brazil learned to live without the African slave trade, but slavery, long extinct in most Latin American countries, ending in Venezuela and Colombia, and about to cause an unparalleled disaster in the United States, was still a powerful institution in Brazil. Few persons gave serious thought to its abolition until such thoughts were forced upon them by changing conditions both at home and abroad.

64. Graham, *Britain and the Onset,* p. 168; Joaquim Nabuco, *Um estadista do Imperio* (4 vols.; São Paulo, 1949), I, 249–250; Nabuco, *O Abolicionismo,* p. 129; *Colecção das leis do Imperio* (1855), pp. 454–455.
65. For brief summaries of the ministerial programs of the period, see *Organizações e programas ministeriais* (2nd ed.; Rio de Janeiro, 1962), pp. 111–139. See also Stein, *The Brazilian Cotton Manufacture,* p. 7.

The slaves, gentlemen,
do not have the incentive of wages,
nor personal security, and the fear of punishment
cannot overcome these facts.

BERNARDO PEREIRA DE VASCONCELOS
in the Chamber of Deputies, 1827

Brazil is coffee and coffee
is the Negro.

AN APHORISM ATTRIBUTED TO SENATOR
SILVEIRA MARTINS OF RIO GRANDE DO SUL

4

THE INTER-PROVINCIAL SLAVE TRADE

THE INTERNAL TRAFFIC

Aggravating the labor problem in some parts of Brazil and alleviating it in others was the flow of slaves to those places where the product of their labor was most valuable. The internal slave trade in Brazil was, in fact, strikingly similar to that which developed in the United States under comparable circumstances. The expanding cotton industry in Alabama, Mississippi, Louisiana, and Texas increased the demand for slaves, elevated slave prices, and turned the less prosperous states from Virginia to South Carolina into exporters and even breeders of slaves.[1] In Brazil, the crop that set off these processes was coffee, but developments were much the same as in the American south.[2] Slave prices rose in response to demand and profits.[3] Slaves were made to migrate, and masters sometimes pulled up stakes and went with their entire work forces into the more promising regions. New frontier areas were opened, and the cultivation of rich new soils expanded production,

1. A. A. Taylor, "The Movement of Negroes from the East to the Gulf States from 1830 to 1850," *Journal of Negro History*, Vol. 8 (1923), pp. 367–374.
2. For an analysis of the situation in the American South, see Robert William Fogel and Stanley L. Engerman, "The Economics of Slavery," in Fogel and Engerman, *The Reinterpretation of American Economic History*, pp. 311–341.
3. For the rise of slave prices after 1850, see Stein, *Vassouras*, p. 229.

heightening the commitment to slavery. The statement attributed to Senator Silveira Martins—"Brazil is coffee and coffee is the Negro"—characterized a Brazilian reality which resembled the relationship that had evolved between cotton and slavery in the American south. If cotton was "king" in a large part of the United States, it was that same nation's breakfast stimulant which greatly determined the course of events in Brazil.

The forced migration of Brazilian slaves, which followed suppression of the African traffic, began on the plantations, farms, and cities of the northern, western, and extreme southern regions of the country and ended with their arrival on the coffee plantations of Rio de Janeiro, Minas Gerais, and São Paulo. The movement continued on a large scale for thirty years—from 1851 until its virtual abolition by the provincial legislatures of the importing provinces in 1881.

The new traffic was not unprecedented. For hundreds of years slaves in Brazil had been moved to whatever part of the country most required them and wherever they brought the best prices. During the sixteenth century, Indian and Negro captives had been concentrated on the great sugar plantations of Pernambuco and Bahia. During the seventeenth century, the legendary *bandeirantes* of São Paulo had ranged over large parts of the South American interior in search of Indians, both pagan and Christian, driving them to coastal markets for shipment to the prosperous northeastern sugar captaincies. In the eighteenth century, despite restrictions on the movement of slaves into mining regions, many black captives were sent to the gold washings of Minas Gerais, Goiás, and Mato Grosso, causing a labor shortage on northeastern sugar plantations.[4] With the decline of mining in Minas Gerais in the late eighteenth century and the subsequent growth of the coffee industry, part of the population of south-central Brazil, both slave and free, shifted to the new coffee regions.[5]

Even before the African slave trade ended, small numbers of slaves from northeastern Brazil were entering the slave markets of Rio de Janeiro to meet the demand created there by coffee cultivation. By as early as 1842 the movement of slaves between the provinces was large enough to require regulation, and by 1847 widespread drought, centered in and about the province of Ceará, had increased the spontaneous flow of northern slaves toward the south. By the latter date, merchants in Rio with commercial connections in north Brazil were "casually" receiving slaves on consignment to meet financial needs of masters in areas

4. Boxer, *The Golden Age,* pp. 42–47; Bastide and Fernandes, *Brancos e negros,* p. 8.
5. Viotti da Costa, *Da senzala à colônia,* pp. 60–62.

afflicted by drought. Similarly, drought in Ceará had stimulated a traffic in Indians, who were forced by famine to sell their children.[6]

With the abrupt suppression of the African trade, the trickle of northern slaves into the south grew into a torrent and began to be regarded as vital to the interests of planters in the coffee region. Prices of slaves at Rio soared in the months just after the suppression of the African traffic, motivating southern planters to look beyond local markets to meet their labor needs, even to acquire slaves in the extreme southern province of Rio Grande do Sul.[7] Almost as soon as it had begun, the government and members of the General Assembly regarded the inter-provincial slave trade as vital and unassailable.[8]

In May 1852, a report of the Justice Ministry used the word "fabulous" to describe the rise in slave prices at Rio. The cost of slaves had doubled in a brief time, so that even those with "vices" and "defects," previously unwanted, were finding buyers.[9] Not only were prices high, but, as Table 7 shows, the volume of slaves entering Rio de Janeiro from northern and southern provinces was also rapidly increasing.

In one of a series of articles protesting the growing internal slave traffic, in April 1852 the anti-slave-trade journal, *O Philantropo,* termed the new trade as scandalous as that which it had replaced.[10] In that month at least 345 slaves had entered the Rio market: 245 from northern ports, 48 from Rio Grande do Sul, and the remaining 52 from nearby ports. Of a total of 1,660 slaves recorded as entering the port of Rio from other parts of Brazil during the first fourth months of 1852, 1,376 were from northern ports (691 from the overstocked port of Bahia alone), and 114 from extreme southern provinces.[11]

In April, *O Globo,* a newspaper of the far northern province of Maranhão, told of a large exportation of slaves to Rio de Janeiro, carried on despite a new export tax of 500 milréis imposed on the exporters for each slave shipped.[12] The growing demand for slaves increased the

6. Howard to Earl of Clarendon, Rio de Janeiro, January 24, 1855, *BFSP* (1854–1855), XLV, 1058–1059; Requerimento dos negociantes desta praça . . . . , BNSM, II, 34, 26, 26; Ewbank, *Life in Brazil,* p. 323.
7. Stein, *Vassouras,* pp. 228–229. In the 1850's there was an exodus of slaves from Rio Grande do Sul, but with the expansion of the *charque* (jerked beef) industry between 1859 and 1863 the province became an importer of slaves. During the 1870's this was again reversed. See Tables 3 and 9 and Cardoso, *Capitalismo e escravidão,* pp. 69–70, 208.
8. *Annaes da Câmara* (1851), II, 319–320.
9. *Relatorio apresentado . . . na quarta sessão da oitava legislatura pelo Ministro e Secretario d'Estado dos Negocios da Justiça,* p. 9.
10. *O Philantropo,* April 16, 1852.
11. *Ibid.,* April 16, 30, May 14, 1852.
12. Cited by *ibid.,* April 30, 1852.

stealing of slaves in the cities; even an illicit cargo landed on a beach in Rio de Janeiro province in 1851 and under police protection was not immune to thieves.[13] The situation was awakening the business sense of persons in the new coffee regions of São Paulo. Early in 1853 the provincial president was informed by a local judge at Campinas, a growing center of coffee production, that "convoys" of slaves had recently arrived to be sold "at a very exaggerated price." One slave dealer had recently arrived with a group "composed of 23 slaves of both sexes, and of diverse ages, all Creoles and *ladinos"* (acculturated Africans), and it was said that another slave merchant was about to return from Santa Catarina with fifteen slaves, all ladinos. "At the present time," said the same report, "the purchase of slaves in distant places is proposed in order to sell them in this district—owing to the exaggerated prices to which they have here risen, and this is what various persons have done, going to buy them even in Goiás." The first group of slaves to which the judge referred was composed "almost entirely of Creoles from Bahia, Alagôas and Sergipe . . . picked out . . . and purchased in Rio de Janeiro." [14] The northern and extreme southern regions of the Empire and even the far interior, as *O Globo* had reported in reference to Maranhão, had become the "coast of Africa" for Rio de Janeiro.[15] The new trade was legal, though for a time the Brazilian government examined inter-provincial cargoes to prevent a renewal of the African traffic under another guise.[16]

The internal slave trade was not often described, but rare accounts suggest that it maintained many of the practical and brutal characteristics of the African trade.[17] The young and the strong were in greatest demand; males were more numerous in shipments, but young women were sought after if physically attractive or useful as wet nurses.[18] Family relationships were no guarantee against separation; husbands and wives

13. See Freyre, *The Mansions and the Shanties,* p. 47; Subdelegate of Quiçamã to Police Delegate of Macahé, February 17, 1851, SECRJ, Documentos para a repressão ao tráfico, No. 33; Conrad, "The Struggle," p. 342.
14. Judge of Campinas to President of São Paulo, Campinas, February 7, 1853, AESP, Caixa-Tráfico de negros.
15. Quoted by *O Philantropo,* April 30, 1852.
16. *Relatorio apresentado . . . na primeira sessão da nona legislatura pelo Ministro e Secretario de Estado dos Negocios da Justiça* (Rio de Janeiro, 1853), pp. 6–7; Termos de exames e averiguações feitas nos escravos vindos de varias localidades, AN, Cod. 397.
17. *Annaes da Câmara* (1854), IV, 349.
18. The *Gazeta da Tarde,* January 5, 1881, denounced merchants who sent shipments of females from impoverished northern provinces to rent them as wet nurses or sell them into prostitution. At 50 milréis per month, it estimated, a wet nurse bought in the north for from 400 to 600 milréis yielded 900 in eighteen months and then was marketable at 1,500 milréis.

and their children were parted, though small children often traveled with their mothers and accompanied their sale. In 1880 a newspaper of Ceará told of a local slave woman named Raymunda who at fifty-six had borne twenty children. Eight of these had been "liberated" by death, and twelve surviving brothers and sisters had been sent to the south.[19]

The internal slave trade produced new slave-trading companies and a new profession: that of the traveling slave-buyer who rummaged the provinces, persuading poor farmers or town residents to part with a servant or two in exchange for cash. Slave buyers went from farm to farm, door to door, said a Bahian member of the Chamber of Deputies in 1854, offering poorer farmers seven or eight hundred milréis for slaves who were providing their masters with annual incomes of from thirty to forty milréis.[20] "All at once a slave-trader comes into the market from Rio de Janeiro," wrote a British official in Bahia in the same year, "buys up from the needy or avaricious masters all those slaves he can obtain, and in most cases is the cause of the separation of a father from his wife and children . . . ."[21]

In 1852 the British Consul at Pernambuco, a Mr. Cowper, reported that the internal traffic was "attended with all the horrors of its prototype. . . ." Most painful scenes were being witnessed at Recife, with the departure of every steamship.[22] The trade between the northern provinces and Rio de Janeiro, he wrote four years later, involved thousands of persons annually. Traders made periodic visits to the port of Pernambuco, returning to Rio with their "unresisting victims." Many of the young females were

bought by these rascals for the express purpose of public prostitution in the capital. . . . A woman who had born (sic) thirteen children and thus considerably increased the means of her master, is now threatened with eternal separation from them . . . ; and a young mulatto man was thus recently sold by his own father, a Portuguese. . . . Could not the law forbid the separation of man and wife, of parent and child, at least beyond the precincts of the province in which they reside? This would not only be an act of humanity, but of policy; it would dry the tears of thousands . . . and *it would stop that drain upon the labour of the northern provinces which cannot fail to be shortly felt.*[23]

---

19. *Gazeta do Norte*, Fortaleza, Ceará, July 27, 1880.
20. *Annaes da Câmara* (1854), IV, 349.
21. Howard to Limpo de Abreu, Rio de Janeiro, April 8, 1854, *Class B., From April 1, 1854, to March 31, 1855*, pp. 90–91.
22. Cowper to Earl of Malmesbury, Pernambuco, May 6, 1852, *Class B., From April 1, 1852, to March 31, 1853*, pp. 278–279.
23. Same to Earl of Clarendon, Pernambuco, October 17, 1856, *Class B., From April 1, 1856, to March 31, 1857*, p. 246. Italics added.

A few months later Cowper claimed that the internal slave trade was as cruel "in its details" as the former African traffic. "The coasting traders have their establishments at the ports, and purchase their slaves from men of the lowest order, generally horsedealers, who bring them down from the interior; this is the real source whence the coasting traffic is derived." [24]

Brazilian sources say much the same. In 1856 a deputy from Maranhão denounced the separation of mothers from their children and husbands from their wives. The slaves, he told the Chamber, were transported "huddled together on the decks of steamers" exposed to sun and rain. Officials sometimes provided canvases to protect them from the weather and invited the sick into their cabins, but too many were being sent south to permit protection for all, and the women and children suffered most.[25] In 1857 the *Jornal do Commercio* of Recife described the conditions of some ninety slaves, including two dozen children ranging in age from one month to two years, who had arrived at Recife on a steamer from Maranhão: "The deck of the steamer appeared like one of those coming from the coast of Africa, loaded with human flesh: we saw one unhappy child combatting with death, and others miserably naked." [26]

Perhaps with the aim of evading the taxes on slaves assessed at the provincial ports of departure, slaves were also marched overland through the interior of Bahia and Minas Gerais to the southern coffee regions. Perhaps the best description of this overland traffic was that of Deputy Marcolino de Moura of Bahia contained in a speech delivered in the Chamber of Deputies in 1880. An eye-witness to what he called "those death troops of tormented innocent persons," he described the overland trade as follows:

Not long ago in the heat of midday, I was passing through one of those desert regions of my native province; the sun burned white-hot. Suddenly I heard a confused clamor of approaching voices. It was an immense caravan of slaves destined for the fields of São Paulo. Among men with chains about their necks walked as many women, carrying on their shoulders their children, among whom were seen youngsters of all ages, the whole march being on foot, bloodying the hot sand of the roads.

Wishing to run from "that painful sight," the witness was stopped by the cry of a mother who "fell breathless by the roadside from the effects of the blazing sun." At night, said the same witness, the encamped slaves

lie extended around a bonfire without distinction of sex or age, and amid the clanging of irons, the wailing of the women and children, are heard the

24. Same to same, Pernambuco, January 24, 1857, *ibid.*, pp. 260–261.
25. *Ibid.*, p. 143.
26. *Class B., From April 1, 1857, to March 31, 1858*, pp. 115–116.

shouts of the guards testing the chains and imposing silence upon those who dare to complain. (*Sensation.*) But beyond the leaping shadows the most unrestrained vice. And if during the night one of those miserable slave women becomes a mother, the next day the march of the convoy is not interrupted, and the cherished fruit of her womb is condemned to die on the first or second day of travel, if it is not thrown before into some corner to die in abandonment . . . . This is the traffic in its most horrendous form . . . .[27]

By the mid-1850's barracoons and slave depositories had disappeared from Brazilian beaches, but convoys of slaves, better treated than their African predecessors, were still to be seen driven through city streets, and business houses still offered them for sale. Creole slaves took the place of "raw" (*boçal*) Africans in the warehouses and on the auction blocks in the main business streets of the capital, on the Rua do Ouvidor and the Rua Direita.[28] Thomas Ewbank described a group of Creole slaves who, along with "new and second-hand furniture, old pictures, Dutch cheeses and Yankee Clocks," were among the "items" auctioned off at a shop on the corner of Ourives and Ouvidor. Of 89 slaves listed in the shop catalog, 53 were males and 36 were females. Unlike the Africans seen a quarter of a century before by British travelers in the Rua do Valongo, many of the slaves Ewbank saw were trained in a craft or profession.[29] Among the males, who generally ranged in age between eighteen and thirty, were

carpenters, masons, smiths, and country hands . . . a sailor, a caulker and boatman . . . two tailors, a coachman, a saddler, a sawyer, a squarer of timber . . . , a shoemaker, cooks, a coffee-carrier, and a baby surgeon, who, like most of his profession, was a musician . . . .

Of the females,

the oldest was twenty-six, and the youngest between seven and eight— washers, sewers, cooks, two dressmakers. Others made shirts, dressed ladies' hair, etc. A couple were wet nurses, with much good milk, and each with a colt or filly, thus: "No. 61, 1 Rapariga, com muito bom leite, com cria."

27. *Annes da Câmara* (1880), V, 38. A similar contemporary account of an overland slave caravan in the United States, without the excesses of the Brazilian example, is quoted in Taylor, "The Movement of Negroes," p. 375. A notable difference in the American arrangement was the supplying of wagons and carriages for transporting whites (presumably migrants too) and any blacks unable to keep up.
28. Perdigão Malheiro, *A escravidão*, II, 119.
29. For descriptions of the old slave market in Rio, see Walsh, *Notices*, II, 322–328; Maria Graham, *Journal of a Voyage to Brazil and Residence There* (London, 1824), p. 229; Chamberlain, *Vistas e costumes*, pp. 198–199; J. B. Debret, *Voyage pittoresque et historique au Brésil* (3 vols.; Paris, 1834–1839), II, 78–79; *Briefe über Brasilien* (Frankfurt am Main, 1857), p. 4. See also Conrad, "The Struggle," pp. 33–38.

Like their African predecessors in Valongo Street, the slaves Ewbank saw were "exposed and examined . . . . The head, eyes, mouth, teeth, arms, hands, trunks, legs, feet—every limb and ligament without are scrutinized, while, to ascertain if aught be ruptured, the breast and other parts are sounded." Unlike the Africans, of course, the Creole "merchandise" was "of every shade, from deep Angola jet to white or nearly white, as one young woman facing me appeared to be." [30] A typical notice of an auction like the one Ewbank attended appeared in a Rio newspaper on July 1, 1854:

SLAVE AUCTION

Today Saturday July 1, on the Rua do Ouvidor No. 90, at 10:30, J. Bouis will have an auction in his house of diverse slaves of both sexes and different ages, they being blacks with trades, ditto of the field, black mucamas, ditto for all service, ditto with children, young black boys (*muleques*), little black girls (*negrinhas*), etc., etc. The honored buyers may examine them before the auction. Those who are not known will put forward a token gesture of 100$000 in the act of bidding on the first slaves. All slaves are attested to be in good health. [31]

In the northern provinces agents or companies regularly placed advertisements in the daily press offering to purchase slaves for shipment south. Typical were the notices in various issues of *A Ordem* of Ceará in which Olympio & Bros. offered "the best prices" for slaves between twelve and twenty for shipment to São Paulo. The Bazaar Primeiro de Dezembro of São Luiz de Maranhão, preparing a shipment for Rio in late 1879, petitioned for slaves in various issues of *O Paiz*. In 1880 an agent established at the Hotel da Europa in São Luiz offered to buy slaves of both sexes and any color, including *filhos ingenuos* (free children of slave women), and later in the same year *O Paiz* ran advertisements announcing that good prices were being paid at the Hotel Porto for slaves of both sexes between twelve and twenty years of age; and that Melchor Brothers & Co. would buy captives without skills and up to fifty years of age. [32]

ECONOMIC CAUSES AND REPERCUSSIONS
OF THE INTER-PROVINCIAL TRAFFIC

The new internal trade was the natural result of the coffee planters' greater capacity to pay, in competition with other Brazilians for a

30. Ewbank, *Life in Brazil*, pp. 282–284.
31. *Diario do Rio de Janeiro*, Rio de Janeiro, July 1, 1854.
32. *A Ordem*, Baturité, Ceará, September 14, 1879; *O Paiz*, São Luiz, October 25, November 27, 1879; February 14, July 7, 8, 1880.

"commodity" in short supply. In July 1852 the Brazilian Naval Minister explained the new traffic in the following manner:

everyone knows that coffee planting occupies more field hands, and with the increasing necessity and high value of the slaves who are employed in that service, the large number of them that come from Bahia is very well explained.

Slaves were coming to Rio de Janeiro from Maranhão and Pará, he continued,

as the result of an economic law, in virtue of which, the object which has less value in one place passes on to another where the price is greater, whatever may be the obstacles which stand in the way of it.[33]

Mr. Webb of the American Legation in Rio reached the same conclusion in 1862:

The rapidly increasing value of the negro in the province of Rio de Janeiro and all the southern provinces of the empire, and the steadily advancing price of coffee, added to the well ascertained fact that the *slave* population is on the *decrease* instead of the *increase,* as with us, . . . is rapidly depopulating the northern provinces of the empire. Every coasting vessel brings its ten to thirty slaves for sale at Rio, for the supply of labor in this vicinity and on the coffee plantations; and the cry is heard from the provinces of Pará, Maranham, Piaui, Parahiba, Pernambuco, and even Bahia, that they are being depopulated for the benefit of the southern provinces, by the inevitable law of demand and supply.[34]

Brazilians with an economic interest in reducing the internal slave traffic quickly envisioned the divisive effects which the movement of population would have upon regional commitments to slavery, and they warned of the consequences of a continuing removal of captive workers from less prosperous regions. In the 1850's coffee planters needed slaves, however, and the dangers of the internal slave trade were remote. Once it had begun, therefore, the traffic continued nearly unrestricted. Over a period of thirty years, it combined with the effects of aging and death to alter the quantity and "quality" of slaves, with particular effectiveness in the less prosperous regions of the country—the dry northern provinces especially, but also the western provinces of Goiás and Mato Grosso and the old mining regions of Minas Gerais, the southern provinces of Paraná, Santa Catarina, and Rio Grande do Sul, and even the less productive coastal zones of the provinces of Rio de Janeiro and São Paulo.

33. *Annaes da Câmara* (1852), II, 211.
34. Webb to Seward, Petrópolis, May 20, 1862, *Message of the President of the United States to the Two Houses of Congress at the Commencement of the Third Session of the Thirty-Seventh Congress* (Washington, 1862), I, 704.

Like other aspects of Brazilian slavery, the internal trade was directly affected by temporary and long-term economic trends. A serious change in the weather or a war on another continent was sufficient cause to uproot new thousands or to reduce the volume of the forced migration. In 1856 the Brazilian Foreign Minister ascribed the drain on slaves from north to south to the failure of Brazilian planters to compete successfully in world sugar markets.[35] Four years later William Christie attributed the trade to the irregularity of the seasons in the north and the resulting poverty of the planters, along with a national financial crisis and the high slave prices at Rio de Janeiro.[36] When markets for northeastern goods improved abroad, the movement of slaves diminished. According to data collected in 1862, 34,668 slaves arrived at the port of Rio from northern and southern provinces between January 1852 and July 1862 —between three and four thousand annually (see Table 8).[37] During 1862, however, a period when the American Civil War offered favorable prospects for Brazilian cotton in world markets and reduced the American coffee market (see Table 26), the exportation of northern slaves to the coffee provinces dropped drastically.

After the American Civil War the annual average rose again, and with the onset of drought in the northeast in 1877 the inter-provincial trade again expanded so rapidly as to endanger the equilibrium of the slave system itself.[38] Prices dropped drastically in the north, particularly in the stricken province of Ceará, and slaveowners, unable to feed their slaves or perhaps even themselves, took what they could get.[39] An indication of the scope of the exportation of slaves from Ceará during the

35. Scarlett to Earl of Clarendon, Rio de Janeiro, October 13, 1856, *Class B., From April 1, 1856, to March 31, 1857,* p. 170.
36. *Class B., From April 1, 1860, to December 31, 1860,* p. 45.
37. The statistics in Table 8 do not include slaves traveling with their masters or sent overland or those sent illegally to avoid taxes. Nor do they include the movement of slaves within provinces, from the mining regions of Minas Gerais to the province's coffee zone, for example. By itself, the growth in the slave population of São Paulo between 1864 and 1874 (see Table 3) seems to prove that the actual movement of slaves was much larger than the number recorded. For statistics essentially in agreement with those in Table 8, see Tavares Bastos, *Cartas do Solitario,* p. 460; Bastide and Fernandes, *Brancos e negros,* p. 36. Ferreira Soares estimated an annual importation of 5,500 slaves into Rio de Janeiro from 1852 to 1859. See Stein, *Vassouras,* pp. 65–66.
38. *Relatorio apresentado a Assembléa Geral Legislativa na primeira sessão da decima sexta legislatura pelo Ministro e Secretario de Estado dos Negocios da Agricultura, Commercio e Obras Publicas Thomaz José Coelho de Almeida* (Rio de Janeiro, 1877), pp. 15–16. Henceforth Agriculture Ministry Reports will be referred to in notes as *Relatorio do Ministerio da Agricultura* with date of presentation.
39. Jorge Freire, *Notas à margem da abolição,* Mossoró, Rio Grande do Norte, 1955), p. 6.

drought of the late 1870's is provided by the unusually large yield which the provincial government collected in 1879 from the tax levied on slaves at the port of exportation. In that year the provincial income from this item was nearly three times what it had been four years earlier. In 1880, however, revenue from this source dropped by nearly half, and in 1881, with the emergence of the radical abolitionist movement in that province, ceased to be recorded.[40]

The economic dominance of south-central Brazil, which inflated slave prices in the capital of the Empire, was not a temporary phenomenon. The value of coffee exported from Brazil from 1840 to 1863 reached 925,000 contos, while the value of sugar, the principal cash crop of the northern provinces, was only 372,000 contos during those same twenty-three years. Producing half of the world's coffee in 1868, Brazil had long before slipped behind in sugar production. In that year, Brazilian coffee exports were worth more in world markets than all other exports combined, while the value of sugar was only about one-sixth of the total value of Brazilian exports.[41] Even during the years when the American Civil War was stimulating Brazilian cotton production, the value of coffee exports remained higher than the value of sugar and cotton exports combined.[42] With the end of the Civil War, of course, the Brazilian share of the world cotton market declined, and the gap between the value of northern and southern exports once more widened. Coffee produced in Brazil in fiscal year 1872/73 was valued at more than 115,000 contos; the combined value of sugar and cotton crops was less than 49,000 contos. In the latter year the total value placed on national production of the same three crops was nearly 170,000 contos, of which more than two-thirds were produced in the four south-central provinces.[43]

The growth or decline of the slave population in the various regions of Brazil depended upon their relative economic success. In the south a major industry, coffee production, was developing and thriving, and was

40. In 1875 the yield from this tax was 44:970$000. In 1879 it produced 125:880$000 and in 1880 66:500$000. At the basic rate of 60 milréis per slave, this indicates that more than two thousand slaves were legally exported from Ceará in 1879, about one in every fifteen slaves in the province. See *Annexos a Falla no dia 2 de Julho de 1877* (Fortaleza, 1877), pp. 4–5; "Annexo B.," *Relatorio com que o Exmo. Sr. Commendador Dr. Sancho de Barros Pimentel passou a administração da provincia do Ceará ao 2º Vice Presidente . . . no dia 31 de Outubro de 1882* (Fortaleza, 1882).
41. William Scully, *Brazil; Its Provinces and Chief Cities* (London, 1868), pp. 19–24.
42. The value of coffee produced in 1864–1865 was set at more than 66,000 contos. The value of sugar and cotton was put at a little more than 48,000 contos. See Perdigão Malheiro, *A escravidão*, II, 68.
43. Rebouças, *Agricultura nacional*, pp. 17, 45–46, 149, 204.

of extraordinary economic importance to the nation as a whole. If traditional attitudes strengthened slavery everywhere, in the coffee region the importance of slavery was further fortified by sound economic considerations. As the following pages will show, this major industry, in need of the most productive labor elements available and financially able to acquire them, favored men over women and the young over the old.

As a consequence of the disproportionately large share of the national wealth produced in Rio de Janeiro, nearly one-fifth of the slaves registered in the Empire in a nationwide enrollment completed in the 1870's were located in that small province: 301,352 of a total of 1,540,829 registered (see Table 2). As São Paulo's coffee production grew after mid-century and burgeoned in the 1860's and 1870's, its slave population also expanded, though by that time the slave population was rapidly declining nationally. (See Figures 2 and 3.) In 1874 São Paulo's slave population of over 174,000, which had risen phenomenally since 1864, was surpassed only by those of Rio de Janeiro and Minas Gerais, though some twenty years before São Paulo had lagged behind eight other provinces in slave population.[44] The losers of slaves were most northeastern provinces, Goiás, Paraná, and the Município Neutro, with the important northeastern provinces of Pernambuco and Bahia spectacularly heavy losers (see Table 3). During the following ten years, while the Empire's slave population dropped by nearly twenty percent, the slave populations of São Paulo and Minas Gerais hardly changed, because the dead were replaced by the forced slave migrants needed to open new areas of coffee cultivation. In contrast, during those same years the slave population of the economically declining province of Rio de Janeiro decreased almost as fast as the national average. By 1874 well over half of the slaves of Brazil were located in the four major coffee-producing provinces, and only about one-third were living in the eleven northern provinces. Ten years later nearly two-thirds of the slaves were in the four south-central provinces, and the portion of the slave population in the eleven northern provinces had been further reduced to somewhat more than one-fourth of the total.

As these statistics imply, in the northern provinces the inter-provincial slave trade hastened the transformation to a free-labor system, but in the coffee regions it delayed that development. The employment of free workers in the north was the inevitable result of a rapid drop in the slave population accompanied by an impressive growth in the number of free inhabitants. In some northern provinces, in fact, the ratio of slaves to free men fell so sharply in the decades after mid-century as to render slaves an almost insignificant element in the total population.

44. Dr. Domingo José Nogueira Jaguaribe Filho, *Assembléa Provincial de São Paulo. Discurso pronunciado na sessão ordinaria de 22 de Março de 1882* (São Paulo, 1882), p. 6.

Population (thousands)

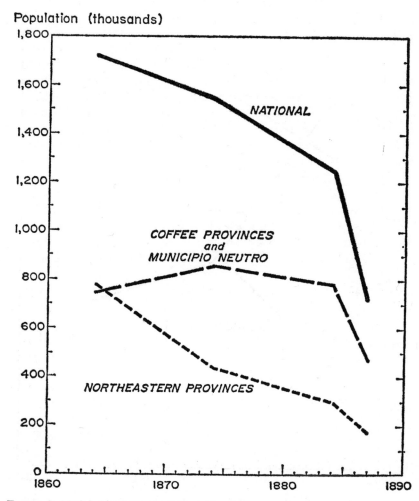

FIGURE 2. National and Regional Slave Populations.

Population (thousands)

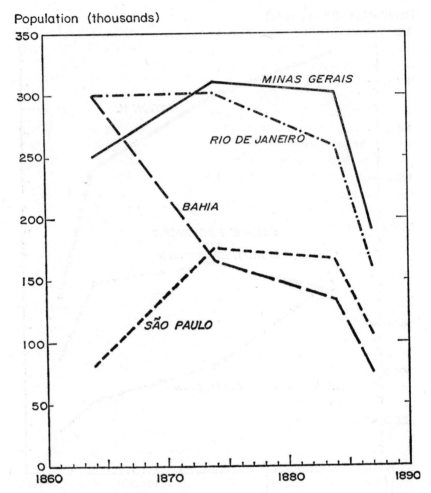

FIGURE 3. Slave Populations of Bahia, Rio de Janeiro, São Paulo, and Minas
Gerais, 1864–1887.

Between 1855 and 1874, for example, the slave population of the northern province of Paraíba decreased from a little more than thirteen to
only seven percent of the population.[45] In the same years the slave population of Pernambuco dropped from a little more than twenty percent of
the population (693,450 free persons and 145,000 slaves) to slightly
more than twelve.[46] (For ratios of slave to free populations in the provinces in 1874, see Table 2.) In comparison to what was happening in
these northern provinces, the change in the ratio of slave to free populations in the province of Rio de Janeiro was not quite so striking. Between
1840 and 1874 the free population of Rio de Janeiro grew rapidly from
183,200 to 456,850, but during the same years the slave population of
that coffee province also expanded considerably, from 224,012 to
301,352.[47] As Table 2 indicates, by 1874 the slave population in many
of the northern provinces and some of those in the exreme south comprised a comparatively unimportant portion of the total population,
while in the coffee-producing provinces it was a much more important
factor.

The relative willingness of the northern provinces to accept emancipation (which began to be manifested in the 1860's and even more in
the 1880's) resulted not only from a reduction in the number of slaves
in those provinces, but also from a decline in the comparative "quality"
of the northern slaves. The female, the sick, the unskilled, and the
elderly were in less demand in the south and stayed at home, whereas
many of the most productive slaves were exported. Mothers often saw
their children shipped away, staying themselves with their old masters.
A British report on slaves exported from Pernambuco in 1856 provided
no information about the health or skills of the persons involved, but
suggested that the proportion of females to males in the inter-provincial
trade was about what it had been in the African trade, roughly two
males for every female. Furthermore, the same statistics suggested that
the old and the very young were in less demand than persons of a
more productive age,[48] and this is confirmed by the unnaturally large

45. The slave population of Paraíba fell from 28,473 in 1855 to 25,817 in 1874.
In that same period its free population grew from 183,479 to 341,643. *Exposição
feita pelo Doutor Francisco Xavier Paes Barreto na qualidade de presidente da
provincia da Parahyba do Norte. Em 16 de Abril de 1855* (Paraíba, 1855), p. 18;
Table 6.
46. *Class B., From April 1, 1855, to March 31, 1856*, p. 239.
47. *Relatorio do Presidente da Provincia do Rio de Janeiro . . . para o anno de
1840 a 1841* (2nd ed.; Niterói, 1851). *Relatorio do Ministerio da Agricultura,*
April 30, 1885, p. 372.
48. The precise figures were 410 males and 196 females. Of these, 86 were between the ages of five and ten, 345 were eleven to twenty, 130 were twenty-one to
thirty, and the remaining 45 were between thirty-one and forty. *Class B., 1856–
1857*, p. 264.

numbers of slaves in their teens and twenties who were located in the coffee provinces during the 1870's. (See Figure 4.) According to the 1872 census, slaves in Minas Gerais between the ages of eleven and twenty outnumbered those under eleven by more than 30,000, though nationwide the young group outnumbered the older by more than 45,000.[49]

The preference for young, highly productive men in the coffee provinces is clearly reflected by a continuing majority of males in that region during a period (1851–1871) when natural birth and the internal slave trade were creating a more normal ratio of males to females in other provinces. The 1872 census clearly showed that most of the excess of 100,000 males over females was concentrated in the four coffee provinces, males outnumbering females in those four provinces by over 81,000.[50] In some districts within the coffee area, males outnumbered females by unusually high ratios. In São Paulo, as Table 16 shows, this predominance of males was characteristic of both the older coffee areas in the Paraíba Valley and central São Paulo, as well as in developing coffee municípios in the north, where the hard work of cutting down virgin forests and establishing new fazendas had already resulted in a particularly wide margin of male predominance by the 1870's. In 1884 male slaves in the four central coffee-producing provinces (see Table 4) comprised about 55 percent of their total slave population, still outnumbering females by more than 70,000. By that date, on the other hand, female slaves outnumbered males by more than 12,000 in the eleven northernmost provinces, although in the Empire as a whole female slaves still comprised less than 48 percent of the captive population. (See Figure 5.)

Evidently the most productive slaves were also greatly concentrated in the south-central provinces. Brazil was "essentially an agricultural country," the defenders of slavery reiterated, but by the 1870's that was no longer a convincing argument for retaining slavery in large parts of the country. In seven of the Empire's major political divisions (Paraná, Alagôas, Rio Grande do Norte, Piauí, the Município Neutro, Amazonas, and Ceará) servants and day laborers were more abundant than agricultural workers (see Table 20). In contrast, nearly 62 percent of the total slave population of the four coffee provinces, including the aged, the women, and the very young, were classified as agricultural workers, while only 14 percent of the slaves of those provinces were servants or day laborers. When we contrast the approximately 170,000 slaves in

49. *Recenseamento da população,* IX, 1084, *passim.* In the United States the flow of slaves from the border states to the southwest had a similar effect upon age groups. See Conrad and Meyer, "The Economics of Slavery in the Ante-Bellum South," p. 355.
50. *Recenseamento da população,* V, 78; IX, 1084; XV, 358; XIX, 433.

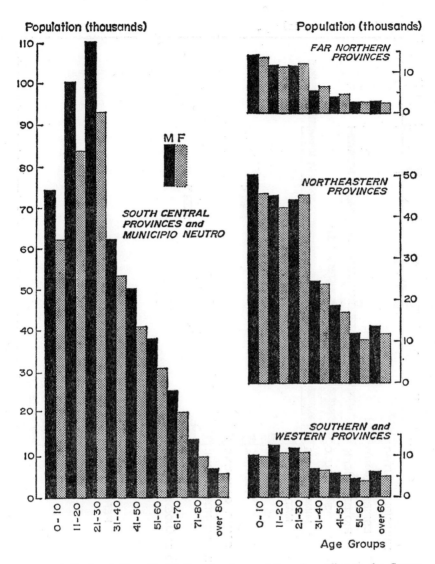

FIGURE 4. Regional Slave Populations by Age and Sex, According to the Census of 1872.

Population (thousands)

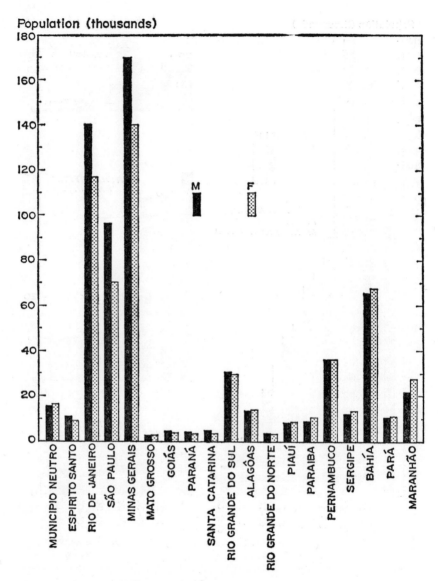

FIGURE 5. Provincial Slave Populations, by Sex, 1884.

the northeastern provinces who were employed as agricultural workers with the 3,750,000 free persons recorded as residing in those same provinces, the small importance of slavery to the agriculture of most of the northeast becomes apparent. In contrast, the 521,879 agricultural workers in the coffee provinces (excluding the Município Neutro) were a more formidable factor when set beside the 2,839,519 free persons of the same provinces. To put it another way, the single province of Minas Gerais (see Table 20 and Figure 1) contained almost as many agricultural workers (278,767) as the sixteen provinces outside the coffee region combined (284,757). Moreover, if we remember that the slaves in the coffee provinces were particularly concentrated in a relatively small number of municípios within those provinces, it becomes apparent that by the 1870's and 1880's slave values were not dispersed throughout the country but were much concentrated in a few areas. Ownership, of course, was also greatly concentrated. In 1883, for example, about one of every 762 slaves in Brazil was owned by the Count of Nova Friburgo, wealthy coffee planter of Rio de Janeiro province.[51]

The conclusion to be drawn from this abundance of facts and statistics is that the agricultural elite of some provinces, particularly northern and western ones, had less reason than the planters of Minas Gerais, Rio de Janeiro, and São Paulo, or even Espírito Santo, to insist upon a continuation of slavery when the institution began to be challenged in the 1860's and again in the 1880's. The challenge, in fact, came in part from the regions that had lost much of their labor force to the south and had been compelled as a result to make an earlier transition to a free-labor system.

POLITICAL REACTIONS

The threat to the slave system inherent in the internal slave trade was recognized almost as soon as that trade began. Yet immediate interests prevailed over problematical dangers. Slaves were needed by the coffee industry, and, therefore, feeble attempts to stop it for the benefit of northern planters were without much effect.

Faced with rising slave prices and dwindling slave populations, unable to stop the exportation of slaves through direct prohibition, northerners quickly conceived the device of imposing heavy taxes on slaves shipped to other provinces. Originating in Pernambuco in immediate response to the sudden southward movement of slaves, this measure

51. Van Delden Laërne, *Brazil and Java*, pp. 339–341. For the Count's extraordinarily lavish way of life, see Alcindo Sodré, "O elemento servil—a abolição," *Terceiro Congresso de Historia Nacional* (Rio de Janeiro, 1941), IV, 124–125.

was soon imitated by the legislative assemblies of other provinces,[52] but failed to stabilize the slave-labor supply in the various regions of the country because many slaveholders were attracted by immediate economic gains. Prohibition of the internal slave trade was desired in the whole of the north, said João Maurício Wanderley in the Chamber in 1854, but the heavy taxes on their exportation imposed by "all the provinces" had failed to stop the trade.[53]

The most serious attempt to end the shipment of northern slaves to the south took the form of a legislative project introduced into the Chamber of Deputies on August 11, 1854, by that same Bahian deputy, João Maurício Wanderley, the future Baron of Cotegipe. Designed to prohibit inter-provincial slave commerce under penalty of the anti-slave-trade law of September 4, 1850, this project aroused a debate in the Chamber which revealed that a conflict of interest had already developed by 1854 between northern and southern planters.[54]

Wanderley's bill was supported by deputies from Paraíba, Pernambuco, Alagôas, and Bahia, all provinces losing slaves to the south, but was strongly opposed by José Inacio Silveira da Mota of São Paulo, an importing province. Silveira da Mota's main arguments were economic. The value of slaves varied from province to province, because slaves employed in coffee production earned more for their masters than slaves employed in the cultivation of sugar cane. To deny a master's right to move his slaves in response to this economic fact would be to deny his right to this difference in value—a violation of property rights. Silveira da Mota warned that prohibition of the internal trade would create a new illegal slave traffic, simply because slaves would continue to be more valuable where coffee was produced.[55]

Wanderley's bill was warmly welcomed by Deputy Araújo Lima of the northern province of Alagôas, whose statements clearly revealed its purpose. He spoke bitterly of depopulation and economic deterioration in the north, implied that southern buyers had lifted the prices of slaves beyond the reach of sugar planters, and warned that the region

---

52. *Relatorio apresentado . . . na quarta sessão da oitava legislatura pelo Ministro . . . da Justiça* (Rio de Janeiro, 1852), p. 9; *Annaes da Câmara* (1854), IV, 246; *Relatorio apresentado a Assembléa Legislativa Provincial do Ceará no dia 1º de Outubro de 1862*, p. 32; *Falla dirigida a Assembléa Legislativa da Provincia das Alagôas em o 1º de Marco de 1855*, pp. 53–54; *Class B., From April 1, 1854, to March 31, 1855*, p. 277; *O Philantropo*, April 30, 1852.
53. *Annaes da Câmara* (1854), IV, 350.
54. *Ibid.*, IV, 124. At the same time, Wanderley introduced a second bill to free slaves who begged and to compel slaveowners who freed aged, sick, or incurable slaves to feed them unless they (the masters) were absolutely without means. Neither project made any significant progress in the Chamber.
55. *Ibid.*, IV, 243–247.

he represented was "menaced with ruin, with perfect decadence." The depopulation and decline of one part of the Empire would create "grave perils" for the whole nation, he warned, including the prosperous south. Would not the prosperity of the coffee region be compromised if most slaves were concentrated there? "Be certain," he said, "that you will have opposite interests, provinces with slaves, provinces without slaves. . . . You will have the kind of struggles and antagonisms . . . which have placed the American Union in such imminent danger." [56]

In defense of his own bill Wanderley argued that northern planters could not compete with those of the southern provinces in the acquisition of workers. Almost none of the northern planters had yet disposed of their slaves, "because they would lose the fixed capital employed in agriculture." Yet a heavy annual mortality of at least five percent would soon force northern planters to buy urban slaves or those of small farmers, whose planting could be done by free men. If, however, these sources of slaves were lost to southern buyers, the north would soon be "reduced to breeders of oxen!" Like his colleague from Alagôas, Wanderley warned of a disastrous regional division of interests:

The consequence of a radical change in the conditions of labor in the provinces will be political antagonism between the provinces of the south and the provinces of the north, because the latter, when they no longer have slaves, will insist that there be none in the south (*applause*); the provinces of the south will desire the opposite, and we will see springing from this clash of interests among us the same dangers which have menaced the . . . United States of America . . . .[57]

The Chamber of Deputies rejected Wanderley's project, but by the 1860's, with the United States involved in civil war, prominent Brazilians even in the coffee provinces finally began to recognize the threat to their system inherent in the widening regional differences caused by the inter-provincial slave trade. "Was it not the case, Gentlemen," asked Silveira da Mota in a major Senate speech in 1862, "that when some years ago in the United States the Northern States abolished slavery, and it remained in the Southern States, the industrial interests of the Southern States became entirely opposed to those of the Northern? Was it not after the creation and growth of this diversity of interests that the explosion took place which has not yet terminated?" If the Brazilian north continued to be deprived of workers, he predicted in this reversal of opinion, the interests of northern and southern provinces would become antagonistic.[58] The growing danger to the slave system implied

56. *Ibid.*, IV, 275–276.
57. *Ibid.*, IV, 346–348.
58. *Class B., 1862*, pp. 115–116.

by the war in North America and rumblings of anti-slavery sentiment within Brazil had alerted this former deputy from São Paulo, now representing Goiás in the Senate, to the dangers inherent in a clash of regional interests.

But by the early 1860's it was already very late for stopping the process. Evidence of important and irreversible economic changes in the north was already available, to be confirmed by the national census of 1872. Soon after the outbreak of the American Civil War a deputy from the northeastern province of Alagôas, Aureliano Cândido Tavares Bastos, began publishing articles in the Liberal Rio journal, *Correio Mercantil,* under the by-line Solitario. These Letters from the Hermit (*Cartas do Solitario*) included several studies of Brazilian slavery which reflected a sincere concern for the plight of the slaves and an enlightened understanding of the interests of his northern constituents. The inter-provincial slave trade was detrimental to the agricultural interests of the north, claimed Tavares Bastos, but would ultimately be recognized as beneficial to that region and harmful to the south. Its moral consequences and the economic revolution which it hastened were already in evidence. In Pernambuco, Paraíba, and Rio Grande do Norte, free men were finding paid employment on sugar plantations, and in Ceará a similar transformation was taking place in the nascent coffee industry. In the northern provinces free labor had been found more productive than slave labor. Despite epidemics of cholera and the loss of workers to the south, northern agriculture had been improved and plows and steam engines introduced, and in some regions the *senhor de engenho* had become a mere processor of sugar crops planted by free tenants.[59]

By 1863 this northern politician and economist, one of the first of the abolitionists, was convinced that slavery was no longer indispensable in at least some parts of the Empire. To hasten its end and to alleviate the rural labor shortage, he proposed a series of reforms which included the emancipation of all slaves in certain provinces selected on the basis of their small captive populations. These were northern provinces, specifically Ceará, Rio Grande do Norte, Paraíba, Alagôas, and Pernambuco, whose slave populations had been reduced in great part by the inter-provincial slave trade.[60] As Tavares Bastos' own opinions sug-

59. The increased agricultural production of Ceará during the American Civil War was the result in part of an improved market for cotton. Yet such able men as Perdigão Malheiro and the historian, Homem de Melo, president of Ceará in 1868, were convinced that the improved economic situation in that province was the result of the growth of free labor and the decline of slavery. See Perdigão Malheiro, *A escravidão,* II, 161.

60. Tavares Bastos, *Cartas do Solitario,* pp. 459–460; Aureliano Cândido Tavares Bastos, *A Provincia* (2nd ed.; São Paulo, 1937), pp. 241–262.

gested, the north, already somewhat less committed to slavery, was to be noticeably more receptive to steps intended to result in a gradual elimination of the slave system, which soon would be recommended to the nation by the Emperor himself.

The . . . war in the United States . . .
reverberated in the Empire like an immense
and frightful thunderclap; it was the voice of God
speaking through the mouth of cannons . . . .

PERDIGÃO MALHEIRO, 1867

5

THE
BEGINNINGS OF
EMANCIPATIONISM

IMPERIAL EMANCIPATIONISM

During the 1860's a significant emancipationist movement developed in Brazil, culminating in 1871 with the passage of legislation freeing the newborn children of slave women. This shift from the do-nothing policy of the 1850's was the result of the recognition by many Brazilians, including the highest authorities, that slavery was a discredited institution in the Western world and could not continue to exist without some serious restrictions upon it. Abolition, it was believed, was impossible under Brazilian circumstances, but equally impossible was continuing silence on a question which greatly concerned the world outside the Empire.

A series of events abroad helped to stimulate the reformist attitudes of the 1860's. The freeing of the slaves in the Portuguese, French, and Danish Empires, the liberation of the Russian serfs in 1861, and the Civil War in the United States, gave the Brazilian slavery question an immediacy unknown since the end of the slave-trade struggle in 1851. Two events, the Emancipation Proclamation and the so-called "Christie Affair," which led during 1863 to a break in British-Brazilian relations, undoubtedly helped to moderate Brazilian attitudes toward the slavery question even before the conclusion of the American Civil War in 1865.[1] But it was the outcome of the military conflict in North America that most greatly undermined Brazilian slavery and awakened opposition to it, for the survival of slavery in the United States had provided

1. On New Year's Eve, 1862, a British naval force began a brief but humiliating blockade of Rio harbor, the immediate result of minor incidents but in fact a consequence of the long British-Brazilian dispute over the emancipados and slavery itself. See Graham, *Britain and the Onset*, pp. 167–171; Bethell, *The Abolition*, pp. 382–383.

the defenders of the Brazilian institution with one of their strongest arguments. The ratification of the Thirteenth Amendment to the American Constitution was an act of great importance not only in the United States, but also for Cuba, Puerto Rico, and Brazil, for it condemned slavery in those places almost as decisively as it did in North America. With the victory of the northern states, Brazil was confronted as never before by the need to take some steps toward ending slavery and initiating a free-labor system. In 1865 only Spain, with her colonies of Cuba and Puerto Rico, accompanied Brazil as a major slaveholding nation, and Brazil was the last of the independent countries of the Americas to carry the "colonial stigma" of chattel slavery. If she was to retain her good reputation, built up during years of peace and development under the leadership of a moderate sovereign, she would have to take some impressive step toward its elimination.

The emergency caused by changing world conditions was felt most immediately, of course, by the Emperor and his councilors and members of the governmental ministries, who were committed to the protection not only of internal interests, but the good name and reputation of Brazil in the world community. After the re-establishment of British-Brazilian relations in 1865, the British Minister in Rio, Sir Edward Thornton, reported "a rapidly growing feeling among the leading men of the necessity of the abolition of slavery." Brazilians were "beginning to be ashamed of the existence of such an institution in their country, and the liberal party now in power confess that it is incompatible with their political principles." Events in the United States had "inspired Brazil with a feeling of isolation and shame that she should be the last on this continent to wipe off such a stain from her institutions, and are producing a moral pressure which it will be difficult for her Government to withstand." [2] Brazil, wrote Perdigão Malheiro not long after in his monumental work on slavery, could not resist the current of world opinion on the slavery question. Resistance was impossible and would even be of the greatest danger.[3]

2. Thornton to Earl of Clarendon, Rio de Janeiro, December 6, 1865, PRO, FO 84/1244. A similar mood, one almost of panic, developed in Cuba and Spain just after the American Civil War. Long almost unmentionable in the Spanish Cortes, the question of emancipation of Cuba's slaves was suddenly taken up there in 1865. "The war in the United States is finished," said one Spanish legislator, "and being finished, slavery on the whole American continent can be taken as finished." See Arthur F. Corwin, *Spain and the Abolition of Slavery in Cuba, 1817–1886* (Austin, Texas, 1967), p. 162. In a pioneering statement on abolition, Richard Graham plays down events in the United States as a factor inducing Brazilian reform, while emphasizing the significance of British pressure. See "Causes for the Abolition of Negro Slavery in Brazil: An Interpretive Essay," *HAHR*, Vol. XLVI (May 1966), p. 131.
3. Perdigão Malheiro, *A escravidão*, II, 156.

The Emperor himself, after perhaps prolonged meditation on the difficulties and hazards involved, made the decision to act against slavery, and Dom Pedro was by far the most important single influence in the passage of the 1871 slavery reform law. His power to respond to world opinion, however, was not unlimited, for the planter class, deriving the greatest benefit from slavery, stood at the foundations of the Brazilian political system, and it was only with the support of that class or with the passive consent of some segments of it that any reform could be adopted and carried out.

To challenge slavery was a fearsome undertaking even for an Emperor in a society still dominated by rural potentates. What was required was a change in the slave system sufficiently impressive to satisfy foreign and native critics without too much immediate offense or harm to the powerful at home. As a result, the solution which the cautious and scholarly Dom Pedro and his advisers adopted and, after years of effort and hesitation, forced through the General Assembly, was moderate, yet dramatic: the liberation of the newborn children of slave women. This "fairest and most gradual method," as a prominent Liberal, José Antônio Saraiva, characterized it for the British Minister in 1865, would "contain a degree of consideration for the rights of property and would meet with the least opposition from the present slaveholders." [4]

Yet even this moderate solution, which Lincoln proposed for Delaware in 1861 and saw rejected by the legislature of that state the same year, could hardly have been imposed upon Brazil if it had not been for the cooperation of northern provinces and their representatives in the General Assembly, who, as will be seen, passed the reform against the combined will of the coffee-producing provinces. There was no irrepressible wave of emancipationist sentiment among the agricultural elite in any part of Brazil in the 1860's, or even among the general population. There was, however, a greater willingness in most areas outside the coffee provinces (approaching enthusiasm among some planters and politicians in Pernambuco) to bow to the will of the Emperor and world opinion and to accept legislation carefully designed to prepare for the inevitable, while doing as little harm as possible to established interests. As a Brazilian scholar recently put it, the resistance to reform was concentrated in the south-central provinces, "while for the North-Northeast, a progressively [slave] exporting region, a program which only remotely affected the volume of the labor force would seem less crucial." [5]

A man of liberal reputation outside his Empire, Pedro II had cau-

4. Thornton to Earl of Clarendon, Rio de Janeiro, December 6, 1865, PRO, FO 84/1244.
5. Paula Beiguelman, *Formação política do Brasil* (2 vols.; São Paulo, 1967), I, 26.

tiously identified himself with emancipation even in the 1850's, and, therefore, when highly placed persons began to speak in favor of emancipation at the height of the American Civil War, few informed Brazilians could have believed that the Emperor was uninvolved.[6]

In September 1863, at a time when Pedro had had almost nine months to ponder the meaning of the Christie Affair and the Emancipation Proclamation, a prominent lawyer with close connections to the Crown publicly proposed the solution to the slavery question that would soon be adopted by the government. "The emancipation of the womb," said Perdigão Malheiro, advocate to the Council of State and page of the Imperial House, was the best solution to the slavery problem. The new generation would be freed, he told a gathering of the prestigious Brazilian Institute of Lawyers, while existing slaves continued to serve their masters "until death and ordinary manumissions have extinguished this cancer of Brazilian society." The slave was a special form of property, "tolerated by civil law for special motives," he added, but the same law could be modified or even extinguished, in obedience to "the most powerful law of the Author of Nature." Hardly a more authoritative voice could have been heard on a legal question in Brazil, and informed Brazilians must have suspected that Perdigão Malheiro had delivered his outspoken message at the request of the Emperor, or at least with Pedro's tacit approval.[7] In the same year,

6. Pedro had agreed in 1856 to serve as protector of the new civic club, the Ipiranga Society, dedicated to freeing slaves on Independence Day, and on September 7 of that year he and the Empress witnessed the first liberation ceremony of that organization in the Carmelite Church in Rio. Scarlett to Earl of Clarendon, Rio de Janeiro, October 13, 1856, *Class B., From April 1, 1856, to March 31, 1857,* p. 171; *Discussão da reforma do estado servil,* II, 142. In her biography of Pedro, Mary Wilhelmine Williams claimed that in 1840 the Emperor freed the slaves included in his inheritance, and that in 1864 he freed those included in the dowry of Princess Isabel. See *Dom Pedro the Magnanimous,* p. 265. Yet as late as 1866 the Emperor "liberated 190 slaves of his private property" for service in the Paraguayan War and was still making use of thousands of government-owned slaves. About that time some 2,500 "slaves of the nation" resided at the Emperor's estate of Santa Cruz, caring for his fields and cattle or hired out to nearby farms. The slaves of Santa Cruz were privileged, receiving a daily wage and education. Slave children there had formed a band and could play the national hymns of the United States, England, and France for the pleasure of foreign guests. See John Codman, *Ten Months in Brazil* (Boston, 1867), pp. 103–106; Benedicto Pires de Almeida, "Tietê, os escravos e a abolição," *Revista do Arquivo Municipal,* Vol. XCV (São Paulo, 1944), p. 53.
7. Agostinho Marques Perdigão Malheiro, *Illegitimidade da propriedade constituida sobre o escravo* (Rio de Janeiro, 1863), pp. 17–24. Aside from the close legal and courtly association with the Emperor, Perdigão Malheiro was also president of the Brazilian Institute of Lawyers, son of the president of the Supreme Tribunal of Justice, and brother-in-law of the Conservative Party leader, Eusébio de Queiroz. See obituary of Perdigão Malheiro in *Gazeta da Tarde,* June 3, 1881; Augusto Victorino Sacramento Blake, *Diccionario Bibliographico Brasileiro* (7 vols.; Rio de Janeiro, 1883–1902), I, 18.

furthermore, Perdigão Malheiro began writing his admirable study of slavery in Brazil, to be published in three volumes in 1866 and 1867 by the National Press.

Only three months after his spokesman proposed the liberation of the newborn, Pedro recommended the same solution in a memorandum addressed to the new Liberal President of the Council of Ministers, Zacarias de Góis. Events in the United States, Pedro told his Prime Minister, compelled the Brazilian government to consider the future of slavery "so that the same does not befall us as with respect to the traffic in Africans . . . ." The most practical solution, he suggested, was the liberation of the newborn.[8]

Although events in the United States made action ever more imperative, a tragic Brazilian involvement in the affairs of neighboring countries caused the Brazilian government to delay initiation of the proposed reform. In October 1864 the Brazilian army intervened in an internal dispute in Uruguay, causing the President of Paraguay, Francisco Solano López, to launch attacks against Brazil, taking the Empire into a conflict which would last until the death of López in March 1870.[9]

With his Empire thus at war and in a state of uncertainty over the slavery issue, in July 1865 the Emperor traveled to the war zone in Rio Grande do Sul. Having conferred there in September with the newly appointed British Minister, Sir Edward Thornton, whose task it was to re-establish normal relations with Brazil, Pedro returned to Rio in early November convinced of the need to adopt some degree of slavery reform.[10] Thornton himself was informed that the Brazilian government was "most anxious to present some measure to the legislature for the abolition of slavery, but . . . that it cannot be done at this moment, nor until the war with Paraguay be concluded . . . ." The delay was required, Thornton was told, in order "that there should be no cause of agitation or division of the country . . . , no excuse for preventing all parties from supporting and aiding the Government heart and soul in the prosecution of the war."[11]

In contrast with previous years, the British position regarding Brazilian slavery was cautious and discreet in 1865, and thus probably not an overriding cause of Pedro's decision to act. As relations were being restored, the Foreign Office ordered Thornton to enquire about a possible revival of the slave trade, the state of the slaves and emancipados,

8. Heitor Lyra, *Historia de Dom Pedro II* (3 vols.; São Paulo, 1938–1940), II, 235–236.
9. For a summary of these events, see Calógeras, *A History of Brazil*, pp. 211–217.
10. Williams, *Dom Pedro the Magnanimous*, p. 121.
11. Thornton to Earl of Clarendon, Rio de Janeiro, December 6, 1865, PRO, FO 84/1244.

and about attempts to acquire new workers through immigration, but he was also told that it was "not the wish of Her Majesty's Govt that you should, on the resumption of Diplomatic Relations with Brazil, enter upon former matters of controversy connected with this question." In turn, Thornton advised his government in December 1865:

I find that among all classes of Brazilians there is extreme sensitiveness as to any pressure on the abolition question from Europe and particularly from England, and . . . I would earnestly deprecate all positive pressure on the part of Her Majesty's Government beyond unofficial and friendly advice; for I believe that it would rather tend to retard than to hasten the end so much to be desired.[12]

Despite the absence of British pressure and the Emperor's involvement in preparations for carrying on the war with Paraguay, soon after the close of the North American conflict he found time to take preliminary steps toward slavery reform. Near the end of 1865 he asked a close adviser, José Antônio Pimenta Bueno, to compose a slavery reform project, and by January Pimenta Bueno (later the Marquis of São Vicente) had prepared a moderate five-point program providing for free birth, the establishment of provincial emancipation councils, slave registrations, and the liberation of state-owned slaves in five years and convent slaves in seven.[13] Opposed, however, by an old-guard Conservative, the Viscount Olinda, then President of the Council, this measure was tabled, and more months passed before Pedro was prepared to try again.

The Emperor's mood, however, was reflected in a series of executive decisions tending to constrict the slave system. Having decreed the long-delayed liberation of the emancipados in 1864, in June of the following year he decided to end the lashing of slaves condemned to labor gangs as a violation of Article 179 of the Constitution which prohibited whipping and all cruel punishment, and early in 1866 the government banned the employment of slaves on government works. Later that year Dom Pedro again revealed his sympathy for emancipation when he granted the prior of the Benedictine monastery a diamond snuff-box in appreciation of the monks' decision to free all children henceforth born to female slaves in their possession. As the owners of some 2,000 slaves, the Benedictines were influential, and their example

12. Foreign Office to Thornton, September 5, 1865, PRO, FO 84/1244; same to same, November 25, 1865, *ibid.;* Thornton to Foreign Office, December 6, 1865, *ibid.*
13. Williams, *Dom Pedro the Magnanimous,* pp. 121, 266; Lyra, *Historia de Dom Pedro II,* II, 238; Nabuco, *Um estadista do Imperio,* III, 26–31.

was expected to be followed by other religious orders and even by private persons.[14]

Soon after, the nation received far more shocking evidence of Pedro's determination to act. In July 1866 a prestigious abolitionist society of Paris (the Comité pour l'Abolition de l'Esclavage) petitioned the Emperor to use his power and prestige to abolish Brazilian slavery. Undoubtedly to the surprise and dismay of slaveholders, the government's official response implied that the new cabinet of Zacarias de Góis was strongly interested in ending slavery, though the liberation of the slaves could not be achieved at once. Emancipation in Brazil, wrote the Foreign Minister in the name of the Emperor, was "nothing more than a question of method and opportunity." When circumstances permitted, the government would consider abolition as an object of the greatest importance.[15] From this statement, it was inferred that the obstacle to emancipation was the war with Paraguay and that the government was determined to act upon the conclusion of that struggle.

Both the war effort and slave emancipation were advanced by a decree of November 1866 granting freedom to government-owned slaves who agreed to serve in the army. Private slaveholders and religious orders, notably the Carmelites and Benedictines, together estimated to own some four thousand slaves in several provinces, were strongly urged to follow the government's example, and Pedro released 190 of his own slaves for service in Paraguay.[16] During the long war, in fact, some twenty thousand persons (including the wives of liberated soldiers) found their way to freedom as a result of voluntary enlistment or through substitution of slaves for their masters in the National Guard; the government even granted titles of nobility to masters who would furnish slaves for the army. Not satisfied with the volume of recruitment, early in 1867 Pedro donated 100 contos (£10,000) of his own wealth to buy the freedom of slaves who would serve in the war against Paraguay.[17]

14. *Colecção das leis do Imperio* (1865), p. 278; Thornton to Earl Russell, Rio de Janeiro, November 2, 1865, *Class B., 1865*, pp. 12–13; same to same, February 1, 1866, *BFSP* (1866–1867), LVII, 1270; same to same, May 29, 1866, *BFSP*, LVII, 1271; same to same, June 27, 1866, *BFSP*, LVII, 1272.
15. Dornas Filho, *A escravidão*, pp. 151–152.
16. *Colecção das leis do Imperio* (1866), Tome XXVI, Part I, p. 313; Oficios e outros papeis da casa imperial, 1801–1868, AN, Cod. 572, Document 6: Thornton to Lord Stanley, Rio de Janeiro, December 7, 1866, *Class B., 1867*, p. 31; Pires de Almeida, "Tietê," p. 53.
17. See Nabuco, *O Abolicionismo*, p. 61; Poppino, *Brazil*, p. 172. Thornton to Lord Stanley, Rio de Janeiro, March 6, 1867, *BFSP* (1867–1868), LVIII, 945. Free men could substitute slaves for duty at the front, and a business in able-bodied males for military service developed. Same to same, Rio de Janeiro,

Though the bloody conflict was probably of greater concern to him than the slavery issue, Pedro continued to associate himself with emancipationism. In February 1867, probably at his instigation, Zacarias de Góis presented the government's reform project, drawn up the previous year by the Viscount São Vicente, and several questions concerning slavery reform to the Council of State for its consideration. These proposals now included, aside from the original measures outlined by São Vicente, the complete abolition of slavery with full compensation to owners on the last day of the nineteenth century, a proposal certain to arouse fear and hostility. The questions put to the Council of State were bold and to the point: Was it desirable to abolish slavery directly and, if so, when and with what safeguards? [18]

The Council of State, meeting with the Emperor early in April 1867, reflected the alarm of the planters. Under pressure from the monarch, most of the councillors granted the need for reform but cautioned against haste, warning of public disorders, race wars, a labor shortage, and huge losses to the economy. Immediate abolition, said Nabuco de Araújo, father of the future abolitionist Joaquim Nabuco, "would precipitate Brazil into a profound and infinite abyss." At least 500,000 persons would be lost to the national labor force. Some freed slaves would work for wages, but others would become vagabonds or move to the cities, and their women would turn to domestic tasks.

Most members of the Council accepted the concept of free birth as a step toward emancipation, but many did so reluctantly. Viscount Abaeté was ready to accept reform, but not ahead of Spain. Viscount Rio Branco—parliamentary leader of the emancipationist movement only four years later—predicted that freeing the newborn would cause unrest on plantations, a scarcity of credit, and decreased production; yet expressed the opinion of the majority of the Council, under the direct pressure of the Emperor. The government, he thought, should prepare its reform so that it could be enacted after the war with Paraguay when military forces would be available to meet the expected threat to public order.[19]

There was no unmistakable regional division in the Council of State on the topic discussed, but the three most clearly emancipationist members had ties to northern provinces. The Liberal Francisco de Montezuma of Bahia (Viscount Jequitinhonha) strongly favored immediate

November 3, 1866, *Class B.*, *1866*, pp. 47–48. Advertisements for slaves suitable for military service appeared in newspapers in Ceará in 1868. See Girão, *A abolição no Ceará*, p. 28.
18. Nabuco, *Um estadista do Imperio*, III, 32.
19. José Antônio Pimenta Bueno, Marquês de São Vicente, *Trabalho sobre a extincção da escravatura no Brasil* (Rio de Janeiro, 1868), pp. 58–72; Nabuco, *Um estadista do Imperio*, III, 38.

liberation of the newborn.[20] Souza Franco, an old Liberal from Pará, was "frankly emancipationist," desiring to set a date for the elimination of slavery.[21] And, finally, it was José Tomás Nabuco de Araújo, representing Bahia, who put forward the arguments and devised the proposals which were to gain general acceptance in 1871.

This statesman, allied by marriage with leading families of Pernambuco, saw the Brazilian situation as more serious than those of some countries which had abolished slavery, for the problem lay within its borders and not in a distant colony. Yet to prevent the issue of slavery from becoming "the prize of demagogues," the government was compelled to take the initiative. To stop the torrent was impossible. To direct it was high policy. Nabuco proposed several measures, some included in the São Vicente project and others new. He favored free birth, an emancipation fund for annual manumissions, and laws to improve the captives' living conditions. To ease the expected labor shortage, he proposed that freedmen be obligated to serve their former masters or persons of their choosing or be declared vagrants.[22] He called for a review of the contract-labor (locação de serviços) laws "to adopt them to the needs of colonization and the consequences of emancipation." Finally, the senator from Bahia recommended measures to remove the slaves from the cities to the countryside, both to give immigrants more opportunities in the towns and to furnish more field hands for agriculture.[23] As his son, Joaquim Nabuco, wrote years later, the suggestions of Nabuco de Araújo were the basis of the complicated legislation that was finally passed on September 28, 1871.[24]

Soon after the meeting with the Council of State, the Emperor appointed a committee headed by Nabuco de Araújo to prepare a bill, and only a month later in his annual Speech from the Throne he urged the General Assembly to take up the question of slavery at an appro-

20. Nabuco, *Um estadista do Imperio,* III, 34. Born in Bahia as Francisco Gomes Brandão, Jequitinhonha had a long liberal career under the adopted name of Montezuma. As Minister of Justice in 1837 he had tried to enforce the ban on the slave trade, and in 1865 he had proposed abolition in fifteen years. To Joaquim Nabuco he was "the first of the abolitionists in the full sense of the word." *Ibid.,* III, 24.
21. *Ibid.,* III, 39.
22. Under Nabuco's plan, such persons would not be punished with imprisonment, "which is what they desire," but would be condemned to labor in penal establishments or disciplinary colonies.
23. Pimenta Bueno, *Trabalho,* pp. 63–67.
24. Nabuco, *Um estadista do Imperio,* III, 43; *Diario Oficial,* Rio de Janeiro, April 9, 1867. Eight members of the Council favored initiation of legislation after the war. Jequitinhonha wanted immediate action on a "free womb" law. Two councillors, Olinda and Muritiba, opposed all reform. See Barão do Rio Branco, *Efemérides brasileiras* (Rio de Janeiro, 1946), pp. 45–46.

priate time. Though couched in moderate terms, this speech, wrote the younger Nabuco sixteen years later, was like lightening in a cloudless sky.[25] The Emperor, concerned with affairs of state and foreign problems, had dared to assert his authority in defiance of the interests of the planter class, but also took the precaution of explaining his aims and reassuring the nation's slaveholders that he had no intention of imposing too rapid solutions. Soon after this historic message, the government printing press published the third volume of Perdigão Malheiro's *A escravidão no Brasil,* containing recommendations for slavery reform nearly identical to those proposed by São Vicente and Nabuco de Araújo and discussed in the Council of State. Brazil should have emancipation, Perdigão Malheiro wrote in his final chapter, but it should not be brusque and imprudent. The treasury should not be burdened with indemnification through immediate emancipation. Immigration should be promoted. Brazil should prepare herself for a future worthy of the century and the respect of the world, but she should proceed with moderation and a decent regard for established order.[26]

Despite the government's cautious approach toward reform, slaveholders were alarmed. Newspapers and politicians remained nearly silent, but planters soon made their bitterness and opposition known to their business associates in the cities in order to solidify the rural-urban opposition.[27] The growing reaction against the government's policies was present in two articles published in the *Correio Mercantil* soon after the Emperor's Speech from the Throne. In the second of these "Letters from a Blind Man," an anonymous writer rebuked the regime for its reply to the French abolitionist society, warned against governmental interference in the slavery question, and scolded the Emperor for his personal intervention. The government's reply to the French society was "rash, because it awakened exaggerated hopes without defining its purposes. . . ." Property values had fallen, and slaves had begun to think adventurous thoughts.[28] Slavery was a mistake, a restraint against nature, said this angry writer, but it was "a sanctioned, tolerated, and legalized mistake." "The government," he warned, "does not know the

25. Pimenta Bueno, *Trabalho,* p. 110; Nabuco, *O Abolicionismo,* p. 63.
26. Perdigão Malheiro, *A escravidão,* II, 191–231.
27. José Maria dos Santos, *Os republicanos paulistas e a abolição* (Rio de Janeiro, 1942), pp. 53–54.
28. In 1866 Thornton reported growing alarm caused by slave violence and "a feeling springing up among the slaves themselves" that they would soon be freed. Thornton to Earl of Clarendon, Rio de Janeiro, January 5, 1866, *Class B., 1866,* pp. 42–43. The British Consul at Pará reported in 1867 that "the prevailing feeling that the emancipation of the slaves . . . is not far distant has the effect of deterring purchasers from placing any large amount of capital in so insecure an investment. . . ." *Class B., 1867,* p. 38.

danger it runs in putting itself like an apostle at the forefront of this idea." [29]

Despite such criticism, Pedro continued on his emancipationist course for more than a year longer, cautiously attempting to accommodate the unreconcilable aspirations of a growing emancipationist movement and foreign opinion with the demands of Brazilian agriculture. On the question of slavery, in fact, Pedro was a pivotal figure, sometimes recommending progressive steps but avoiding rapid action, occasionally even abandoning his emancipationist posture in favor of other considerations. On May 3, 1868, for example, in another Speech from the Throne, he informed the nation that the slavery question had been the object of "serious study" and that a proposal would be submitted to the Assembly for its consideration at an "opportune time." [30] Soon after, however, the war with Paraguay, which had already justified postponement of slavery reform for more than two years, motivated Pedro toward actions which implied a near abandonment of his emancipationist policy. Faced with an unresolvable clash between his Liberal Prime Minister, Zacarias de Góis, and the commander of the armed forces in Paraguay, the Duke of Caxias, Pedro chose in July to accept Zacarias' resignation and to ask a Conservative to form a cabinet.[31] This arbitrary but legal decision enraged Liberals, who held a majority in the Chamber, and was taken as an affront to the growing number of persons who had become sympathetic to emancipationism. While Zacarias was committed to the government's proposals, the new cabinet was identified with opposition to slavery reform. With such a government in power, an emancipationist bill was not likely to reach the Chamber of Deputies. The Liberal Chamber, in fact, was dissolved on July 20, and in subsequent elections was replaced by a Chamber composed almost unanimously of members of the Conservative Party.

POPULAR EMANCIPATIONISM

A result of this sudden reversal of imperial policy was a strengthening and radicalization of the emancipationist movement, which the Emperor's earlier acts had helped to stimulate, and which by 1868 had become a significant force in its own right. Pedro, of course, was not the only Brazilian who had been responsive to outside events or internal

29. "Cartas de um cego," *Correio Mercantil,* May 25, 29, 1867.
30. Nabuco, *Um estadista do Imperio,* III, 55–71; Santos, *Os republicanos paulistas,* p. 48.
31. In his own defense, the Emperor later claimed that it was in fact the war that had determined this important decision. See Nabuco, *Um estadista do Imperio,* III, 104.

changes. The Civil War in the United States and slow economic and demographic evolution within Brazil had begun to generate an emancipationist spirit in scattered parts of the Empire between 1862 and 1865, and the movement had been further stimulated by the Emperor's message to the French abolitionist society and his other public statements on the slavery issue. Already in 1862 the British Consul at Bahia had reported to his government that as a result of the great drain of the labor resources of the northern provinces, slavery was greatly concentrated in the province of Rio de Janeiro. The war in North America, he reported, and "the principles which seem to govern that mighty contest" were being "viewed in the proper light" by influential persons in Bahia. A senator from that province had recently declared that events in the United States would sooner or later react with irresistible force upon Brazil. Dependent upon the planters of Rio de Janeiro for its support, slavery would become a burden once the northern supply was exhausted, and then its elimination would become an advantage to the entire nation.[32] Soon after, an ex-Confederate traveler, no doubt sensitive to regional differences, was reporting that an anti-slavery "party" had appeared in the Brazilian north from Amazonas to Pernambuco and was "constantly pressing its views upon the government." Having freed themselves in part from slavery through the sale of their slaves to the south, he noticed with a touch of scorn, northern Brazilians were manifesting virtuous indignation at the sins of those who had paid them so liberally for their slave property. In contrast, the southernmost districts of Bahia and the provinces of Rio de Janeiro and São Paulo were holding on to the institution "with South Carolinian pertinacity." [33]

The fledgling emancipationist movement of the 1860's, which would arise again full-winged in the 1880's, produced a spate of polemical writings in the form of projects, articles, and books, some of them apparently instigated by the Crown, but others reflecting the views of independent reformers. Such publications often included proposals for reform or the eventual elimination of slavery; these Tavares Bastos summed up in 1865 in a letter to the British Anti-Slavery Society. The most common proposals suddenly put to the country after many years of apathy did not call for abolition of slavery, but recommended prohibition of the public sale of slaves or the separation of slave families, the liberation of captives owned by the government, the clergy, or foreigners, and the abolition of the inter-provincial slave trade. These and

32. Morgan to Christie, Bahia, June 14, 1862, *Class B., 1862,* p. 123; same to Earl Russell, Bahia, September 24, 1862, *ibid.,* p. 124. Similarly, the British Consul in Rio Grande do Sul informed London "that even the Brazilians themselves are becoming alive to the evils of slave labour. . . ." Collan to Earl Russell, Rio Grande do Sul, January 31, 1864, *ibid.,* pp. 83–84.
33. Codman, *Ten Months in Brazil,* pp. 154–155, 184.

similar measures were perhaps intended to make slavery less offensive to foreigners, to stop the loss of slaves in the outer provinces, and to concentrate the working population onto the plantations where it was most needed. Other proposals, put before the country even before the Emperor and his advisers had revealed their own plan of reform, were intended to end slavery within the lifetime of existing generations, either through liberation of the newborn or by the establishment of a terminal date (usually thirty or fifty years in the future).[34]

Some suggestions were more radical. Only weeks after the surrender of Lee at Appomattox, for example, the elderly Francisco de Montezuma of Bahia proposed to the Senate the total abolition of slavery within fifteen years, and, soon after, this member of the Emperor's Council of State published a series of articles in the *Jornal do Commercio* proposing emancipation without indemnification.[35] In contrast, a writer from Maranhão, aware that the war in the United States had delivered a fatal blow to Brazilian slavery, frankly advocated a new form of serfdom that would have had the important advantage of preventing the sale of workers of Maranhão to the coffee planters of the south. Slavery was finished, he believed, but slaves lacked instruction and the will to work except when driven by fear of the whip. His solution to this dilemma was a law declaring Brazilian slaves serfs of the soil (*escravos da gleba*), with their sale to be prohibited. Thus, the "free" descendants of Brazilian slaves would remain subject to their old masters as tribute-paying *colonos,* "owing to their incapacity to manage their own affairs."[36]

Widespread support for slavery reform, instilled in Brazilians in part by the Emperor's leadership, made his policy reversal in 1868 particularly unacceptable. Perhaps not since 1848 had a political crisis aroused such invective against the monarch and the imperial system, coming now from a new force in Brazilian society: a revived liberalism identified with democratic reforms including the liberation of the slaves. The Emperor's dismissal of the Liberal cabinet and the appointment of a Conservative ministry aroused strong reformist sentiments among students, writers, Liberal politicians, and a portion of the informed urban population.

---

34. Perdigão Malheiro, *A escravidão,* II, 356–361. Tavares Bastos added to these proposals gradual abolition by provinces, beginning with those bordering foreign territories and those where free labor had been adopted on a large scale, thus repeating proposals he had made in *Cartas do Solitario.*
35. Evaristo de Moraes, *A lei do Ventre Livre* (Rio de Janeiro, 1917), p. 8; Perdigão Malheiro, *A escravidão,* II, 101.
36. F. A. Brandão, *A escravatura no Brasil* (Brussels, 1865), pp. 52–56. For other writings and proposals on slavery of the period, see Perdigão Malheiro, *A escravidão,* II, 99–103.

It was Nabuco de Araújo who in 1868 placed himself at the head of the opposition to the Conservative ministry, while upholding the cause of emancipationism. In a Senate speech delivered the day following the imperial coup, Nabuco denounced the Emperor's choice of the Viscount Itboraí, an elderly Conservative leader, to head a new cabinet. Like slavery, he admitted, the ministry was legal. The Emperor possessed the right to nominate and dismiss ministers of state. Yet, also like slavery, the *legitimacy* of the Emperor's act was open to question. Slavery, said Nabuco de Araújo, was "authorized by law," but it was "condemned by divine law . . . , by the entire world." [37] Nabuco's speech was a bold attack upon both the Emperor's constitutional powers and the institution of slavery by one of the most respected of Brazilian statesmen.

In October, under the leadership of Nabuco de Araújo, the newly established Liberal Center, composed of Liberal and independent senators, endorsed the emancipationist program so arduously formulated in the Council of State, and during the following March the Center issued a manifesto demanding electoral reform, abolition of the National Guard and recruitment, and emancipation of the slaves. A basic purpose of this radical program, or so it blustered in an apparent attempt to frighten the government and the planters into concessions, was the prevention of social upheaval, and a new Liberal propaganda organ, *A Reforma,* soon affirmed that position.[38]

The first issue of *A Reforma,* which appeared in Rio in May 1869, outlined the slavery reform bill now being proposed by the Liberal Center, which included the emancipation of children of slave women followed by "the gradual liberation of existing slaves in a manner to be announced at an appropriate time." In the same issue, Tavares Bastos expressed impatience with the Conservative regime on the slavery question and noted the Emperor's failure to mention the subject in his latest Speech from the Throne.[39] Emancipationist rather than abolitionist, the publishers of *A Reforma,* the first anti-slavery paper since *O Philantropo,* established a journalistic precedent which in 1880 would serve the publishers of *O Abolicionista,* organ of the Brazilian Anti-Slavery Society. There was, moreover, a continuity of editorial direction between the two reformist papers. Joaquim Nabuco, son of Nabuco de Araújo, was closely associated with both, as was Joaquim Serra, a

37. Nabuco, *Um estadista do Imperio,* III, 108.
38. *Ibid.,* III, 119, 129–133.
39. *A Reforma,* Rio de Janeiro, May 12, 1869. Later issues of *A Reforma* were more conciliatory on the slavery question (see the issue of May 30, 1869) and by July its "moderation" had encouraged slaveholders to advertise in its pages for the return of runaways, some of them Africans too young to have been taken to Brazil before November 7, 1831. See *ibid.,* July 20, 1860.

journalist from Maranhão who joined the staff of *A Reforma* in 1868 and remained committed to the cause of liberation until slavery ended twenty years later.[40]

The Emperor's adoption of an emancipationist policy and his apparent abandonment of that policy in 1868 helped to foment reformist activities at institutions of higher learning, particularly at the Law Faculties of Recife and São Paulo. Already in 1865, an eighteen-year-old student at the Law Faculty in Recife, Antônio de Castro Alves, was lauding in verse the liberation of the slaves in North America and urging Brazilians to follow the example. Soon the young northeasterner was depicting the suffering and personal misfortunes of romanticized slaves, lamenting the fate of a young girl sold to a distant province or of a slave woman longing for Africa.[41] Quickly famous, the young poet joined an emancipationist society in Recife which included among its members the law student, Rui Barbosa. In Recife Castro Alves wrote an anti-slavery drama, *Gonzaga,*[42] which was received with a public enthusiasm presaging the abolitionists "meetings" that in a few years would be held regularly in Rio and other Brazilian cities.

In 1868 Castro Alves entered the Law Faculty at São Paulo, where he joined Rui Barbosa, Joaquim Nabuco, and other students who had already made known their anti-slavery views. The young liberals, each a leader himself, were led and inspired by the poet and teacher, José Bonifacio de Andrada e Silva, grandson and namesake of the independence leader.[43] However, the abolitionism of the São Paulo Academy, which attracted students from the entire country and even from abroad, did not reflect the attitudes of São Paulo's leading citizens, politicians, and landowners. An "alien body" in the heart of a plantation community where chattel slavery was growing in importance in the late 1860's, the Law Faculty was a center of intellectual ferment, "ever ready (according to Richard M. Morse) to disjoint the narrow patterns of provincial life"; to introduce "political ideas and passions transcending local issues. . . ."[44] It was in this academic environment, surrounded by a disapproving populace, that Castro Alves wrote and recited his poem *O Navio Negreiro,* a "Dantesque dream" of a slave ship crowded with men and women dancing to the threatening crack of a whip.

40. Fernando Segismundo, *Imprensa brasileira, Vultos e problemas* (São Paulo, 1962), pp. 193–202.
41. See his *Os escravos.*
42. Raymond S. Sayers, *The Negro in Brazilian Literature* (New York, 1956), p. 143.
43. Antônio Gontijo de Carvalho, "Prefacio," *Obras Completas de Rui Barbosa,* Vol. I, Tome I, p. xvi.
44. Morse, *From Community to Metropolis,* pp. 55–56, 95–96.

The fall of the Liberal cabinet on July 16, 1868 radicalized the young Liberals of the São Paulo Law Academy, already committed as they were to emancipationism. Joining forces with older opponents of slavery, they created the Club Radical and a journalistic voice, *O Radical Paulistano,* with an editorial board including Rui Barbosa and the poet, lawyer, and ex-slave, Luiz Gama.[45] Supporting the entire program of the Liberal Center, *O Radical Paulistano* was an academic equivalent of Nabuco de Araújo's *A Reforma.* In an essay published in its first issue, the editors of the new weekly claimed that decisive reforms were essential if catastrophe was to be avoided. "Only a radical policy, truly defined, bearing on its banner the urgent reforms for which the country can no longer wait, will manage to save us," the new paper claimed in the same alarmist style used earlier by *A Reforma.*[46] In the new radical journal and in public lectures, the members of the newly formed "America" lodge directed their anger against the imperial system, blaming it for the perilous condition of the nation and the government's desertion of its emancipationist program. What was the government doing, asked the boyishly enthusiastic Rui Barbosa in an article published in 1869, in the face of an imminent social revolution? The government had deserted the cause of emancipation, he claimed, while the provinces were hoisting the banner of freedom. Only a federative system, only provincial initiative and emancipation could rehabilitate the country. The abolition of slavery was near at hand, he concluded, whether the government wished it so or not.[47] For the first time in Brazilian history, in fact, a true anti-slavery movement had appeared, and by 1870 there were many signs of unprecedented activity: the proliferation of emancipationist clubs, the beginnings of anti-slavery journalism, and frequent anti-slavery meetings.[48] The situation had developed to the point, in fact, that the need to undercut the growing radicalism became an important argument for reform in 1870 and 1871.

THE EVE OF REFORM

Even before the end of the Paraguayan War, preliminary steps were taken to reassure the public that the government intended to return

45. Carvalho, "Prefacio," p. xxiv.
46. *Obras Completas de Rui Barbosa,* Vol. I, Tome I, p. 34.
47. Ibid., pp. 108–111. In a speech delivered forty years later, Barbosa hinted at the existence of an unbridgeable gap between the views of the students and those of the permanent provincial inhabitants. In São Paulo at the time, he said, the theme of abolition "could have been dealt with only by the petulance of a student playing the antics of liberal radicalism, with his case resting on excessively little judgement." Cited by Morse, *From Community to Metropolis,* p. 147.
48. *Discussão da reforma do estado servil,* II, Appéndice, p. 46.

to its emancipationist policies. From May to July 1869, many projects to liberalize slavery were presented to the Chamber of Deputies.[49] Most were not even debated, but one bill to eliminate the most sensational aspects of slavery received the support of the ministry and was passed into law. Eight years earlier, a bill to prohibit the public auctioning of slaves and the separation of married couples and their children under fifteen had passed the Senate, and in June 1869 this project was finally sent to the Chamber of Deputies, where it was passed into law on August 25. The first significant legislative restriction on the slave system since 1850, it prohibited public and commercial slave auctions under penalty of a fine of from 100 to 300 milréis. Private sales, however, were permitted, and thus the new law had no important effect upon the inter-provincial slave trade, which continued at a large volume for another ten years. Also allowed, moreover, were "judicial auctions" of slaves, to be supervised by local authorities, for the discharging of debts or the division of property among heirs, such auctions to be announced a month in advance to allow bidding. In all slave sales, either private or judicial, the separation of a husband from his wife or a child from his mother was to be prohibited, except when the child had reached the age of fifteen. Finally, the law ruled that if inventoried slaves could offer an amount of money equal to their judicial evaluations and no claims of heirs or debtors existed, the judge in charge could grant them certificates of emancipation.[50]

With the end of the Paraguayan War in sight, on September 12, the Imperial Government provided more evidence of its emancipationist aims. At his headquarters in Asunción, the Count d'Eu, son-in-law of the Emperor and commander of the Brazilian armed forces in Paraguay, urged the provisional Paraguayan government to abolish slavery in that country, an easy task complied with almost at once. The young commander was obviously aware that the freeing of a few Paraguayan slaves, if any slaves in fact existed after five years of war and an extraordinary loss of population, would not be the most important result of his action. Not only was it intended to appease the Brazilian and

---

49. These proposed, among other reforms, to substitute imprisonment with labor for condemnation to labor gangs (the galleys) for slaves convicted of crimes, to punish buyers of slave women intended for prostitution, to create an emancipationist lottery, to establish a national slave registration, to free the newborn, to abolish corporal punishment, to allow slaves to buy their freedom, to free slaves owned by the government and those given in usufruct to the Imperial Family, to liberate females of child-bearing age, and to prohibit the use of slaves in towns. *Annaes da Câmara* (1869), I, 124–125, 143; III, 135; *ibid.* (1870), I, 59–60; V, 47; Godoy, *O elemento servil*, pp. 437, 442, 453.

50. *Colecção das leis do Imperio* (1869), Tome XXIX, Part I, pp. 129–130.

international anti-slavery movements, but it also obligated the Brazilian government to take a similar step at home.[51]

In March 1870, with the death of the Paraguayan president, Francisco Solano López, the war ended, and with its conclusion the thoughts of Brazilians turned to the government's commitment to take up the cause of emancipation. With the opening of the new legislative session in May, members of the Assembly reminded the government of that commitment. One result of the war, however, had been the rise to power of a Conservative ministry strongly opposed to slavery reform, and that government refused to lend its authority to the anti-slavery cause. In reply to demands for emancipationist legislation from the Chamber of Deputies, Viscount Itaboraí reminded the legislators of the great economic and national interests associated with slavery, of the need to proceed slowly and cautiously to avoid offense to the rural proprietors and the legitimate interests associated with them. Nothing could be done without thought and preparation, said the President of the Council, particularly since the Empire had just endured a destructive war.[52]

Soon, however, an important reform of the slave regimes of Cuba and Puerto Rico strengthened the voice of the Brazilian emancipationists and underlined the need for similar changes in Brazil. In the summer of 1870, with Cuba in a state of rebellion and under growing threat of intervention by North American forces on the side of the rebels, the legislature of Spain had passed a law granting freedom to both the newborn and the aged slaves of Cuba and Puerto Rico.[53]

Influenced by the Spanish example, in mid-August 1870 a special committee of the Chamber of Deputies urged action on a reform project like that elaborated in the Council of State in 1867 and 1868, recommending as well the introduction of free workers as "substitutes for the present instrument of agricultural production . . . ." One member of the committee, Rodrigo da Silva of São Paulo, opposed the majority opinion, however, on the usual plea of the economic necessity of slavery. Brazil, he thought, was in the same circumstances as his province, where slavery was essential. "The interests of agriculture are the interests of our society; it cannot have others more important because all its vitality is there." The least shock, the least disturbance of these interests could crumble this "beautiful edifice" in ruins.[54]

51. *O Abolicionista*, Rio de Janeiro, December 1, 1880; Nabuco, *O Abolicionismo*, p. 65; *Discussão da reforma do estado servil*, II, Appéndice, p. 50.
52. *Annaes da Câmara* (1870), I, 12, 25–26; Nabuco, *Um estadista do Imperio*, III, 148; Godoy, *O elemento servil*, p. 433.
53. Corwin, *Spain and the Abolition of Slavery in Cuba*, pp. 246–251.
54. Godoy, *O elemento servil*, pp. 419–430.

Viscount Itaboraí obviously shared the views of the deputy from São Paulo, and therefore no further action could be taken until his ministry was replaced by one more willing to lead the reform project through the Assembly. That this would soon occur was, in fact, anticipated in Rio de Janeiro, where in late August there were rumors that Pedro was "determined to have the slavery question brought forward this session," and would replace the ruling ministry if it refused to act.[55] A major question facing the Emperor, however, was whether to appoint a Liberal regime to champion the reformist legislation, or to avoid the political crisis certain to result from another sudden change of national leadership by appointing a more cooperative Conservative to guide the bill through the Assembly.

It was Nabuco de Araújo who helped to settle the question, who in fact was publicly identified with the fall of Itaboraí and the rise of a more conciliatory Conservative ministry. Aware of the emancipationist sentiments of many members of the Conservative Party in the Assembly and opposed on principle to the Liberal Party's rise to power through another imperial *coup d'état,* Nabuco was willing to allow the more accommodating wing of the Conservative Party to enact anti-slavery legislation. More than power, Nabuco had said in a major speech in July, the Liberal Party wanted the reforms which only the leadership of a segment of the Conservative Party could then achieve.[56]

The immediate cause of the resignation of the Itaboraí cabinet was Nabuco's proposal to apply 1,000 contos of the expected budget surplus to the liberation of slaves. Signed by nine senators, this amendment was defended in the Assembly by its author. The Liberal Party had patiently awaited a governmental solution, he said, but nothing had been done. The Liberal Party, consequently, could not watch the Assembly session end "without a protest against the procedure of the government in respect to a matter of such importance." Now that Spain had decreed the gradual emancipation of the slaves of Cuba, Brazil had become the only American nation, the only Christian nation, to maintain the status quo of the colonial era. Only the Itaboraí ministry impeded reform, claimed Nabuco de Araújo, while the Chamber of Deputies, the provincial assemblies, the Council of State, the people, and even the slaveowners were ready for prudent legislation.[57] Near the close of September, with the Council of Ministers divided on the slavery question, the Itaboraí ministry resigned under pressure, to be replaced by a Conservative Party government led by the Viscount São Vicente, a senator closely

55. See William Hadfield, *Brazil and the River Plate, 1870–76* (London, 1877), p. 74.
56. Nabuco, *Um estadista do Imperio,* III, 148–153.
57. *Ibid.,* III, 153–157.

associated with emancipation since his preparation of the reform project of 1866.

Called by the Emperor to direct the legislation through the Assembly, committed by his own program to seek a "prudent solution," São Vicente was uncertain, however, of his own ability to provide the leadership needed to accomplish the important work.[58] Against the will of the Emperor, he resigned after five months in favor of Viscount Rio Branco. A Conservative senator from Bahia, a member of the Council of State, editor, and diplomat, Rio Branco had recently returned from a special mission to Uruguay and Argentina, where he had allegedly been convinced that reform in Brazil could no longer be postponed.

Although few concrete achievements toward slavery reform were made during the five years following the American Civil War, an important shift in national attitudes had occurred. A hearty liberalism encompassing in its program the government's slavery reform project had made itself felt. Meanwhile, too, many slaves had been freed to fight in Paraguay, some to die there but others to return to freedom, their contribution to the war effort perhaps subtly altering the opinions of their fellow-soldiers.[59] National leaders such as Rio Branco, who only a few years earlier had seen little justification for change, had been swung over by the Emperor, by their experiences abroad, and by growing internal demands. Any reform, however, even one intended to give the slavery system a few more decades of undisturbed life, was certain to be opposed by some politicians, particularly those who represented parts of the country where slaves were greatly concentrated by 1871.

58. *Ibid.*, III, 171–181; *Organizações e programas ministeriais*, p. 157.
59. Ianni, *As metamorfoses do escravo*, p. 217. For effects of the war on slavery, see also Charles J. Kolinski, *Independence or Death, The Story of the Paraguayan War* (Gainesville, Florida, 1965), pp. 195–196.

*I know for myself
how often the permanence
of this odious institution in Brazil
vexed and humiliated us
before foreigners.*

VISCOUNT RIO BRANCO IN 1871.

Before the slave is born he suffers inside his mother.

JOAQUIM NABUCO IN 1870.

6

THE
EMANCIPATION OF
THE NEWBORN

THE RIO BRANCO LAW

In 1871 the emancipation of the newborn children of slave women seemed a feasible solution to the Brazilian problem. Recommended in print as early as the eighteenth century[1] and occasionally after, legislated in Chile in 1811, by Gran Colombia in 1821, by Portugal in 1856, by Spain for her Caribbean colonies in 1870, and even recommended by Abraham Lincoln for Delaware in 1861, the "free womb" was sanctioned by precedent.[2]

The project introduced into the Chamber of Deputies on May 12, 1871, and passed almost unchanged into law on September 28 contained much more, however, than a free-birth provision. The bill was complex because it was expected to alter the status quo in a manner satisfactory to critics of slavery while guarding the rights of the slaveholders. It was intended to set the stage for evolution toward a free-labor system without causing much immediate change to agriculture or economic interests. It was expected to patch up a failing institution while eliminating its last source of renewal, to protect the interests of the living generation of masters while it redeemed the impending gen-

---

1. See Ribeiro da Rocha, *Ethiope resgatado*
2. For a valuable study of the abolition of slavery in Venezuela see John V. Lombardi, *The Decline and Abolition of Negro Slavery in Venezuela, 1820–1854* (Westport, Connecticut, 1971).

eration of slaves. Hailed as a great reform, it was an intricate compromise. Yet it contributed significantly toward the collapse of slavery seventeen years later.

Passed under the Conservative administration of Rio Branco, the legislation freed the newborn children of slave women, obligating their masters to care for them until the age of eight. In exchange for any expense or trouble involved in such responsibilities, masters were given the choice of receiving from the state an indemnification of 600 milréis in six-percent thirty-year bonds or of making use of the labor of the minors (*ingenuos*) until they reached the age of twenty-one. The law created an emancipation fund to be used for the annual manumission of slaves in all the provinces. For the first time in the history of the Empire, the slave was granted the legal right to keep the savings (*peculio*) which he might acquire through gifts and inheritances and, with the consent of his owner, by his own labor. With his savings thus guaranteed, the slave was assured the privilege of buying his own freedom when he could present a sum of money equal to his "value." The law freed slaves owned by the state, including those held in usufruct by the Imperial Family. It freed persons included in unclaimed inheritances or abandoned by their owners. It placed liberated persons under governmental supervision for five years, with the obligation to contract their services or, if living as vagabonds, to work in public establishments. Finally, the new law ordered a nationwide registration of all slaves, to include their names, ages, marital status, aptitude for work, and parentage, if known. Slaves whose masters failed through neglect to register them within one year of the special registration were to be considered free.[3]

REGION AGAINST REGION

Although rarely recognized in the oratory of the day, the debate on the Rio Branco Law pitted region against region. As a group, the coffee-growing provinces were unprepared in 1871 for even moderate changes in the labor system, and southern planters, therefore, carried on what Joaquim Nabuco later called "an organized war against the Government and the Emperor. . . ."[4] In contrast, political leaders in most other provinces were amenable to a mild reform. Some northerners in and out of the General Assembly staunchly defended the status quo, and the coffee regions, notably the cities of Rio de Janeiro and São Paulo, produced their avid reformists. Yet the debate in the Senate and Cham-

3. These are the most important provisions. For the full text, see Appendix II.
4. Nabuco, *O Abolicionismo,* pp. 60–61.

ber of Deputies and the votes taken in the lower house on the legislation
(see Table 21) revealed that the core of the resistance was located in
the coffee provinces, the inevitable result of the concentration of slaves
in the same area. In fact, slave population statistics for the period correspond logically with the voting behavior of provincial delegates in the
General Assembly (see Tables 2, 3, and 21).[5] The long debate on the
law, moreover, reveals much the same. Of twenty-five senators and
deputies who delivered major speeches in opposition to the project, nineteen represented a major coffee province or the Município Neutro.[6]

Occasionally the regional character of the dispute was pointed out.
Perdigão Malheiro, who had proposed free birth in 1863 but opposed
that reform in 1871 as a deputy from Minas Gerais, stated frankly in
the Chamber that Rio de Janeiro, Minas Gerais, and São Paulo, with
their eight or nine hundred thousand slaves, had the best reasons to
oppose the bill. Legislation which could be applied to Amazonas or
Ceará, he warned, was not applicable to those provinces or to Bahia and
Pernambuco, with their hundreds of thousands of slaves.[7] According to
Rio Branco, some planters of the north were so much in agreement with
the bill that they were already conforming with its provisions.[8] A senator
from São Paulo claimed that too much importance was being given to
northern spokesmen who favored the reform and that opposing southern
voices merited more influence because of their region's greater contribution to national wealth. Accused of adventurism, northerners responded
by portraying themselves as the cautious reformers that they were.[9]

The debate of 1871 was characterized by intra-party dispute. The

5. It might be surmised that these votes were more a reflection of the Emperor's
will than that of the regional electorate, but in regard to slavery and other important economic issues, politicians exercised independence from party and monarch, and were much beholden to local landlords. For a similar view, see P. N.
Evanson, "The Liberal Party and Reform in Brazil, 1860–1889" (unpublished
Ph.D. dissertation, University of Virginia, 1969), p. 55.
6. *Discussão da reforma do estado servil*, II, Appéndice, pp. 143–149.
7. *Annaes da Câmara* (1871), III, 115, 122. Perdigão Malheiro replied to the
charge of inconsistency on the slavery issue with the explanation that his works
on slavery were "books of the study and of doctrine; and who is not aware of
the distance between a book of the study and of doctrine and the work of the
legislator?" *Annaes da Câmara* (1871), III, 118.
8. *Discussão da reforma do estado servil*, II, 75. In 1869 Liberal deputy Pedro
de Araújo Beltrão announced in the Pernambuco Provincial Assembly that he
and his immediate relatives would free all children henceforth born to their slaves.
The same planter supported the program of Nabuco de Araújo's Liberal Center
and invited "all true Liberals" to support the principle of free birth. See "Abolition of Slavery in Brazil," *South American Journal*, July 14, 1888. For other decisions of northern planters to "free the womb," see Rebouças, *Agricultura nacional*,
pp. 176–178.
9. *Discussão da reforma do estado servil*, II, 98, 314.

Conservative Party controlled the Chamber, but the ruling ministry could not depend upon this advantage alone to rush its bill through the lower house because the regional interests of many of its members took precedence over party loyalty. The Conservative Party schism in the Chamber was so complete, in fact, that the minority faction rejected the leadership of Rio Branco in open debate, even threatening to form a new party.[10] In the final vote on the law, forty-five deputies (two-thirds from coffee provinces) opposed the bill. In contrast, as Table 21 shows, the Conservative ministry was able to rely upon the support of most deputies from provinces north and west of Minas Gerais to pass the free-birth law over the opposition of most of their colleagues from the coffee region. Among the western and southernmost provinces, only Rio Grande do Sul voted against the reform, but there too, as Table 2 shows, was a large and valuable concentration of slaves comprising more than twenty-one percent of the provincial population.

In the Senate, less responsive to local considerations, the small contingent of Liberal senators led by Nabuco de Araújo joined the bulk of the Conservatives from all the provinces to pass the government's bill. However, five of the seven senators who voted against the project represented coffee provinces, and one of two northerners who did so was the former Liberal President of the Council, Zacarias de Góis of Bahia, who rejected the bill for partisan reasons. Zacarias was not opposed to the bill itself, Rio Branco claimed, but resented the Conservative Party's initiative and its support of a measure which "by right" belonged to him and the Liberal Party.[11]

THE NATIONAL DEBATE

The slavery reform bill of 1871 set off an almost unprecedented national debate. Perhaps no question had aroused so much popular interest since the abolition of the slave trade or the achievement of independence. Opponents and supporters of the reform used every reasonable means to advance their views. Friends of the reform argued their cause in the legislative chambers, in the press, and in public meetings in the theaters of Rio de Janeiro and other cities, where speakers sometimes attracted audiences estimated in the thousands.[12] While the aroused nation

10. *Ibid.*, II, 125, 212–213.
11. *Ibid.*, II, 260.
12. André Rebouças, *Diário e notas autobigraficas* (Rio de Janeiro, 1938), p. 287; Carlos Bernardino de Moura, *Considerações feitas pelo cidadão Carlos Bernardino de Moura na conferencia no dia 2 de Julho corrente no Theatro de S. Pedro* (Rio de Janeiro, 1871).

awaited the reform with impatience or fear, many persons published their opinions and proposals.[13] Newspapers of Rio de Janeiro and the provinces increasingly turned their attention to the controversy as the legislative debate continued week after week. To support its cause the government subsidized the press, including staid commercial papers like the *Jornal do Commercio,* and even distributed propaganda leaflets in the provinces.[14] Major dailies of most regions supported the government's cause, and some radical papers like *O Abolicionista* and *A Imprensa Academica* of São Paulo demanded far more than the moderate bill. According to one "Spartacus," a supporter of the project, only two minor Brazilian papers and one major one, the *Diario do Rio de Janeiro,* opposed the government's reform. Fifty-seven papers, large and small, representing most of the provinces from Pará to Rio Grande do Sul, were listed as supporters of the Rio Branco bill, though others, notably those of Espírito Santo and the hinterland of Rio de Janeiro, were silent at a time when silence on the slavery issue was tantamount to opposition.[15]

Evidence of resistance to the project is perhaps as abundant as documents favoring action. Between May and mid-September 1871, agricultural and commercial organizations of Rio de Janeiro, Minas Gerais, and São Paulo sent at least twenty-two petitions to the two chambers of the Assembly in support of the status quo, all published in the legislative annals.[16] In Rio, members of the Conservative Party, hostile to the ruling ministry, created the influential Club da Lavoura e do Commercio (Commercial and Agricultural Club) in July to defend slavery against the reform-minded faction of their own party.[17]

The revitalization of republicanism, quiescent since the 1840's, was in part at least a reaction of coffee planters to the emancipationist sentiments of the Emperor and the programs of Liberal and Conservative ministries. Slaveowners undoubtedly received Pedro's statements of 1867 and 1868 and the emancipationist programs of Liberal cabinets with some dismay. But the rise to power at the Emperor's bidding of a Conservative Party cabinet openly committed to slavery reform apparently

13. See for example Elzeario Pinto, *Reformas: emancipação dos escravos* (Salvador da Bahia, 1870); T. de Alencar Araripe, *O elemento servil. Artigos sobre a emancipação* (Paraíba do Sul, Rio de Janeiro, 1871); *Analyse e commentario da proposta do Governo Imperial ás câmaras legislativas sobre o elemento servil por um magistrado* (Rio de Janeiro, 1871). In 1870 Joaquim Nabuco, then only twenty-one, wrote his first analysis of slavery in which he denied the legitimacy of slave property. See "A escravidão," pp. 4–106.
14. *Discussão da reforma do estado servil,* II, 19, 34, 302; *Annaes da Câmara* (1871), III, 167, 236, 251.
15. *Discussão da reforma do estado servil,* II, 39–40.
16. *Ibid.,* II, 337, 368–369.
17. Gouveia, *Historia da escravidão,* pp. 219–221.

shook the confidence of many in the imperial system itself. There was a practical side to republican ideology which did not escape the attention of party leaders and recruits in São Paulo and neighboring provinces. Republicanism implied federalism—a weak central government and provincial legislatures with power to determine slavery policy in a way consistent with provincial conditions, without the dictation of a powerful executive or national legislature. A republican movement had begun to form in the coffee provinces in the late 1860's, gathering strength in response to the emancipationist program of Zacarias de Góis, and flowering into an organized party in 1870.[18] The Republican Manifesto of the third of December of that year, published some two months after the cabinet of São Vicente revealed its program of slavery reform, avoided references to the slavery question, but denounced the Emperor's power to choose cabinets at will and outspokenly demanded a decentralization of power.[19] As the threat to slavery increased during 1870 and 1871, republicanism grew apace, and when the Rio Branco Law was passed by the Assembly against the will of the coffee provinces, it brought a new contingent of planters into the provincial republican movements of the coffee zone.[20] Joaquim Nabuco later declared in the Chamber, with some exaggeration, that in 1871 the only opposition to the Rio Branco bill was that of the planters and the Republican Party.[21]

THE OPPOSITION

The arguments used against the government's project were abundant and complex. Ranging from clever to spurious, they tell much about Brazilian slave society. Most opponents of the bill would have agreed that slavery was condemned by religion and the opinions of mankind, but they asked difficult questions regarding the consequences of an emancipationist measure. Perdigão Malheiro admitted the need to end slavery, while asking only that it be achieved by the safest and most convenient

18. Santos, *Os republicanos paulistas,* pp. 12–13.
19. *Brazilian Republican Address* (Rio de Janeiro, 1871), pp. 9–11. Significantly, each of the authors of the Republican Manifesto, Quintino Bocaiúva and Salvador de Mendonça, also wrote books in which they advocated importation of inexpensive Chinese laborers to work on coffee plantations. See Bocayuva, *A crise da lavoura;* Mendonça, *Trabalhadores asiaticos.*
20. Santos, *Os republicanos paulistas,* pp. 118–119; *Annaes da Câmara* (1888), II, 65.
21. *Ibid.,* II, 407. For an outline of the party program of the Paulista Republicans, strong on provincial autonomy and the need for new sources of labor, but hesitant on the question of slavery, see Morse, *From Community to Metropolis,* pp. 158–159.

method. No one, he claimed, desired to resolve the problem through "absolute justice." [22]

Most opponents, however, attacked the heart of the project: the liberation of the children of slave women.[23] Brazilian laws, said a senator from Minas Gerais during the long debate, "have recognized and still recognize not only ownership of the slave woman, but also of the child whom she might bear." The property right over the child was "an extension of the right of property over the slave woman, and of the same nature." Indemnification of the child's small value seemed of little financial significance to the General Director of Public Revenue, but he feared the consequences of opening "a breach in the fortress walls" of property rights.[24]

With some legal accuracy opponents of the bill sometimes compared the slave with other living possessions, particularly plants and animals capable of reproduction or of bearing fruit. Barros Cobra of Minas Gerais claimed that the acquired right of the master to the fruit of the slave womb was as complete as the proprietor's right to the fruit of the tree or to the offspring (*cria*) of any animal in his possession. Between these two forms of property there was "a perfect identity of conditions." The slave born of a slave was capital and an instrument of labor.[25] To free the children of slaves by legislation, said an old advocate of the slave traders, J. M. Pereira da Silva, representing Rio de Janeiro in the Chamber, was "to offend the right of property guaranteed . . . by the Constitution . . . and respected by all existing laws." Rejecting the concept that slave property was different from other forms of property, as claimed by the Minister of Agriculture, Pereira da Silva asked where the Constitution and the laws distinguished this new species of property. Were not the fruit of the tree, the product of the land, and the yield of

---

22. *Annaes da Câmara* (1871), II, 51–52; III, 115.
23. *Discussão da reforma do estado servil*, II, 302.
24. *Annaes da Câmara* (1871), V, 139–140. The defensive arsenal of pro-slavery legislators included abstruse legal arguments, the result of the legal training possessed by at least fifteen of the twenty-five members of the Assembly who delivered major speeches against the bill. Some legal arguments were specious or based upon an incomplete grasp of the facts. Viscount Itaboraí, for example, learnedly distinguished between Natural and Positive Law and theorized that when a parliament revoked legislation contrary to reason and Natural Law it was obliged to indemnify the losses of private persons, because such persons were not legally responsible. The violence of slavery had not been committed by the Brazilian planter, he claimed, but by the African chief. Brazilians might have prohibited the purchase and sale of Africans, he admitted, forgetting the law of 1831 and two decades of illegal trading in slaves, but such transactions had been permitted and the buyers of Africans were therefore not at fault. *Annaes do Parlamento Brasileiro. Senado* (hereafter *Annaes do Senado*) (1871), V, 140.
25. *Annaes da Câmara* (1871), III, 258–259

the planting the property of those who owned the tree, the land, and the seed?[26]

Opponents of the bill posed many non-legal objections to emancipation of the newborn. The indemnification which the government proposed to pay the masters who chose to surrender children when they reached the age of eight seemed inadequate to some, though masters were to have the alternative of using the labor of such children for another thirteen years. The most favorable statistics showed, said Baron da Villa da Barra of Bahia, that barely half of the children born of slaves reached the age of eight, and, therefore, the real indemnification for the rearing of ingenuos (as free-born children were to be called) was a mere 300 milréis, and not 600 as stated in the project. Barros Cobra calculated that six-percent simple interest over thirty years was only 1,080 milréis, a sum which a slave could earn for his master in two or three years. Indemnification through the labor of the ingenuos seemed to him illusory because masters could not be reimbursed with services already guaranteed to them under the law. Deputy Capanema of Minas Gerais recalled that in the capital of the Empire, slave masters sent the offspring of their slave women to the foundling house (*casa dos expostos*) and then rented their mothers as wet nurses, earning five to six hundred milréis in a single year. Under these circumstances, the government's bonds were patently unattractive.[27]

A surprising number of pro-slavery theoreticians argued that freeing the newborn was tantamount to murder, applying to the bill the epithet of "Herod's Law" and predicting the abandonment and death of thousands of unwanted babies.[28] A pamphleteer predicted that the law would not grant a life of freedom to the children of slave women, because, as a result of its provisions, most would die. Disgusted masters, calculating the loss of labor during and after pregnancy and the costs of rearing useless children, would not provide sufficient care; thus half or more would be sacrificed so that some might be free.[29] Capanema thought that the bill would create a situation like that which had existed before the abolition of the slave trade, when slaves were cheap and ninety-five percent of the children, neglected and unwanted, died before they reached the age of eight. The young would be sacrificed again, he predicted, because they would not be wanted. The law would be resisted or ignored, predicted Perdigão Malheiro, and the result would be "a true

26. "Discurso sobre a proposta do governo acerca do elemento servil," *Discursos do Deputado J. M. Pereira da Silva* (Rio de Janeiro, 1872), pp. 89–137.
27. *Annaes da Câmara* (1871), III, 95, 173–174, 259.
28. *Discussão da reforma do estado servil*, II, 313.
29. *Reflexões sobre a emancipação em relação á lavoura patria e sobre a mesma lavoura* (Bahia, 1871), p. 27. The same writer, nonetheless, proclaimed the kindness of the Brazilian slave master.

hecatomb of innocent ones!" If the material or pecuniary interest of masters in children born into slavery was already inadequate to prevent a "prodigious mortality," reasoned Barros Cobra, the reduced proprietary incentive caused by the law would greatly increase the death rate. Masters would have no interest in rearing and educating free children, and abandonment would occur on the greatest imaginable scale.[30] The death rate among slave children, said Pereira da Silva, "however kind and charitable the owners may be," had been calculated at seventy percent. If only thirty of every hundred children were then reaching the age of eight, how many children, for whom masters would have "no interest" and "no affection," could survive? "Instead of humanitarianism," he concluded, "will you not have slaughter?" [31]

The exact status which ingenuos were to have also troubled opponents of the bill. Some dreaded the consequences of rearing in a slave environment children destined for freedom and the rights of citizenship, or wondered if ingenuos were to be subjected to the same punishments as slaves.[32] Barros Cobra developed a tortured legalistic argument concerning the dangerous and unconstitutional status that the free-birth law would grant to the children of slave women through their designation as ingenuos. The Constitution had adopted the Roman precedent according to which an ingenuo was a person born of a free womb and a *liberto* was one born of a slave womb who later gained his freedom. Under this definition, the child born of a slave woman could not be an ingenuo because the law would liberate the fruit of the womb and not the womb itself. The person freed by the legislation, it followed, would be at best a liberto, and, therefore, unqualified to enjoy the full political rights which the Constitution granted to persons born in Brazil to free mothers.[33]

Opponents also warned that freeing some of the slaves would foment a rebellious spirit among the others. Perdigão Malheiro foresaw a general slave revolt. José de Alencar spoke of "sad days, with all their attendant crimes, horrors, and scandalous scenes." The idea of emancipating the children, said Capanema "will completely rupture the ties of subordination, will divide the servile population on our agricultural estates into two classes, making it impossible to continue under the system of passive obedience, which is the only one possible as long as slavery exists in our country." The slaves were not so brutalized, he added, that they did not

30. *Annaes da Câmara* (1871), III, 123, 173, 258. Charity, said Barros Cobra, should not be relied upon when legislating for mankind.
31. "Discurso sobre a proposta do governo," pp. 89–137.
32. *Discussão da reforma do estado servil*, II, 304; *Annaes da Câmara* (1871), III, 96–97; *Annaes do Senado* (1871), V, 137.
33. *Annaes da Câmara* (1871), III, 258–259.

know that parents should enjoy the same right to freedom as their children.[34]

Opponents also deplored the expected economic consequences of the law. As early as May, in response to the Emperor's Speech from the Throne, Paulino de Souza of Rio de Janeiro was blaming the project for a loss of confidence among rural proprietors. In the same debate Pereira da Silva recalled that public and private income was still derived almost exclusively from the large estates dependent for labor almost solely upon slaves. Andrade Figueira warned that the government could not upset the established order without a response from consecrated interests. The mere introduction of the bill into the Chamber, it was claimed, had already caused great harm to agriculture. Property values had fallen sharply and credit was already hard to obtain.[35]

To other deputies the reform seemed to threaten the national existence. The law would stir up the most dangerous elements of the population, sacrifice the most important interests. Brazil, it was said, could no more free her slaves than Britain could destroy her machines. Agriculture and related interests needed time to prepare for the liquidation of slavery and the acquisition of a new labor force. The greatest peril, many opponents of the bill were saying, was not the loss of the slave, but the loss of the worker; not the loss of property, but the capital which it represented. The reform bill was even likened to an immense boulder set precariously on a mountain top threatening to roll down into a valley to crush the innocent people below. The ministry which pledged itself to toppling that stone, admonished a deputy, was either blind or had failed to look down into the valley.[36]

Finally, the Emperor was frequently blamed. The project, it was said, lay in the shadow of "Caesarism." To support it was tantamount to an act of subservience to the imperial will. Pedro had imposed his ideas upon the ministry, and both he and the Council of State had overstepped their constitutional powers through initiation of a legislative project. The Emperor, said a deputy from Minas Gerais, did not have the right to express opinions on matters of state. José de Alencar accused Pedro of abandoning the neutral position assigned to him by the Constitution. "He takes sides," said the romantic novelist, "he loses the character of the judge and takes on that of the dictator." Since 1866, said Capanema, when the Emperor pledged to free the slaves, much had changed, including his own devotion to monarchist principles. Since then "simple mor-

34. Moraes, *A campanha abolicionista,* p. 1; *Annaes da Câmara* (1871), II, 51–52; III, 171–173; *Annaes do Senado* (1871), V, 197.
35. *Annaes da Câmara* (1871), I, 102, 116; III, 113–114; V, 26.
36. *Ibid.,* III, 175; V, 72; *Reflexões sobre a emancipação,* pp. 23–26; *Discussão da reforma do estado servil,* II, 13, 48, 563–564.

tals" had lost their ability to act and think in conformity with needs and circumstances, while he who saw things from "inaccessible heights" could only march forward to his high place in the pantheon of heroes.[37]

At times opponents showed a desire to compromise. Some favored indirect measures leading toward full freedom by the end of the century. Deputy Calmón was ready to accept the emancipation of slaves reaching sixty-five and the gradual indemnified manumission of selected women and children. Such measures were better than the free-birth provision, it was reasoned, because they respected the rights of property, honored the will of masters, conceded a reasonable indemnification, and would even diminish the last source of new slaves through the liberation of women of child-bearing age.[38]

The arguments of the opposition were varied, complex, and self-righteously expressed, but they did not convince the ministry or the majority of the legislators, who saw the bill as a reasonable and needed compromise. Better this bill, claimed the Rio Branco regime, than further economic and social uncertainty, or continuing radicalization of the country.

THE SUPPORTERS

In a series of speeches delivered between early May and late September, Viscount Rio Branco revealed the principal aims of the legislation. It offered, he contended, the most moderate and reasonable solution possible under the difficult circumstances facing the nation. It was designed to re-stabilize the economic and social life of the country, to reverse the damage that the dispute over slavery had inflicted upon agriculture, to restore the confidence of the planters and to revitalize agricultural credit. Further resistance to change would have the effect of arousing public discontent to the level that a moderate measure would no longer be enough. The national situation had become so dangerous that indirect measures of the kind acceptable to the bill's opponents would merely arouse passions and create dangers which the Assembly was trying to avoid. The project had great virtues favoring the interests of the proprietors. It represented the "complete solution," condemning slavery to slow extinction while it preserved the labor force.[39]

Members of the Rio Branco ministry also clearly explained the government's position to the Assembly. Sayão Lobato, Minister of Justice and a senator from Rio de Janeiro, argued that the project was intended

37. *Ibid.*, II, 42–46, 58, 583–584; Gouveia, *Historia da escravidão*, p. 191; *Annaes da Câmara* (1871), III, 170, 241.
38. *Ibid.*, I, 117; III, 99–100, 241.
39. *Discussão da reforma do estado servil*, II, 22–23, 29, 47–50, 74, 274.

to maintain organized the labor force which cultivates the lands, to guarantee existing slave property, which will never be taken from the slave master . . . without just indemnification . . . , but at the same time to declare that the future generation of female slaves, now destined for captivity, will be born free, will not increase the number of existing slaves.

The most important provision of the bill—the free-birth provision— guaranteed the status quo for eight years, said the Justice Minister, and for as long as twenty-one years if planters so decided. The child brought up on the plantation by his mother's master would acquire a respectful attitude and accustom himself from birth to "maximum subjection." [40] The government's plan did not sacrifice the proprietors' interests, said the Minister of Agriculture, but rather reconciled those interests to the greatest possible degree with the principle of equality. The bill "respected the past and corrected only the future." In promoting the legislation, the ministry was not rigorously following the principle of human equality but was slightly sacrificing that principle in the search for a solution. In confiding the ingenuos to the care of their mothers' masters, said another supporter, the government had in mind their future employment as rural workers. Confined to the agricultural properties under the law, they would become habituated to the narrow world of the plantation on which they were born and to which all their sentiments would be linked. They would learn to serve and to produce that which Brazil most needed: the wealth of the soil.[41]

Like its opponents, supporters of the bill used arguments which revealed the harshness of slave life. Deputy Junqueira was convinced that "the precarious hygienic conditions" under which Brazilian slaves were forced to live were responsible for an enormous death rate among both children and adults and a consequent loss of labor to the nation. A free-labor system, said Viscount São Vicente, induced a more equitable distribution of wealth, while slavery retarded the growth of the population and the development of culture. "It is sufficient," he claimed, "to compare the mortality of slaves with that of the free population to deduce the consequences. Slavery, he charged, was "moral and legal inequality carried to an extreme." [42]

Supporters claimed that free labor was more productive than slave labor. Free men contributed more than slaves to the public welfare. Free men gave of their capital and intelligence as well as their labor, while slaves, motivated solely by fear, contributed only labor. Free workers provided a pool of manpower useful in war time, while enslaved workers constituted a permanent national threat. Statistics showed that produc-

40. *Ibid.,* II, 345–349.
41. *Ibid.,* II, 208, 570.
42. *Ibid.,* II, 193–194, 329–331.

tion increased in proportion to the decline of the slave population. As proof of the economic superiority of free labor, a deputy from Pernambuco cited abundant statistics on the economic development of the free and slave states of North America. Alencar Araripe recalled the failure of Europeans to emigrate to Brazil, despite repeated efforts of Brazilian governments to attract them through the establishment of colonies and the distribution of fertile and accessible land. "The reason," he said, "is that the European . . . fears the contagion of slavery." [43]

Defenders of the project also expounded upon the political and international ramifications of the bill. Enacting reform, Brazil could avoid a civil war of the kind which had stricken the United States and Cuba.[44] Brazil stood nearly alone in the world in maintaining slavery. The opinion of civilized and Christian nations compelled reform. "I know for myself," said Rio Branco in a speech recounting diplomatic experiences in Uruguay, Argentina, and Paraguay, "how often the permanence of this odious institution in Brazil vexed and humiliated us before foreigners." [45]

Proponents of the bill did not neglect moral and religious arguments. Property based upon an infraction of human rights, said Alencar Araripe, could not be permanent. The living generation, said Junqueira, was obliged to deliver future generations from the nightmare of slavery. "Can Brazil," asked Fernandes da Cunha, "a Catholic nation . . . in free America, provide a sad and hateful exception among all her sister countries? After Europe resolved the question, after the American republics, and particularly the United States, resolved it . . . is it not time to subdue the monster?" [46]

More than one supporter of the bill distinguished between the proprietor's right to possess a *thing* and his right to possess a *person*. The second form of property, it was said, was legal but not legitimate. *Things* were defined as entities without rights or responsibilities, which could be appropriated and used without restrictions, while *persons* were "moral beings with rights and obligations granted by their Creator." The natural right to possess *things* had its origin in the moral order of creation and was legitimate. Such property could be "used and abused," was never subject to modification by the legislator, and offended no one. The property right over slaves, however, was subject to legal restrictions and could be revised or revoked in response to public need.[47]

Perhaps the most brilliant and uncompromising speech delivered dur-

43. *Ibid.,* II, 168–188, 329–331, Appéndice, pp. 28, 39.
44. *Ibid.,* II, Appéndice, pp. 9–11. In the case of Cuba, the reference was to the first war for independence, which had begun in 1868 and was to last for ten years.
45. *Ibid.,* II, Appéndice, p. 104.
46. *Ibid.,* II, 557, Appéndice, pp. 18, 26.
47. *Ibid.,* II, 316–320.

ing the debate was that of Senator Francisco Sales Torres-Homem, a veteran of radical politics who in 1871 represented Rio Grande do Norte. Sales Torres-Homem, himself a probable descendant of slaves, placed the seizure and subjugation of a black man in Africa and the enslavement of the Brazilian infant on the same level of iniquity. In the latter case, the master awaited his new property at the door of life itself. This was "piracy carried on about the crib." He refuted the major arguments of opponents. Property over human beings, "far from being founded upon natural law, is . . . its most monstrous violation." Human beings could not be compared "to the colt, the calf, to the fruit of the trees, and the animate objects of nature subject to the domination of mankind." He challenged the claim to the unborn children of slave women with a dramatic reminder that the dust of which their bodies would be composed was still scattered over the earth, that the souls already claimed by the masters for the hell of slavery still reposed "in the lap of the creative power . . . ." Those who spoke so loudly of property rights, he charged, had forgotten that most of the slaves who worked their lands were the descendants of persons "whom an inhuman traffic criminally introduced into this country with an affront to laws and treaties." [48]

The debate was not always orderly. Opponents often interrupted defenders of the bill. As it made its way through the Chamber, they demanded nominal votes on unimportant articles. Andrade Figueira (Rio de Janeiro), Antônio Prado (São Paulo), Perdigão Malheiro (Minas Gerais), and others filibustered or resorted to interpellations to delay progress. To slow down debate, the minority faction regularly refused to enter the Chamber until the bare government majority had arrived to form a quorum, forcing every advocate of the bill to be in attendance at every session.[49] During the last month of the debate in the lower house, the government could depend upon only sixty-two supporters, the exact number needed to open a session and to assure passage of the legislation. At times the decorum of the Chamber was disrupted by exchanges of accusations, notably on August 2 after passage of the article which gave the slaves the right to their savings and their freedom when they had collected their price. Throwing charges, deputies left their seats to swarm about the hall, as spectators rose to their feet to stand in silence. "Not since the agitated days of [1840] was the precinct of the Chamber the theater of such scenes," said a report of the debates, "and the government's project was passed only after a struggle unprecedented in our parliamentary annals." [50]

48. *Ibid.,* II, 282–297.
49. *Ibid.,* II, 11, 18–19, 59–60, 62, 64, 81–82, 112, 229; Duque-Estrada, *A abolição,* p. 66.
50. *Discussão da reforma do estado servil,* II, 5–15, 255.

The Senate session of September 27, 1871, was solemn. The galleries and the floor were crowded with spectators awaiting the final vote, long delayed by the speech of a senator from Bahia. At last, the President of the Senate announced that the project had been approved, bringing prolonged applause and cascades of flowers from the galleries. Outside demonstrations honoring Rio Branco, Nabuco de Araújo, Sales Torres-Homem, and other legislators set off several days of boisterous public celebrations.[51]

Despite the sense of triumph, the immediate effects of the victory were small. The law was complex, but brought no immediate change in the lives of most slaves, and even the children whose freedom it guaranteed could not derive much practical benefit from their status until they reached their legal maturity. By then, as defenders of the bill had argued, reared and trained in an environment of slavery, the ingenuos would be slaves by disposition if not by law, ill-equipped and little motivated for much more than a life of labor and servility on the plantations of their mothers' masters.[52]

Portentous remarks regarding the effects of the law had marred the last days of the debate. Nabuco de Araújo regretted deletion of a provision to end slavery at the end of the century. The emancipation fund, he predicted, distributed thinly about the country, would not be effective, though concentration of its assets in such provinces as Ceará and Rio Grande do Norte might have created free areas from which the provinces occupied by slavery could have been steadily reduced. Nabuco foresaw violations of the law. Children born after its enactment would be enslaved through substitution of others born before, and free persons would be registered as slaves.

Nabuco was joined by the historian from Maranhão, Cândido Mendes de Almeida, in deploring the failure to provide educational opportunities for children whom the law would free.[53] This failure, of course, was deliberate. The question of education was not debated, but Brazilian history reveals little inclination on the part of the master class to grant educational opportunities to plantation workers or to prepare their ex-slaves for citizenship. To have done so in 1871 would have been to enact a reform far more radical than anything included in the Rio Branco Law, for effective education might have transformed Brazil's social and economic system even more than the abolition of slavery.

As it turned out, an important result of the Rio Branco Law was the

51. *Ibid.*, II, 583–586.
52. Regarding this "defect" of the law, see Ianni, *As metamorfoses do escravo,* pp. 215–216.
53. *Discussão da reforma do estado servil,* II, 498–531. For a later evaluation of the Rio Branco Law by the son of Nabuco de Araújo, see Nabuco, *O Abolicionismo,* pp. 72–87.

postponement of true abolitionism, as the Rio Branco government had hoped it would. To this extent, the legislation was a moderate success, but only moderate, for the debate and the new status of the children also undoubtedly had liberalizing effects upon Brazilian opinion.[54] The press campaign in favor of the law, which carried the message of the government to every part of the country, identified the goal of emancipation with patriotism and the nation's future, undoubtedly undermining the authority of the slaveholders and the national commitment to the slave system. It is more difficult, of course, to evaluate the effect of the debate upon the attitudes of the slaves, but Joaquim Nabuco later claimed that the Rio Branco Law was "a tremendous deception" for them because the Emperor and even the Liberal Party had spoken openly of emancipation.[55] In at least one province a surge of unrest among slaves was explained in 1872 by their belief that the Rio Branco Law had freed all slaves and that they were unjustly held.[56]

Despite its omissions, the Rio Branco Law was a victory for reform. Abolitionists felt an immediate sense of achievement, and therefore the passage of the law was followed by an anti-climactic silence. Within the decade, however, anti-slavery agitation would begin anew and this time would not be stopped until it brought the collapse of the slave system.

54. Ianni, *As metamorfoses do escravo,* pp. 216–217.
55. Nabuco, *O Abolicionismo,* pp. 69–70.
56. *Relatorio da presidencia da provincia de Sergipe em 1872* (Aracajú, 1872), pp. 5–10.

In our country,
where there is so much negligence,
so many facilities for indulgence and protection,
only a rigorous law . . .
can be effective.

NABUCO DE ARAÚJO
in the Senate, September 26, 1871

. . . the world [continues]
to believe that slavery is ending in Brazil,
without realizing that this is happening
because the slaves
are dying.

JOAQUIM NABUCO
O Abolicionismo

7

THE
RIO BRANCO
LAW

THE GOVERNMENT APPLIES THE LAW

Though more effectively carried out than the legislation of November 7, 1831, the Rio Branco Law had little more than passive support from the planter class whose cooperation had been thought essential.[1] Under these circumstances, it was not within the power of the central government to impose observance. The result, in the words of Joaquim Nabuco, was "another epoch of indifference for the fate of the slave, during which even the government could forget to comply with the law which it had passed." [2]

In the weeks following the debate, the government took steps to set the law in motion. Yet from the beginning there were signs that it would not be consistently enforced. Article 6 of the Rio Branco Law promised liberty to all government-owned slaves. A decree interpreting this article, issued by Rio Branco on November 11, established the policy to be followed in the liberation of the slaves owned by the state, including

1. *Annaes da Câmara* (1871), III, 123.
2. Nabuco, *O Abolicionismo*, p. 3.

those used by the Emperor and his family. Slaves of the nation employed in public works or on state-owned plantations were to be allowed to seek employment elsewhere, and those choosing to remain on government properties were to receive salaries and to be supervised and protected by provincial presidents. Another directive, however, issued and signed by Rio Branco just ten days later, reminded those same presidents that when setting salaries they were to keep in mind the government's need to derive a sufficient profit from rural properties. *The former slaves were to have the right to seek employment elsewhere only if this did not deprive the estates of needed workers.*[3]

Other acts of the government seemed to envision a policy of strict enforcement while revealing doubt that officials and slaveowners would comply with their legal obligations. Article 8 ordered a national registration of all slaves and ingenuos. A decree of December 1, 1871, established rules for these registrations. Local tax collectors or customs officials were to advertise the masters' obligation to enroll their slaves and ingenuos in a general registration to begin on April 1, 1872, and to end on the last day of September. Copies of these announcements were to be sent to parish priests, who were to pass on the information to their congregations. Places of registration were to be open on all work days from 9 A.M to 4 P.M throughout the period. The books were to be closed and tallied on September 30, 1872, but masters were to be allowed to register slaves for one year thereafter without incurring fines or the loss of unreported slaves. Following this period, any slave not registered was to be considered free, unless his master could prove that he was not responsible for the infraction of the law. Officials who were to carry out the registrations were to compile reports on slaves and ingenuos registered, specifying their sex, age, marital status, profession, and place of residence, and changes were to be reported from time to time to keep the statistics current.

The same decree threatened fines for non-compliance. Owners neglecting to register slaves or ingenuos or failing to report changes in their status were to be fined as much as 200 milréis. Officials charged with registering slaves were to be fined one-fourth that amount if they failed to carry out their duty. Priests neglecting to inform their congregations of the regulations were subject to fines of ten milréis for every Sunday and holy day they were remiss. Officials not imposing such penalties were themselves to be heavily fined by provincial presidents.[4]

Article 3 provided for the establishment of an emancipation fund to be created by taxes on slaves, national lotteries, fines, and contributions. More than a year after promulgation of the Rio Branco Law, on Novem-

3. Veiga, *Livro do estado servil*, pp. 205–211.
4. *Ibid.*, pp. 33–44.

ber 13, 1872, the Minister of Agriculture decreed regulations for the use of the emancipation fund. Families were to be preferred for liberation over individuals, particularly family members owned by different masters, and preference was to be given to parents of ingenuos, free children, and slave children in that order. In selecting individuals for manumission, mothers and fathers with free children and slaves between the ages of twelve and fifty were to be preferred, beginning with the youngest of the females and the oldest of the males.[5] This would liberate child-bearing women while it kept the most productive males at work.

The same decree ordered the creation of classification councils (*juntas de classificação*) in each município, to be composed if possible of the president of the municipal chamber, the public prosecutor, and the tax collector. These councils were to meet each year throughout the country on the first Sunday in July to classify and select slaves for liberation, the first such meetings to take place on April 1, 1873. Here too fines were to be levied for failure to comply. A council member neglecting to attend meetings without justifiable cause would forfeit from 10 to 50 milréis, and negligent masters would be punished by imprisonment for from ten to twenty days. The values of slaves to be freed were to be established through arbitration, and persons freed were to receive certificates of emancipation.[6]

A system of registration and classification was thus established on paper, but the government did little to assure that the work would actually be accomplished in the hundreds of municípios from Rio Grande do Sul to Amazonas. Instead of granting salaries, for example, or other incentives to the local officials charged with the work, the government, anticipating some shirking of duty, threatened officials with punishments which it could hardly have had the power to impose throughout the far-flung regions of the country.

The registration and classification therefore proceeded with astonishing slowness, despite the penalties for non-compliance. Nearly seven months after the registration was to have been concluded, the Minister of Agriculture announced that he had received reports from municípios in only eleven provinces, recording only 198,814 slaves, less than one-seventh of those who would be included in the final count. The law had been carried out, he reported, as fast as circumstances permitted. The following September, less than two weeks before the second and final deadline for registration, the Agriculture Minister informed Rio Branco of his decision to allow holders of mortgages to register the slaves of

5. To facilitate the classifications, a simpler system was decreed on September 20, 1876. For an outline of the still complex system of classification as it existed in 1886, see Ianni, *As metamorfoses do escravo*, pp. 224–225.
6. Veiga, *Livro do estado servil*, pp. 51–72.

debtors who refused to comply with the law, and two months after the close of the registration he was still seeking information from provincial presidents concerning the results of the registrations and classifications.[7]

The report of the Ministry of Agriculture of 1874 was pessimistic. Both the registration and the classifications had encountered obstacles. Classification councils had failed to meet on time. A new date for compliance had been set and had long since passed, but only a little over a million slaves had been registered.[8] By May 1875 the situation had slightly improved. The latest information gathered by the Ministry of Agriculture put the total number of registered slaves at 1,431,300, and the count went on. The first provincial distribution of the emancipation fund was expected soon, though fewer than 200,000 slaves had thus far been classified. The classification councils of many districts had not reported, despite repeated demands and threats of punishment. The failure, thought the Minister of Agriculture, resulted from the lack of salaries for officials who had the responsibility, and the great distances which persons were forced to travel to reach the registration places.[9]

This was an accurate appraisal, though apathy and widespread scorn for the regulations also contributed to the inactivity. Many explanations for the lack of progress (probably representative of the nation as a whole) are contained in letters from classification councils of Sergipe to the president of the province. One council informed the executive that its meeting had been delayed for three months owing to a lack of notebooks. Another reported suspension of its work due to the want of a prosecutor, and another reported that the refusal of a notary to participate had delayed the work. Still another junta de classificação of Sergipe had held regular sessions, but had been unable to establish any value for the 524 slaves of the município because of a total unwillingness of the local masters to attend its meetings. Some of the municípios of Sergipe submitted their reports in 1875, but others continued to find reasons for non-compliance the following year. In August 1876 a council ascribed its inability to function to the fault of a secretary, a position lacking any form of salary. It was impractical, a local official explained, "to suppose that any citizen could lend himself to such a service, fleeing his daily occupations to submit himself to labor which deprives him of his means of subsistence." A report of the same period from the município of Divina Pastora announced that the council of that place had not met on the designated first Sunday in July "in consequence of finding myself ill and in such a state that I am unable to rise from bed . . . ." A junta of Itabaiana reported that it had not met because the prosecutor was

7. *Ibid.*, pp. 83, 93; *Relatorio do Ministerio da Agricultura*, May 13, 1873, p. 5.
8. *Relatorio do Ministerio da Agricultura*, May 14, 1874, pp. 5–7.
9. *Ibid.*, May 2, 1875, pp. 7–8.

busy in the município of Simão Dias and the notary was busy with "no less important business." [10]

The tone of the report of the Minister of Agriculture of May 1876 suggests that the problems encountered in Sergipe were like those in districts elsewhere. Slave classification was "a most difficult task and even unachievable. . . ." Nowhere had it been completed on schedule in the course of five years.[11] The special registration had continued beyond the legal deadline and in fact had been extended officially in November 1875 by a decision of the Emperor in consultation with the Council of State. Pedro and his advisers had concluded that slaves not yet registered by September 30, 1873, were not to be freed in accordance with the decree of December 1871, because their non-registration in many districts had resulted from a lack of officials or a deficiency of notebooks, "which, though sent on time, did not arrive at the said localities within the legal period." [12] The registration was completed and closed soon after, but the government's decision to extend the deadline probably resulted in the registration of many slaves who would have been legally free if the Rio Branco Law had been interpreted strictly and rigidly applied.

THE FAILURE OF THE EMANCIPATION FUND

The slowness of the registration and classification delayed the application of the emancipation fund. By May 1874 more than 3,000 contos had been accumulated in the fund, enough to free nearly 6,500 slaves at an average price of 500 milréis. Yet the assets of the fund could not be distributed to the provinces, said the Minister of Agriculture, because the distribution depended upon completion of the registration, hindered in some places by a lack of fiscal stations and in others by a shortage of personnel.[13]

In May 1876, *nearly five years after the Rio Branco Law was passed*, the government at last announced that the first 1,503 slaves, about one of every thousand registered, had been freed by the fund, and it was expected that another 2,500 would be freed soon.[14] By mid-1877, only

10. Escravos, APS. The failure of the *juntas de classificação* in Brazil was similar to that of the *juntas de manumisión* established earlier in Venezuela for the same purpose. See Lombardi, *The Decline and Abolition of Negro Slavery in Venezuela*, pp. 61–72.
11. *Relatorio do Ministerio da Agricultura*, January 15, 1877, p. 13.
12. Veiga, *Livro do estado servil*, p. 195.
13. *Relatorio do Ministerio da Agricultura*, May 14, 1874, pp. 5–7.
14. *Ibid.*, January 15, 1877, p. 14.

755 more had been freed by the fund, making a total of only 2,258 slaves during a period of nearly six years. More than 6,000 contos had gone into the fund during five fiscal years, but less than 1,295 had been applied directly to the freeing of slaves. The explanation for the poor results was still the same: the unwillingness of government employees to accept added duties without added pay.[15]

By late 1878 another 1,800 persons had been freed, the average price rising from 562$630 to 843$343. Despite this high cost, only a small part of the fund was actually being applied to the liberation of slaves. Though the shortage of notebooks and personnel persisted, nearly one-fifth as much money had been spent by 1878 on notebooks, "gratifications," and other unspecified costs as had been applied directly to the manumission of slaves. Well over half of the total assets of the fund remained unused either in the provinces or in the capital (see Table 22).[16]

While the bureaucracy remained thus nearly inactive, thousands who might have been freed remained enslaved. In the four and one-half months just prior to May 1879 a mere 245 slaves were freed at an average price of 742$778. A balance of more than 4,182 contos had accumulated in the fund by that date, but the Minister of Agriculture opposed a second distribution to the provinces on the grounds that unreported changes in the slave population had rendered the government's statistics inaccurate.[17] During the following year only 201 slaves were freed through the fund, and no additional distribution was made.[18]

With the reawakening of abolitionist sentiment in 1880, the government suddenly stepped up its application of the fund. Within a period of sixteen months in 1880 and 1881, second and third distributions totaling 6,750 contos were made, and 5,413 more slaves were freed.[19] By 1885, more than 23,000 persons had been liberated by the fund at a cost of 14,520 contos, not including approximately 600 contos contributed by the slaves themselves to their own freedom.[20] The average price of about 663 milréis (see Table 23), though not particularly high for an active male slave, was greater than the price normally received on the open market for women and children, who made up the

15. *Ibid.*, June 1, 1877, pp. 6–8.
16. *Ibid.*, December 27, 1878, pp. 12–15.
17. *Ibid.*, 1879, pp. 11, 27.
18. *Ibid.*, May 14, 1880, p. 22.
19. *Ibid.*, January 19, 1882, p. 13.
20. *Ibid.*, April 30, 1885, p. 375; *Jornal do Commercio*, Rio de Janeiro, July 3, 1885. The regulations of November 13, 1872, forced slaves to contribute any donations, bequests, or inheritances which they had received for this specific purpose. Those unwilling to do so were to lose their place in the classification and be passed up. See Veiga, *Livro do estado servil*, p. 57.

great majority of the liberated.[21] Slaves over seventy were freed, according to an abolitionist source, at prices high enough to pay for half a dozen young slaves.[22] Prices in the coffee provinces were the highest, reflecting the greater productive capacity of slaves in that area, while the prices in the northeast were much lower, particularly in Ceará. In Rio de Janeiro province one slave was released at the unheard-of cost of 2,900 milréis.[23]

The fund was abused in ways other than the obvious recourse to high prices. Maurilio de Gouveia has pointed out that the masters' right to select the persons to be freed gave them opportunities to dispose of sick, blind, useless, and troublesome slaves.[24] To make their least valuable slaves eligible for sale through the fund, masters were known to have arranged marriages between the elderly and the very young, between useless and incorrigible slaves and free persons lured into the arrangement by money.[25] The deaths of slaves often went unrecorded in order that they might be "liberated" by the fund.[26] The emancipation fund allegedly served as a source of electoral campaign money, and in some isolated communities annual distributions went regularly to five or six influential persons.[27] In areas where slaves were in great demand, masters were reluctant to exchange them even for high prices. São Paulo's share of the third distribution, received there in September 1881, did not reach the municípios until nearly a year later. In the município of Campinas in the central coffee zone of São Paulo, slaves were in such great demand that three distributions went unused until planters, forced to comply with the law, freed thirty-one slaves at an exorbitant average of 1,566 milréis.[28]

Many more slaves were freed gratuitously or conditionally after 1871 than were freed by the fund. Private emancipation was probably stimulated by the example of the monks of the Benedictine and Carmelite orders, who freed their several thousand slaves soon after passage of

21. Of 1,567 persons freed by the fund in the Município Neutro, 854 were under twenty-one and 585 were women over twenty-one. Of the 121 adult males listed, 78 were over forty. The ages of seven persons were not revealed. Escravos. Junta qualificadora para libertação, 1873–1886, DPHAG, 6-1-39.
22. *O Christianismo, a civilisação e a sciencia protestando contra o captiveiro no Brasil* (Bahia, 1885), p. 104.
23. *South American Journal,* September 29, 1881.
24. Gouveia, *Historia da escravidão,* p. 227. This right of masters to select slaves to be freed was contained in Article XXVII of the decree of November 13, 1872. See Veiga, *Livro do estado servil,* pp. 52–53.
25. *Annaes do Senado* (1885), I, 11; *O Christianismo, a civilisação e a sciencia protestando,* pp. 94, 104.
26. *Annaes do Senado* (1885), I, 11–12.
27. *Gazeta da Tarde,* December 14, 1883.
28. *Rio News,* July 15, 1883.

the Rio Branco Law.[29] By May 1880, when the new liberation movement was just beginning to show signs of vitality, a little more than
35,000 slaves were known to have been freed by their masters inde-
pendently of the fund since passage of the Rio Branco Law, most of
these gratuitously.[30] By 1885, with the popularization of manumission
in such provinces as Ceará and Rio Grande do Sul, this figure had
surged to 131,794, of whom 87,221 were said to have been released
without compensation to their masters. The number of slaves who had
died since the beginning of the special registration was put at 214,860.[31]

The emancipation fund failed to achieve impressive results for at
least two major reasons. First, the government did not provide the
necessary incentives to accomplish the work in the provinces. The idea
of freeing slaves by this means was not genuinely popular during the
1870's and participation therefore was sluggish where distances were
great, conditions primitive, slaveholders powerful local lords, and public
officials in need of something more than legal responsibility and official
threats to make them act. Secondly, the fund was never large enough
to liberate many slaves, particularly at the high prices decided upon
locally through arbitration. The money for the purpose, according to
the Rio Branco Law, was to come from taxes, lotteries, fines, and contributions, but these sources of income were never enough to free more
than a small portion of the slave population. The emancipation fund
was not expected to be more than a humanitarian gesture, a minor
instrument of liberation, or evidence of good intentions. At worst, it was
a means for masters to rid themselves of their least useful slaves at
gratifying prices.

THE NEWBORN

Perhaps the most serious criticism brought against the Rio
Branco Law was its failure to grant the average ingenuo a life much different from that of the average slave. A member of the Emperor's Council of State publicly affirmed in 1884 that the free children of slave
women, who were also referred to in the jargon of the day as *riobrancos,*
had been kept "almost in their totality in the same servile condition as
the rest (*sic*) of the slaves, lacking the indispensable and deserved in-

29. Henrique de Beaurepaire Rohan, *O futuro da grande lavoura e da grande
propriedade no Brasil* (Rio de Janeiro, 1878), pp. 13–15; Homens livres reduzidos
a escravidão, AHI, 235-7-19; Veiga, *Livro do estado servil,* pp. 31, 295.
30. *Relatorio do Ministerio da Agricultura,* May 14, 1880, p. 20.
31. *Ibid.,* April 30, 1885, p. 372. For somewhat different but analagous statistics,
see Nabuco, *O Abolicionismo,* p. 86.

struction and deprived of the tutelar protection of the public authority." [32]
Article 18 of the regulations of November 13, 1872, implied the master's
right to inflict corporal punishment upon an ingenuo if that punishment
was not "excessive." The services of the ingenuos were not normally
transferable, according to another article, but could be assigned to a
second master if the child's mother was sold or the transfer was agreed
to in the presence of an *ad hoc* trustee and approved by the judge of
orphans. The ingenuos' services, moreover, could be legally "rented"
to another person.[33]

In the Brazilian milieu of the 1870's and 1880's the result of such
legal ambiguities was the open buying and selling of the present and
future "services" of free children and their advertisement in the public
press. Africans too young to have been imported before 1831 and children too young to have been born slaves were openly placed on sale
together in the province of Rio de Janeiro and advertised in the Rio
press. The *Jornal do Commercio* ran notices of government-regulated
slave sales in the interior town of Valença, listing Africans whose ages
certified by public notaries proved their illegal importation and the
illegality of their de facto slave status. Such advertisements contained
the names, ages, and "evaluations" of ingenuos similarly certified by
public notaries. One such list, published in 1881, included ten ingenuos
whose prices ranged from 400 milréis for a nine-year-old boy to 10
milréis for a male child of two, and a later list included a riobranco
named Luiz expected to change hands for a mere 5 milréis.[34] Despite
repeated protests in the press and to the government itself, the "sale"
of ingenuos continued until 1884. In May of that year, Andrew Jackson
Lamoureux, the American editor of *The Rio News,* called attention to
an advertisement in the *Jornal do Commercio* for the sale of fourteen
ingenuos at Valença. At that time the question of the legality of the
practice had been before the Council of State for eighteen months, legislation to prohibit the sale of ingenuos was being considered in the
Chamber of Deputies, and the Minister of Agriculture had just assured
the country that no further sales of the kind would be permitted.[35]

The statistics which the Ministry of Agriculture pieced together on
the births and deaths of ingenuos do not indicate unusually high infant
mortality or the widespread abandonment of ingenuos, as predicted by

32. *Acta da conferencia das secções reunidas dos negocios da fazenda, justiça e
imperio do Conselho do Estado* (Rio de Janeiro, 1884), p. 17.
33. Veiga, *Livro do estado servil,* pp. 50, 69.
34. *Rio News,* February 15, May 5, 1881; December 24, 1882; *Gazeta da Tarde,*
February 23, 1883. See also Nabuco, *O Abolicionismo,* p. 121; Joaquim Nabuco,
Cartas a amigos (2 vols.; São Paulo, 1949), I, 76–78.
35. *Rio News,* May 24, 1884; *Annaes da Câmara* (1884), I, 35.

opponents of the Rio Branco Law in 1871.[36] Yet the statistics do not disprove the pessimistic predictions either. What they show is that the children of slave women *registered as ingenuos* were far fewer than the number of children that those women might naturally have given birth to. By the end of the seventh year after passage of the law, only 278,519 babies had been registered, of whom 218,418 were recorded as living. The census of 1872, however, recorded 439,027 female slaves between the ages of eleven and forty, or about two women of child-bearing age for every ingenuo who was born, registered, and survived between 1871 and 1879.[37] Similarly, in 1883 there were 835 women slaves on the nine coffee plantations of the Count of Nova Friburgo, but only 337 ingenuos.[38]

These statistics indicate either a very high death rate among the children of slaves, which was certainly to be expected, or a low birth rate, or both, and these inferences are supported by the small number of slave children ten years of age or younger recorded in the census of 1872—only about 365,000 in a total slave population of more than one and a half million, which included more than 375,000 women between 15 and 40.[39] Undoubtedly some children born as slaves and many ingenuos, particularly those whose lives were brief, were never registered. Many, perhaps, were abandoned, as members of the General Assembly warned they would be, and others delivered to the Church's houses of charity or, less likely, even sent "to die of hunger in houses which for a small price perform infanticide without a trace," a charge made by abolitionists in 1883.[40] Evidently, too, many children were denied ingenuo status through false registration, since, again according to opponents of slavery, "apparently no children were born of slave mothers just after the 28th of September, 1871, while the [fazenda records]

36. For the pessimistic impressions of a foreigner concerning the registration of ingenuos, see C. C. Andrews, *Brazil, Its Condition and Prospects* (New York, 1887), pp. 312–313.
37. *Recenseamento da população*, XIX, 4; *Relatorio do Ministerio da Agricultura*, May 14, 1880, pp. 12–13. In contrast, according to the Brazilian census of 1950, 60.1 percent of Brazilian women 15 or older were prolific, and the average number of live births per prolific woman was 5.2. For "brown" and Negro women the average number of live-born children was 5.5 and 5.3 respectively. See Francisco M. Salzano and Newton Freire-Maia, *Problems in Human Biology, A Study of Brazilian Populations* (Detroit, Michigan, 1970), p. 63.
38. Van Delden Laërne, *Brazil and Java*, p. 341. In contrast, in their calculations of the profitability of slavery in the United States, Conrad and Meyer assume that each "prime field wench" might have produced five to ten marketable children during her lifetime, and that successful pregnancies were spaced two years apart. See "The Economics of Slavery in the Ante-Bellum South," p. 349.
39. *Recenseamento da população*, XIX, 4.
40. *Manifesto da Confederação Abolicionista*, p. 16.

show an unheard-of increase of births for 1870." [41] Whatever their fate, it is probable that the half million ingenuos thought to be alive when slavery was abolished in 1888 comprised a slender percentage of those born to slave women during the preceding seventeen years.[42] Despite the provisions of the law intended to create accurate statistics on this class of children, despite the heavy penalties decreed for non-compliance, their fate could not even then be known.[43]

Most of the ingenuos who did survive remained on the plantations under the supervision of their mothers' masters. Possessing the right to choose between employing the labor of the children after their eighth birthday or surrendering them for government bonds, masters overwhelmingly chose to use their labor, in part because this option required from them no action whatever. Of the more than 400,000 ingenuos registered by 1885, only 118 had been delivered to the government in exchange for the ornate certificates which the regime had printed for the purpose (see illustration number 25), and during the following year only two more ingenuos were so exchanged. In accordance with the decree of November 13, 1872, the few ingenuos which the government did receive were, like the "free Africans" a few years earlier, turned over to private persons, who also possessed the right to use their services or to hire them out to others. By 1885 more than 9,000 ingenuos had passed into a state of unencumbered freedom along with their mothers, but the great majority of surviving children undoubtedly remained, in conformity with the law, in a state of de facto slavery until they were freed along with the slaves on May 13, 1888.[44]

THE BROADER MEANING OF THE LAW

A decade after passage of the Rio Branco Law its failure to produce impressive immediate results was widely recognized. Even proslavery spokesmen admitted that the law had not been implemented en-

41. Trail to Frelinghuysen, Rio de Janeiro, May 21, 1884, *Papers Related to the Foreign Relations of the United States* (Washington, 1885), p. 29.
42. This figure of 500,000 was used by the Baron of Cotegipe in the Senate in May 1888. See *Extincção da escravidão no Brasil. Lei nº 3353 de 13 de Maio de 1888. Discussão na Câmara dos Deputados e no Senado* (Rio de Janeiro, 1889), p. 69. In 1886 there were 439,831 registered ingenuos in Brazil. *Relatorio do Ministerio da Agricultura*, May 14, 1886, p. 36.
43. Even recently population statistics have been poorly kept in parts of Brazil, but it is known that mortality rates, particularly among Negroes, infants, and rural people (categories to which ingenuos generally belonged) are tragically high. See Smith, *Brazil*, pp. 107–117; Salzano and Freire-Maia, *Problems in Human Biology*, pp. 66–76.
44. *Relatorio do Ministerio da Agricultura*, April 30, 1885, p. 376; *ibid.*, May 14, 1886, p. 36. For a similar view, see Ianni, *As metamorfoses do escravo*, pp. 215–216.

ergetically, that its provisions no longer corresponded with national aspirations, and that its results were insignificant when compared with the effects of private initiative and the high costs of administration.[45]

Yet the law had great effects upon attitudes. Its inadequacies were both deplored and exploited by the abolitionists. Joaquim Nabuco characterized it as a great deception for the slaves, who expected more.[46] "The plain truth is," wrote Lamoureux in *The Rio News* with some exaggeration, "that there never was a greater sham enacted by a national legislature. . . ."[47] The authors of the Manifesto of the Abolitionist Confederation of Rio de Janeiro, José do Patrocinio and André Rebouças, condemned the slaveholders for their bad faith and lack of patriotism. The masters were guilty, they charged, of terrible crimes, despite the extraordinary privileges which the Rio Branco Law had bestowed upon them.[48]

The response of the coffee planters to the law was mixed. Generally opposing it before its passage, they later looked upon it as the last word on the slavery question and therefore an instrument of protection. Under the shadow of its provisions, they added to their slave inventories well into the 1880's with an almost traditional defiance, which was only tempered by recognition that the immediate solution to their labor needs was no longer to be a permanent one. In the face of the abolitionist wave of the 1880's, moreover, the Rio Branco Law served as a strong new argument: it had condemned slavery to extinction, and no other measures would be necessary to assure its disappearance within the life span of existing generations. What was needed, slaveowners would argue, were legislative solutions to economic problems caused by the rapid aging and dying of indispensable field hands—not a further curtailment of the rights of masters.

While the demand for new sources of cheap labor was thus growing more insistent, a new opposition to servile labor in any form was also developing, inclined to reject all the arguments the masters could produce. This was perhaps the most positive effect of the Rio Branco Law. It had subtly undermined slavery, identifying emancipation with the best interests of the nation. The debate on the law had clearly underlined the inequity of slavery for all to understand. Of great practical importance too was the liberation of half a million children, many of whom in the 1880's were entering productive age and, as slaves, would have represented a strong incentive for a prolongation of the traditional labor system.

45. *Annaes da Câmara* (1884), III, 172; *Diario do Brasil,* Rio de Janeiro, September 29, 1882.
46. Nabuco, *O Abolicionismo,* p. 70.
47. *Rio News,* February 5, 1881.
48. *Manifesto da Confederação Abolicionista,* pp. 15–16.

Part Two : 1879–1888

*Unfortunately, the revolutionary spirit had to accomplish in a few years
a task which had been scorned
for a century.*

JOAQUIM NABUCO
Minha formação

8

THE PROVINCES
ON THE EVE OF
ABOLITIONISM

In 1879, on the eve of uncompromising abolitionism, the demographic imbalance that had resulted from the inter-provincial slave trade was already causing reactions that would soon help to destroy slavery. The main deciding factors were the quantity and "quality" of slaves present in the various provinces and districts and the degree of conversion to a free-labor system which had taken place. Where slaves were many, valuable, and at work on the land, slavery was righteously defended, but where they were few and "worth" very little or found as often in kitchens as in the fields, populations became indifferent to slavery or even began to oppose it. Free workers were recognized as an acceptable alternative to slaves in places where captives were few and large numbers of free men and women were already employed in agriculture. In contrast, where slaves were still abundant, planters lacked opportunities to observe free men at work on the land, and their experience seemed to reinforce the old theory that free Brazilians could not be relied upon to provide a steady and dependable labor force. As abolitionism began to appear and grow in the 1880's, in fact, this alleged incapacity of free workers became a major pro-slavery argument.

THE NORTH

The most important regional differences, of course, were those between producers of sugar and cotton in the north and the coffee growers of the south. For northerners generally, abolition would mean some loss of privileges and assets, but for them the process had started long before. During the half century between the abolition of the legal African slave traffic in 1831 and the advent of uncompromising abolitionism, many northern planters had made the necessary psychological and practical adjustments—including the employment of free workers—that would permit them to accept the abolition of slavery with philosophical forbearance.

As shown in an earlier chapter, slavery was no longer very important in many parts of Brazil when the 1872 census was taken, but equally important as a cause of emancipationist sentiment was the subsequent drastic decline of the slave population in the same areas. Between 1874 and 1884, according to official statistics, the national slave population declined by a little less than 20 percent (see Table 10), but in eight northeastern provinces the rate of decline was nearly 31 percent during the same period and even higher in the far north and in the western and extreme southern provinces. In contrast, the slave populations of the south-central provinces, even including the city of Rio de Janeiro, where the fall was rapid, dropped by only 9 percent, and in São Paulo and Minas Gerais the reduction was kept at between 3 and 4 percent. Of all the provinces, logically, São Paulo, a major importer before 1881, was the one best able to prevent a rapid drop in slave population between 1874 and 1887 (see Tables 10 and 11 and Figure 3). The statistics collected by the Brazilian government show, in fact, that the *male* slave population of São Paulo actually increased by more than 8,000 between 1874 and 1884, whereas in every other province there was a substantial decline of male slave population during those same years. (See Figure 6.)

To reach conclusions that would place them among the liberal and forward-minded, northern slaveowners had merely to make a few simple calculations in 1879, the year that northern members of the General Assembly renewed the parliamentary slavery debate. Many of the best slaves had been sent to the south, and those who remained were aging and dying. Merely to inspect the inhabitants of the slave huts was to

Population (thousands)

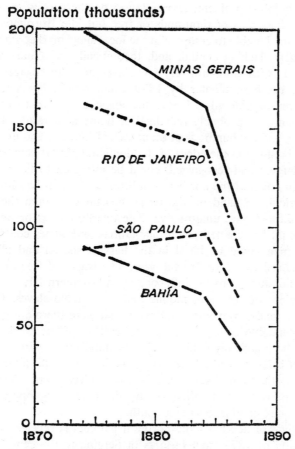

FIGURE 6. Male Slave Populations of Bahia, Rio de Janeiro, São Paulo, and Minas Gerais, 1874, 1884, 1887.

recognize that slavery was nearly finished. Children under eight were free, or would be in thirteen to twenty-one years, and by then most of their elders would be beyond their prime. A significant part of the enormous capital invested in slaves had already "depreciated" or had been converted into cash or other forms of property. Money that formerly would have gone to the purchase or maintenance of slaves was already being used to pay wages and salaries.

In both the north and south there were serious labor shortages that would speed the progress of emancipation, though the response to the problem also differed from region to region. While coffee planters held on stubbornly to their slaves, continued to purchase those of the north until 1881, and looked desperately to Europe and Asia for new solutions to their labor problem, less endowed northerners were attracting more of the hundreds of thousands of free but idle Brazilians to their establishments. Unable to compete in the local slave market with wealthier southerners, lacking capital, and, theoretically, a climate attractive to Europeans, with comparatively few slaves actually engaged in agriculture, the northern planter by 1879 could reasonably look to two future sources of plantation labor: the ingenuos grown to adulthood, most of whom had probably remained at home as a result of the Rio Branco Law, and the hundreds of thousands of indigent and unemployed free men subsisting on the edges of the dominant export economy. Such workers, planters had recognized, could be attracted to their establishments, for in much of the northeastern littoral free men had little access to good agricultural land on the fertile coastal strip, and the arid interior was difficult and unattractive. The overflow of poor people and ex-slaves could be directed to the plantations and wages could be kept low.[1] Free men could be hired in the harvest season and allowed to fend for themselves the rest of the year. The wages of free men, moreover, were not subject to the influence of the southern labor market, as were the prices of the more mobile and marketable slaves. Free men could not be made to migrate southward and were therefore potentially a more dependable source of labor. Liberation of the work force, in fact, might be practically equivalent to its stabilization within the provinces, might bring an end to the large-scale loss of useful male workers, which the northeast had suffered for nearly thirty years, although this advantage for some was still offset by the continuing opportunity of others to acquire good prices in the south.

The attitude of at least some northern planters is revealed in a published petition of 1877 from farmers of Sergipe to the central government. This message blamed a growing labor shortage upon the Rio Branco Law and the inter-provincial slave trade, and pointed out that in one important sugar-growing município of Sergipe, the loss of able-bodied slaves due to all causes had been thirty percent in less than five years. With captive workers obviously doomed to rapid extinction, the petitioners expressed opposition to slavery and suggested reforms to win over the idle population. Free men willing to work for wages or under contract might be exempted from military service. "Private liberalized concessions" could be offered to attract workers, including the granting of comfortable housing, an increased cultivation of cereals and other food crops, and the establishment of night classes where farm workers could learn to read and write. "Motivated by these advantages and the idea of an assured wage, the proletarians [would] incorporate themselves onto the rural properties and abandon . . . the breeding

1. Furtado, *The Economic Growth of Brazil,* p. 151.

grounds of idleness and vice. . . ." [2] The message from Sergipe was particularly significant because in that northeastern province slavery was still strong and vital in comparison to the institution in some neighboring provinces.

There was, then, on the whole a greater willingness in the north of Brazil to see slavery end, but within those vast regions the commitment to slavery also varied. In the far northern province of Maranhão, where slaves were comparatively numerous and the non-white population outnumbered the white by nearly two to one,[3] influential citizens were less inclined to give free rein to abolitionist sentiments. Though less recalcitrant than the south-central provinces, Maranhão and even neighboring Pará never took a prominent role in the abolitionist effort, and both provinces remained important slaveholding areas until the eve of abolition. In contrast, the provinces located on the northeastern hump of Brazil (notably Ceará, Rio Grande do Norte, Paraíba, Pernambuco, and even parts of Bahia) were exporters of large numbers of slaves (see Table 9), and this large and important part of the country was perhaps the least inclined to defend slavery.[4]

Within the Brazilian north abolitionism found particularly fertile soil in two provinces. Amazonas, rich in rubber and with few Negro slaves, would solve the problem quickly in 1884 with great public enthusiasm, for in that province, where most of the work was done by Indian and *caboclo* labor, there was little to do to end Negro slavery, and the urge to do it was consequently great. The poor drought-stricken province of Ceará had long been a major source of slaves for the southern market, and this commerce had increased during the 1870's in response to drought. Thus, by 1879, Ceará was ready to become a center of agitation which during the next five years would inspire abolitionists throughout the country. Within the northern provinces, of course, even Ceará, there were individual planters and politicians who opposed abolition much as did their counterparts in the south. Broadly speaking, however, the will to resist in this region was weaker, and the desire to see slavery swept away was remarkably well manifested, despite the backward character of the regional cities and their obvious dependence upon the agricultural sector of their economies.

Only eight years after passage of the Rio Branco Law, the evolution

2. *Representação da lavoura de Sergipe aos altos poderes do estado* (Rio de Janeiro, 1877).
3. *Recenseamento da população*, XIX, 1.
4. Some southern and western provinces, including perhaps Goiás, Paraná and Santa Catarina, were in much the same situation. Rio Grande do Sul had many slaves, but during the decade 1874–1884 its recorded slave exports exceeded even those of Ceará. Abolitionism became powerful there, but, as will be seen in Chapter 13, fashioned a compromise with slavery.

toward a free-labor system, which had been particularly rapid in much of the north, had created signs in that region of a new emancipationist mood. Both in the General Assembly and within the region itself, there were indications that prominent and influential persons were no longer satisfied with the gradual system of liberation established by the legislation of 1871. On the eighth anniversary of the Rio Branco Law, in the midst of a tragic drought, a small group of middle-class citizens of Fortaleza, the capital and port of Ceará, created an emancipationist society which in a little more than a year evolved into a powerful abolitionist organization. According to an American traveler whose book was published in 1879, a strong emancipationist movement supported by prominent citizens had also appeared in Pernambuco by that date, the result of the loss of slaves to southern provinces. Coffee plantations in the province of Rio de Janeiro, the same writer reported, were often manned by as many as three or four hundred slaves, whereas the sugar plantations of Pernambuco and Pará rarely possessed a fifth of that number. "Now mark the result," came the conclusion:

At Rio there is a constant cry for workmen; the slaves are not sufficient, yet free laborers cannot compete with forced ones; the planters work their negroes as they would never work their mules, yet complain that they reap no profits. In the northern provinces, there is free labor, enough and to spare; poor men have a chance in the world; rich ones are content with the fair returns that their money brings them; society is far more evenly balanced, and the level of private character is far higher than in the south.[5]

Even an ardent abolitionist could find some kind words for the northern slaveholder. In 1880, José do Patrocinio called attention to the disequilibrium between the northern and southern provinces on the slavery question. The north, he told an abolitionist audience, "much kinder to the slave, rids itself of the dreadful merchandise as fast as it can. The remaining slaves live with the masters in amicable relationships which are truly patriarchal." The south, on the other hand, "ambitious, obstinate, aristocratic, barbarous, and cruel to the slave, drunk with the game of coffee, has been buying the fatal merchandise at whatever cost." The north was abolitionist, said Patrocinio, while the south, indebted to the banks and coffee merchants, knew no way of life but slavery.[6]

5. Herbert H. Smith, *Brazil: The Amazons and the Coast* (New York, 1879), pp. 469–470.

6. *Gazeta da Tarde,* December 27, 1880. For the same reasons that Brazilians of northern provinces were to play an important role in the abolitionist movement of their country, Puerto Ricans became "an essential driving force in Spanish abolition." Slavery had never been as deeply rooted in Puerto Rico as in Cuba. The slave trade to the smaller island had ended by 1835, owing to the inability of Puerto Ricans to compete with Cuba for contraband slaves, and an inter-island

THE COFFEE PROVINCES

But even in the coffee regions there were differing degrees of commitment to slavery. In the Empire as a whole, the anti-slavery movement was stronger in urban than in rural areas, but in the region of coffee cultivation the clash between the comparatively sophisticated cities and the distinctly pro-slavery hinterland was particularly bitter. This was especially true after 1886 when such key towns as São Paulo, the neighboring port of Santos, Campos in eastern Rio de Janeiro province, and the capital of the Empire itself served as centers of agitation, as hiding places for runaway slaves, and even as headquarters for abolitionist assaults upon slavery in surrounding rural areas. The slave population of the city of Rio and neighboring districts was large and valuable, and the defenders of the status quo were quick to organize when an abolitionist movement appeared there in 1880. Despite strong opposition, however, the imperial capital was the center of the national anti-slavery movement during eight years of struggle, because it was there that politicians gathered from every region, that the organs of government were established, that abolitionist newspapers, books, and other works of propaganda could best be published, and that a large and sophisticated public could best make known its views before the holders of authority.

In Brazil as a whole, as Joaquim Nabuco wrote in 1883, slavery was strongest in the coffee districts of the south-central provinces,[7] but within these provinces were large areas where that profitable crop was not grown and where slavery was consequently no longer as deeply rooted as in the coffee districts. This was particularly true of sprawling and populous Minas Gerais, which contained a small pro-slavery coffee zone bordering on similar areas of Rio de Janeiro and São Paulo, where a large part of the province's slave population was concentrated.[8] Farther inland, however, were poorer mining and cattle-producing regions that, like the northeast, had lost slaves to the coffee zones and continued to

---

slave trade subsequently developed. By 1860 the proportion of slaves to free persons in Puerto Rico was one to thirteen, whereas in Cuba it was one in four. As northeastern members of Brazilian legislatures were more inclined than those of Rio de Janeiro to vote for emancipation, in the Spanish Cortes of 1871–1872 most Puerto Ricans were emancipationists. The Spanish legislature found it expedient to abolish slavery in Puerto Rico in 1873, though it survived in Cuba until 1886. See Corwin, *Spain and the Abolition of Slavery in Cuba*, pp. 154–157, 282–291; Knight, *Slave Society in Cuba*, pp. 141, 171, 184–186, 190–192.

7. Nabuco, *O Abolicionismo*, pp. 218–219.

8. For the slave populations of the municípios of Minas Gerais, see *Recenseamento da população*, IX (2), 1074–1078.

do so on a large scale during the last years of slavery (see Table 12).[9] Within Minas Gerais, therefore, interest in the servile system varied much as it did in the Empire as a whole—coffee districts defending the labor system, larger but poorer non-coffee areas displaying less concern for its survival or even eager to see it end. Joaquim Nabuco was conscious of the differing attitudes toward slavery in the various parts of the province when he wrote of the decadence of the old mining towns and described the coffee districts as "the opulent part of Minas Gerais."[10] Much the same situation existed in São Paulo and Rio de Janeiro provinces where coffee municípios continued to attract slaves at the expense of non-coffee municípios, as well as from regions outside those provinces[11] (see Tables 13, 14, and 15).

Even among the coffee districts, as historians have recently pointed out, there were differing attitudes toward slavery caused by differing levels of development and prosperity. The coffee economy of Rio de Janeiro was declining by 1879. Its planters still owned many young and valuable slaves, and three-fourths of the province's captives were engaged in agricultural labor.[12] Yet the lands of the province could no longer produce the wealth of earlier years. Deeply in debt, threatened with ruin by the new wave of abolitionism, with scenes of agitation only a few miles away in the imperial capital, their defiance was to be of the bitterest kind.

The coffee economy of São Paulo, on the other hand, was expanding into new areas, and the province as a whole was enjoying an economic boom. For the planters of São Paulo abolition could mean financial losses, but in the end the Paulistas—particularly those of the developing northern parts of the province—were more flexible because they were riding a wave of prosperity, and the means to solve their problems were at hand. Rich and optimistic, they were better prepared to ward off the abolitionist pressure, to take successful steps toward solving the labor problem, and then, when overwhelmed by the unexpected success of extra-legal abolitionist methods in 1887, to turn and move in harmony with the liberation movement, despite the many slaves on their fazendas. Both before and after mid-1887, when the slave system suddenly col-

9. Viotti da Costa, *Da senzala à colônia*, pp. 60–62. In the late 1860's Richard Burton wrote that most of the slaves of São João d'El-Rei, Minas Gerais, had been "sold off to the agricultural districts of Rio de Janeiro, which still calls for more." See his *Explorations*, I, 115

10. Nabuco, *O Abolicionismo*, p. 154

11. Samuel Harman Lowrie, "O elemento negro na população de São Paulo," *Revista do Arquivo Municipal*, Vol. XLVIII (São Paulo, 1938), pp. 11–15.

12. Of 276,195 slaves registered in Rio de Janeiro province in June 1881, 117,251 were from ten to twenty-one years of age, 149,099 were twenty-one to sixty, and 9,845 were registered as over sixty. Of the total, 203,037 were engaged in agricultural labor. *South American Journal*, March 16, 1882.

lapsed in São Paulo, Paulista planters acted to protect their economic interests. Before that date their determined support of slavery was based upon large slave inventories, high profits from slave investments, and fear of a shortage of field hands for the clearing and planting of new lands and the harvesting of crops. After that date, as will be apparent, the Paulista slavocracy swung headlong toward emancipationism, with the expressed aim of protecting their imperiled economic interests and restoring the stability of their society.

As the abolitionist decade began, however, Paulista coffee planters and their neighbors in Minas Gerais and Rio de Janeiro were particularly determined to maintain slavery for years to come, perhaps as long as thirty years. Their captive workers were in part choice people from the north, whose importation during the 1870's, in the words of a British observer, had "corresponded with the gradual extension of new coffee fields and the increase of the shipments of coffee." As a class, the slaves in the coffee provinces were "robust and healthy," said the same writer, adding some explanations:

The slaves brought from Africa were generally young. The most of the native Africans one meets were brought over when they were boys and girls of 12 to 18 years old. The gangs of slaves brought from the northern provinces to the south, were young. The dealers would buy only those that would sell highest to the planters of São Paulo and Rio de Janeiro. The purchaser had to calculate in his own mind how many years work he could get out of the negro before he bought him. Looking at a gang of slaves working on a coffee plantation, one is struck with the large proportion of young and strong-looking people amongst them. Were I asked to say what would be the average number of years of work that could be got out of the gangs I have seen working on the coffee estates . . . I would be safe in calculating thirty years as the average workable time.[13]

There were various levels of economic success among planters in the coffee provinces which elicited somewhat different responses from district to district to the challenge of abolitionism. In his major study of the capital city of São Paulo, Richard M. Morse states that as coffee cultivation spread into new areas of São Paulo after mid-century, the new planters—unlike those of the Paraíba Valley—were inclined to reject slavery and to turn to immigration as the solution to their labor needs. The ending of the African slave trade, he explains, would have made the traditional system "illusory," though he later states that the early immigrationist experiments failed to provide an alternative labor force and that, "as Brazil's center of economic gravity swung south into the paulista coffee lands, thousands of slaves were transferred, at ex-

13. A. Scott Blacklaw, "Slavery in Brazil," *South American Journal,* July 6, 20, 1882.

orbitant prices, from Minas Gerais and from the north," doubling the provincial slave population of 80,000 between 1866 and 1873.[14]

Richard Graham has also attributed to the new "landed entrepreneurs" of São Paulo a tendency to reject the seignorial past along with slavery. The new planters, writes Graham, "demonstrated their innovating spirit by adopting a new crop [coffee?], using novel techniques to process it, demanding a more plentiful and flexible source of labor than could be provided by slavery, and enthusiastically welcoming the railroads, which they often built themselves." Along with modernized urbanites and industrialists, the new Paulista planters, he claims, were an important factor in the elimination of the slave system. Both Morse and Graham, now backed by Eugene Genovese, have attributed the alleged progressiveness of the newer Paulista planters to bourgeois tendencies acquired as a result of their origins and their late arrival upon the economic scene, and they support this explanation with the argument that the newer planters understood that slavery was an obstacle to the large-scale European immigration that was needed to replace an inadequate slave population.[15]

Abundant evidence shows, however, that the new planters of São Paulo, many of whom were in fact wealthy migrants from the older plantation regions of Rio de Janeiro, Minas Gerais, and even the northeast, overwhelmingly adopted slavery as the immediate solution to their labor needs rather than turning to free labor, and there is no reason to believe that they did so reluctantly or involuntarily or with much hope that any other solution in fact existed.[16] The flow of slaves into São Paulo continued well into the period when coffee cultivation was being extended into new northern and western areas of the province, and in fact it was in just those zones where the growth of the slave population was particularly impressive during the last decades of slavery, in the face of a rapid national decline of the slave population.[17] (See Tables 14 and 15, particularly the statistics for Casa Branca, Descalvado, São Carlos, Pirassinunga, and Amparo.) In the new and little-exploited Paulista north and west, wrote Samuel Lowrie, "economic interests

14. Morse, *From Community to Metropolis,* pp. 114–115, 146.
15. Graham, *Britain and the Onset,* pp. 31, 161–162. For similar views, see Warren Dean, *The Industrialization of São Paulo, 1880–1945* (Austin, Texas, 1969), pp. 35–36, 41; Beiguelman, *A formação do povo,* pp. 52–53; Eugene D. Genovese, *The World the Slaveholders Made* (New York, 1969), pp. 81–88; Robert Brent Toplin, "The Movement for the Abolition of Slavery in Brazil," (unpublished Ph.D. dissertation, Rutgers University, 1968), pp. 26–30, 100.
16. Dean, *The Industrialization,* p. 39. According to an American observer, the high price of coffee "has tempted many planters in the northern provinces to sell or bring their slaves into the coffee-growing region. . . ." Partridge to Fish, Rio de Janeiro, May 21, 1876, *Papers Related to the Foreign Relations of the United States,* December 1, 1876, pp. 26–27.
17. Lowrie, "O elemento negro," pp. 13–15.

favoring the maintenance of slavery were more powerful than those of any other region." The relative importance of slavery to the various parts of the province, he added, was the result of regional economic conditions during the last quarter of the nineteenth century: "decadence on the coast, relative stability in the North (Paraíba Valley) and Center; and rapid development of the Mogiana-Paulista Zone. Under the influence of these economic conditions, the slaves were transferred from the least progressive to the more prosperous zones." [18]

Planters and their representatives explained this late accumulation of slaves, which affected all major coffee zones of the province at the expense of poorer coastal regions, by citing slavery's continuing profitability in the production of coffee. Even if legal slavery were limited to three years, said a member of the Chamber of Deputies in 1880, "we would still buy slaves at two *contos de réis*," since a coffee-producing slave paid his purchase price in two years.[19] Claiming that half or even more of the slaves in Minas Gerais and São Paulo had been acquired from the north since 1871, Prudente de Morais, future president of the Republic, put the annual income from a slave's labor in the coffee provinces at 300 milréis in 1885.[20] The situation of the northern Paulista municípios on the eve of abolition is illustrated by the example of Mogi-mirim. In late 1886 that município contained seventy-four plantations producing about 55,000 sacks of coffee. Almost all the work on the estates was done by some 3,000 slaves, and there were not more than 800 free workers in the município.[21] "Having recourse to the slave," as Martinho Prado, Jr., put it in 1884, the coffee planters of São Paulo had shown little interest in employing free national workers.[22] As late as 1886, planters in the Paulista município of Limeira were observed bidding as much as 1,600 milréis (£160) on a single slave.[23]

The hour was late for slavery, but such speculation would not have surprised the coffee merchants of Santos or Rio de Janeiro, who knew that fazendeiros, with little confidence in free workers, could reasonably anticipate rich returns from slaves employed in coffee cultivation, income which might otherwise have been entirely lost. Ironically, since

18. *Ibid.,* p. 15.
19. *Gazeta da Tarde,* September 11, 1880. For an earlier statement on the quick profits to be derived from slaves in coffee production, see Freyre, *The Mansions and the Shanties,* p. 131.
20. *Annaes da Câmara* (1885), I, 254–255. On the same occasion, another future president, Campos Sales, agreed that "certainly more than half" had been imported from northern provinces.
21. *South American Journal,* November 27, 1886.
22. Martinho Prado, Jr., *Circular de Prado Junior, candidato republicano á Assembléa Geral pelo 9º districto da Provincia de S. Paulo* (São Paulo, 1884), p. 14.
23. *South American Journal,* May 1, 1886. In 1882 the large sum of 500 milréis was offered by a planter of Tietê, São Paulo, for the return of a male runaway. See Pires de Almeida, "Tietê," p. 50.

slavery was moribund in the 1880's owing to the abolitionist threat, as a short-term investment slaves may have been unusually attractive for coffee planters, since the anti-slavery turmoil had reduced slave prices without reducing their productive capacity.[24] If it is true, as the Brazilian economic historian, Roberto Simonsen, has claimed, that a "good slave" could produce twenty-five sacks of coffee per year,[25] and if it is also true, as claimed by Afonso de E. Taunay, that the average price of a sack of coffee in 1886/87 was 30$770 (see Table 26), the slave purchased in São Paulo early in 1886 for 1:600$000 could have produced coffee worth 769$250 in the first year, and probably would have earned his master much of his original cost before the Paulista slave system began to crumble in mid-1887. If, however, slavery had survived for another thirteen years, as was expected of it in 1886, a slave acquired that year could have produced his original price several times over before his liberation. Buying a slave in Brazil in 1886 was admittedly a reckless act, but it was not an entirely unreasonable one.

The distinction between the old and new agriculture of São Paulo is valid, but neither the special situation of the new planters nor their alleged tendency to reject the past was able to convert them into precocious abolitionists, or to deter them from buying many slaves.[26] As will be seen, quite different circumstances were to turn them into emancipationists. Like their predecessors in older Brazilian agricultural regions, they manned their plantations with black slaves, doubted their ability to attract free Brazilians and Europeans, and, like proprietors anywhere, defended their investments when they came under attack.

To understand São Paulo's role in the abolitionist decade, we must distinguish, as Nabuco did, between the planters' ability and their willingness to adopt a new labor system.[27] To gauge their relative posi-

24. The opposite situation had existed in the United States before the Civil War, and thus the short-term return on slaves was evidently much lower. Slave prices in the United States had, of course, been determined not only on the basis of the immediate income they produced, but by long-term prospects, including the reproductive potential of females. See Fogel and Engerman, "The Economics of Slavery," p. 328; Conrad and Meyer, "The Economics of Slavery in the Ante-Bellum South," pp. 342–361.
25. Simonsen, "Aspectos da história econômica do café," p. 267.
26. See Morse, *From Community to Metropolis,* p. 146; Freyre, *Order and Progress* (New York, 1970), pp. 195–196.
27. The planters of São Paulo were in a position to be more flexible on the slavery question than those of the Paraíba Valley, wrote Nabuco in 1883. Paulista planters had employed a large part of their capital in the purchase of slaves from the north, and their province was the bulwark of the slave system. Yet its agriculture, as Nabuco noted with remarkable clairvoyance, was not as dependent upon slavery *for its solvency* as the debt-ridden plantations of Rio de Janeiro and Minas Gerais; São Paulo, moreover, possessed the climate to attract Europeans and the capital to pay free workers. See *O Abolicionismo,* pp. 154–155.

tion on the slavery issue, the attitudes of Paulista planters in the several parts of the province must be compared not only with those of other coffee planters but with those of representative Brazilians throughout the country. The Paulista conversion to emancipationism came late and was motivated not by their desire to liberate blacks or to make way for Europeans, but, paradoxically, to keep their slaves at work under an emergency situation, even under an altered status. European immigration, moreover, was less a cause of their sudden switch to emancipationism in 1887 than a fortunate and tardily affected solution to their labor problem. Though immigration schemes were vigorously initiated at last in 1885 and 1886 and began to provide a large supply of European plantation workers in 1887, before that date immigrationist efforts had been feeble and nearly entirely unsuccessful. Beginning in the 1830's, many attempts had been made to attract Europeans, and some had in fact arrived. Yet the census of 1872 put the foreign-born population of São Paulo at only 29,622, of whom 15,227 were Africans (more than 13,000 still enslaved), and only 1,132 were Italians.[28] As late as 1884 the number of colonists employed on coffee plantations in São Paulo was estimated at only 1,000 households.[29]

As a result of many early failures, until well into the abolitionist decade the planters of São Paulo had little faith either in Europeans or in free Brazilians as substitutes for their slaves. In 1879, Antônio Moreira de Barros of São Paulo, in a plea for Chinese workers, denied that Europeans could ever be persuaded to work beside slaves on coffee plantations.[30] Senator Joaquim de Godoy of São Paulo sent a questionnaire concerning the future of labor to the Paulista municípios in 1884. The replies indicated that attitudes toward slavery and immigration differed little in the various parts of the province. Most of the responding municipal chambers rejected unindemnified liberation of slaves over sixty (then under consideration by the Brazilian legislature), and most favored laws to force ex-slaves and unemployed free Brazilians to work on their plantations. Absent were calls for European immigrants, though at least one chamber asked for Chinese workers. Making no reference to Europeans himself, Senator Godoy claimed in his message to the municípios that the only immediate answer to the labor problem in São Paulo was the Brazilian worker, who had not yet been able to accommodate himself "to the mental state of the planters, who believe that only slave labor is productive." [31]

Thus, on the eve of the final abolitionist struggle, the elites of São Paulo, Rio de Janeiro, and Minas Gerais had a greater interest in the

28. *Recenseamento da população*, XIX, 430, 434.
29. Van Delden Laërne, *Brazil and Java*, p. 139.
30. *Ibid.*, p. 141; Evanson, "The Liberal Party," p. 163.
31. Godoy, *O elemento servil*, pp. 57–198.

survival of slavery than most Brazilian planters elsewhere. "In the coffee cultivation," wrote a correspondent of *The London Times* at Jundiaí, São Paulo, in 1883, "there are employed about 500,000 slaves, who at this work are worth at least £120 a head, or a total of £60,-000,000 . . . ." [32] In contrast, much of the rest of Brazil had already moved far toward a complete transformation from a slave to a free-labor system, and the economic motivation to maintain slavery had therefore been largely removed. Some resentment had undoubtedly built up in the northern provinces, moreover, from the loss of slaves to the south, and this migration may well have helped to motivate the anti-slavery rumblings of 1879.

In the coffee zones, by contrast, slaves were still the principal source of labor on plantations, and capital was still flowing into slave investments. Immigration—both Chinese and European—had failed to provide an alternative work force, and marginal and vagabond Brazilians were still looked upon as unemployable. Relying upon the guarantees contained in the Rio Branco Law and acting in the traditional and accepted manner, coffee planters had done little to convert to a free-labor system; most therefore were entirely unprepared to accept the implications of the new reform movement of the 1880's.

32. *South American Journal,* August 16, 1883.

> *There is nothing more difficult*
> *than to evaluate the relative importance*
> *of the diverse factors of a movement which becomes national.*
> *The last of the apostles can become the first,*
> *like St. Paul, in services and proselytism.*
> *All in abolition is joined together.*
> *Its history cannot be written*
> *ignoring any of its links.*
>
> JOAQUIM NABUCO
> *Minha formação*

9

THE
ABOLITIONIST MOVEMENT:
FIRST PHASE

THE BEGINNINGS OF ABOLITIONISM

It is not surprising that it was a representative of a northeastern province who renewed the abolitionist debate in the General Assembly in 1879, and that the first negative response came from a deputy representing São Paulo. Both historians and contemporary participants in the abolitionist campaign agree that a speech by Deputy Jeronymo Sodré, framed in advance in Bahia and delivered on March 5, 1879 in the Chamber of Deputies, was the spark that ignited the tinder.[1] To the astonishment of his fellow legislators, Sodré denounced the Rio Branco Law as a disgraceful and mutilated reform. Brazilian society, he declared, was standing atop a volcano. Brazilian Liberals were compelled to go beyond the work of the Conservatives, to declare to the nation that all Brazilians were citizens, that all were free. Following an unparliamentary outburst of comments and commotion, Sodré concluded his historic speech with an appeal for the total and rapid extinction of slavery.[2]

1. Joaquim Nabuco, *Minha formação* (São Paulo, 1947), p. 170; Fonseca, *A escravidão, o clero e o abolicionismo*, pp. 18–19; Dornas Filho, *A escravidão*, p. 169.
2. *Annaes da Câmara* (1879), III, 194–195. As a student in the 1850's, Sodré had been a member of the emancipationist "Sociedade 2 de Julho," founded in Bahia in 1852 by students of the Medical Faculty to liberate slaves. See Fonseca, *A escravidão, o clero e o abolicionismo*, pp. 245–246.

In his quick reply to Sodré, Martim Francisco Ribeiro de Andrada of São Paulo not only defended slavery, but even implied that coffee interests would prefer to dismember the Empire rather than to see the labor system destroyed by a legislature dominated by the deputies from other regions. "We, the representatives of the Southern provinces of the Empire," said this Paulista grandson of the independence leader, José Bonifacio de Andrada e Silva, "appreciate the integrity of this vast country, but not so much so that, in order to preserve it, we are willing to tolerate the general liquidation of fortunes and the violent destruction of slave property, for so great have been the large shipments of slaves from the provinces of the North who sell [them] to us for a heavy sum." [3]

Joaquim Nabuco, elected to the Chamber in 1878 from Pernambuco, was soon revealing an inclination to follow Sodré's example.[4] In August and September, in two speeches, Nabuco accused the British-owned São João d'El-Rei Mining Company of Minas Gerais of holding two hundred persons in illegal slavery for twenty years.[5] In a brilliant address delivered in October, Nabuco joined Sodré in demanding new legislation to replace the law which his father had so strongly supported only a decade before, a law which in the opinion of the younger Nabuco no longer corresponded to the aspirations of the nation. Within the Chamber itself, he claimed, a new abolitionist force was growing, principally among members of the Liberal Party.[6]

In contrast with the ideas of Nabuco and a few northern supporters,[7] Martim Francisco once again defended the status quo. Slavery, he said, in a reply to Nabuco's speech, was a constituted fact and could not be quickly abolished. Labeling the young northerner's opinions "exaggeratedly radical," he asked Nabuco to refrain from placing his "beautiful oratorical gifts . . . at the service of a cause which can greatly harm our

3. Cited by Evanson, "The Liberal Party," p. 228; Evanson reasonably interprets Martim Francisco's words as constituting "one of the earliest examples of modern Paulista separatism."
4. Nabuco to Barão de Penedo, Palmeiras, January 22, 1879; same to same, Rio de Janeiro, May 8, 1879, in Nabuco, *Cartas a amigos,* I, 30–31.
5. *Rio News,* October 15, 1879; *Annaes da Câmara* (1879), V, 256–257. In October a judge of Rio das Velhas, Minas Gerais, decided that the persons held as slaves by the British company had been legally free since 1860 and were entitled to wages, but the company's last 28 slaves were not freed until June 1882. *Rio News,* November 5, 1879; *South American Journal,* August 3, 1882.
6. *Annaes da Câmara* (1879), V, 311.
7. Carolina Nabuco, *The Life of Joaquim Nabuco* (Stanford, California, 1950), p. 56. Dornas Filho and Carolina Nabuco listed a total of eleven deputies in the Chamber in 1879–1881 who supported slavery reform: one each from Maranhão, Sergipe, and Paraíba; two each from Amazonas and Bahia; and three from Pernambuco. Correio Rabello of Minas Gerais was the only one listed who represented a coffee province. See *ibid.,* p. 64, and Dornas Filho, *A escravidão,* p. 169.

country." [8] Both descendants of outstanding Brazilian statesmen who had earlier fought for slavery reform, both scions of traditional Liberal families, Martim Francisco and Joaquim Nabuco seemed to epitomize at that moment the regional differences on the question of slavery which had once again emerged into the open.

The legislative session of 1879 produced little more than skirmishes, but the session of the following year coincided with a wave of popular abolitionism. As early as April the public had been informed that Nabuco intended to propose legislation to end slavery by the end of the decade.[9] The bill he would introduce would not become law at once, he predicted in a letter to the British and Foreign Anti-Slavery Society, but would be offered to every legislative session "in a Liberal house by myself or some of my friends, and in a Conservative house by some prominent Conservative abolitionist, like Mr. Gusmão Lobo"—a deputy from Pernambuco in the Conservative Assembly of 1878. Gaining more votes each year, Nabuco predicted, it would one day pass.[10]

In the same month (April 1880), a former pharmacist turned journalist praised Nabuco in one of a series of weekly articles in the Rio paper, *Gazeta de Noticias.* Nabuco had raised the banner of abolitionism, wrote José do Patrocinio, had staked his political career upon its success, proposing a moderate reform which the Assembly nevertheless received with indifference.[11]

Soon after, individuals who objected to slavery began to organize clubs in order to take action against the institution and to make their feelings known. At the end of May a society for the liberation of slaves was inaugurated at the Military School in Rio.[12] On July 25 the Normal School sponsored an "abolitionist conference," the first of a series of weekly Sunday meetings. This first gathering was highlighted by a speech delivered by one Vicente de Souza, and participants contributed a total of 160 milréis for the *peculio* (personal liberation fund) of a Creole slave named José. At a second meeting the following week, at the request of the opera-composer, Carlos Gomes, another meeting was called for the benefit of his slave, Margarida, who had served as a wet nurse for the composer's son in Bahia. A third conference, held in the

8. *Annaes da Câmara* (1879), V, 312–313.
9. Nabuco may have been motivated by the passage of a law to end slavery in Cuba. In lieu of indemnification, this Spanish law obliged ex-slaves to undergo eight years of tutelage (*patronato*) under their former masters, but even this extension of forced labor was terminated by a royal decree on October 7, 1886. See Corwin, *Spain and the Abolition of Slavery in Cuba,* pp. 301–305; Knight, *Slave Society in Cuba,* pp. 177–178.
10. *Rio News,* April 24, 1880.
11. *Gazeta de Noticias,* April 26, 1880
12. *Rio News,* June 5, 1880.

São Luiz Theater, allegedly attracted nearly 700 persons, but produced contributions totaling only a little more than 84 milréis. These gatherings continued through the month, and at the meeting of September 5 musical entertainment was added to the program as a permanent feature. Before the end of August the Associação Central Emancipadora, soon to be dominated by the vigorous and appealing journalist, José do Patrocinio, had been organized in Rio to systematize the abolitionist movement throughout the country.[13]

With an anti-slavery movement thus developing almost spontaneously in the capital in apparent response to the initiatives of Sodré and Nabuco, the latter deputy brought the issue back to the General Assembly, though the session of 1880 was nearing its end. On August 24 Nabuco asked the Chamber to grant urgency to an emancipationist bill of his creation to permit action upon it during the current session. Thirty-eight members of the Chamber agreed to permit immediate discussion, but, under pressure from dissident representatives, the Council President threatened to resign if the bill was discussed, and the Chamber sessions were therefore suspended for several days.[14]

The project which so upset the normal procedures of the Chamber was a strong attack upon slavery, designed to abolish the institution by the end of the eighties, with full indemnification for masters of remaining slaves. The buying and selling of captives would have ceased at once, thus ending the trade between the provinces. Slave markets of all kinds would have been closed, and persons transporting slaves from one province to another punished in accordance with the slave-trade law of November 7, 1831 (see Chapter 2). Associations organized to emancipate captives were to be granted land, according to Nabuco's bill, for the establishment of colonies for the benefit of freedmen. Mothers were no longer to be separated from their children to be rented as wet nurses, as servants, or for any other purpose. Many slaves would have been freed outright, according to Nabuco's bill, including the elderly, the blind, the incurably sick, and all those born in Africa, whatever the date of their importation. The older brothers and sisters of ingenuos would have been freed in two years. Primary classes would have been established for slaves in all towns and cities, with planters required to send their slaves and ingenuos to schools to acquire a knowledge of reading, writing, and "the principles of morality." Among other provisions of Nabuco's bill was one to prohibit the use of irons and chains and every form of corporal punishment.[15]

13. *Associação Central Emancipadora. Boletin N. 2, 28 de Outubro de 1880; Gazeta da Tarde,* August 21, 1880.
14. *Annaes da Câmara* (1880), IV, 366; Blacklaw, "Slavery in Brazil."
15. *O Abolicionista,* January 1, February 1, 1881.

Angered by the delay of the legislature and the obvious decision of the Liberal cabinet to stand firm, on August 30 Nabuco asked the ministry to express an opinion on the reported rise of a separatist movement in the southern provinces, provoked by northern abolitionism. Arousing a noisy reaction among spectators and deputies, Nabuco then declared his political independence and predicted the triumph of his cause:

On the question of abolition, . . . in the conviction that it is necessary to march beyond the law of September 28, I would separate myself not only from the cabinet, not only from the Liberal Party, not only from public opinion and from the general conspiracy of the country, but from everything and everybody.

He would make an alliance with the future, he promised, for no one— neither the Council President nor the cabinet—could prevent abolition. Even the Emperor himself understood that the hour had arrived to grant freedom to one and a half million slaves.[16]

The response to Nabuco's oratory came this time from Martinho Campos of Minas Gerais, who righteously accepted for himself the label of "slavocrat" ("I declare quite deliberately that it is not my fate to be an emancipationist"). Claiming that slave labor was necessary on coffee fazendas, Martinho Campos denounced Nabuco's proposals as impractical, and the request for urgency was then overwhelmingly rejected by seventy-seven deputies. Fourteen of the eighteen deputies who supported Nabuco's request were from northern provinces, seven from Pernambuco alone.[17]

Five days later Nabuco tried to attach anti-slavery articles to the budget project, including measures to abolish the inter-provincial slave trade and to create regional charity funds (*caixas de piedade*) for the purpose of freeing slaves. These he proposed to name for José Bonifacio, the famous grandfather of one of Nabuco's more recalcitrant Paulista opponents, who fifty-seven years before had proposed the creation of caixas de piedade in a speech intended for the Constituent Assembly.[18]

Three days later abolitionism took another step forward with Nabuco again in the leadership. On the fifty-eighth anniversary of Brazilian independence, a small anti-slavery group met at Nabuco's home on Flamengo Beach to organize the Sociedade Brasileira contra a Escravidão (the Brazilian Anti-Slavery Society). According to a contempo-

16. *Annaes da Câmara* (1880), IV, 437–440.
17. The measure was supported by only three deputies from coffee provinces, two from Rio de Janeiro and one from Minas Gerais. The last vote favoring urgency was cast by a deputy from Rio Grande do Sul. *Annaes da Câmara* (1880), IV, 437–448.
18. *Ibid.,* V, 36.

rary account, the evening of September 7 was stormy; the waves of the harbor crashed loudly against the ruined quays at the water's edge. Nabuco's voice inside the house, accompanied by a volley of cannon commemorating independence, sounded above the salvos and seemed to deny, to the romantic mind of the witness, the message of the guns. "There is no liberty or independence," Nabuco seemed to be saying at that dramatic moment, "in a land of one and a half million slaves." [19] Three weeks later a second meeting was held in Nabuco's residence, where the Brazilian Anti-Slavery Society was officially inaugurated. The members of the new organization resolved to publish a newspaper and to communicate with other anti-slavery organizations in Europe and America.[20]

The Brazilian Anti-Slavery Society, according to Carolina Nabuco, was created to fight slavery through propaganda, and the propaganda quickly came.[21] The society's Manifesto, written by Nabuco, was published in pamphlets and newspapers in English, French, and Portuguese. While its purpose was to convince Brazilians that slavery was no longer necessary, it also denounced "the infinite cruelties" of the institution. Attempting to associate abolitionism with patriotism, it identified its cause with the ideas of the Pernambucan revolutionaries of 1817, with José Bonifacio, and with an emancipationist tradition in parliament reflecting "the noblest and most enlightened part of the Brazilian conscience. . . ." The Manifesto praised the Rio Branco Law, but denounced its "superstitious" respect for the interests of the masters and its implied acceptance of slavery for another three-quarters of a century. Accusing the General Assembly and the Liberal ministry of ignoring the plight of the slaves, appealing to national pride, to the Emperor, and to every class, the Manifesto ended with a reminder that "Brazil would indeed be the very last among the countries of the world, if having slavery, she had not also an abolitionist party. . . ."[22]

On November 1, 1880, the first issue of O Abolicionista, the organ of the Brazilian Anti-Slavery Society, appeared in Rio, claiming that its very existence proved how far the public had gone toward acquiring abolitionist sentiments. With new denunciations of the government and the Chamber, the monthly began its campaign of propaganda with an attack upon the legality of slavery itself, undermined as it was by the colossal and continuing violation of the law of November 7, 1831. The paper lashed out at the economic institutions of the country, at slavery, "the one cause of the economic and industrial backwardness" of Brazil,

19. *Gazeta da Tarde,* September 16, 1880.
20. *O Abolicionista,* November 1, 1880. In November the British and Foreign Anti-Slavery Society offered its co-operation. *Ibid.,* January 1, 1881.
21. Nabuco, *The Life of Joaquim Nabuco,* p. 75.
22. Quoted by *Rio News,* October 15, 1880.

at the latifundia spread over the entire country, with their hundreds of slaves enriching their owners, without religion, morality, or family life. The public was sick, said *O Abolicionista*, "of the spectacle of wealth criminally accumulated above the general misery by the exploitation of one and a half million persons." In the cities of Brazil, it charged, "we are the object of study by foreigners" intrigued by "the advertisements for the purchase and sale of human creatures, for the capture of runaway slaves; the commission houses, real brothels and at the same time market places for human beings. . . ." These and other abuses *O Abolicionista* pledged to denounce in a continuing crusade.[23]

THE HILLIARD INCIDENT

Seeking friends wherever they might be found, on October 19 Nabuco wrote to the American Minister in Rio, Henry Washington Hilliard, a southerner and former Confederate, enclosing several copies of the Manifesto of the Anti-Slavery Society. In his letter Nabuco asked the American's opinion regarding the effects of abolition in the southern states, setting off events which would advance the abolitionist cause and draw up the lines of battle. Hilliard replied from the American legation in Rio, drawing a brief summary of the history of slavery in the United States, of the crisis leading to the Civil War, and the problems of Reconstruction, all published along with Nabuco's letter in the *Jornal do Commercio*.[24]

Particularly interesting to the Brazilian public were Hilliard's thoughts on slavery and free labor. A former slaveowner and Congressman from a large and opulent plantation district of the south, where slaves had been employed "exclusively" in the years before the Civil War, Hilliard claimed that the abolition of slavery had brought great benefits to the south, including improved relations between the races and (in 1880) the largest cotton crop in memory.[25] Contrary to the pessimistic pre-war predictions of southerners, he told Nabuco, the abolition of slavery had not brought economic ruin, the loss of the plantation labor force, and the

23. *O Abolicionista*, November 1, 1880.

24. For the Nabuco-Hilliard correspondence and other documents concerning the incident, see Henry W. Hilliard, *Politics and Pen Pictures at Home and Abroad* (New York, 1892), pp. 411–435.

25. On the American slavery question Hilliard was allegedly a leader of southern moderates, but he had strongly opposed the abolitionists in the United States before the Civil War, had been involved in persuading Tennessee to secede from the Union, and had commanded a Confederate unit in the war. See Toccoa Cozart, "Henry W. Hilliard," *Transactions of the Alabama Historical Society* (Montgomery, Alabama, 1899–1903), IV, 277–299.

destruction of the agricultural system. Southern Negroes were working well, "with patience and fidelity." For Brazil, Hilliard recommended what he called a cautious program of emancipation with full payment to the masters, to end in the complete liquidation of Brazilian slavery in seven years.[26]

Responding to this encouragement, the abolitionists staged a banquet in the American's honor at the fashionable Hotel dos Estrangeiros in the Catete district, decorating its mirrored room (ironically for a former Confederate soldier) with a large portrait of Abraham Lincoln in the act of reading the Emancipation Proclamation to the members of his cabinet. That same day André Rebouças announced in the *Gazeta da Tarde* that for the first time the Brazilian abolitionist family was meeting "to distribute the sacred bread of the Eucharist in favor of those who suffer in the irons of captivity. . . ." Fifty abolitionists were to attend the banquet, "but round about them in spirit will be 1,500,000 brothers awaiting the delicious bread of freedom." The menu on this occasion, which roused the fury of the slavocrats, included *Bouchées de Dame à la Monroe, Jambon d'York à la Garrison, Poisson Fin à la Washington,* and *Pudding diplomate à la Hilliard.* In an undiplomatic fashion, Hilliard gave a rousing speech favoring emancipation and accepted honorary membership in the Brazilian Anti-Slavery Society.[27]

Undiplomatic, at least, is how the enemies of abolitionism judged Hilliard's letter and his attendance at the abolitionist banquet. In the January issue of *O Abolicionista* Nabuco wrote that nothing but the Hilliard letter had produced "such an outcry from the camp of the slavocrats as the banquet which we offered to that eminent statesman." [28] The outcry, in fact, was immediate. Two days after the gathering at the Hotel dos Estrangeiros, Moreira de Barros of São Paulo alluded in the Chamber to a "clear and manifest intervention of a foreign nation in an entirely domestic question," suggesting too that Hilliard had been acting on orders from his government, which was seeking revenge for Brazilian friendliness toward the Confederacy.[29]

It became known in Rio on November 24 that the following day the government was to be interpellated in the Chamber on the Hilliard incident, and on that afternoon the Chamber galleries were filled to capacity.

---

26. *Jornal do Commercio,* October 31, 1880.

27. *Sociedade Brasileira contra a Escravidão. Banquete offerecido ao Exm. Sr. ministro americano Henry Washington Hilliard, a 20 de Novembro de 1880* (Rio de Janeiro, 1880); Moraes, *A campanha abolicionista,* p. 22; *O Abolicionista,* December 1, 1880. For Hilliard's own description of the banquet, see *Politics and Pen Pictures,* pp. 398–399

28. *O Abolicionista,* January 1, 1881. Even the foreign press reflected disapproval of Hilliard's involvement. See *South American Journal,* January 6, 1881.

29. *Annaes da Câmara* (1880), VI, 309–310.

The interrogator, Belfort Duarte of Maranhão, was fulfilling, he said, the duty of a representative of a province "where wealth is the slave." Referring to abolitionism as "a sinister idea," he demanded to know if the government approved of the emancipationist propaganda exhibited in public meetings and political banquets, specifically the "manifesto" of a foreign diplomat. To these and related questions, Saraiva, President of the Council, replied that Hilliard's letter was an expression of personal views. The members of his cabinet, he said, all believed that the Rio Branco Law provided the complete and safe solution to the problem of slavery, though the ministry was also required to respect all legally expressed opinions to the contrary.[30]

The incident in the Chamber was inconclusive, but revealed a growing public interest in abolitionism, the determination of slavocrats to resist, at the expense perhaps of constitutional guarantees, and a total unwillingness of the Liberal government of José Antônio Saraiva to be moved toward further anti-slavery acts.

VARYING COMMITMENTS TO ABOLITIONISM

As the reaction to the Hilliard incident suggested, abolitionism was indeed growing and spreading. Yet the leaders could hardly have been satisfied with the public response to their efforts. Emphasizing the irrefutable argument that slavery as constituted in Brazil was all but illegal, the abolitionists frightened slaveholders during the first few months. Yet their power appeared to spring more from intelligence, determination, and the validity of their arguments than from the size of the following they attracted.

Only a small minority of the population became involved during the first three years of the struggle, except in the northern province of Ceará, where the movement quickly triumphed and seemed to claim the support of almost the entire population. Anti-slavery clubs and societies eventually appeared in even the smallest Brazilian towns, and near the end of the struggle the movement even invaded the countryside and the plantations; but in the beginning abolitionism involved a relative few and was essentially a phenomenon of the cities.[31]

At first there was reluctance to become involved even in the major towns, the result both of ingrained traditional values and of the dependence of city residents upon the government or the landed elite for their

30. *Ibid.,* VI, 355–357; *Gazeta da Tarde,* November 24, 1880.
31. Florestan Fernandes, *The Negro in Brazilian Society* (New York, 1969), pp. 32–33; Beiguelman, *Formação política,* I, 186; Viotti da Costa, *Da senzala à colônia,* pp. 428–433; Graham, *Britain and the Onset,* pp. 161 ff.

livelihood and security. The slaveholder was still an awesome and over-shadowing force in the early 1880's to the inhabitants even of larger cities like Rio de Janeiro, Salvador, and São Paulo. As a result, the movement failed at first to attract large numbers of ex-slaves, Negroes, and working men.[32] Even the free laborer was "a pro-slavery man," according to one foreign observer, since he believed that emancipation would reduce his wages. "The free labourer (said the same writer) looks down on the slave and does not look forward to the time when they will be on equal terms. . . . The free labourer now and then comes in for a handsome sum for catching runaway negroes," and furthermore, "he is afraid to tamper with the negro in the way of pointing out to him the benefits of freedom. He knows that punishment would be death, if he were found intriguing." [33] In 1884 Joaquim Nabuco regretted the in-difference of black people and rural workers to abolitionism, claiming that the movement was working to make them independent farmers and landowners,[34] and after his electoral defeat of 1886 in which many free Negroes voted for his opponent, Nabuco wrote to a friend:

> this unconcern of the free negroes in Brazil to the question of Abolition so soon as they cease to be slaves and leap at once to the dignity of citizens and electors is another sign of how deeply the humiliation of slavery has penetrated the mind and heart of the slave people, and will give you some idea of the difficulty the Abolitionist movement has to fight against in Brazil. Instead of a solid negro vote, as in North America, for the party that raised the cry of Abolition, we here see many negroes following the party banner of their old masters in the true servile spirit.[35]

As late as 1887 a northern writer explained the anti-abolitionist senti-ments of the free colored of Bahia by their belief "that hating the African race, helping to persecute it," they would themselves appear to be with-out ties to Africa.[36]

As a group, even the urban middle class did not quickly commit itself to abolitionism, for it was "too much dependent on the wealthy coffee planters to openly stand for abolition." [37] For every merchant, doctor, bureaucrat, or lawyer who participated in the early years, there were many who did not. The results of an election held in Rio in late 1881 showed that most voters in the capital (government employees, mer-chants, proprietors, and professionals) were still unwilling to commit

32. Viotti da Costa, *Da senzala à colônia*, p. 438.
33. Blacklaw, "Slavery in Brazil."
34. See *Campanha abolicionista no Recife (Eleições de 1884). Discursos de Joaquim Nabuco* (Rio de Janeiro, 1885), p. 10; Viotti da Costa, *Da senzala à colônia*, pp. 433–434.
35. Quoted by *South American Journal*, February 20, 1886.
36. Fonseca, *A escravidão, o clero e o abolicionismo*, p. 143.
37. Blacklaw, "Slavery in Brazil."

themselves to the cause of liberation. Even the dynamic and personable Nabuco, running against a Conservative pro-slavery lawyer, could attract only ninety votes of a total of 1,911 cast in the first electoral district of the city. The election of 1881, in fact, was a shocking disappointment to abolitionists, because nationwide the victors were slavery's defenders or uncommitted candidates.[38] For abolition, wrote A. Scott Blacklaw by way of explanation, "there is a great want of moral support from among the public men in Brazil. The influential people of the nation seem to disregard it. Nearly every Brazilian who can afford it has slaves; if he has not, his relations and friends have." [39]

There is little reason to believe, moreover, that industrialists and capitalists as a class were sympathetic to abolitionism. Although merchants and the owners of industries stood to profit from an end to slavery, as an interest group they did not back the movement. In its infancy during the 1880's, in fact, industry was best established in those parts of Brazil where resistance to abolitionism was most tenacious, and it is not surprising that commercial and industrial groups allied themselves closely with landlords and slaveholders in such pro-slavery organizations as the Associação Commercial and the Club da Lavoura e do Commercio, with its banches in rural communities in São Paulo, Rio de Janeiro, and Minas Gerais.[40] Most members of the Brazilian entrepreneurial class, writes Warren Dean, referring principally to São Paulo, came from the planter elite,[41] and there is no reason to suppose that their outlook toward slavery differed much from that of their compadres and clients.

In support of the hypothesis that industrialists played an important role in abolitionism, Richard Graham singles out the committed reformist, André Rebouças, as representative of those men associated with industry who joined the movement. Although Rebouças, as will be seen, believed in industrialization, he was not representative of industrialists. He was not opposed to slavery, as Graham conjectures, because he was associated with business interests, but rather because he was "a puritan moralist," as Graham himself puts it in a recent article.[42] An engineer and teacher, a sensitive intellectual who by 1874 had abandoned his

38. Nabuco, *The Life of Joaquim Nabuco*, p. 91; *Rio News*, November 15, 1881. Of 5,928 electors in the Município Neutro, 2,211 were public employees, 1,076 were merchants or commercial employees, 516 were proprietors, and most of the rest were doctors, lawyers, and other professionals. Nabuco, *O Abolicionismo*, p. 179.
39. Blacklaw, "Slavery in Brazil."
40. Viotti da Costa, *Da senzala à colônia*, p. 433.
41. Dean, *The Industrialization of São Paulo*, pp. 36–38, 46.
42. Richard Graham, "Landowners and the Overthrow of the Empire," *Luso-Brazilian Review*, VII, 2 (December 1970), 49. See also Ignacio José Verissimo, *André Rebouças através de sua auto-biografia* (Rio de Janeiro, 1939), p. 162.

efforts to organize construction companies after encountering frustrating
resistance from established interests, Rebouças was instead strongly committed to a radical reordering of Brazilian society, including a reform of
the land system.[43] His distaste for the large agricultural estate, a central
theme of his writings, cannot be explained by an alliance with industrialists and capitalists, many of whom were the owners of large estates as
well as investors in railroads or textile factories.[44] It is true, as Graham
writes in support of his theory that industrialists played an important
role in abolition, that the students and professors of the engineering
school, where Rebouças taught, formed an abolitionist society of their
own;[45] but, to avoid exaggerating the significance of this fact, it must be
pointed out that such societies were also formed in medical, military,
and law schools and, as abolitionism gained strength, in institutions of
learning throughout the country. Moreover, if industrialists as an interest
group supported abolitionism, it was not through large and frequent
contributions, although Rebouças himself gave of his limited funds. "Unfortunately," wrote Nabuco from London in 1882, "the abolitionist party
lacks only one thing, but that is the sinew of press propaganda: money.
Talent, heart, courage, self-denial, independence we have; but what we
lack is money." [46]

There were undoubtedly many factors contributing to a personal decision to join the abolitionist movement—factors of temperament, boldness, personal interest, chance acquaintances, or intellectual experiences
—but it can hardly be denied that for city people the degree of commitment to slavery of the neighboring rural area was often an important if
not overriding factor. For reasons already explored, it was more acceptable in many parts of the northeast for leaders and politicians with links
to the plantations and slaveholding interests to associate themselves with
emancipationism than it was for their counterparts in the coffee zones,
as regional voting records and the high ratio of northerners in the national leadership prove. Representatives of every class and profession
eventually became involved in abolitionism—slaves and the owners of

---

43. Verissimo, *André Rebouças*, pp. 73, 112–114, 131; Rebouças, *Agricultura
nacional*, pp. 1–7, 111–112, 120, 367–368.
44. Perhaps a more authentic representative of the Brazilian industrial class was
Felicio dos Santos, a politician from Minas Gerais with interests in textile and
paper industries who supported tariff protection through the agency of the Associação Industrial and was an ardent opponent of abolitionism. See Nícia Vilela
Luz, *A luta pela industrialização do Brasil* (São Paulo, 1961), p. 61.
45. For Graham's arguments, see *Britain and the Onset*, pp. 161–162.
46. In 1882 Nabuco could not acquire enough money to establish an anti-slavery
journal in Rio, and in 1880 and 1881 his press campaign was practically limited
to the publication of the monthly *O Abolicionista.* Nabuco to Domingos Jaguaribe,
London, November 16, 1882; same to Joaquim Serra, London, November 17,
1882, *Cartas a amigos,* I, 86–89.

slaves, laborers and landlords, actors, musicians, and entertainers, capitalists and railroad workers, merchants, lawyers, teachers, soldiers and students. The middle and upper sectors of society and talented upstarts like José do Patrocinio provided the bulk of the leadership, not because they were particularly pursuing the interests of their social classes, but because they were qualified to confront the wielders of power on their own level.

Much of the press of Brazil was directly or indirectly linked to agriculture and commercial interests, and the abolitionists therefore gained little support from established and "responsible" journals during the first phase of the struggle.[47] Although there were significant exceptions, the tendency of editors, both monarchist and republican, was to ignore the movement as long as possible, then to attack it or even to impugn the motives or the moral character of the major abolitionist leaders.[48] In most areas of Brazil some elements of the press eventually sympathized with abolitionism, and some papers gave a powerful boost to the cause, but newspapers in general remained aloof, rejected rapid emancipation on economic grounds, or upheld the pro-slavery position. The first of the major abolitionist papers of the period was Ferreira de Araújo's *Gazeta de Noticias,* which, along with *O Abolicionista,* awakened public interest in 1880, but this pioneering journal was quickly superseded by the more radical *Gazeta da Tarde* under the brief control of José Ferreira de Menezes. Until replaced as the principal abolitionist paper in 1887 by *A Cidade do Rio,* the *Gazeta da Tarde,* owned and edited by José do Patrocinio after mid-1881, was the one reliable source of information in the capital to a public hungry for news of the progress of liberation.

If the national press was laggard in the first few years, at least two foreign editors in Rio offered immediate encouragement to the abolitionists and consistently granted the movement the aura of prestige and authority which foreign opinion conveyed. The *Revista Illustrada,* a *Punch*-like weekly started in 1876 by a gifted Italian caricaturist, Angelo Agostini, placed its stimulating cartoons and comments on the side of abolitionism from the beginning of the struggle, arousing the ire of the slavocrats who styled it the "Red Review." [49] Almost as effective, despite the language barrier, was *The Rio News,* outspokenly abolitionist from the time it replaced *The British and American Mail* in Rio in 1879. Edited by a brilliant and liberal American, Andrew Jackson Lamoureux, *The Rio News* supported Nabuco in 1879 and 1880, and from then on

47. *Rio News,* August 5, 1881.
48. See *A Provincia de São Paulo,* São Paulo, December 1, 1880; *O Atirador Franco,* Rio de Janeiro, February 17, 1881; *O Paiz,* São Luiz de Maranhão, January 28, 1881.
49. Toplin, "The Movement," p. 127.

was the constant anti-slavery muckraker, finding enslaved Indians in the upper reaches of the Amazon or the jungles of Colombia, exposing the illegal sale of ingenuos or "free Africans" in the provincial towns of Rio de Janeiro and Minas Gerais, dissecting the sophistries of slavocrat politicians, censuring such traditional practices as the parasitical dependence upon rented slaves, or condemning a Paulista lynch mob led by unreconstructed Confederate exiles.

The abolitionist meetings held in Rio during the second half of 1880 were gay and exuberant affairs, but attendance was rarely mentioned in the press or in the abolitionist bulletins, and reports of contributions hint at small and intimate gatherings or some poverty or tight-fistedness among those attending. The contributions collected at nineteen weekly conferences totaled only a little more than two and one-half contos, enough perhaps to have purchased the freedom of two or three slaves at current prices. In 1882, for example, a man of twenty-eight, his wife and two children were placed on sale at Juiz de Fora, Minas Gerais, evaluated together at 2:600$000, a few milréis more than the total amount of the contributions during four months of abolitionist meetings.[50]

Talent, impecuniosity, revolutionary enthusiasm, and a contrasting bourgeois exuberance were the qualities most in evidence at the weekly meetings. At a conference held early in September in the São Luiz Theater, the speakers were applauded enthusiastically when they called for "subdivision of the soil" or demonstrated mathematically that the Brazilian slavemasters had run up an enormous debt to the nation through their violation of the law of 1831 during the previous half century. Yet the collection taken at the same meeting amounted to a little more than a hundred milréis.[51] The conferences continued nonetheless, developing an appealing routine which put them among the most attractive public spectacles in Rio. The meetings were characterized by a well-meant bourgeois enthusiasm. Literary and musical performances preceded the oratory, arousing the zeal of the participants by degrees. Occasionally a slave was granted his freedom, giving the public a chance to see and applaud the persons profiting from their donations.[52] Following these preliminaries, José do Patrocinio, Nicoláo Moreira, or some other well-known speaker rose to the stage amid showers of rose petals, the audience eager to applaud each assault upon the slavocracy.

50. *Associação Central Emancipadora. Boletin N. 4, 28 de Dezembro de 1880;* Gazeta da Tarde, April 6, 1882.
51. *Gazeta da Tarde,* September 6, 1880; *Associação Central Emancipadora. Boletin N. 2, 28 de Outubro de 1880.*
52. *Gazeta da Tarde,* January 31, 1881.

Typical, perhaps, was a meeting held at the São Luiz Theater early in 1881, one of the last of the meetings described in detail in the *Gazeta da Tarde* during this first phase of the abolitionist campaign. The entertainment began with a rendition of "the splendid overture of the dramatic *Salvator Rosa*" by Carlos Gomes, performed by two professors from the Conservatory. This was followed by a four-handed performance of a Gomes waltz, "Paulo e Virginia," by the pretty sisters, America and Maria Clapp, "a juvenile effort favoring those who groan in the chains of captivity" received with "delirious applause" and cascades of rose petals.

Other highlights of the program included a musical selection performed by the Mendelsohn Classical Trio, Mrs. Angelina Accioli's rendition of "a difficult Phantasy from *Aida,*" and, between bravos and bursts of applause, recitals of the poems "Liberdade" and "Ave Cezar" by their authors, Arthur Brazilio and Dr. Melo Morais.[53] The best of the speakers, delivering their exhortations after these rousing preliminaries, left the stage of the São Luiz amid a barrage of flowers tossed from the stalls and boxes. Music and poetry were written to support the movement: works like the "Ingenua Polka Brilhante" composed for the Associação Central Emancipadora by the music student, Horacio Fluminense, "A Escravidão e o Christo" (Slavery and Christ) recited for the abolitionist public by its author, Ernesto Sena, and "Essencialmente Agricola," a polka-ized spoof on a common pro-slavery argument dedicated to José do Patrocinio by an anonymous lady abolitionist and advertised in the *Gazeta da Tarde.*[54]

Abolitionist activity was not confined to the capital during its first months. The movement had begun to appear spontaneously in towns and cities at scattered points in every region of the country. The Abolitionist Club of Pelôtas was founded in late August in the rich cattle region of Rio Grande do Sul near the Uruguayan border, and the area soon had its own abolitionist journal. At the same time an Emancipationist Commission was inaugurated in Natal, Rio Grande do Norte, to purchase the freedom of slaves. In September, members of the Literary and Republican Union paraded through the streets of Diamantina, Minas Gerais, followed by a band and a great throng of people requesting donations for the liberation of a slave woman. In November, the Sociedade Abolicionista Maranhense was formed in São Luiz de Maranhão. On the first of the same month an abolitionist paper of Bahia, also titled *Gazeta da Tarde,* undertook the sponsorship of a short-lived series of anti-slavery meetings. While students in São Paulo were establishing the Sociedade

53. *Ibid.,* November 15, 1880.
54. *Ibid.,* November 15 and December 8, 1880.

Abolicionista Academica, others in Rio were creating the Associação Emancipadora da Escola Polytechnica.[55]

Of special importance for abolition were the events occurring in the northern province of Ceará, stricken by drought and by now possessing few slaves. The Liberal *Gazeta do Norte* of Fortaleza, lukewarm on the slavery issue when it was founded in June, had evolved by late November 1880 (along with public opinion in the northern capital) into an abolitionist paper. The change was completed in time for the newspaper to laud the creation of the Sociedade Cearense Libertadora, the abolitionist club of Ceará, which held its organization meeting on December 8 and was soon initiating a campaign to liberate all the slaves in the province.

55. J. I. Arnizaut Furtado, *Estudos sobre a libertação dos escravos no Brasil* (Pelôtas, 1882), p. 58; *O Abolicionista*, November 1, 1880; February 1, 1881; Documentos relativos a escravatura, 1815–1880, AN, Cod. 622; *A Idea Nova*, Diamantina, October 8, 1880; *Gazeta da Tarde*, November 27, December 13, 1880.

. . . *in my opinion*
the emancipation of the slaves and the ingenuos
is only the beginning of our work.

JOAQUIM NABUCO
O Abolicionismo

São Paulo prefers the republic to abolition.
Let the Emperor decide.

DEPUTY COSTA PINTO
of São Paulo in 1880

10

ACTION AND
REACTION

THE ABOLITIONISTS

The men and women who set off this simmering national revolt formed a diverse group whose common qualities were talent, enthusiasm, and dedication. Three interlocking organizations had quickly formed in Rio in 1880, one centered around José do Patrocinio and Nicoláo Moreira and the Associação Central Emancipadora, another around José Ferreira de Menezes and the *Gazeta da Tarde,* and the third about the figure of Joaquim Nabuco and his Brazilian Anti-Slavery Society.

Though it published the monthly *O Abolicionista,* Nabuco's wing of the movement was less directed toward the Brazilian populace, held public meetings less frequently because of a lack of funds, and never acquired a powerful and popular daily paper like the *Gazeta da Tarde.* Short of finances but possessing great prestige and personal magnetism, Nabuco directed his efforts at the legislature during the periods when he held a seat in the Chamber, toward raising support in the intellectual centers of Europe, and even eventually toward enlisting the aid of the Pope and a laggard Church on the side of the abolitionist cause.[1] Nabuco's greatest single piece of propaganda, *O Abolicionismo,* written during a prolonged stay in Europe and published in 1883, was "a book

1. For Nabuco's own account of his audience with Pope Leo XIII in 1888 and its mixed results, see *Minha formação,* pp. 191–205. For the failure of the Catholic Church to take a significant anti-slavery stand, see Toplin, "The Movement," pp. 89–92.

of tranquil disputation," in the words of the more demagogic *Gazeta da Tarde,* a book to be studied as a civic duty.[2]

Descended on his father's side from a political family which since the 1820's had constantly supplied representatives to the national legislature, and on his mother's side from old and powerful planter families of Pernambuco, Nabuco possessed useful advantages. Despite his lineage, this descendant of slaveowners was hardly less revolutionary than his associates, the descendants of slaves: Ferreira de Menezes, André Rebouças, Luiz Gama, and José do Patrocinio. Under his father's influence, Nabuco had joined the struggle in his youth, translating abolitionist articles from English into Portuguese, serving as lawyer for a young Negro assassin in a legal battle directed against both slavery and capital punishment,[3] writing an inspired abolitionist treatise when still a student at the Law Faculty in Recife, aiding his father on the staff of the Liberal *A Reforma.* Nabuco's democratic blaze was dimmed after the victory of abolitionism, but while the struggle lasted he championed more than freedom for the blacks. Like Rebouças, Patrocinio, and other abolitionists, as will be seen, he fought for broader reforms intended to transform Brazil into a democratic nation. Brilliant, possessing unusual oratorical gifts, socially well-placed, trained in law, "tall, well-proportioned, the head and the face possessing a purity of sculptural line, magnificent eyes, an expression at once gentle and virile, a noble blend of force and grace" —this was the oversized hero who aroused the fear of the slaveholders and landlords.[4]

José do Patrocinio's background was very different, but, like Nabuco, he was influenced by a talented father. The son of a slaveowning priest and fazendeiro, Father João Carlos Monteiro,[5] and a black fruit vendor, Justina Maria do Espírito Santo, Patrocinio was born in 1853 in his father's home in Campos dos Goitacazes in the sugar-growing region of eastern Rio de Janeiro province. Brought up in the vicarage of Campos and on a nearby fazenda, he left his parental home while still a boy in 1868 to serve an apprenticeship in the Misericordia Hospital in Rio de Janeiro, finally entering the Faculty of Medicine as a pharmacy student. Completing the course but lacking money to establish himself in his pro-

2. *Gazeta da Tarde,* September 25, 1883.
3. "A Escravidão," pp. 40–42; Nabuco, *The Life of Joaquim Nabuco,* pp. 19 ff.
4. The words were those of Affonso Celso, Jr., quoted by Duque-Estrada, *A abolição,* p. 281. *El Demócrata* of Madrid said of the visiting Nabuco in 1881: "His eloquence is enhanced by natural gifts. A commanding figure, a sympathetic expression, a good voice, and the freshness of youth, enable him at once to claim the attention of all his hearers, whilst he describes the condition of slavery with all the enthusiasm of a philanthropist and the calmness of a statesman." Quoted by *Rio News,* April 5, 1881.
5. For a biographical sketch of Patrocinio's father, see Moraes, *A campanha abolicionista,* pp. 377–382.

fession, Patrocinio was saved from destitution by an opportunity to tutor the children of a wealthy owner of lands and buildings, one Captain Sena, and eventually married one of the captain's daughters.[6]

Patrocinio joined the staff of Ferreira de Araújo's *Gazeta de Noticias* in 1877 on the strength of his poetic skill and was associated with that paper during the period when it was the pioneer voice of abolitionism. Already famous at twenty-eight, he left that paper in 1881 in protest against its increasingly conservative views,[7] but quickly acquired a paper of his own as a gift from his father-in-law, Captain Sena. This was the *Gazeta da Tarde,* the Rio daily which under the direction of Ferreira de Menezes had become the most uncompromising and effective abolitionist paper in the city, practically the only abolitionist paper at the time of its editor's death in 1881.

No one was better qualified than Patrocinio to take charge of the *Gazeta da Tarde* after the death of Ferreira de Menezes. A fiery and effective speaker at abolitionist meetings, the author of thousands of words on the slavery question, Patrocinio possessed the reputation of an uncompromising reformist. Influenced by the writings of Pierre Proudhon, he had adopted the battle cry: "Slavery is theft!" and continued to act until 1888 as though he truly believed the aphorism. With bulging eyes, sparse beard and moustache, corpulent face and body, unruly brown hair, and skin described as the color of a ripe Havana cigar, Patrocinio, in the words of Nabuco, was "the expression of his epoch." [8] Emotional, highstrung, theatrical, romantic, he reached his audiences, both in public and through the press, with a raucous wit and powerful emotional appeals. "It was emotion which inspired him to great performances," wrote Carolina Nabuco, "such as throwing himself, sobbing, at the feet of the Imperial Princess in an irresistible impulse of gratitude. He did not deliver his speeches. He acted them out with extraordinary power, but they possessed a communicative ardor and a vibrant spontaneity which hid his exaggerated dramatics . . . ." [9]

6. See Patrocinio's own summary of his life in *Gazeta da Tarde,* May 29, 1884, reproduced in Moraes, *A campanha abolicionista,* pp. 361–363. For a fuller account of Patrocinio's life during these years, see Osvaldo Orico, *O tigre da abolição* (Rio de Janeiro, 1956), pp. 21–73.
7. See *Gazeta da Tarde,* August 25, 1881.
8. Moraes, *A campanha abolicionista,* p. 382; Nabuco, *Minha formação,* pp. 178–179.
9. *The Life of Joaquim Nabuco,* p. 382. Performing best before an audience, Patrocinio could also display a sardonic humor in his writing. Confronted at the height of his career by an anonymous unstamped letter addressed aggressively to "the overseer of the plantation of the Simple-minded, the black man and day laborer (*jornaleiro* instead of *jornalista*), José do Patrocinio," he admitted in his column, "Semana Politica," the right of the anonymous correspondent to call him black, white, "or anything that comes to his head." Patrocinio complained, how-

José do Patrocinio and Ferreira de Menezes were not the only descendants of slaves who emerged as leaders. One of the most admirable of them was André Rebouças, a thin, dark, soberly dressed engineer and teacher of botany, calculus, and geometry at the Polytechnical School, writer and learned analyst of the nation's economic and social problems.[10] Lacking oratorical gifts or the will to speak in public, Rebouças was effective through the press or in conversations with the powerful men of his time, with Nabuco, Senator Dantas, Taunay the novelist and immigrationist, Patrocinio, and particularly the Emperor and his daughter Princess Isabel.[11] Rebouças was a contributor to the *Gazeta da Tarde,* a co-founder of the Brazilian Anti-Slavery Society, and co-author with Patrocinio of the strongly-worded Manifesto of the Abolitionist Confederation of 1883. A constant participant in the struggle, an organizer of clubs and associations, a financial contributor, and a "propagandist everywhere," [12] Rebouças did not rest when the slaves were freed. With that achievement in the past, he feared the resurgence of reaction, and so used his reputation and influence in support of Brazilian Rural Democracy, the continuation of the abolitionist revolution to its "logical conclusion." [13] "Rebouças incarnated like no other one of us," wrote Nabuco years later, "the anti-slavery spirit: the entire spirit, systematic, absolute. . . ." [14]

At least one of the major abolitionists had known the experience of illegal enslavement. This was Luiz Gama, a man with a background even more bizarre than Patrocinio's. Gama's father was a member of a wealthy Portuguese family of Bahia, fond of horses, hunting, and fishing. His mother was a free, rebellious African woman from the Mina Coast, the pretty "pagan" Luiza Mahen, a vegetable peddler, like Patrocinio's mother, who was accused of involvement in a revolutionary plot in Bahia and exiled in 1837 allegedly to Rio, though perhaps her true destination was west Africa.

Gama was born free in 1830, but three years after his mother's disappearance his father sold him into slavery as a result of sudden impoverishment. Shipped to Rio and later to Santos, the port of São Paulo, Gama ascended the steep Serra do Mar, barefoot and hungry, accom-

---

ever, of the financial extortion represented by the cost of postage, which he had paid. "I am a black man, but no longer a slave. I am free, and, as such, I am not obliged to work for the fantasies of the anonymous gentleman." *Gazeta da Tarde,* September 27, 1884.

10. Verissimo, *André Rebouças,* p. 82; Rebouças, *Agricultura nacional.*

11. See his *Diário e notas.*

12. André Rebouças, "Abolição da Miseria," *Revista de Engenharia,* Rio de Janeiro, November 28, 1888; Verissimo, *André Rebouças,* pp. 192–193, 200–203.

13. *Ibid.,* pp. 209–211.

14. Nabuco, *Minha formação,* pp. 172–173.

panied by a hundred others like him. He was employed as a servant in São Paulo, where he learned to read with the help of a student; but he soon fled his master's home, conscious of the illegality of his enslavement as the son of a free woman.[15] Gama subsequently spent six years in the militia, but in 1854 was again in São Paulo city, where he worked as a secretary and was soon making a career as a journalist, poet, satirist, lawyer, and early abolitionist along with the dynamic students of the Law Academy, Rui Barbosa, Castro Alves, and Joaquim Nabuco.[16] As a lawyer, Gama's specialty was the liberation of persons held, as he had been, in illegal slavery, particularly Africans kept as slaves in violation of the law of November 7, 1831. By 1880, not long before his death, the former slave, by then the unchallenged leader of the anti-slavery movement in São Paulo, was said to have aided the liberation of more than a thousand persons, and was still applying his talents in the provincial courts to establish the principle that every African under sixty-two was free.[17]

Other abolitionists who rose to national fame included the Paulista, Antônio Bento, a well-born rebel and man of God who created "a religious order under the invocation of Nossa Senhora dos Remedios, and made the cult a medium of abolitionist propaganda." [18] Editor of *A Redempção,* a rough-hewn abolitionist paper of São Paulo, Bento was the leader of the radical "caiphazes," activists unsatisfied with the results of propaganda, who in 1886 and 1887 went to the plantations to uproot slavery in its strongholds and bring the system abruptly down.[19]

The abolitionists included the leaders of religious Positivism, Miguel Lemos and R. Teixeira Mendes, who argued the cause in pamphlets and letters, influencing a select but powerful few.[20] They included Rui Barbosa, active as a student in 1869 and emerging again in 1884 as one of the most dynamic and effective leaders in the press, in the General Assembly, and before the public. A small, thin man with a dark moustache and a weak chin—inoffensive in appearance—Barbosa could be a dynamo at an abolitionist conference, able to bring an audience to tears or laughter with the turn of a phrase.

15. See the obituary of Luiz Gama in the *Gazeta da Tarde,* August 25, 1882.
16. Morse, *From Community to Metropolis,* pp. 146–147.
17. *Gazeta da Tarde,* December 15, 1880; Antonio Manoel Bueno de Andrada, "A abolição em São Paulo," *Revista do Arquivo Municipal,* LXXVII (June–July, 1941), 262–265.
18. *Cidade do Rio,* Rio de Janeiro, February 17, 1888.
19. Viotti da Costa, *Da senzala à colônia,* pp. 429–431.
20. See Lemos, *O Pozitivismo e a escravidão moderna;* Miguel Lemos and R. Teixeira Mendes, *A liberdade espiritual e a organização do trabalho. Considerações historico-filosoficas sobre o movimento abolicionista* (2nd ed.; Rio de Janeiro, 1902). See also João Cruz Costa, *A History of Ideas in Brazil* (Berkeley and Los Angeles, 1964), pp. 105–107.

The leaders of the movement in the Rio area included João Clapp, a descendant of North Americans—merchant and owner of Clapp & Filhos, a china shop on the Rua dos Ourives specializing in fine porcelain, crystal, and tea sets. A constant participant in meetings and a co-founder of the Abolitionist Confederation in 1883, Clapp was also the director and one of the instructors at a night school in Niterói maintained by the Freedmen's Club of that city for the education of newly liberated slaves.[21]

The number of abolitionists in parliament was to increase over the years, but in 1880 there were already at least a dozen in the Chamber of Deputies who sympathized and several more in the Senate. Those in the Chamber included José Mariano, editor of *A Provincia,* an anti-slavery paper established in Pernambuco in 1872, and principal leader of the movement in Recife in the 1880's; Joaquim Serra, journalist and writer from Maranhão who had worked with the Nabucos on *A Reforma* in 1869, and was to become one of the most prolific of anti-slavery writers.[22] They included Joaquim Saldanha Marinho of Amazonas, Grand Master of the Masonic Order, a leading Republican as early as 1870 and political activist after the fall of the Empire;[23] Marcolino de Moura of Bahia, author of fiery anti-slavery speeches in the Chamber in 1880; and Jeronymo Sodré of the same province, the man who allegedly initiated the abolitionist decade with his denunciation of the Rio Branco Law in March 1879.

THE AIMS OF ABOLITIONISM

The goals of the movement's major leaders were broader in scope than those adopted gradually during the 1880's by a large part of the informed Brazilian public. The "abolitionism" of the majority, particularly those who were converted during the culminating years of the struggle, was generally limited to an acceptance of the need for liberation and an expectation that an end to slavery would bring some immediate benefits to the entire nation. Abolition, it was thought, aside from releasing hundreds of thousands of persons from an unjust bondage, would stimulate European immigration, advance industry and agriculture, and elevate the nation's moral character, so long corrupted by the evil influences of servile black dependents. Slavery, according to this view, as-

21. For an advertisement of the shop's merchandise, see *Novidades,* Rio de Janeiro, March 17, 1887. For Clapp's abolitionist activities, see *Gazeta da Tarde,* April 17, 1883.
22. Nabuco, *Minha formação,* p. 177.
23. See George C. A. Boehrer, *Da monarchia à republica* (Rio de Janeiro, n.d.), p. 172; Rio Branco, *Efemérides brasileiras,* p. 183; José Maria Bello, *A History of Modern Brazil, 1889–1964* (Stanford, California, 1966), pp. 35–36, 77.

siduously propagated by the abolitionist press, was irrational and evil, a survival of Portuguese colonialism, unpatriotic, an obstacle to national self-respect, rejected by the international community, incompatible with natural law and natural rights.

Most Brazilians, however, even sincere idealists whose anti-slavery convictions were strongly held, probably gave little thought to the kind of society that was to exist after slavery was defeated. The need to pursue new reforms or to prepare ex-slaves for citizenship was perhaps not self-evident in a society where former bondsmen were expected to remain at work on the masters' lands, where education had always been reserved for the few, and even the Constitution restricted political participation to a small minority. In such an environment it would be unreasonable to expect a widespread adoption of goals intended to create an egalitarian system. Abolition, in fact, was a "white" revolution, to use Octavio Ianni's term, a political movement not intended by most of its adherents to transform slaves into citizens, but limited to the replacement of slavery by a free-labor system.[24]

For at least a limited few, however, the ideology of abolitionism encompassed much more than the emancipation of the slaves. Most of the more prominent leaders identified their cause with a broad range of reformist goals, which taken together were nothing short of revolutionary. Emancipation alone, abolitionists argued on many occasions, would not solve the nation's problems.[25] Abolition would take precedence over other reforms, as Nabuco put it, but other social changes would have to be attempted once this fundamental step had been taken. Slavery meant more than the relationship between the master and his human property, Nabuco wrote in *O Abolicionismo*. "Slavery" was "the sum of the power, influence, capital, and patronage of all the masters; the feudalism established in the interior, the dependence of commerce, religion, the poor, industry, parliament, the Crown, and . . . the State" upon the aristocratic slaveholding minority. The goals of abolitionism were not limited to the liberation of the slaves. Abolitionism, rather, was to be a continuing struggle against the power of the landlord class and all the harmful effects, "demoralization, inertia, servilism, and irresponsibility," of three centuries of slavery. "The task of annulling those influences," wrote Nabuco, "is certainly beyond the ability of one generation, but as long as this work has not been concluded, Abolitionism will have a reason to exist. . . . The struggle between Abolitionism and Slavery is of today," he warned, "but it will be greatly prolonged. . . ."[26]

24. Ianni, *As metamorfoses do escravo*, p. 235; Bastide and Fernandes, *Brancos e negros*, pp. 133–136.
25. See Lemos, *O Pozitivismo e a escravidão moderna*, p. 28.
26. *O Abolicionismo*, pp. vii, 4–7.

Nabuco outlined the broader aims of the movement in the preface to this same work. Written in 1883 during a prolonged residence in London, *O Abolicionismo* was intended to be the first of a series of studies to promote a group of related causes: the abolition of slavery, administrative decentralization, religious equality, broader political representation, European immigration, improved foreign relations, and economic and financial reforms.[27] Radical abolitionists like Nabuco, André Rebouças, José do Patrocinio, Antônio Bento, Rui Barbosa, Senator Dantas, and others hoped that extension of education to all classes, mass political participation, and a broadening of economic opportunities for millions of blacks and mulattoes and other underprivileged segments of Brazilian society would enable these groups to assume a place of equality in a homogeneous and more prosperous nation.[28] That this did not occur was not the fault of the leaders of abolitionism, who refused to disband the Abolitionist Confederation after its major goal had been achieved in 1888 but maintained the organization as a center for the promotion of new reforms. It was the result, rather, of a powerful reaction of the former slaveholders in the months just after abolition, of the scattering of the radical reform movement after the fall of the Empire in 1889, and of the reconsolidation in ensuing years of traditional arrangements and the retention of much of the spirit and organization of the old regime.

Often, however, during the years of agitation the abolitionists called for the advancement and democratization of their country, and education was high on the list of needs. "To emancipate and to instruct," wrote Tavares Bastos in 1870 in an appeal for popular education, "are two intimately linked tasks." [29] André Rebouças longed for the day when there would not be a single village in all Brazil without a school. It was indispensable, he argued, "to teach every Brazilian citizen to read and write and to give him a profession." [30] Nabuco's first antislavery bill of 1880 contained a provision for the establishment of primary classes in all the towns and cities of the Empire for the education of slaves.[31] Rui Barbosa wrote a massive study of Brazilian primary education, *Reforma do ensino primário,* published in 1883, which condemned the low level of Brazilian learning, called for the creation of

27. *Ibid.,* p. vii. The last two issues Nabuco hoped to deal with himself, but he asked Sancho de Barros Pimentel, a former deputy from Sergipe and president of Ceará, to write one of the works on political reform; he hoped that Rui Barbosa would do the book on religious liberty and that Rodolfo Dantas would author a work on education. See Nabuco, *Cartas a amigos,* I, 103–104.
28. Fernandes, *The Negro,* pp. 41, 44; Nabuco, *O Abolicionismo,* pp. 19, 204.
29. Tavares Bastos, *A Provincia,* pp. 256–261.
30. Rebouças, *Agricultura nacional,* pp. 300, 375.
31. *O Abolicionista,* January 1, February 1, 1881

a Ministry of Public Education, compulsory school attendance, and a system of public instruction independent of the Catholic Church.[32] Even after the abolition of slavery, the reformist wing of the Liberal Party and the last cabinet of the Empire, still under the spell of abolitionist fervor, aspired to create a free and improved educational system, to extend the ballot, to establish provincial autonomy and freedom of worship, and even to promote legislation which would facilitate the acquisition of land, a program which encompassed most of the reforms Nabuco mentioned in the preface to *O Abolicionismo.*[33]

Aside from an end to slavery, the cause that the abolitionists probably supported most enthusiastically, particularly after May 13, 1888, was "the democratization of the soil." This slogan implied the dismantling of large agricultural estates and the creation of small farms where immigrants, poor Brazilians, and freedmen could find some economic and social independence and prosperity. That this idea would emerge in Brazil was inevitable, given the reality of the traditional landholding system, and, in fact, calls for agrarian reform were heard long before the 1880's.[34]

In his remarkable "Memoir on the Slave Trade" of 1823, José Bonifacio de Andrada e Silva had proposed that all free men of color without a means of acquiring their livelihood receive from the state "a small grant of land for cultivation" as well as government aid in establishing themselves on those properties.[35] The great landed estate, wrote A. P. Figueiredo of Pernambuco in 1847, was a barrier to prosperity, to immigration, to the emergence of a middle class, and to the functioning of constitutional government in his province; he recommended a tax on land to encourage its distribution to an impoverished and expanding population.[36] In 1861 Tavares Bastos published *Evils of the Present and Hopes of the Future,* in which he proposed a whole series of re-

32. See Rui Barbosa, *Reforma do ensino primario: Parecer e projeto* (Rio de Janeiro, 1883); Barbosa, *Obras Completas,* Vol. X; Evanson, "The Liberal Party," pp. 207–211.

33. *Annaes da Câmara* (1889), I, 142. In "The Role of the Planters in the Fall of the Brazilian Empire," a paper delivered at a session of the American Historical Association meeting of 1967, I suggested that fear of an abolitionist-inspired land reform, which was included in the Liberal Party program of 1889 and in the program of the Ouro Preto government, was among the causes of the fall of the Empire in 1889. Recently Richard Graham has advanced the same theory. See his "Landowners and the Overthrow of the Empire," pp. 47–56.

34. José Arthur Rios, "The Development of Interest in Agrarian Reform in Brazil," in T. Lynn Smith (ed.), *Agrarian Reform in Latin America* (New York, 1967), pp. 95–99. On the land system in Brazil, see Smith, *Brazil,* pp. 257–356.

35. Andrada e Silva, "Representação," pp. 53–54, 58.

36. A. P. Figueiredo, "The Need for Agrarian Reform in Brazil (1847)," in Smith, *Agrarian Reform,* pp. 67–72.

forms that abolitionists and Liberals adopted as their own in the 1880's.[37] In 1866 the same deputy from Alagôas introduced legislation into the Chamber to liberate slaves belonging to the Brazilian government and to grant them land, equipment, and cattle, and in 1870 he called for a tax on estates to promote popular education and the sale and distribution of unused lands. "Only the rural property tax and previous expropriation of uncultivated areas along future railroad routes," he wrote, "can resolve the enormous difficulty which was bequeathed to us by the improvident land-grant policy." [38]

During the abolitionist years, land reform was often and urgently proposed. Even before abolitionism André Rebouças wrote a series of articles to advance the cause of "rural democracy." Under Rebouças' plan, landowners would sell or rent plots of land of twenty hectares (nearly fifty acres) to freedmen, immigrants, and farmers, keeping the core of their properties as the location of a mill or a processing plant. Traditional export crops would continue to be grown on the smaller plots, and, once harvested, would be turned over for a good price to the former landowners, now rural industrialists, whose factories in the field would prepare crops for final consumption. Before export, coffee, sugar, cotton, tobacco, and cacao would be processed into coffee extract or powder, refined sugar, textiles, cigars, cigarettes, and chocolate, thus assuring a maximum profit to Brazilian farmers and manufacturers. Each *engenho central,* according to this plan, was to have its own school, where children would receive technical and industrial education. Each independent property was to be large enough to permit crop rotation and to provide pastures and forests.[39]

Resembling the modern *usinas,* or sugar factories, established in sugar-producing regions of Brazil after the abolition of slavery, Rebouças' *engenhos centrais* would have differed greatly from the modern Brazilian plantations in both purpose and organization. According to his plan, there was to be a division of land into small plots instead of the consolidation of family-owned sugar *fazendas* into gigantic corporate-controlled plantations. Rebouças foresaw independent and industrious farmers, in control of the land, instead of the hired hands, sharecroppers, squatters, migrant workers, and tenants now employed or subsisting on large estates.[40]

37. A. C. Tavares Bastos, *Os males do presente e as esperanças do futuro* (São Paulo, 1939), pp. 25–53. See also his "Memoria sobre immigração" of 1867, *ibid.,* pp. 55–127, in which he argued the advantages of abolition, political decentralization, an improved legal system, better communication routes, religious equality, and "subdivision of the large property."

38. Godoy, *O elemento servil,* p. 479; Tavares Bastos, *A Provincia,* pp. 327–332.

39. Rebouças, *Agricultura nacional,* pp. 1–7, 111–112, 120, 367–368.

40. Smith, *Brazil,* pp. 345–351.

Rebouças' plan for "rural democracy" was supported before 1880 by at least one other writer. Viscount Beaurepaire Rohan, a friend and associate of Rebouças, wrote in 1878 in a report presented to the Ministry of Agriculture that "the division of the great territorial property is indeed indispensable to the development of our agriculture, and even more when slavery is completely extinct." The solution to the problems of agriculture, he wrote, lay in the establishment of "central factories" on lands retained by estate owners after the division of the greater part of their lands into small properties. The central area would serve as a processing center and as a population nucleus, with a school, a church, shops, "and everything else which can make comfortable the lives of the farmers." [41]

With the beginning of the abolitionist era, land reform was often called for in the press and even at public meetings.[42] Nabuco's slavery reform bill of 1880 included a provision to set aside land for freedmen's colonies, and the first issue of his anti-slavery monthly, *O Abolicionista,* denounced the latifundia. In December 1880, the *Gazeta da Tarde* published a series of unsigned articles written by André Rebouças which denounced "latifundia, feudal barons, landlords, and Landocracia," and demanded the establishment of "rural democracy," central mills, and small agricultural properties. The Rebouças articles demanded the liberation of one and a half million "brothers," a distribution of land to ex-slaves, a land tax, and laws to encourage the sale and subdivision of "the enormous territorial properties of the nefarious landocratic barons of this Empire." [43]

As the abolitionist decade proceeded, reform of the land system continued to be associated with the liberation movement. The abolitionist society re-founded at the Escola Polytechnica in Rio in 1883, where André Rebouças was employed as a teacher, called for a tax on uncultivated lands located within twenty kilometers of lines of communication, evidently intended to hasten the sale and distribution of large estates.[44] The Dantas Project of 1884, a major reform bill intended to free slaves who had reached the age of sixty, stipulated that freedmen would eventually become owners of the land they worked.[45] In the same year, in an appeal to voters in Recife, Nabuco associated the establishment of the small property with the goals of abolitionism. That move-

41. Beaurepaire Rohan, *O futuro da grande lavoura,* pp. 10–11.
42. *Gazeta da Tarde,* September 6, 1880; *Associação Central Emancipadora. Boletin N. 2, 28 de Outubro de 1880.*
43. *O Abolicionista,* November 1, 1880; Rebouças *Diário e notas,* pp. 291–292; *Gazeta da Tarde,* December 3, 4, 7, 8, 9, 10, 11, 1880.
44. *Rio News,* August 15, 1887. For another call for "the small farm, the democratic farm," see *O Cruzeiro,* March 15, 1883.
45. *Obras Completas de Rui Barbosa,* Vol. XI, Tome I, pp. 300–301.

ment, said Nabuco, signaled "the beginning of property for the small farmer." The abolitionists, he claimed, were struggling to give the rural poor "an honest independence and a few fathoms of land which they can cultivate as their own, protected by laws executed by an independent magistracy, in which they may have a redoubt as impregnable for the honor of their daughters and the dignity of their character as any *senhor de engenho.*" There was "no other possible solution for the chronic and profound ills of the people," he told the electorate of Recife, "than an agrarian law to establish the small property." The solution to Brazilian poverty, he believed, was "the democratization of the soil." [46]

The same phrase—democratization of the soil—was to be heard again in the months just after abolition, as leading Liberals and abolitionists promoted this new reform as "the logical consequence" of the law of May 13, 1888. Only two months after abolition, the Conservative senator, Leão Veloso, charged that abolitionists were repeatedly expressing the view that it was "necessary to end territorial feudalism to establish agricultural democracy," and in the same debate Senator Dantas declared that small landholding would come "through the natural order of things." [47] Dantas, in fact, worked actively for agrarian reform in the months just after abolition, both as a leader of the Liberal Party and a member of the Senate.

At a meeting of the Abolitionist Confederation in August 1888, Dantas outlined the Liberal Party program of the future, which was to include, among other reforms, the division of the large estates. Only a month later the same senator spoke again in the upper chamber of the need to provide land for colonists near transportation facilities, and of breaking up the large estates.[48] Even the Emperor, much influenced by Rebouças and other members of the Abolitionist Confederation[49] and perhaps by the writings of Tavares Bastos, favored a reform of the landholding system as a means of attracting European immigrants.[50] Acclaimed the Patriarch of the Abolitionist Family in celebrations held in Petrópolis and Rio on the first anniversary of the abolition of slavery,[51] the Emperor chose to commit himself and his heiress, Princess Isabel,

46. Nabuco, *Campanha abolicionista no Recife,* pp. 10, 48–49; Viotti da Costa, *Da senzala à colônia,* p. 433. For another of Nabuco's statements on the land question, see his *Henry George, Nacionalização do solo* (Rio de Janeiro, 1884), pp. 5–10.
47. *Annaes do Senado* (1888), III, 188–189.
48. *Rio News,* September 5, 1888; *Annaes do Senado* (1888), V, 226–227.
49. Rebouças, *Diário e notas,* pp. 328–329.
50. *Annaes da Câmara* (1889), I, 16.
51. Rebouças, *Diário e notas,* p. 335. Rebouças, who sailed with the Emperor into exile after the fall of the Empire, later addressed Pedro as "the sublime Martyr of Abolition." See Nabuco, *Minha formação,* pp. 173–175.

. A slave market on Valongo Street, Rio de Janeiro.

The return to town of a rural proprietor.

3. A shoemaker's shop.

4. The iron collar, punishment for runaways.

Negro carriers.

Slaves moving a cart used for transporting heavy loads.

7. A small sugar-cane press in a shop in Rio de Janeiro.

8. Slaves sawing boards near Rio de Janeiro.

A shackled slave gang stopping at a tobacco shop.

A public whipping, a daily occurrence at the Praça de Sant'Anna in Rio de Janeiro.

11. Slaves in the stocks, a form of punishment used most often on rural plantations.

12. Overseers punishing slaves on a rural estate.

13. *Above, left.* The Emperor Pedro II, whose long reign was plagued by the slavery issue.

14. *Above, right.* José da Silva Paranhos (the Viscount Rio Branco), Conservative senator from Bahia, editor and diplomat, head of the cabinet which in 1871 sponsored the free birth law.

15. *Left.* Luiz Gama, who spent some of his childhood years in illegal slavery, became a poet, journalist, and lawyer in later years, and acted as legal advocate for hundreds of Africans held in bondage in violation of the law of November 7, 1831.

16. *Above, left.* Joaquim Nabuco, scion of a powerful northeastern political family, brilliant writer and orator, one of the most effective opponents of slavery; "a noble blend of force and grace...."

17. *Above.* José Ferreira de Menezes, journalist, founder of the *Gazeta da Tarde*, and outspoken abolitionist until his sudden death in June 1881.

18. *Left.* José do Patrocinio, son of a white fazendeiro and a black fruit vendor, was a fiery speaker at public meetings, owner and editor of the most effective abolitionist newspapers of Rio de Janeiro; author of thousands of words on the slavery issue, he was regarded as the leader of the Brazilian abolitionist movement.

Above. André Rebouças, teacher, economist, engineer, essayist, friend of the powerful; unwavering reformist, prophet of "Brazilian Rural Democracy."

Above, right. Rui Barbosa devoted his extraordinary talents to the abolitionist movement in the press, on the public podium, and in the Chamber of Deputies.

Right. José Mariano, a leader of the antislavery movement in Pernambuco, edited the abolitionist journal, *A Provincia,* of Recife, and represented his province in the Chamber of Deputies from 1878 to 1886.

22. *Above, left.* João Mauricio Wanderley (the Baron Cotegipe), Bahian sugar planter, opponent of the inter-provincial slave trade in 1854, head of the Conservative government which passed the revised sexagenarian law in 1885; an enemy of the abolitionist cause until the end of his long life.

23. *Above.* Antônio da Silva Prado. A coffee planter, banker, publisher, and Conservative politician from São Paulo, his late conversion to the anti-slavery movement was a key event in the collapse of slavery.

24. *Left.* Princess Isabel, the Redeemer. In 1871 the heiress to the Brazilian throne signed the Rio Branco Law, freeing the newborn, and in 1888 she sanctioned the bill which abolished slavery. On November 15, 1889, she was deprived of her succession by the uprising which created the First Republic. "'Senhor Rebouças,' said the Imperial Princess on board the *Alagôas*, which carried them together into exile, 'if there were still slaves in Brazil we would return to liberate them.'"

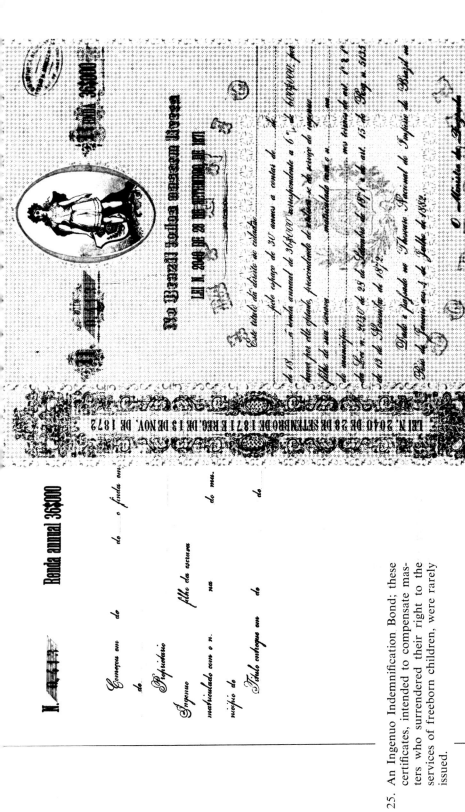

25. An Ingenuo Indemnification Bond; these certificates, intended to compensate masters who surrendered their right to the services of freeborn children, were rarely issued.

26. Francisco do Nascimento as portrayed by Angelo Agostini on the cover of the *Revista Illustrada*. "At the head of the jangadeiros of Ceará, Nascimento blocks the traffic in slaves sold to the south· from the province of Ceará."

to the continuing reform movement, and thus probably hastened his fall from power.

The abolitionists, then, promoted collateral reforms after May 13, 1888, but until that date their principal goal was to put an end to slavery. In the beginning and for several years they tried to achieve this basic goal by legal and peaceful methods—by propaganda and legislative action—and they continued to use these methods until their cause was victorious. Having failed by 1885, however, to win satisfactory concessions by these methods alone, and disappointed with the solutions which the planters and the parliament found acceptable, they turned as well to illegal methods, apparently reasoning that if masters could not be persuaded to give up their slaves, slaves could perhaps be urged to leave their masters. Illegal abolitionism—the incitement of slaves to abandon plantations for pre-arranged places of refuge—was not attempted on a large scale, however, until after the resistance to legal abolitionism had created enough anger and frustration to drive men to these more dangerous methods.

THE PRO-SLAVERY REACTION

The first abolitionist wave which struck Rio receded early in 1881. Yet during the first brief phase of the movement the slave masters and their representatives in parliament and in the press responded strongly in defense of threatened interests. The reaction, in fact, appeared to command the loyalty of most of the population, the result, in Nabuco's opinion, of the complicity of the commercial sectors and the slaveholders' monopoly over labor, land, capital, the law enforcement agencies, and dependent educated classes.[52]

The Liberal ministry of the Bahian senator, José Antônio Saraiva, committed to electoral reform and a balanced budget, led the defense of the status quo, brandishing the free vote in one hand, in the words of a critic, and the lash of slavery in the other.[53] As early as August, the Minister of Agriculture in the Saraiva government set forth its position with arguments that were used by defenders of slavery in ensuing years. All Brazilians were emancipators, according to this logic. No Brazilians enjoyed owning slaves, and only necessity forced them to do so. Like every Brazilian, the government desired to see an end to slavery, but for economic and social reasons would promote that goal only by means of the Rio Branco Law: the peculio, manumissions, and "the action of death." Accelerating rapidly, these processes would eliminate

52. *O Abolicionista,* January 1, 1881.
53. *Gazeta da Tarde,* August 26, 1880.

slavery in twenty years, peacefully, safely, and unobstructed by government interference.[54]

With the ministry thus committed to permanent inaction on the slavery question, part of the press began a campaign of slander directed against the principal leaders of the abolitionist movement.[55] Manoel Peixoto de Lacerda Werneck of Rio de Janeiro, soon to represent his province in the Chamber, responded to Nabuco's emancipationist bill with a series of articles in the *Jornal do Commercio,* accusing the "naturally ambitious" young Pernambucan of a desire to aggrandize himself "before the ephemeral judgement of the multitudes." [56] According to *O Corsario* of Rio de Janeiro, Nabuco had chosen abolitionism as a means of gaining recognition in foreign countries after suffering personal and political disappointments, including his failure to marry a wealthy woman.[57] *O Paiz* of Maranhão referred to Nabuco as a man "without the authority of good sense, . . . without the sound conscience of the patriot." Nabuco, it hypothesized, "declaims against slavery through a lust for glory, for vanity alone, . . . more to be applauded abroad than because of a true love of liberty." [58] As Nabuco himself later observed, "slavery tried by every means to identify itself with the nation, and in the imagination of many people it succeeded. To attack the black flag is to insult the national. To denounce the regime of the slave huts is to defame all Brazil." [59]

In December 1880, the Republican daily, *A Provincia de São Paulo,* denounced the *Gazeta da Tarde* as "that sheet which fortunately only appears here brought from the capital as a curiosity," while it ridiculed José do Patrocinio as "that orator . . . who supposes himself placed in a superior atmosphere, beyond the reach of the mortals of this country, the most brilliant reformer of absolutely everything, the omniscient, the all-seeing, the wise, the celebrated and fêted orator [who] would

54. *Ibid.,* August 16, 1880.

55. *Ibid.,* September 18, 1880.

56. Manoel Peixoto de Lacerda Werneck, *Questão grave. Artigos a proposito do annunciado projecto do Sr. Deputado Joaquim Nabuco, fixando prazo fatal á existencia do elemento servil, publicados no Jornal do Commercio* (Rio de Janeiro, 1880), p. 5.

57. *O Corsario,* Rio de Janeiro, October 2, December 4, 1880.

58. *O Paiz,* January 28, 1881.

59. Nabuco, *O Abolicionismo,* p. 248. Nabuco was often accused of lack of patriotism and of close ties with foreign interests or with the emancipationist Emperor. After returning from Europe in 1884, he was accused of making a reputation for himself in Europe at the cost of his country and of being the *enfant gaté* (spoiled child) of imperial policies. See *Manual do subdito fiel ou cartas de um lavrador á sua magestade o imperador sobre a questão do elemento servil* (Rio de Janeiro, 1884), p. 51.

cause all the illustrious men of this nation to bow before his genius." [60]
An apparent attack upon Patrocinio's racial origins was commented
upon in a letter from Luiz Gama published two days later in the *Gazeta
da Tarde*. "In us even color is a defect," commented Gama, "an un-
pardonable vice of origin, the stigma of a crime." But the critics forgot
"that this color is the origin of the wealth of thousands of thieves who
insult us; that this conventional color of slavery, . . . so like that of
the earth, hides volcanoes under its dark surface, where the sacred fire
of freedom burns." [61]

There were angry reactions to the abolitionists in the Chamber of
Deputies. In August, Martinho Campos of Minas Gerais, one of the
most ardent of the parliamentary rearguard, declared himself a slavocrat
in the interest of his slaves. [62] In November, cheered and complimented
by a host of colleagues, Campos demanded respect for law and order,
denounced the "socialists" and "modern reformers" who were sub-
verting the world, and deplored their alleged exaggerations, falsehoods,
and open calls for rebellion. "To this cry of abolition," he suggested,
"let the planters respond with revolver in hand." "To speak of the
emancipation of the slaves is not to be able to see an inch in front of
your nose," quipped Deputy Moreira de Barros on another occasion.
"Such negrophiles are playing with fire," warned the Baron of Cotegipe,
a defender of slavery until the last days of his long life. [63]

The abolitionists became the objects of harassing tactics and even of
physical abuse. Reporters of the *Gazeta da Tarde* were denied the right,
normal for members of the press, to attend the sessions of the legislature,
and issues of the *Gazeta* sent to interior subscribers via the Pedro II
Railway were unaccountably delayed en route. [64] As the crisis deepened
in the following years, as abolitionism spread into a hundred towns and
districts and even plantations were no longer secure from its influence,
the violence and harassment grew more frequent. The most common
targets of anti-abolitionist attacks were the editorial offices of reformist
newspapers, with their expensive and fragile equipment.

As in 1871, pro-slavery politicians and planters in 1880 institutional-
ized their resistance through the formation of agricultural associations,
both in the cities and in rural communities. The most important of

60. *Provincia de São Paulo,* December 1, 1880.
61. *Gazeta da Tarde,* December 3, 1880.
62. *Ibid.,* August 31, 1880. The *Gazeta da Tarde* thought he would have been
more accurate and honest if he had declared himself a slavocrat in the interest
of his creditors.
63. *Annaes da Câmara* (1880), VI, 259; *Gazeta da Tarde,* September 25, 1880.
64. *Gazeta da Tarde,* November 15, 1880; February 22, November 7, 1881; September 22, 1882; June 4, 1883; *Rio News,* June 5, 1883.

these was the Centro da Lavoura e do Commercio (Commercial and Agricultural Center), created with the announced purpose of directing the slavery question toward a calm solution.[65] *O Cruzeiro* of Rio was chosen as the press organ of the new conservative center, which described itself as "an association of planters, merchants, and representatives of allied classes intending to protect the legitimate agricultural interests of Brazil and to comply with the reform of the present labor system under the influence of the law of September 28, 1871, without an alteration of public and private security, a decline of national production, and other social disturbances." The aims of the center, according to its constitution, were to be carried out in the provinces by local clubs, while in Rio its work would be delegated to a permanent executive committee charged with promoting press propaganda, delivering petitions to government, and maintaining contacts with local clubs.[66] More effective than the Club da Lavoura of 1871, the Centro soon had regional branches in dozens of communities in the three major coffee provinces and a few more in the north, and by 1884 was sufficiently powerful to call a large meeting of provincial representatives in the capital.[67] Closely allied with the Commercial Association of Rio by common opinions and an interlocking membership, the Centro acted as a powerful pressure group dedicated to combating abolitionists and preventing further legislative steps toward freedom.[68]

Not all planter organizations were unreservedly opposed to change, though the Paulista Club da Lavoura e do Commercio of Campinas, with its extraordinary concentration of slaves (see Table 16), was regarded as a good example of the majority that were. According to abolitionists, there was a second class of agricultural clubs made up of "prudent and progressive planters" who asked only for time and the means to affect a transition to free labor. Representative of this more progressive class was the club of the município of Pindamonhangaba in São Paulo, located not in the north or west of the province but in the Paraíba Valley. In 1880 the planter club of that community announced its intention to study the practical means of bringing free workers into the region and to take other steps to prepare for the inevitable abolition of slavery.[69]

Pro-slavery arguments of 1880 were much the same as those of 1871,

65. *Gazeta da Tarde,* November 15, 1880.
66. "Bases organicas do Centro da Lavoura e do Commercio," *ibid.,* December 10, 1880.
67. Moraes, *A campanha abolicionista,* pp. 61–62.
68. *Ibid.; Associação Commercial do Rio de Janeiro. Elemento servil; 1ª representação da commissão especial nomeada, em assembléa geral extraordinaria de 2 de Maio de 1884* (Rio de Janeiro, 1884), p. 14.
69. *Gazeta da Tarde,* October 20, 1880; *O Abolicionista,* November 1, 1880.

altered only by new circumstances and a new devotion to the Rio Branco Law. Theoretically no one hoped to perpetuate slavery in Brazil, only to prolong it. No one supported slavery in theory, as Nabuco put it in 1885, but many people sustained it in practice.[70] The law of 1871, once furiously fought, had become by 1880 the untouchable charter of slavery, used even to justify the continued slave status of Africans imported after November 7, 1831.[71] The slaves were unprepared by education and experience for rapid emancipation, defenders of slavery argued. They had first to be educated, for, brutes that they were "they lack all ambition other than to free themselves from that labor which brings them nothing but exhaustion." [72] Abolition would mean lost income for the state, pro-slavery spokesmen claimed, as they had for sixty years. Agriculture was dependent upon the slave, and until a free-labor force could be recruited, further steps toward emancipation were unthinkable. Abolition would be illegal and even immoral if imposed upon planters without indemnification. Slavery was advantageous to the slave, who would be helpless if he suddenly found himself free. If abolition were suddenly decreed, the freedmen would not work, would not produce, would be consumers only and an element of social unrest. As in 1871, it was again predicted in 1880 that, once freed, the former slaves would rise up in revolt.[73]

Pro-slavery spokesmen occasionally resorted to arguments then almost taboo in Brazil—to a racism that became more fashionable after the fall of the Empire. The freedman, according to a petition of the Commercial Association, was "incompatible with any regime of economy and order, of labor and morality." [74] In Brazil, said the industrialist Felicio dos Santos in the Chamber in 1882, the Negro was an absolute necessity, despite his inferior "cerebral conformation." [75] In a pro-slavery article published in the Republican *A Provincia de São Paulo,* the Positivist philosopher, Luis Pereira Barreto, author of abstruse works on metaphysics and theology, theorized that for the Brazilian of European descent, whose predominance was founded upon "natural conditions," slavery was "a necessary evil," because "we find ourselves dislocated from the line of evolution of the most advanced part of humanity." For "the unhappy children of Africa," on the other

70. *Annaes da Câmara* (1885), II, 212.
71. See the statement of Senator Ribeiro da Luz of Minas Gerais, *Annaes do Senado* (1883), III, 19.
72. *Diario de Noticias,* Rio de Janeiro, February 4, 1882; Nabuco, *Conferência a 22 de Junho de 1884,* p. 32.
73. *Diario de Noticias,* February 5, 1882; *Brazil,* Rio de Janeiro, April 12, 1885; *Annaes da Câmara* (1882), I, 416.
74. Quoted by Nabuco, *Conferência a 22 de Junho de 1884,* pp. 30–31.
75. *Annaes da Câmara* (1882), I, 416.

hand, slavery was "incontestably a relative good," since their transportation to Brazil from Africa had guaranteed their lives and those of their offspring.[76]

Some of the more stubborn defenders of slavery were even unhappy about the Rio Branco Law. *O Diario do Brazil* not only condemned abolitionists as "ingrates" who raised their voices against the beneficent hand that fed them; it called too for effective counter-propaganda and a program of action to impede the process of emancipation as long as a free-labor system was not functioning, to demand that the law of 1871 not be executed in a manner unnecessarily harmful to the slave masters, to repel the aggression directed against agriculture, and "to expose the falseness of the seditious and loathsome calumnies spread abroad in order to wound the honor of the planters." [77]

The defenders of slavery in and out of parliament produced an extraordinary number of quotable aphorisms which the staff of the *Gazeta da Tarde* collected during 1880 and published near the end of the legislative session: "Brazil is coffee," said Silveira Martins of Rio Grande do Sul, "and coffee is the Negro." "Slavery is convenient," said Liberal Senator Sinimbu from Alagôas, "even for the slave." "I love my country more than I love the Negro," confessed Saraiva, President of the Council of Ministers. "The planter should merit more care from the public powers than the slaves," thought Martim Francisco Ribeiro de Andrada. "What was done on the 28th of September," said Ferreira Vianna of Rio de Janeiro, a strong opponent of the Rio Branco Bill in 1871, "is already too much: go back! go back!" "São Paulo prefers the republic to abolition," was the opinion of the monarchist, Costa Pinto, of that province, "let the Emperor decide." "The slave among us is a true proletarian gentleman," remarked the old slavocrat, Andrade Figueira of Rio de Janeiro. "Rigorous measures [are needed]," warned Paulino de Souza of the same province, "and at once, to contain the insubordination of the plantations and to cause dangerous impatience to wither away." [78]

The pro-slavery reaction was not confined to the statements of politicians. It showed up in the elections of November 1881, in which nearly all candidates running as abolitionists were defeated. The new cabinet established early in 1882 was headed, in fact, by Martinho Campos, the deputy from Minas Gerais who had suggested confronting the abolitionists with gun in hand. Nabuco, running against a known slavocrat in the capital, was overwhelmingly defeated, and so left for

76. Beiguelman, *Formação política*, I, 160–161. Pereira Barreto was a prominent philosopher with a decided anti-democratic bent; see Cruz Costa, *A History of Ideas in Brazil*, pp. 88–96.
77. *Diario do Brazil*, February 10, 1882.
78. *Gazeta da Tarde,* September 25, 1880.

Europe to carry on the struggle there.[79] "It is clearly evident from these results," commented *The Rio News*, "that the country does not desire emancipation, and that it fears even the simple discussion of the question." Slavocrats believed that the anti-slavery agitation would be crushed by the verdict at the polls.[80]

There was, then, a powerful reaction to abolitionism which showed up in the Assembly, in the press, and, most convincingly perhaps, in the 1881 elections. The abolitionists, having dramatically revealed their presence in 1880, slackened their pace the following year, perhaps startled by the rage of their opponents. The anti-slavery meetings, held weekly in 1880, ceased in 1881, and abolitionist clubs either disbanded or carried on less publicly. The supporters of slavery, on the other hand, had also been frightened by the energetic abolitionist activities, and the new and unexpected threat caused the provincial legislators in the coffee provinces to take action to end the inter-provincial slave trade in order to strengthen slavery in the northern provinces. In so doing, they inadvertently helped to set off the most powerful of the provincial abolitionist movements, that of the poor northeastern province of Ceará.

79. *Rio News,* December 3, 1881.
80. *Ibid.,* November 15, 1881.

*From the port of Ceará
no more slaves will be embarked.*

THE PEOPLE OF FORTALEZA
January 27, 1881

11

THE
MOVEMENT
IN CEARÁ

THE END OF THE INTER-PROVINCIAL SLAVE TRADE

As early as August 1880, the pro-slavery reaction in the coffee provinces had begun to take a form which, contrary to its purpose, shortened the life of slavery in Brazil. For decades slaves had been moved southward from the northern provinces into the coffee zones with little attention directed toward their condition, and as late as September 1880 southbound voyagers on ships of the Brazilian Steamship Company could be almost certain of having as fellow-passengers slaves destined for sale in the south.[1] Northern deputies had tried in 1854, as related in Chapter 4, to stop the southward traffic through legislation, but southern coffee planters had then been unwilling to be influenced by predictions of impending national disunity on the slavery question and had opposed an end to the free flow of slaves from region to region.

In 1878, however, some southerners had become aware of the threat to their interests inherent in the north-south trade, and they tried to stop it. In that year, Antônio Moreira de Barros, an ardent pro-slavery politician, introduced a bill into the São Paulo Provincial Assembly to impose a prohibitive tax upon slaves entering São Paulo from outside the province. The aim of Moreira de Barros' proposal was not to limit the influx of slaves into São Paulo. Its purpose, rather, was to close off the São Paulo slave market in order *to restrict the outflow of slaves from other provinces,* specifically those of the north that were rapidly divesting themselves of their slave populations. Moreira de Barros' motivation was not humanitarian but expedient, as was João Mauricio Wanderley's in 1854, when the interests of Bahia and other northern provinces seemed to require an end to the inter-provincial slave trade. If Wanderley had hoped in 1854 that abolition of the traffic between the provinces

---

1. *Annaes da Câmara* (1880), V, 35.

170

would protect the slave resources of Bahia, Moreira de Barros was reasoning in 1878 that abolition of that traffic would re-fortify the declining commitment of northern slave-exporting provinces to the slave system, and thereby prolong the life of slavery. The legislation passed the Provincial Assembly, but the provincial president, responding to protests from planters who still were eager to acquire even more northern slaves, declined to sanction the measure.[2]

The national division on the slavery question, foreseen in 1854 and again in 1878, had indeed become a reality by August 1880 when the same Paulista legislator, Moreira de Barros, now representing his province in the national Chamber, introduced a bill there to prohibit the transportation of slaves from one province of the Empire to another, infractions of the law to be punished under penal provisions of the anti-slave-trade law of 1850, including heavy fines and imprisonment.

Paula Beiguelman, arguing the theory that Paulista planters were early abolitionists, has recently hypothesized that São Paulo sought to end the inter-provincial slave trade because the newer coffee regions of that province were no longer interested in maintaining the slave system.[3] However, this theory is contradicted by Moreira de Barros himself, who declared in defense of his policy that both of his bills, the provincial legislation of 1878 and the national project of 1880, were intended to promote "the political advantage of curbing the antagonism which regretfully I see developing between the two parts of the Empire over this matter [of slavery], and placing all provinces on the same level of interest in order to resolve, at an opportune time, the great question of the servile element."[4] The attempt to end the inter-provincial slave trade was not made because newer and more progressive planters of São Paulo had decided to reject slavery in favor of free labor. Rather, as Moreira de Barros himself revealed, the proposed legislation was intended to stop that traffic in order to shore up the fast eroding commitment of northern proprietors to the slave system. To the clever A. Scott Blacklaw, a spokesman for the coffee interests of Ceylon, it seemed

2. Prado Jr., *Circular*, p. 11; *Provincia de São Paulo*, August 15, 1880; *Annaes da Câmara* (1880), IV, 194–195.
3. See Beiguelman, *A formação do povo*, pp. 52–53. Warren Dean explains the Paulista anti-slave-trade legislation of 1878 as an attempt to end slavery quickly "in order to encourage the flow of free labor." Slavery, he says, citing percentages rather than absolute numbers to prove his point, had declined in the province of São Paulo between 1854 and 1873. See Dean's *The Industrialization of São Paulo*, p. 41, and his "The Planter as Entrepreneur: The Case of São Paulo," *HAHR*, XLVI (May, 1966), 144. It is true that the free population of São Paulo grew much faster than the slave population during those years. However, as has been seen, *in real numbers* the slave population of that province also grew significantly.
4. *Annaes da Câmara* (1880), IV, 194. The two co-signers of the national bill also represented São Paulo. *Provincia de São Paulo*, August 15, 1880.

"uncharitable" to suppose that the real aim of the lawmakers was the prolongation of slavery, but there was "strong circumstantial evidence that it was so." [5]

The bill failed, however, to achieve the purposes expected of it— by this date all but unachievable. The legislation, in fact, was stopped in the Chamber by a coalition of deputies that included a significant bloc of northerners, who put pressure on the government to shelve the project.[6] Revealing the source of the opposition and admonishing the government and the recalcitrant northern deputies, the pro-slavery organ of Republicanism, *A Provincia de São Paulo,* commented: "The ever-increasing disproportion between the numbers of slaves of the northern and southern provinces makes increasingly necessary a prohibitive measure to preserve the uniformity of the interests of the whole country." If there were not a quick end to the traffic, the article concluded, the slave population of the northern provinces would soon be so reduced "that the northern deputies, who form a majority in the Chamber, will be able to decree emancipation *without compromising or even affecting the interests of their respective provinces . . . .*" [7]

With the measure blocked in the Chamber by the north, only the provincial assemblies of the coffee provinces possessed the legislative power to erect a barrier to the southward movement of slaves. By mid-December the provincial assembly of Rio de Janeiro, composed, as the *Gazeta da Tarde* put it, of "fazendeiros, slave masters, and their clients," had levied a tax of 1:500$000 (approximately the price of a healthy male slave) on each captive coming from other provinces. The aim of the law, said the *Jornal do Commercio,* was "to prevent aggravation . . . of the entirely disequal distribution of the slave population among the various sections of the national territory." Predicting that Minas Gerais and São Paulo would soon pass similar restrictive legislation, the *Jornal do Commercio* concluded that the three provinces most interested in slavery had the duty to organize a legal resistance to the invasion of slaves from the north, for as soon as the other provinces had dispatched their last slave they would become abolitionist and, with their united votes, would eliminate slavery throughout the nation.[8] Thus, members of the São Paulo assembly, of the General Assembly, and at least two major newspapers of the coffee region had all recognized that the inter-provincial slave trade was destroying the equilibrium of slavery and threatened its very existence.

5. Blacklaw, "Slavery in Brazil." For the same opinion, see Van Delden Laërne, *Brazil and Java,* p. 85.
6. *Gazeta da Tarde,* September 17, 1880; *Provincia de São Paulo,* September 11, 1880.
7. *Ibid.* Italics added.
8. *Jornal do Commercio,* December 21, 1880.

São Paulo and Minas Gerais followed Rio de Janeiro in the enactment of anti-slave-trade laws. Minas acted almost at once, in late December, imposing a tax of two contos on each entering slave.[9] The São Paulo provincial assembly, now under pressure from the press and the planters, including the Club da Lavoura of Campinas—the same forces that had opposed the provincial bill two years before—passed a law in January 1881 requiring registration of all slaves entering the province and a registration fee of two contos, with heavy penalties for non-compliance. Introduced on January 17, the bill had been passed and sanctioned by the twenty-fifth of the month with little discussion of its aims.[10] These were described some months later, however, during a debate on a project to exempt a planter from the registration fee on thirty slaves. "What we wanted to avoid," said the legislator, Rodrigo Lobato, "was that the provinces of the north, after discharging all their slaves into the province of São Paulo, would be the first to give the cry of emancipation. This was the principal motive of the law of January 25 of this year." [11]

With abolitionism breaking out around them, southern legislators had at last become convinced of the danger of the constant removal of slaves from northern provinces, and so they had legislated a virtual end to this traffic.[12] Thirty years before, when the trade was just developing, this legislation might have contributed more to the stabilization of the slave population in the northern provinces and to prolonging the life of slavery nationwide. Legislated in late 1880, however, and by the southern provinces against some northern resistance, it had the ironic effect of strengthening northern abolitionism.

This was the case, at least, in Ceará, where the value of slaves was almost totally dependent upon the existence of the southern market. Brazilians hoping to prolong slavery through maintenance of the balance between north and south might have been worried by the comments of

9. *Rio News,* January 24, 1881; Viotti da Costa, *Da senzala à colônia,* p. 209. The passage of laws against the inter-provincial slave trade by Rio de Janeiro and Minas Gerais, provinces whose planters have never been suspected of holding progressive or abolitionist views, seems to disprove conclusively the theory that the legislature of São Paulo passed its anti-slave-trade bill because the province's planters rejected slavery as a solution to their labor needs.

10. *Provincia de São Paulo,* September 11, 1880; *Gazeta da Tarde,* December 14, 1880; *Colecção de leis e posturas municipaes promulgadas pela Assembléa Legislativa Provincial de São Paulo no anno de 1881* (São Paulo, 1881), p. 3; *Annaes da Assembléa Legislativa Provincial de São Paulo* (São Paulo, 1881), pp. 11–25.

11. *Annaes da Assembléa . . . de São Paulo, 1881,* pp. 314–318.

12. Before the end of 1881 there were reports that the importation of slaves into Rio de Janeiro had ceased and that the exportation of slaves from Pernambuco had "greatly diminished" as a result of the heavy taxes. *South American Journal,* August 18, September 29, 1881.

The Rio News published the day before the ratification of the São Paulo bill. If the coffee provinces refuse to permit the purchase of slaves from other parts of the Empire, said the English-language paper, "the value of the slaves in the exporting provinces will soon decline and they will become strongly in favor of abolition, in order to be rid of an unprofitable institution and to make way for free labor. . . ." The planters had opposed all direct steps toward abolition, said the American paper, but had *"wholly overlooked the simple fact that this repression of the slave traffic is sure to accomplish the same result."* [13]

The sudden appearance of a powerful abolitionist movement in Ceará in January 1881 was soon attributed, in fact, to both the near exhaustion of the slave supply of that province and to the erection of the southern barrier to the trade. In the Chamber of Deputies in 1882 João Penido of Minas Gerais bitterly accused Ceará of having turned to abolitionism only after selling its slaves.[14] Walter J. Hammond, a frequent correspondent to *The Rio News* with strong Paulista sympathies, cynically observed in 1883 that "until São Paulo shut her doors to receiving slaves from the northern provinces, the northern men carried on quite a brisk traffic in slaves with their more industrious and go-ahead brethren in the south." [15] The provincial taxes, a pro-slavery writer claimed in 1888, "far from mitigating, exacerbated the abolitionist wrath, and notably in the province of Ceará. . . ." [16]

DROUGHT AND EMANCIPATIONISM IN CEARÁ

Nature as well as the legislators of the southern provinces had precipitated the surge of northern abolitionism. From 1877 to 1880, drought had devastated both life and property in much of the northeast. The worst sufferer, in the opinion of *The British and American Mail,* had been the northern farmer, who had lost his cattle, his cotton, and even his seed, and, possessing only slaves, was selling them to subsist.[17] In

13. *Rio News,* January 24, 1881. Italics added.
14. *Annaes da Câmara* (1882), IV, 441.
15. Letter from Walter J. Hammond, Jundiaí, São Paulo, dated February 28, 1883, in *Rio News,* March 15, 1883. "It must . . . be remembered," wrote another foreign sympathizer of the slaveholders about 1886, "when the northern provinces boast of being in advance of the southern as to abolition, that a few years since some hundred thousand slaves were exported from the north and sold in the south." Charles Hastings Dent, *A Year in Brazil* (London, 1886), p. 288.
16. *O abolicionismo perante a historia ou o dialogo das tres provincias* (Rio de Janeiro, 1888), p. 56.
17. *British and American Mail,* March 9, 1878.

the north by 1880 the slaves had become, in the words of a well-to-do southerner, "the only money in circulation." [18]

The drought, particularly serious in Ceará, caused a sharp increase in the outward flow of slaves.[19] Between 1871 and 1881 more than seven thousand captives, more than a fifth of the whole slave population, had been officially exported from the stricken province, and undoubtedly many more were exported illegally. Of the registered deportees, nearly three thousand were shipped from the port of Fortaleza, the provincial capital, in 1877 alone, some of them purchased in the interior for as little as two sacks of flour.[20] As food grew scarce, it became more valuable than the people it was intended to feed. The answer was disposal at low prices. During the decade preceding the rise of the abolitionist movement in Ceará, that province exported a larger percentage of its slave population than any other province. Only Rio Grande do Sul exported *a larger number.*[21]

By 1880, slaves constituted for some Cearenses the only remaining transferable property. As late as December of that year—the month of the first provincial anti-slave-trade laws—slave prices were still propped up in Fortaleza by the southern market, though for a decade and longer most of the agricultural labor of Ceará had been performed by free workers.[22] The rewards offered for the return of runaways in 1878 and 1879 indicate that values had remained much higher than was warranted by local economic conditions. As late as April 1879 an advertisement offered 150 milréis for the return of a male fugitive of twenty-five, and only a week before passage of the anti-slave-trade law of Rio de Janeiro province a slave was freed at an abolitionist meeting in Fortaleza for the price of a conto.[23] Ceará, in fact, was still an emporium of the northeastern slave trade in 1880, gathering to its

18. *Annaes da Assembléa de São Paulo, 1880*, p. 263.
19. The drought allegedly cost the province almost half of its people and two-thirds of their fortunes. Three hundred thousand died, and 250,000 refugees from the interior crowded into the town of Fortaleza with its normal population of 25,000. See Roberto Attila do Amaral Vieira, *Um herói sem pedestal* (Fortaleza, 1958), pp. 45, 55–56.
20. Girão, *A abolição no Ceará*, p. 63; *Relatorio do Ministerio da Agricultura*, January 19, 1882, p. 5.
21. *Relatorio do Ministerio da Agricultura*, May 7, 1884, p. 187.
22. *Associação Commercial do Rio de Janeiro. Elemento servil*, p. 4; *Annaes da Câmara* (1869), III, 56; *Rio News*, September 24, 1879.
23. *Cearense, Fortaleza*, April 30, 1879; Duque-Estrada, *A abolição*, p. 111. An advertisement in the *Cearense* (November 22, 1878) offered 100 milréis for the return of a woman of 22. Another in the *Pedro II* (October 31, 1878) offered 50 milréis for the return of a man, and an extra 150 milréis if he was found outside the province.

beaches the slaves of neighboring provinces as well as those of its own hinterland for deportation to the south.[24] The southern provincial laws struck most effectively there, drastically reducing the monetary assets of the persons still owning slaves and providing an extraordinary incentive to budding abolitionism.

Emancipationism had developed early in Ceará, the result perhaps of a widespread use of free labor in a province where as early as 1845 slaves were "comparatively scarce." [25] In 1868 the Provincial Assembly had authorized the spending of fifteen contos for the emancipation of a hundred babies, giving preference to females, and an improved bill of the same kind was passed in 1870. In that same year, with "free birth" increasingly under consideration in the capital of the Empire, emancipationist clubs appeared in the provincial towns of Baturité and Sobral, much as they had at scattered points in other parts of the country.[26]

Yet the existence of the southern market and the apathy of most of Brazil on the slavery question were obstacles to a significant upsurge of abolitionism in Ceará after passage of the Rio Branco Law. Like the rest of the nation, the northern province was silent on the slavery question between 1871 and 1879 while, from the sandy beaches of its capital city, captives were regularly carried out to waiting ships on the primitive *jangadas,* flat-bottomed sailing boats first fashioned by the Indians and used by generations of northeastern fishermen—the only practical means of carrying merchandise to ships anchored off shore. Before 1879, with thousands of hungry and desperate people migrating from the interior to the provincial capital, with tens of thousands dying of disease and famine in suburban shanty towns, there were no significant protests against the familiar sight of slaves, uniformly dressed in blue cotton and accompanied by a "corrector" being marched down to the harbor for conveyance to the ships.[27]

THE RISE OF ABOLITIONISM IN CEARÁ

In 1879, however, amid the distress of the last year of drought, there were signs of a renewed interest in the slaves. On the eighth anniversary of the Rio Branco Law, a small emancipationist and humanitarian organization called Perseverança e Porvir (Perseverance and Futurity), a name reflecting the hardships of the times, was organized in Fortaleza by a group of young men, nearly all of whom were involved in

24. Tristão de Alencar Araripe, *O Ceará no Rio de Janeiro* (Fortaleza, 1884), p. 26.
25. Kidder, *Sketches,* II, 225.
26. Girão, *A abolição no Ceará,* pp. 53–60.
27. *Ibid.,* p. 63.

the commercial life of the city.[28] For the first year of its existence the new group seemed hardly different from the familiar emancipationist clubs inaugurated from time to time in the towns and cities of Brazil with great fanfare and limited objectives, holding a few meetings, attracting the attention of a local liberal journal, and then dropping out of sight.

Late in 1880, however, the members of Perseverança e Porvir decided to form a new organization dedicated not only to emancipation but to abolition, and on December 8 the founding session of the Sociedade Cearense Libertadora was held with the cooperation of the provincial president, André Augusto Padua Fleury. "The most distinguished ladies and gentlemen of the society of Ceará attended the brilliant festival without distinctions as to party," said a report in the *Gazeta da Tarde,* proving that in Ceará abolitionism was acceptable to a major part of the ruling class.[29]

The first public conference in Ceará resembled those still being held weekly in Rio de Janeiro. Speeches were heard, poems recited, contributions collected, pledges of dedication to abolitionism received with fervent applause, and slaves were ceremoniously freed. "All the speeches were terminated in the midst of general applause," stated a witness's report of the meeting, "combined with the harmonies of the military bands of the Police and the Fifteenth Battalion, who performed in the adjoining hall." [30] This was not a revolutionary conspiracy, but a public meeting of wealthy and distinguished members of Cearense society, supported by the police and national army and the highest authorities, all apparently acting in response to rapidly changing local and national conditions. On the first day of 1881, the first issue of *Libertador,* organ of the Sociedade Cearense Libertadora, appeared in Fortaleza, dedicated to abolitionism with the support of most of the conventional press of Fortaleza.[31]

---

28. *Libertador,* Fortaleza, September 28, 1881; *Gazeta da Tarde,* March 24, 1884; Girão, *A abolição no Ceará,* pp. 63–66.
29. Girão, *A abolição no Ceará,* p. 81; *Libertador,* January 1, 1881; *Gazeta da Tarde,* March 24, 1884.
30. Girão, *A abolição no Ceará,* pp. 75–82.
31. *Libertador,* January 1, 15, 1881. The *Libertador* ridiculed the *Pedro II* and the *Gazeta do Norte,* two papers which continued to publish advertisements for the return of runaways, with a parody of the typical slave advertisement:

> Sustentam o captiveiro
> Para lerem annuncios neste gosto,
> Que nos abatem ante o estrangeiro,
> E fazem o rubôr chegar ao rosto:
> > Fugio do Alagadiço
> > O escravo José,
> > Fulo, de 40 annos, que quando anda
> > Arrasta muito o pé

The passage of São Paulo's law restricting the entry of slaves into that province helped to bring on even more surprising events in Ceará. On the afternoon of January 26, five days after passage of the São Paulo bill and the day following its official transformation into law, José do Amaral, president of Perseverança e Porvir, attempted to persuade a slave dealer to free a group of slaves recently brought from the interior, evidently on the grounds that their value had anyhow plummeted owing to the loss of their principal market, the province of São Paulo. Failing to convince the dealer, Amaral then allegedly conceived the idea of closing the port of Ceará to the slave traffic in order to lower still further the profits of the merchants.[32]

That same evening in a Fortaleza theater, between the acts of a play, Amaral and a companion won the audience's approval of a plan to force a ban on the exportation of slaves from Ceará.[33] The president of Perseverança e Porvir also gained the support of two ex-slaves, popular leaders of the port workers, whose names were soon published in newspapers in Rio de Janeiro. These were the *jangadeiros,* Francisco José do Nascimento, the port pilot, soon to be known as "the sea wolf" or "the dragon of the sea," and José Napoleão, a leader of the boatmen famous for having freed himself along with members of his family.[34]

The following morning, January 27, the merchant ship *Pará* arrived at Fortaleza from the north to take on a shipment of slaves. But before the cargo could be loaded José do Amaral and his followers had met with the jangadeiros on the sandy beach below the city and persuaded them that to transport slaves to the ships was degrading to their profession. In response the boatmen, reassured by their leaders, refused to

---

Do qual partio um osso.
Natural de Loanda;
Tem marcas de chicote, e no pescoço
Levou a gargalheira,
Dá-se trinta mil reis e não mais
Ao paysano ou soldado
Que leval-o a rua do Aquiraz
Numero 14, sobrado.

32. *Gazeta da Tarde,* March 24, 25, 1884. Paula Beiguelman has noticed that the anti-slave-trade laws of the south-central provinces stimulated the abolitionist movement in Ceará, but she does not reveal the immediacy of the repercussions in the north. See *A formação do povo,* p. 54. Beiguelman errs when she hypothesizes the existence of an anti-slavery axis formed by "the newer Paulista west," "an area still not provided with slaves," and the Brazilian north, deprived of its slaves by the inter-provincial slave trade.

33. *Acta da sessão magna que celebrou a associação Perseverança e Porvir em 20 de Maio de 1888 pela extincção do elemento servil no Brazil* (Fortaleza, 1890), p. 19; Girão, *A abolição no Ceará,* p. 91

34. *Gazeta da Tarde,* March 24, 25, 1884; *Gazeta do Norte,* January 28, 1881.

load the *Pará*. With that decision, the slave trade which had long flourished at Fortaleza came to an end.

News of the strike on the beach spread to the town, and soon an estimated fifteen hundred persons had assembled at the harbor. As their numbers grew a cry rose up spontaneously in response to the futile attempts of slaveholders to persuade jangadeiros to load their property. *"No porto do Ceará,"* the shout began, soon becoming a chant, *"não se embarcam mais escravos!"* "From the port of Ceará no more slaves will be embarked!" [35]

The *Libertador* claimed complete spontaneity for the slogan. "It was not even known who first uttered it," the abolitionist paper reported more than a week after the events on the beach. "It was an idea that was on every mind, a sentiment that sprang from every heart." The slave merchants had resorted to every expedient, "offerings, promises, bribes, threats," but all in vain. When asked to help the slave dealers, the police also refused to cooperate, on the grounds that they could not force the boatmen to perform a service that they found repugnant. Later, however, when it was learned from a passenger of the *Pará* that a woman who claimed to be free was aboard the ship, the police helped her and five other slaves to get ashore, presumably aboard a jangada. Before the end of the day the *Pará* had sailed from Fortaleza with only part of its cargo, as the demonstration continued on the beach and a wave of manumissions took place in the town above.[36]

With the arrival three days later of the steamship *Espírito Santo,* the struggle was continued. This time a cargo of thirty-eight slaves had been brought to the port for shipment to the south, but again the jangadeiros, who had since resolved at public meetings to maintain their strike, refused to transport slaves. This time more than three thousand persons reportedly assembled at the beach to chant the new abolitionist watchword: *"No porto do Ceará não se embarcam mais escravos!"* Again the slave dealers tried by every means to load the ship, buying jangadas but finding no one to man them, offering bribes (as much as one conto for the transportation of five slaves), appealing to the army, which would do no more than send a small force to the beach to keep order. Not a slave was put aboard the *Espírito Santo* on January 30, and on the evening of the same day there were festivities in Fortaleza, the celebrants shouting praises to "the men of the sea." [37]

With these successes, abolitionism suddenly grew into a mass movement in Ceará, threatening slavery nationwide. Less than two months

35. *Gazeta do Norte,* January 28, 1881.
36. *Ibid.; Gazeta da Tarde,* March 24, 25; *Libertador,* February 7, 1881.
37. *Gazeta do Norte,* January 28, 1881; *Gazeta da Tarde,* March 24, 25, 1884; *Libertador,* February 7, 1881; Edmar Morél, *Dragão do mar—O jangadeiro da abolição* (Rio de Janeiro, 1949), p. 74.

after the victories on the beach, with the slave trade at an end at Ceará, a mass celebration featuring the liberation of thirty-five slaves was held at Fortaleza. Thousands participated as the thirty-five paraded through town to the Passeio Publico, a plaza overlooking the sea. One slave (according to the description in the *Libertador*) carried a flag blessed by the abolitionist priest, Father João Augusto da Frota. Rockets exploded and military bands played as the throng marched into the plaza, which was decorated with flags, carpets of flowers, and triumphal arches.

After the slaves arrived inside a nearby theater, speeches and poems were recited to the usual applause, and a rendition of the hymn of the Sociedade Cearense Libertadora by the two military bands aroused a delirious response. A representative of the thirty-five offered "the flag of liberty" to the leaders of the abolitionist society, each slave then receiving a certificate of emancipation. "Victims of the impetuous sensation of happiness. . . ," said the report of the *Libertador,* "some of those receiving their liberty seemed to swoon at the dazzling contact with freedom." The emancipation of thirty-five slaves all at once was interpreted as a sacrifice which only the abolitionists of Ceará had made. "Of all the abolitionist societies of the Empire," it was announced, "none in richer provinces had done as much." [38]

The success of the Cearense movement brought fear to the central government and those southern politicians who had hoped to control northern abolitionism by shoring up the region's commitment to slavery. A week after the giant abolitionist rally of March 25, the provincial president, Padua Fleury, an opponent of slavery, was replaced by Senator Leão Veloso of Bahia, a politician with no known sympathy for the abolitionist cause. In 1881 Ceará also acquired a new police chief, Torquato Mendes Viana, who soon proved to be an enemy of abolitionism.

The clash between the newly appointed authorities and the populace of Ceará was delayed for months, however, as the movement continued to grow and even the provincial government took steps to control and limit slavery within the province. By mid-1881, liberation societies had appeared in six provincial towns, including Fortaleza. Early in June the provincial president ordered the lowering of prices of slaves to be freed by the emancipation fund in recognition of the reduced market value of slaves in the province. [39] In August, Leão Veloso decreed a heavy tax

38. *Libertador,* April 3, 1881; Girão, *A abolição no Ceará,* pp. 97–107.
39. The average price of liberations in Ceará by means of the first emancipation fund quota was 437 milréis, but after the jangadeiro strike the fourth fund distribution freed slaves in Ceará at an average price of 85 milréis, about $37.00 U.S. Trail to Frelinghuysen, Rio de Janeiro, May 21, 1884, *Papers Related to the Foreign Relations of the United States,* December 1, 1884, p. 30.

on every slave entering Ceará and a fee of 50 milréis on each slave transported from one município to another for the purpose of sale.[40]

Early in August, however, new hostility began to develop between the abolitionists and the presidential palace. By that date it was apparent that the low prices of slaves in Ceará had roused the greed of speculators, who saw an opportunity to profit in the market of Belém, Pará, where the demand for slaves continued strong after the trade had ended in other northern ports, and where every steamer still brought slaves as late as 1882.[41]

Those interested in re-opening the port of Fortaleza to the slave trade included the new police chief, Mendes Viana, who on August 30, 1881, appeared on the beach with a large force of policemen to assure the boarding of slaves on the steamship *Espírito Santo,* one of the two vessels involved in the first encounter of the previous January. The abolitionists responded in their usual dramatic style. A leaflet entitled "Corra Sangue!" (Let the blood run!) appeared in the city calling on supporters to die with honor rather than allow the port of Ceará to be disgraced by a renewed exportation of slaves. The government, the abolitionists later claimed, was trying to ship slaves from Fortaleza in an effort to reestablish the value of slave property in the province.[42]

The leaders of the Sociedade Cearense Libertadora did more than publish leaflets. While some six thousand persons assembled on the beach, chanting their slogan, and while the customs inspector attempted to persuade the police chief to desist in the face of the popular menace, two slave girls bought for the market of Belém were stolen away in a carriage by a group of abolitionists, allegedly including the "dragon of the sea," Francisco José do Nascimento.[43]

The outcome of the incident on the beach was revealed in a telegram from José do Amaral to Joaquim Nabuco:

The slavers tried yesterday to embark slaves for the north. The abolitionists prevented it, despite direct intervention of the armed force. There was no disorder. Great movement of abolitionism here. The president suspended the inspector and other customs employees. Other officials are threatened with suspension.

On the same day, Dr. Frederico Borges, vice-president of the Sociedade Cearense Libertadora and public prosecutor in Fortaleza, singled out as

40. *Libertador,* June 7, August 26, 1881
41. *Diario do Gram Pará,* cited by *Gazeta da Tarde,* July 20, 1882.
42. *Manifesto da Sociedade Cearense Libertadora ao Governo e ao Paiz* (Fortaleza, September 7, 1881)
43. See the report of Mendes Viana of August 31, 1881, in Morél, *Dragão do mar,* pp. 82–85; and Girão's account of the events of August 30 in *A abolição no Ceará,* pp. 115–121.

a trouble-maker in the report of the police chief, telegraphed Rio announcing his dismissal "for being among those members of the Libertadora who in behalf of the honor of the name of Ceará prevented the infamous embarkation of slaves." Following the clash on August 30, the government took revenge on members of the armed forces and civil services as well, including Francisco do Nascimento, who lost his position as port pilot.[44] Even the *Libertador* practically suspended publication after the events of August 30, appearing on the tenth anniversary of the Rio Branco Law, again in December, but not again during the first ten months of 1882.

In the capital of Brazil, in fact, little was heard again from the Sociedade Cearense Libertadora before November 1882, though telegrams from that organization published in the *Gazeta da Tarde* early in June told of government suppression and a threat to exterminate the abolitionist movement in Ceará.[45] The abolitionists of Rio, including Patrocinio, expressed solidarity in a cabled reply, but the movement in Rio was almost equally powerless in mid-1882, apparently able to do little more than survive after its near collapse in 1881.

44. Girão, *A abolição no Ceará,* pp. 110–111; Morél, *Dragão do mar,* pp. 80–81; *Gazeta da Tarde,* September 1, 2, 1881.
45. *Gazeta da Tarde,* June 8, 9, 1882.

12

*Ceará is the hero of abolition;
São Paulo is the stronghold of
putrid slavery.*

JOSÉ DO PATROCINIO
in the "Gazeta da Tarde," May 31, 1883.

THE
ABOLITIONIST MOVEMENT:
SECOND PHASE

AN UNEASY CALM

With the exception of Ceará, there was little to hearten the abolitionists during most of 1882. In January the Emperor had delivered a particularly noncommital Speech from the Throne to usher in the ministry of Martinho Campos, a known slavocrat from Minas Gerais who governed allegedly without a program, but with obvious aversion to the abolitionists. Succeeding Martinho Campos in July, the Viscount Paranaguá promised to speed the transition to a free-labor system through expansion of the emancipation fund, a tax on slave sales, and a ban on the movement of slaves from province to province.[1] Yet during almost a year in power he accomplished nothing.

The editor of *The Rio News* described the plight of abolitionism in August:

It is now more apparent than ever how completely the abolitionists were defeated in the last election. The really active and energetic leaders of the movement were overwhelmingly defeated at the polls, the anti-slavery society from which so much was expected soon went out of existence, the movement was almost totally crushed. A few societies built upon social or local bases have continued to exist, but their work has been spasmodic and of little influence outside of the organizations themselves. In the General Assembly, where the work must largely be carried on, there seems to be not one single abolitionist worthy of the name.[2]

1. *Rio News*, January 24, 1882; *Organizações e programas ministeriais*, pp. 191–192.
2. *Rio News*, August 24, 1882. In November 1881 Nabuco had written from London of the need of the Sociedade Brasileira Contra a Escravidão to meet at least once a month, for even if it had only seven or eight members, he was determined not to see it die. Nabuco to Gusmão Lobo, London, November 12, 1882, *Cartas a amigos*, I, 83.

Joaquim Nabuco analyzed the causes of the movement's decline after its first brief but exultant phase in 1880. Slavery enjoyed the support of "most of the constituted social forces . . . ," he explained. It controlled the land, dominated the rural population, controlled commerce and capital, and commanded "a formidable clientele of every profession, lawyers, doctors, engineers, clerics, professors, government employees. . . ." And yet this appearance of power, Nabuco added optimistically, was a mere shadow. Opposition to slavery was growing and would have its impact upon the government, which would gladly see it end "if it were not for the coffee districts of São Paulo, Minas Gerais, and Rio de Janeiro." It was only a matter of time, he predicted, before the national conscience would force the government to act against slavery as it had in 1871.[3]

The major abolitionist events of 1882 outside the General Assembly were few but significant. On May 21, the Centro Abolicionista Ferreira de Menezes was organized in Rio with the usual performances, speeches, and manumissions to replace the defunct abolitionist clubs, but it never achieved the importance of the earlier abolitionist organizations or of the powerful Abolitionist Confederation, which absorbed it in 1883. In July 1882 the abolitionists of Rio were holding raffles to raise money for a local emancipation fund, the "Caixa Emancipadora José do Patrocinio." Before the death of Luiz Gama in August, a delegate from the *Gazeta da Tarde* had traveled to São Paulo, where he had founded the Centro Abolicionista de São Paulo, creating a propaganda sheet known as *Ça Ira* with the help of local members.[4]

The latter developments were perhaps linked to the major slave revolt which broke out in São Paulo in November, an event that aroused angry comments from planters and the press of São Paulo and Rio and was strong evidence that the abolitionists, frustrated in their use of legal processes, had already gone underground, were already working among the slaves, particularly in the key province of São Paulo. Some months earlier an observant British agent for Ceylonese coffee interests had observed publicly that abolitionists could easily enter the slave quarters on the plantations to inform the slaves that there was no force which could prevent them from seizing their freedom and putting the whole country "in a blaze." The police and the army were entirely inadequate to quell a widespread uprising of slaves, the same writer believed, and the government had not prepared for such an event. "A slave rebellion will not happen," he added, "unless influence from outside the plantations were brought to bear on the minds of the slaves." [5]

It was perhaps because the slaveholders were conscious of these facts

3. Nabuco, *O Abolicionismo*, pp. 215–219.
4. *Gazeta da Tarde*, May 22, June 1, 1882; Duque-Estrada, *A abolição*, p. 91.
5. Blacklaw, "Slavery in Brazil."

that they reacted with near panic to news of the revolt. The *Diario do Brasil,* an unabashed defender of slavery, described the uprising with alarm, noting that after taking over the plantation the slaves had walked to the town of Campinas, killing six persons on the way before surrendering to the police. "Most of them displayed the greatest cynicism," said the paper, "telling all the facts with the most admirable sangfroid." [6] Pro-slavery groups saw the revolt as a signal for action and repression. The Club da Lavoura of Campinas, the town where the slaves had surrendered, petitioned the provincial president and the Minister of Justice to take measures to assure the security of the planters, including an increase in the public security force and the supplying of carbines to the auxiliary police. "In view of the very grave and deplorable event," said the *Diario do Brasil,* ". . . is it not time to react vigorously against the insensate and deadly abolitionist propaganda?" [7] *Opinião Liberal* of Campinas warned: "Public opinion can no longer be deceived. . . . Within the country there exists a factious group disposed to the greatest excesses, concealed by the sympathetic banner of emancipationism, but whose aims are the destruction of the conservative elements of society." [8]

Giving his own account of the revolt, the editor of the *Rio News* also suspected that the rebels had been influenced by outsiders. The slaves had shown signs of defiance before the fighting had begun, said the American paper, and some thirty armed men had consequently attacked their quarters with the intention of seizing their leaders. Armed and with communications dug between their barracks, the slaves had repulsed the attack, killing one and wounding several of the assailants. Conscious of their plight, seventy-three men, women, and children had then set out for Campinas to surrender, shouting salutes to emancipation and republicanism on the way. To the *Rio News,* the "revolt" appeared deliberate and well-organized. The slaves had fought well, "even against equal numbers of the dominant race. . . ." More significant, they had displayed an unexpected understanding of political events. In the light of these facts, the American paper concluded, "the planters may well inquire how it has been possible for these slaves to prepare themselves so well for an uprising, and how they have obtained these ideas of emancipation and government. And it may not be amiss to inquire just how far these ideas have extended among the slaves." [9]

The slave uprising near Campinas was perhaps spontaneous, but to slaveholders and their sympathizers it seemed proof that the abolitionists were plotting acts of destruction even more harmful to established soci-

6. *Diario do Brasil,* November 8, 1882.
7. *Ibid.*
8. Quoted by *ibid.,* November 22, 1882.
9. *Rio News,* November 15, 1882.

ety. In fact, at just that period, José do Patrocinio, now the recognized national leader of the abolitionist movement, was planning a new attack on slavery at its weakest point: the restless province of Ceará.

THE DESTRUCTION OF SLAVERY IN CEARÁ

In October, Patrocinio, now known as "the Black Marshal" or "the tiger of abolitionism," set out from Rio for the north on the steamship *Ceará,* stopping at Bahia and Pernambuco and landing at last by jangada on the beach at Fortaleza. After a triumphant harbor reception, which included an escorting flotilla of jangadas, Patrocinio was met on shore by Francisco José do Nascimento. "Well, then, comrade," he is said to have remarked to the jangadeiro, "the port is still blocked?"—to which Nascimento replied that there was no force in the world that could reopen the port of Ceará to the traffic of the slave traders.[10]

Patrocinio's stay in Ceará, which lasted more than three months, coincided with the opening phase of a systematic program of liberation through concentration on geographic areas: on streets, city blocks, towns, municípios, provincial capitals, and finally provinces.[11] Perhaps conceived by Patrocinio, the new system, later used throughout the Empire, focused first on the município of Acarape, chosen because of its accessibility by rail from Fortaleza and its small slave population.[12] On the first day of 1883, with Patrocinio on hand, Acarape was declared free after only a few weeks of concentrated effort, setting off an avalanche of manumissions that affected communities throughout the province. Early in February 1883, with Patrocinio en route back to Rio, two more Cearense municípios were declared without slaves.[13] Near the middle of the month, the *Gazeta da Tarde* noted the extraordinary progress of abolitionism in Ceará and predicted an early end to slavery in the province. "In all the municípios," the paper reported, "humanitarian organizations are being created; from every point emissaries are being sent to the Libertadora Cearense with the purpose of accelerating the emancipationist spirit. . . ."

The movement was contagious. A simple proclamation was enough to set a locality in motion. "Adherents pour in from all sides," said the *Gazeta,* "a nucleus of emancipation is created, and abruptly a new club

10. *Gazeta da Tarde,* October 10, 19, December 1, 12, 1882; Girão, *A abolição no Ceará,* pp. 131–132.
11. See Duque-Estrada, *A abolição,* p. 112.
12. Girão, *A abolição no Ceará,* p. 135. According to the 1872 census, there were 11,725 free persons and only 140 slaves in the município of Acarape. *Recenseamento da população,* IV, 172–173.
13. *Gazeta da Tarde,* February 3, 1883.

is formed, its birth marked by a handful of liberations." [14] Slaves were being freed voluntarily and without compensation, or by popular subscription when masters demanded payment. "The enthusiasm springing from the movement," said *The Rio News* late in February, "has been something marvelous, for it has pervaded all classes and has extended into every part of the province. Hundreds of slaves have been offered to the various liberation societies for the nominal price of 50$ and 100$ each, and the societies are accepting them just as rapidly as their subscription receipts will permit. . . . In strong contrast," added the American paper, "we regret to note the dilatory results accomplished in the province of São Paulo." In poor Ceará, scene of a drought and famine only a few years before, "the slaves are being liberated for nearly nominal sums, and principally through the voluntary and spontaneous work of the people themselves. In São Paulo there is not only no enthusiasm, but there seems to be a decided opposition to emancipation." [15]

As in 1881, the central government tried to discourage the abolitionist fervor of the Cearenses. In mid-February, after the Fifteenth Army Battalion stationed at Fortaleza declared itself an abolitionist society, the War Minister ordered the unit transferred to Pará, replacing the Ceará garrison with the Eleventh Battalion from Belém. The central government took this unusual action despite the claim of the officers that a telegram from the Emperor congratulating the Sociedade Cearense Libertadora for its success in liberating Acarape had motivated them to convert their battalion into an abolitionist society.[16] Later that month the abolitionists of Ceará were sending telegrams to Rio telling of government threats and the defiant liberation of another 228 slaves in scattered municípios. A few days later they were "surrounded by a terrifying war machine—two battalions of soldiers in the province (the Eleventh of Pará had arrived to replace the abolitionist Fifteenth) and in the harbor the transport ship *Purus* and the corvet *Trajano*." The response to this "provocation" was the freeing of 200 slaves in Icó (where only 785 had existed in the 1870's) and an announcement of the expected liberation of the entire town of Baturité on March 25. On the seventh of that month the men of the Fifteenth Battalion embarked for Pará, seen off by an estimated fifteen thousand persons. The ovation was extraordinary, according to a telegram from Fortaleza, but, contrary to

14. *Ibid.*, February 13, 1883.
15. *Rio News*, February 24, 1883. Concerning São Paulo, the *Rio News* added: "In the interval between the last and the present General Assembly there were only 23 slaves freed, and those at a cost of 21,238$. São Paulo has a slave population of 174,722, larger than either Pernambuco or Bahia; and yet while those two provinces have liberated 1,400 and 1,000 slaves respectively through the fund, São Paulo falls considerably below the smaller total. . . ."
16. *Gazeta da Tarde*, February 14, 22, 1883.

government expectations, order was maintained throughout the day.[17]

By early May the campaign to liberate Fortaleza had begun, the abolitionists systematically taking the city block by block and house by house, locating every slave and his master and buying the former's freedom or persuading the latter to release him without compensation—in Fortaleza no longer a large financial loss. On May 7 the Rua do Major Facundo, location of the headquarters of the Sociedade Cearense Libertadora, was without slaves, and on May 24 the capital was free after only a few weeks of concentrated effort.[18] A major Brazilian city—the first— was entirely without slaves, but others would soon equal the achievement as abolitionism spread into the most vulnerable parts of the country.

In the following months there was little more resistance to the movement in Ceará. All the newspapers except the "Liberal" *Cearense* supported the movement,[19] as did most of the population. In an effort to persuade malingerers to accept the popular judgment, the Provincial Assembly placed a tax of 100 milréis on every slave in Ceará, and a charge of one and a half contos on all slaves exported. This, it appeared, was an official recognition of the closing of the port of Ceará to the slave trade and, more important, a virtual abolition of slavery in the province, since the tax of 100 milréis was more than the average price which masters were accepting for slaves from the abolitionist committees.[20]

By mid-February 1884, twenty-five of the fifty-seven municípios of Ceará were free, and complete emancipation of the province was being predicted for June 1. Less than three weeks later the date of total liberation had been set for March 25, the sixtieth anniversary of the Imperial Constitution. On the 16th of that month, the *Jornal do Commercio*, calling attention to the target date, announced that the slave population of Ceará was confined to sixteen municípios, two with only three slaves each. By the 22nd nearly all the slaves of Ceará were free, and the festivities scheduled for the 25th had already started. On the 24th the abolitionists of Ceará sent the following telegram to Rio:

To "Gazeta da Tarde"—Rio. We have won the first battle. Inform the Emperor, whose abolitionism we respect, that in spite of the government's persecution, Ceará is free.[21]

17. *Ibid.,* February 22, March 6, 7, 1883; *Recenseamento da população,* IV, 172–173.
18. *Gazeta da Tarde,* May 8, November 2, 1883.
19. *Annaes da Câmara* (1883), V, 104.
20. *Relatorio com que o Exm. Sr. Dr. Satyro de Oliveira Dias passou a administração da provincia ao 2º Vice-Presidente Exm. Sr. Commendador Dr. Antonio Pinto Nogueira Accioly no dia 31 de Maio de 1884* (Fortaleza, 1884), p. 28; *Rio News,* November 15, 1883.
21. *Rio News,* February 15, 1884; *Gazeta da Tarde,* March 4, 22, 25, 1884; *Jornal do Commercio,* March 16, 1884.

The statistics of the Ministry of Agriculture, as reliable as any, indicate the effectiveness of the sixteen-month campaign of liberation in Ceará. Of 31,975 slaves registered there after 1871, 2,211 had died by 1884, and a net total of 7,104 had been sent out of the province. The balance of 22,660 persons was cautiously accepted by the Minister of Agriculture as the number freed, the great majority during the frenzied period after November 1882. "In spite of the low price of slave property in the province of Ceará," said the report, the emancipation of all its slaves in such a short time was "a highly creditable fact for private humanitarianism." [22]

Yet slavery did not entirely cease to exist in Ceará on March 25, 1884. In February 1886 the *Jornal do Commercio* reported that 298 slaves were still being held in the Cearense município of Milagres, and more than two years later a report of the Ministry of Agriculture, dated the day after the abolition of Brazilian slavery, placed the captive population of Ceará at 108.[23] Nevertheless, the events in the northern province were remarkable, and they served like a detonator to set off a chain of abolitionist explosions that would begin to destroy slavery from the Amazon to the Uruguayan border.

THE MOVEMENT SPREADS

Long before the conclusion of the liberation campaign of Ceará, the events there had begun to affect surrounding regions. Already in May 1883, Ceará was a refuge for runaways from neighboring provinces, the area affected spreading outward until the attraction of the "Terra da Luz" (Land of Light, as Patrocinio called it) was felt as far south as São Paulo. Complaints against the protectors of fugitives in Ceará began to come in from Pernambuco, Rio Grande do Norte, and Piauí, the three provinces bordering Ceará, and soon the protests were heard from as far away as Rio de Janeiro.[24] The southern abolitionists, adopting bold tactics, particularly after the creation of the Abolitionist Confederation in May 1883, secretly established a Brazilian Underground Railroad with its origins in São Paulo, Minas Gerais, and Rio de Janeiro and its

22. *Relatorio do Ministerio da Agricultura*, May 7, 1884, pp. 183–189. In contrast with the number freed in Ceará, during twelve and a half years the emancipation fund of the Rio Branco Law freed only 18,900 slaves in the entire country.
23. *Jornal do Commercio*, February 21, 1886; *Relatorio do Ministerio da Agricultura*, May 14, 1888, p. 24.
24. *Annaes da Câmara* (1883), I, 56; *Rio News*, February 15, 1884; *Manual do subdito fiel*, p. 16; *South American Journal*, September 13, 1883; Toplin, "The Movement," p. 72.

ideal destination in distant Ceará. As a kind of personal salute to the northern province, André Rebouças drew up an imaginary escape route to the north with its first station in São Paulo at the tomb of Luiz Gama and later resting places along the rivers and streams of the backland wilderness before arrival at the ninth and last station "in paradise, in Free Ceará." [25] The luring of slaves from plantations did not develop on a large scale in 1883—as it did in 1887—and the escape route to the north was probably not much more than a dream, but early in 1883 advertisements began to appear in *O Cruzeiro* in Rio de Janeiro which implied that slaves had been lured away or were being protected by abolitionists.[26] Later the abolitionists would develop this tactic to a high level, providing runaways with escorts, forged certificates of freedom, hiding places, and even railroad transportation to the cities.[27]

By early 1883, as Brazilians became increasingly conscious of the example of Ceará, abolitionism was again erupting at scattered points throughout the country. In February, the provincial president of Pernambuco wired the central government for aid to meet the challenge of abolitionist propaganda so effective that it was allegedly causing local military rebellions.[28] By July one of several abolitionist clubs in Pernambuco, the Sociedade Nova Emancipadora, had created an emancipation committee to liberate the provincial capital by slow, calm, and legal methods. The same committee, dissatisfied with the cautious program of the newly-installed ministry of Lafayette Rodrigues Pereira, recommended to the Chamber of Deputies a more radical program, including the liberation of men over fifty and complete enforcement of the law of November 7, 1831—a policy which would have virtually eliminated slavery throughout the country.[29]

By March 1883, abolitionism was making great strides in the western province of Goiás, where a leading proprietor announced his decision to

25. See Nabuco, *Minha formação*, p. 175.
26. *O Cruzeiro*, February 17, 21, 1883.
27. Moraes, *A campanha abolicionista*, pp. 37–38; Nabuco, *The Life of Joaquim Nabuco*, p. 103.
28. *Gazeta da Tarde*, February 22, 1883.
29. *Annaes da Câmara* (1883), IV, 53. Emancipation societies had appeared in Pernambuco twenty years before the beginning of the national abolitionist movement, and as early as 1879 the new abolitionism had developed in Pernambuco with the creation of the Club Democrata, dedicated to the liberation of slaves. In 1881 the Club Abolicionista was formed in Recife, a group instrumental in the abolition of capitães-do-mato in the province and in the suppression of runaway-slave advertisements in the press of Recife. On September 26, 1881, the important Sociedade Nova Emancipadora was founded in Recife, and by 1884 a rash of anti-slavery organizations had appeared in Pernambuco. See Francisco Augusto Pereira Costa, "A idea abolicionista em Pernambuco," *Revista do Instituto Arqueológico, Histórico e Geográfico de Pernambuco*, 42 (October, 1891), 262–266.

free all his slaves in ten years if they continued to serve him well during that time.[30] An early example of "contract manumission" soon to be popular throughout the Empire, this act implied that the relationship between master and slave was already so weakened by public pressure and discontent among the captives that a supplementary contract was needed, all but annulling the former unrestricted relationship. Many slaveholders would soon be adopting this policy as a practical solution to the immediate challenge of abolitionism, particularly in Rio Grande do Sul, maintaining their control over an unpaid labor force for a settled period of time, giving their slaves an incentive to labor, and gaining a degree of public respect all with one "humanitarian" act. By July 1884, Goiás was well on the way toward total liberation, the vice-president and some of the major landholders joining the cause with the emancipation of their slaves.[31]

The abolitionist movement also developed a presence in Pará, where thousands allegedly turned out in Belém to cheer the abolitionist Fifteenth Battalion on its arrival from Ceará in 1883.[32] In late April of the following year, with a powerful abolitionist movement about to arise upriver in Manaus, the Club Amazonia was founded in Belém with the express purpose of directing the abolition of slavery in the Amazon River Valley.[33] In Rio Grande do Norte a powerful organization liberated the last slave in the city of Mossoró before the end of 1883.[34] The town of Amarração in Piauí was free the following July, and in late September, as the system of geographical emancipation caught on from one end of the Empire to the other, three cities of Paraná—Curitiba (the provincial capital), Paranaguá (the leading port), and Antonina—were nearly free of slaves.[35] In the latter province three abolitionist organizations were founded in 1883, and "grand abolitionist celebrations" were held in the São Theodoro Theater in Curitiba. As elsewhere in Brazil, in Paraná middle- and upper-class citizens were particularly active, as was the large immigrant sector, German and Italian, which expressed its opposition to slavery through its organizations and foreign-language newspapers.[36]

With the return of Patrocinio to Rio in late February 1883, the sys-

---

30. *Tribuna Livre*, Goiás, March 3, 1883, quoted by *Gazeta da Tarde*, April 21, 1883.
31. *Ibid.*, August 18, 1884.
32. Morél, *Dragão do mar*, pp. 80–81. In the Chamber in 1883 Deputy Cantão of Pará claimed that the movement in his province was almost as well developed as in Ceará. *Annaes da Câmara* (1883), I, 50.
33. *Manifesto do Club Amazonia fundado em 24 de Abril de 1884* (Pará, 1884), pp. 17–18.
34. *Rio News*, December 15, 1883.
35. *Gazeta da Tarde*, July 21, October 1, 1884.
36. Ianni, *As metamorfoses do escravo*, pp. 225–227.

tematic liberation of the imperial capital had been attempted, though with so little success that the slaveholders were briefly amused and re-assured.[37] The heart of the Empire was not yet ready for the radical solutions successful elsewhere, but the *Gazeta da Tarde* continued its lone press campaign against the slavocracy, thrusting at ingrained day-to-day practices, inciting the population to greater participation.

In late February 1883 appeared the first of the *Gazeta*'s parodies of fugitive-slave advertisements, easily recognized by the tiny sketch of a hiking runaway carrying a bundle tied to a stick borne over one shoulder —the symbol attracting the eye of slave catchers for decades. The notices in the *Gazeta* were like those still appearing regularly in newspapers in Rio de Janeiro, employing the same blunt physical descriptions, though in these sham announcements it was the slaves who searched for the masters seeking redress for years of unjust captivity. Using real names of masters and slaves drawn from advertisements in the *Cruzeiro* and other newspapers, the *Gazeta* sought to create a public awareness of the baseness of traditional practices. The following example published on February 23 illustrates the style:

100$000

The citizen João, for thirty years despoiled of his rights of a free man, will award the above-mentioned sum to anyone delivering the slavist, Luiz Gomes de Aguiar, who resided or still resides in Campo da Gramma, a place preferred for its magnificent pastures.

This fellow is tall, well placed in the feet, and carries on his neck an ulcer the size of a pigeon egg.

He habitually wears a large felt hat and has various occupations, the principal one that of exploiting his own brothers. . . .

According to the same notice, Gomes de Aguiar could be found along with his friends in the Imperial Palace.[38] More aggressive yet was this "advertisement":

37. *Gazeta da Tarde,* February 20, 1883; *Rio News,* May 3, 1884.
38. *Gazeta da Tarde,* February 23, 1883. This sham notice was obviously inspired by the following authentic advertisement which appeared in the *Cruzeiro* on the same day:

100$000

Fled from the plantation Piabanha . . . the slave João, mullato, thirty years old, regular height and body, small feet, sullen, wears a moustache, has the mark of a knife wound near his stomach, an ulcer the size of a pigeon egg on the right side of his neck, lacks one tooth in front and speaks paulista; works as tailor, stonecutter, servant, and quilt maker; wore a hat with a high crown, a calico shirt, shoes, and a coat of Petrópolis cotton and carried more clothes in a bundle; any-one bringing him to his master Luiz Gomes de Aguiar in Campo da Gramma, or to Benedictino Street No. 10, will be rewarded with the above sum. . . .

Francisco Antonio da Silva, judge of the third civil district of the capital, makes known to the public that the services of the following slavemasters will be auctioned:

Manoel Alves, married, 40 years old, without occupation, developed abdomen, fat legs and swollen eyes.

Maria Antonia, wife of the former, stout and strong, with milk for suckling, littered six months ago. . . .

The services of this couple will be hired out for seven years to pay the indemnity which they owe to the free man João, whom they criminally kept in captivity for fifteen years.[39]

THE MOVEMENT IS RENEWED IN RIO DE JANEIRO

By May 1883 abolitionism was at last reviving in Rio. Early that month, at a meeting in the Hotel Bragança, João Clapp, José do Patrocinio, and Lieutenant Manoel Joaquim Pereira of Ceará conceived the idea of uniting the many abolitionist clubs of the nation into an abolitionist alliance.[40] Soon after, representatives of many abolitionist groups met in the editorial room of the *Gazeta da Tarde* where the new organization —called the Abolitionist Confederation at the suggestion of Patrocinio —was established. Within three months the Confederation consisted of seventeen separate clubs representing at least five provinces and the capital, and including the abolitionist societies of two military schools (those of Pernambuco and Rio de Janeiro), one printers' organization, a medical school, and an association of commercial employees.[41]

In August the Manifesto of the Abolitionist Confederation, written by the two radical abolitionists, André Rebouças and José do Patrocinio, was read before nearly two thousand persons in the Pedro II Theater in Rio de Janeiro. In attendance were two senators and six deputies representing Ceará, Goiás, Rio Grande do Sul, Pernambuco, and Bahia, all agreeing to present the Manifesto to the General Assembly. Accordingly, the Assembly, as a group still unwilling to take further steps toward reform, heard a long historical account of Brazilian slavery which was intended to show that, as it existed in Brazil, the institution was both brutal and illegal.[42] It was obvious to those legislators who listened that the abolitionists, organized now in a national alliance, were more powerful and determined than ever before, and no longer willing to compromise.

39. *Gazeta da Tarde*, February 24, 1883.
40. João Clapp, "Relatorio do estado e das operações da Confederação Abolicionista," *Gazeta da Tarde*, May 29, 1884.
41. See *Manifesto da Confederação Abolicionista*, pp. 21–22.
42. Duque-Estrada, *A abolição*, p. 104; *Annaes da Câmara* (1883), IV, 18–29.

In August 1883, students and teachers at the Escola Polytechnica organized a new abolitionist society with statutes calling for the establishment of similar organizations in all the educational institutions in the country. Under the influence of André Rebouças, a faculty member, the organization also called for a tax on uncultivated land located within twenty kilometers of lines of communication, taxes on slaves of from twenty to one hundred milréis per year, and a maximum emancipation price of six hundred milréis.[43] In November another organization which seemed to threaten the status quo—the Sociedade Central de Immigração—was founded in Rio. Headed by the novelist and senator from Paraná, Alfredo d'Escragnolle Taunay, with the cooperation of the omnipresent André Rebouças, this immigration society with a radical bent was not satisfied with the importation of droves of servile Europeans and Asians for the plantations of the Empire. Instead, it opened a struggle for the reforms its leaders believed were needed to foment a wave of free European immigrants and the establishment of the small agricultural property. It was one more manifestation of the nineteenth-century battle against the latifundia.[44]

As 1884 began, the abolitionism of the capital of the Empire took on for the first time the character of a mass movement. The new meeting place was the Polytheama Theater, which the public jammed to hear such speakers as João Clapp complaining of the high cost of freeing slaves or Deputy José Mariano of Pernambuco praising the city of Rio for its growing abolitionist mood.[45] It was the emancipation of Ceará, however, that brought the movement out into the streets with a Carnaval spirit, halted the normal activities of Rio for three days, and created a momentum that would soon result in liberation of parts of the city. The members of the Municipal Chamber were warned of what was coming by a letter of March 22 from the Sociedade Abolicionista Cearense requesting permission to lift pavement stones along the Rua Gonçalves Dias and the Carioca Plaza in the heart of Rio for the setting up of pennants and flag posts to ornament a gift bazaar at the Guarda Velha Garden. Promising to replace the stones at the end of the celebration, the abolitionists also asked permission to illuminate the Francisco de Paula Plaza and to post signs in various parts of the city announcing a regatta to be held at Botafogo Bay.[46]

One of several centers of the huge celebration was the Polytheama Theater, where at noon on March 25 a great *Kermesse*—a combination

43. *Rio News,* August 15, 1883.
44. See Louis Couty, *Pequena propriedade e immigração europea* (Rio de Janeiro, 1887), particularly the notes appended by Senator Alfredo d'Escragnolle Taunay, pp. 71 ff.
45. *Gazeta da Tarde,* January 14, 1884.
46. DPHAG, Cod. 6-1-1.

carnival and fair—began. The theater was adorned, according to the *Gazeta da Tarde,* with magnificent escutcheons surrounded by wreathes of flowers, the flags of the abolitionist societies lining both sides of the hall along with the names of such deceased reformers as Ferreira de Menezes, Luiz Gama, and Viscount Rio Branco. The entertainment was like that offered at the public meetings of 1880, though with popular additions: the reading of a letter from Joaquim Nabuco, still in Europe, orchestral renditions of the National Hymn, the Symphonia do Guarani by Carlos Gomes, the "Marseillaise of the Slave," composed by Dr. Cardoso de Menezes, musical solos, one-act plays, comic scenes, an open-air chorus, and the dancing of a rousing tango. By late afternoon the Rua do Lavradio, the site of the Polytheama, was so thronged with people that ticket sales were suspended by official order, the crowds allegedly creating a public hazard.[47]

A high point of the festivities was the public acknowledgement of the abolitionists of Ceará. This was accomplished by a gigantic parade that wended its way through the old city from the Rua Primeiro de Março to the Passeio Publico, a fashionable park at the edge of the bay, stopping along the way to award a gold crown to a representative of the Sociedade Cearense Libertadora. All this was done with a degree of public participation unprecedented anywhere else in Brazil, except in Ceará itself. The celebrations began on a Sunday morning and, like the Carioca Carnaval, ended at dawn on Wednesday, with the reported participation of more than 10,000 persons.[48] Abolitionism had at last become a popular movement in the capital of the Empire.

With the festivities hardly ended, abolitionist leaders of Ceará sent a joint cable to João Clapp in Rio recommending exploitation of public enthusiasm to attempt the liberation of the entire slave population of the city, and a few days later at a meeting of the Abolitionist Confederation it was unanimously decided to make the effort. To end slavery in Rio was a much more formidable task, however, than the liberation of Ceará, for the slaves in the Município Neutro numbered more than 32,000 and were of much greater value in terms of milréis than the slaves of the northern province. Despite the difficulties they faced, however, the abolitionists divided the city into sections, each under the supervision of a liberation committee, and each committee received a list of captives and their addresses and the mission to accomplish their liberation through calm persuasion.[49]

On April 5 the *Gazeta* announced that the abolitionists had decided to concentrate on two streets in the heart of the commercial district.

47. *Gazeta da Tarde,* March 25, 26, 1884.
48. Duque-Estrada, *A abolição,* pp. 116–118; *Gazeta da Tarde,* March 26, 1884.
49. *Gazeta da Tarde,* March 27, April 3, 1884.

These were the Rua do Ouvidor and the Rua da Uruguayana, the latter the location of the editorial offices of the crusading abolitionist daily. On the same date the *Gazeta* promised that in forthcoming issues it would publish the names of the slaves in the target area along with those of their masters. Two days later the public learned that the abolitionist committees had been well received in the designated blocks, where they had found twelve slaves. Seven of these had been rented from owners outside the area, but their masters were found and their liberation accomplished. Residents of these two streets were persuaded to sign a statement promising never again to employ slaves in their homes. By April 21 another block of the Rua da Uruguayana, extending from Rua 7 de Setembro to the Carioca Plaza, was free, the occupants pledging to stop using slaves in their establishments.

As the days passed, the liberation movement in the capital developed strength. Aided by students of the Escola Polytechnica, it spread to new streets, and the liberation of each block became justification for a public celebration—the massing of happy Cariocas at the liberated site, lanterns illuminating houses, balconies, store fronts. Fireworks burst intermittently above the narrow streets, as music bands encouraged impromptu singing and dancing. Near the end of April block rallies were occurring almost every night in the heart of the capital.[50]

Popular at last in Rio, abolitionism reached the chambers of the Municipal Council. On May 1 this body issued regulations for the employment of a "Livro de Ouro," a municipal emancipation fund intended to finance the annual liberation of slaves in the Município Neutro. "The emancipation movement," wrote a member of the Council, reacting to events in the city, "must be reflective if it is to be orderly. The great national interests represented by agriculture and commerce . . . should be the directors of that movement, before which any reactionary effort is a crime." By creating the Livro de Ouro, the same official explained, the Municipal Chamber was attempting to direct the liberation of the município, to serve as a "conciliating element," to channel the emancipationist forces toward orderly and legal procedures.[51]

The campaign to liberate the slaves of Rio lasted for several weeks, but lost momentum, and was finally given up as people turned their attention in May and June to a promising effort on the part of the Imperial Government to regain control of the emancipationist process through a legislative compromise: the Dantas Bill for the liberation of slaves of sixty years of age and older. Despite the greater strength of

50. *Ibid.,* April 5 through 26, 1884.
51. DPHAG, Cod. 6-1-41. The Municipal Chamber had decided to create the Livro de Ouro (Book of Gold) in February. *Rio News,* March 15, 1884.

this second attempt to free the city, it had not gone far toward the accomplishment of its purpose. Slavery was still too strong in the capital of the Empire, surrounded as it was by the coffee provinces, to be destroyed by enthusiasm and good intentions alone. As late as 1887 there were still nearly 7,500 slaves registered in the Rio area.[52]

The abolitionism of Ceará and the imperial capital nevertheless stimulated other movements from one end of the country to the other. Early in May 1884, the students of the Law Academy of São Paulo, emulating the students of the Escola Polytechnica, organized an Academic Liberation Commission for the purpose of freeing the slaves in the blocks surrounding the institution. As in Rio de Janeiro, however, slavery was still adamantly defended in the city of São Paulo, though the province's slaves were by this time greatly concentrated in rural areas in the performance of agricultural labor. As a result, the efforts of the students encountered strong resistance in the coffee capital and accomplished very little.[53]

A more vigorous abolitionist movement sprang up in May and June in the city of Campos in the sugar-producing region of eastern Rio de Janeiro province. Its most important force was a new abolitionist newspaper, the *Vinte e Cinco de Março,* which first appeared on May 1. Owned and edited by Carlos de Lacerda, a radical enemy of slavery, the new paper hinted in its first issue that the abolitionists of Campos would use violent methods if necessary to serve their cause.[54]

By mid-June the Club Abolicionista Carlos de Lacerda was liberating major streets of Campos, and a few owners, confronted by abolitionist committees, were settling for moderate prices. Yet the agricultural community as a whole reacted strongly to this abolitionist attack at the heart of the rich sugar-growing Paraíba delta. The Club da Lavoura of Campos allegedly armed "disguised assassins" in municipal police units, persecuted abolitionists, and even threatened their lives, while papers controlled by agricultural interests called for a "revolution." In May a pro-slavery crowd gathered menacingly at the editorial offices of the *Vinte e Cinco de Março*—a prelude to serious armed clashes that were to erupt in Campos in 1887 between abolitionists and their opponents.[55] Until then the abolitionists of Campos carried on surrounded by a hostile rural

52. *Relatorio do Ministerio da Agricultura,* May 14, 1888, p. 24.
53. *A Onda,* São Paulo, October 17, 1884; *Gazeta da Tarde,* May 3, 1884; Bastide and Fernandes, *Brancos e negros,* p. 55. The last government report of the slave population, giving statistics collected in 1886 and 1887, put the urban and rural slave populations of São Paulo at 4,926 and 102,403 respectively. See *Relatorio do Ministerio da Agricultura,* May 14, 1888, p. 24.
54. *Vinte e Cinco de Março,* Campos, Rio de Janeiro, May 1, 1884.
55. *Ibid.,* June 17, 19, 1884; *Rio News,* May 24, 1884.

region, eventually beginning to employ the violent methods which Carlos de Lacerda had threatened to use in the first issue of his paper. These allegedly came to include the burning of sugar fields and agitation among plantation slaves, which in 1887 turned Campos into a refuge for hunted runaways and, briefly, a battlefield between the contending forces.

13

SHOCK WAVES
OF CEARÁ: AMAZONAS AND
RIO GRANDE DO SUL

THE END OF SLAVERY IN AMAZONAS

The most effective provincial liberation movements directly spurred by the emancipation of Ceará were those of Amazonas and Rio Grande do Sul. The situation of Amazonas was particularly favorable to abolitionism. In the 1860's and 1870's a small elite in that province had grown rich on an accident of nature: abundant forests of natural rubber trees tapped by free Indians, mestiços, and migrants from the Brazilian northeast spread thinly along the waterways of the Amazon basin. The northern province, "a prodigious emporium of natural riches," was indifferent to the question of slavery, André Rebouças had written long before the eruption of the movement in that province.[1] The wealth of the river valley had attracted a net influx of slaves from other areas (see Table 9), but only 1,501 were registered there at the beginning of 1884, the majority employed in urban centers as household servants. Manaus, the provincial capital, was alone the residence of 571 slaves, more than a third of the provincial total, and over half of these belonged to masters owning one or two personal servants. In the entire city there were only 308 masters, whose average slave holdings consisted of fewer than two persons each.[2] In the rubber-producing areas of the province there were fewer than 500 slaves, and many of these were used in domestic service.[3]

1. *Agricultura nacional,* pp. 49–50.
2. *Relatorio com que o presidente da provincia do Amazonas . . . entregou a administração da mesma provincia ao 1º vice-presidente . . . em 16 de Fevereiro de 1884* (Manaus, 1884), pp. 29–30; *Relatorio do Ministerio da Agricultura,* May 7, 1884, p. 187; *Amazonas,* Manaus, May 4, 7, 9, 14, 16, 1884.
3. Baron de Santa-Anna Nery, *The Land of the Amazons* (London, 1901), pp. 211–212.

Despite this scarcity of bondsmen in Amazonas, the example of Ceará and the leadership of the highest provincial official were required to goad the province into action. The legislature at Manaus had set aside funds each year from 1869 to 1872 for the emancipation of slaves, and in 1882 it had placed a tax of two contos on slaves imported into the province. Yet little more was accomplished before 1884.[4] Like other provinces, Amazonas had not made full use of its emancipation fund quotas. Six distributions totaling nearly twenty-six contos had reached the province and filtered down to the municípios, but only six slaves had been freed by the fund during the seven years before March 1883. There were few slaves to classify in Amazonas, but classification councils had performed their duties with the reluctance common in other parts of the country.[5]

It was the provincial president who finally initiated and led the abolitionist movement in the province. Newly installed in his office on March 25, 1884—the same day that Ceará was declared free of slaves—President Teodureto Souto informed the Provincial Assembly that the problem of slavery in Amazonas could be solved legally and without much loss to owners. The Assembly lacked the authority to abolish slavery outright, but did possess the means to indemnify masters. With a balance of more than 972 contos in the treasury, the president requested the creation of an emancipation fund for the liberation of the entire provincial slave population.[6]

Two days later a bill to allocate 500 contos for that purpose was presented to the Assembly. Opposition appeared—even in Amazonas—but a modified law was passed by a unanimous vote on April 24, giving rise to a scene much like that witnessed in the Imperial Senate on September 27, 1871: enthusiastic applause, a rain of flowers from the galleries, and a rendition of the National Hymn by the music band of the Third Artillery Battalion. The bill provided 300 contos for the liberation of the slaves (not 500), but set aside 200 alone to eliminate slavery in Manaus by September 5.[7] On the day the law was passed, prominent ladies of Manaus established a new society, the Amazonenses Libertadoras, in the Government Palace in the company of the provincial president and other prominent civil and military leaders. The purpose of the new organization, said its statutes, was the rapid liberation of the

4. *Amazonas,* May 4, 24, 1884.
5. *Relatorio apresentado á Assembléa Legislativa Provincial do Amazonas . . . em 25 de Março de 1883, pelo Presidente José Lustosa da Cunha Paranaguá* (republished in *Amazonas,* May 2, 1883).
6. *Exposição apresentada á Assembléa Legislativa Provincial do Amazonas na abertura da primeira sessão da decima setima legislatura em 25 de Março de 1884* (Manaus, 1884), p. 4.
7. *Amazonas,* April 16, 1884. The date set for freedom in Manaus was the thirty-fourth anniversary of the establishment of Amazonas as a separate province.

slaves of Amazonas by every means at hand. To hasten the achievement, each lady promised to contribute an item of jewelry, potentially a major source of liberation funds, since the members of the emancipationist organization were drawn from the cream of Manaus society.[8]

With comparatively little to do, the abolitionists of Amazonas compressed the task of liberation into a brief event-filled period following passage of the anti-slavery legislation. Tasks requiring months and even years in other provinces were carried out in days in Amazonas.

On May 1 the provincial president decreed regulations for execution of the new law. The work of abolition was to be accomplished in the shortest possible time, hopefully by September 5. The president himself was authorized to appoint liberation committees for the capital and other parts of the province, including traveling liberators for isolated places. Drawn from every class and profession, these committees were to begin their work as soon as possible, using every legal means to free slaves at the lowest possible cost without causing disturbances or offending established rights. Notices containing the name of every slaveholder in the province were to be published in the press and posted in public places, and masters were to be invited publicly to send written proposals to the government within thirty days specifying the amounts they would accept for the emancipation of their slaves.[9]

Within three days the names of forty-one masters had appeared in the press of Manaus, and by April 16 the name of every slaveholder in the city had been put before the public. Under such pressure, a leading slaveholder of the province quickly announced his willingness to liberate his fifteen slaves at 400 milréis each, and many soon followed the example, offering their slaves to the government for as little as 100 milréis.

Like the abolitionists of other provinces, those of Amazonas organized clubs and societies. Between April 24 and May 14 at least nine abolitionist societies appeared in Manaus, and on May 14 these organizations banded together with the editorial boards of four newspapers, the Provincial Assembly, the Municipal Chamber, two Masonic lodges, and other organizations to form an Abolitionist Congress, meeting under the chairmanship of the provincial president in the Municipal Chamber palace. The creation of each club provided an opportunity for a public meeting, keeping the city of Manaus in a state of festivity during much of May.

Sunday, May 11, was devoted almost entirely to the kind of public demonstrations now identified with the victorious phases of abolitionism. The Plaza Dom Pedro II, the Presidential Palace, the headquarters of

8. *Ibid.*, April 27, 1884.
9. *Ibid.*, May 4, 1884.

the Third Artillery Battalion, the normal school, the Municipal Chamber, private homes, and even the city jail were decorated with lanterns and flags. In the morning the students of the lyceum and the normal school jointly created the Crusade of Liberation. Later that day the Liberation Society 25th of March held its first meeting at the Presidential Palace. At that session, representatives of the *catraeiros,* the boatmen of Manaus, responding to efforts to hasten slaves down river, where their value would be increased, followed the example of the jangadeiros of Ceará and declared the port of Manaus closed to the slave traffic. The day's activities not yet terminated, the abolitionists later converged on the Plaza 28 de Setembro, parading through the streets of the city accompanied by the Third Artillery band, saluting the editorial offices of the anti-slavery press. The abolitionist movement of Manaus had developed "colossal proportions," declared an article in *Amazonas*. Even the inmates of the jail had supported the cause, contributing more than forty-seven milréis to the work of liberation.

On the same day, impressed by the strength of the movement, the editors of *Amazonas* proposed a new goal: the total emancipation of the slaves of the capital by May 24, eighteenth anniversary of a major Brazilian victory in the Paraguayan War and a year after the liberation of the capital of Ceará. Three days later, at its first session, the Abolitionist Congress of Amazonas accepted the ambitious target, and the following day, at a special session of the combined clubs, the systematic liberation of the city was planned through its division into six districts, each with a liberation committee.

By May 18 the liberation movement in Manaus had altered the life of the provincial capital. "Amidst the most profound agitation" manumissions were taking place throughout the city, though some masters were trying to commit their slaves to service contracts pledging them to further labor for long periods of time—the system of "liberation" soon to be common in Rio Grande do Sul. Manumissions were occurring in outlying communities as well. The residents of the município of Teffé, where the census of 1872 had recorded sixty-seven slaves, responded to the arrival of a liberation committee from the capital by releasing all of its six slaves in eight days, completing the liberation of one more Brazilian município.

The fourth week in May was a memorable one in Manaus. On the afternoon of the twenty-third, citizens assembled at the Plaza Dom Pedro II at the newly erected Pavilion of Liberty, where Dr. Teodureto Souto, the provincial president, distributed 186 certificates of freedom to the last slaves of the city. A tropical storm delayed the celebrations on the morning of the twenty-fourth, but already at 6 A.M. a twenty-one-gun salvo honored the leading abolitionist organizations and rocket wheels were set off at thirty-minute intervals throughout the morning.

After the storm, abolitionists, including the members of the Provincial Assembly, marched from the Plaza 28 de Setembro to the Pavilion of Liberty. At the head of the procession walked the president of the Abolitionist Congress accompanied by twenty youths on horseback. Behind came a richly decorated carriage pulled by twenty freedmen dressed in white suits and straw hats. Inside the coach, escorted by four horsemen and two shield-bearers rode "a pure Indian girl," who symbolized the free city of Manaus. Gathered at the Pavilion of Liberty, the crowd waited in silence as Dr. Souto solemnly declared the end of slavery in the city. Concerts and parades with mass participation kept Manaus in a state of commotion during the rest of the day, and the celebrations ended as scheduled on the twenty-fifth.[10]

The liberation of the rest of Amazonas was planned for September 5, but the reaction of the central government to the developments in the northern province hastened the event. A little more than a week after slavery was officially ended in Manaus, an order originating with the central government removed the president of Amazonas from his position, as the president of Ceará had been removed from his after the first sudden outburst of abolitionism there. Attributing Dr. Souto's dismissal to his abolitionism, the *Gazeta da Tarde* condemned the attitude of the regime. The nation understood, said the abolitionist paper, that the government did not wish to act in conformity with public opinion, that it did not intend to recognize the autonomy of the provinces. The people of Manaus had freed the city's slaves by legal means and with payment to the masters, the *Gazeta* concluded, but "the representatives of the black trinity of the south (São Paulo, Minas Gerais, and Rio de Janeiro) will not permit the provinces of the north to think and to settle matters according to the will of civilized man. . . ."[11]

The Rio News recorded the final events of the abolitionist drama in Amazonas. "The 5th of September had been chosen as the date for the total liberation of the province," said the American paper on July 24, "but when the news was received that the president, Dr. Theodureto Souto, had been dismissed by the government because of his action in signing the provincial emancipation act, the people at once arranged a popular manifestation to him for the 10th of July, and then celebrated that day by the most honorable and praiseworthy act in their power—the liberation of every slave in the province. A more significant and dignified rebuke to the government could not have been made."[12]

The liberation of the slaves of a second province had evidently been hastened by the resistance of the central regime to another powerful

10. *Ibid.*, issues of May 1884.
11. *Gazeta da Tarde,* June 2, 1884
12. *Rio News,* July 24, 1884.

advance of abolitionism, but even this resistance could not have brought such a sudden and complete solution to the slavery question if the huge tropical province had teemed with black slaves. The use of "a pure Indian girl" to symbolize the free city of Manaus was appropriate in a way perhaps not considered by the organizers of the celebration of May 24, for it was Indian labor—often forced Indian labor—that had made black slaves little more than household luxuries in Manaus.[13] The sudden decision of Amazonas to set at liberty all its slaves (to paraphrase Adam Smith) was proof that the few that existed there were of little importance to the provincial economy.

COMPROMISE IN RIO GRANDE DO SUL

In Rio Grande do Sul slavery was of greater importance than in Amazonas, but it was undermined by several peculiarities of the province. The proximity of the Spanish-speaking republics, where slavery had long since ceased to exist, and the presence of a large foreign-born population showing little enthusiasm for slavery undoubtedly had liberalizing effects upon the native population.[14] Furthermore, Rio Grande do Sul had suffered a heavy manpower loss through the inter-provincial slave trade during the 1870's (see Table 9). Slavery remained important in the charque or jerked beef industry,[15] and the captive population of the province was still large in 1884. Yet its peculiar situation had made Rio Grande do Sul nearly as vulnerable as Amazonas to the shock waves of Ceará. Impressed by the major victories that abolitionism had achieved in the north during the first half of 1884, reacting to the economic panic and falling slave prices caused by Ceará, fearing perhaps a total loss of the future labor represented by the province's large slave population, the Riograndenses reached an astute compromise with abolitionism which permitted them to make use of the labor of their slaves, while placing upon them the nominal label of "free" men and women. The economic shock was thus minimized, as the province gloriously added itself to the ranks of the emancipationist provinces.

The liberation movement, which reached a peak of intensity in Rio Grande do Sul in August and September 1884, was not, then, so clearly idealistic, or even as complete, as those of Ceará and Amazonas. In a matter of months two-thirds of the sixty thousand slaves of the southern

13. For comments on the ill-treatment of Indian labor in Amazonas, see Santa-Anna Nery, *The Land of the Amazons*, p. 313.
14. The German community of São Leopoldo, for example, registered only 1,546 slaves in the census of 1872 and 29,314 free persons. *Recenseamento da população*, XVII, 205–206.
15. Cardoso, *Capitalismo e escravidão*, pp. 239–240.

province were granted free status, but most were compelled to continue giving unpaid labor to their former masters for from one to seven years. "The movement in Rio Grande do Sul," as *The Rio News* put it in late 1884, "must be distinguished from those of Ceará and Amazonas, as it is far less liberal and unselfish in character. Nearly all the liberations are being granted on conditions of time service, or apprenticeship, which are in great part for the period of five years." [16]

This system of "liberation" was based upon the fourth article of the Rio Branco Law, which declared that, in order to gain his freedom, the slave could hire out his labor to a third person for not longer than seven years. The liberation of a slave by such a labor contract was not to be annulled by his failure to keep the agreement, but he could be compelled to complete his contract in a public establishment or under contract with another private employer.[17]

The formula for liberation used in Rio Grande do Sul was explained by prominent provincial leaders. Senator Silveira Martins declared in the Senate that slaveowners deserved indemnification, but could renounce it. If they were unwilling or unable to make this sacrifice, however, the slave might buy his freedom with his labor. "Give him his freedom," the senator recommended to the masters, "with the condition that he work another three, four, or five years (never more), according to the amount which you think due you. Thus you will not disorganize your work force, and you will have time to prepare for transition to paid labor. . . ." [18]

Early in the liberation campaign, the president of Rio Grande do Sul clarified the legal questions involved in freeing slaves through labor contracts, and suggested ways of forcing slaves to comply with the arrangement. The mere inclusion of the master's statement in the certificate of liberation specifying the length of service was as valid as the labor contract agreed to with a third person, wrote the provincial president, "the slave acquiring in both cases his immediate freedom. . . , remaining, however, subject. . . to the granting of his services. . . under penalty of being compelled to perform them in public establishments or, by

16. *Rio News*, October 24, 1884.
17. Luiz Francisco da Veiga, *Livro do estado servil*, p. 28. The regulations of the Rio Branco Law of November 13, 1872 added that the freedman failing to complete his labor contract was subject to the provisions of the contract-labor law of 1837 intended to force immigrants to fulfill their contracts. The latter law provided for forced labor on public works or penal servitude until the contract was fulfilled. The regulations of 1872 also stated that when there was danger that the freedman would flee or when he had in fact abandoned his master, he was subject to imprisonment for not more than thirty days. *Colecção das leis do Imperio* (1872), Part II, Vol. III, pp. 1067–1073; *ibid.* (1837), I, 76–79.
18. *A Reforma*, Pôrto Alegre, October 12, 14, 1884.

contract, with private persons. . . ." Soon after, the Minister of Agriculture gave his full approval to this interpretation of the law.[19]

A Reforma, a leading emancipationist paper of Pôrto Alegre, explained in economic terms the system of liberation that had been adopted by the province. Owners who believed that they had already been indemnified by the labor of their slaves could free them unconditionally, but the master who thought he deserved further compensation "restored his illegitimate property to society and freedom, while requiring indemnification of his capital through the services of the ex-slave." Evaluating the average slave's services at 240 milréis per year, the paper estimated that three years' labor represented the average slave's value, "not today but formerly when the *merchandise* still brought a good quotation in the market." [20] In the words of the provincial president, the system of liberation had the effect of abolishing the slave while conserving the worker in Rio Grande do Sul.[21]

The southern province thus adopted a cautious and illogical system of emancipation that was open to criticism by purists on both sides of the issue. Enemies of slavery could argue that most slaves had already given—not three or five years of service—but eight or fifteen, and that therefore they had already paid their masters several times over for their investment, particularly at present market prices. Defenders of slavery, on the other hand, could point out that liberation through a service contract was a denial of the master's right to the labor of his slave. How could a slave repay his master, it was asked, with that which the master already legally possessed: the right to the labor of his slave without conditions whatsoever? Accepting this logic, the publishers of *O Conservador* of Pôrto Alegre sent letters to all the municípios of the province in October 1884 counseling slaveholders to keep their slaves on the grounds that indemnification through the labor of the slave was illusory. The abolitionists had fooled the people, said *O Conservador,* hoping "to destroy property and leave in misery the persons who confided in their words." [22] An abolitionist, on the other hand, declared in 1887 that those who profited most from the contract-labor system were the masters. While all the evils of slavery remained, he pointed out, masters gained in several ways. They protected themselves against the possible abolition of slavery in the immediate future, hoping that the labor contract would remain valid after the end of slavery. They de-

19. *Ibid.,* September 14, October 15, 1884.
20. *Ibid.,* August 17, 1884. Italics in original.
21. Cardoso, *Capitalismo e escravidão,* p. 260. Cardoso interprets this to mean in reality: "to abolish the legal condition of the slave, conserving his real condition."
22. Cited by *A Reforma,* October 8, 1884.

prived the abolitionists of their arguments. And, finally, they satisfied their vanities, enjoying the eulogies of the press.[23]

Liberation through service contracts was an intricate compromise. Yet from its beginnings the system aroused the same enthusiasm as the more liberal practices used in the northern provinces. Despite the half-way solution, in fact, there was genuine anti-slavery idealism in Rio Grande do Sul, and the movement adopted the showmanship and the tactics used in other provinces. For example, the Abolitionist Club of Pelôtas, founded in 1881, provided daily educational classes for in-genuos. The Club Nihilista Carnavalesco, founded in the town of Itaqui in February 1884, seemed to express an easygoing radicalism in the choice of its name. Already by April *A Reforma* of Pôrto Alegre was reporting mass liberations in the southern cattle town of Pelôtas and predicting the rapid manumission of every slave in the province. In the same month an Abolitionist Club was organized in Pôrto Alegre for that purpose, and in May the people of the town of Uruguayana were liberating their streets and plazas.[24]

By early August the movement in Rio Grande do Sul had developed much the same momentum seen earlier in Ceará and Amazonas. On August 6 the members of the Abolitionist Club met in Pôrto Alegre to name committees to liberate the slaves in three parts of the city, and by the middle of the month the press of Pôrto Alegre was printing the names of hundreds of persons who had agreed to free their slaves, the majority owners of one or two personal servants. Several streets in the center of the city were quickly freed, and the abolitionists, trooping from house to house, celebrated their achievements on the same streets, just as the people of Rio had done a few months before.

By the third week in August the accomplishment of Pôrto Alegre seemed greater than that of Manaus. There was not a slave in the city, said *A Reforma,* whose freedom could not be purchased by September 7, the date set for manumission of the last slave in the city. What had seemed impossible a week earlier had been done: a large city with more than two thousand slaves had been freed in a matter of days. Only rarely had the liberation committees met resistance, and the funds needed to pay the masters demanding monetary indemnification were available. The movement had spread to other cities and towns: to

23. Fonseca, *A escravidão, o clero e o abolicionismo,* pp. 576–580. For a critical analysis of the system of liberation, see Cardoso, *Capitalismo e escravidão,* pp. 253–268.
24. Serafim Antonio Alves, *Relatorio apresentado na Sessão Magna da Associação Emancipadora Club Abolicionista em 21 de Agosto de 1882* (Pelôtas, 1882), p. 9; *Jornal do Commercio,* March 6, 1884; *A Reforma,* April 10, 14, 1884; *Gazeta da Tarde,* May 26, April 13, 1884.

Viamão, Rio Grande, the German community of São Leopoldo, São Sebastião do Cahy, the latter proclaiming the liberation of all its slaves in mid-August.[25]

The celebrations in Pôrto Alegre on September 6 and 7, 1884 were described as more splendid than any that had taken place there in the history of the city. As in Fortaleza and Manaus, the festivities to celebrate the liberation of the last of the city's slaves absorbed the energies of much of the population, including public officials and members of the more prosperous classes. The main parade on the sixth, witnessed by large and enthusiastic crowds, was composed of "a brilliant retinue . . . of ladies and gentlemen in carriages and on horseback accompanied by every music band in the city."

On the following morning the liberation committees of the Abolitionist Club met at the Municipal Palace, where after oratory and the singing of hymns, Pôrto Alegre was formally proclaimed free of slaves. The Municipal Assembly then passed a motion of praise for the movement's leaders, Colonel Joaquim Pedro Salgado and Dr. Joaquim de Sales Torres-Homem, and in response a book containing the names of the ex-slaveholders of Pôrto Alegre and the flag of the abolitionists were handed over to the president of the Chamber. Following these ceremonies, in which the slaves themselves were cast in the shadow of their masters' liberality, selected military and civic organizations gathered at the cathedral, where the Bishop celebrated a *Te Deum* rendering praise for the extinction of slavery in the city.[26]

In the evening a grand Kermesse began in the Plaza Pedro II, where all the government buildings were illuminated and several bands entertained the gathering public. Abundant and costly contributions collected in the preceding weeks were auctioned off at good prices. Kiosks were named in honor of the leaders of the abolitionist movements, provincial and national. At the José do Patrocinio stall, which specialized in flowers, the merchandise was hotly disputed, yielding a profit of 800 milréis. At the kiosk dedicated to Luiz Gama, an abolitionist drank champagne, shattered the glass, and auctioned off the fragments for 15 milréis, the proceeds presumably going to the cause of liberation. A well-known politician paid the extraordinary price of 20 milréis for a special issue of the *Jornal do Commercio*. Cigars and even raffle tickets were sold at exorbitant prices, said *A Reforma*, "while identical objects were bought for the prices marked by the less prosperous classes, who also wanted to keep a token of the great festival of charity." [27]

25. *A Reforma*, August 1, 8, 15–17, 21, 23, 1884.
26. *Gazeta da Tarde*, September 8, 1884; *A Reforma*, August 31, September 10, 1884.
27. *A Reforma*, August 28, September 11, 1884.

In the weeks that followed, town after town in the southernmost province of Brazil reported the establishment of emancipation clubs, the liberation of hundreds of slaves, or the complete eradication of slavery. By the thirteenth anniversary of the Rio Branco Law, eleven cities, seventeen towns, and six municípios had been declared entirely free. On October 17 the important cattle town of Pelôtas proclaimed the liberation of the last of its five thousand slaves, with the president of the province, José Julio de Albuquerque Barros, on hand to reveal the extent of the sacrifice to its slave masters. Those most affected were the owners of charqueadas, the dried beef factories that constituted the town's most important industry. Of the five thousand slaves of the town, two thousand had been domestic servants or port workers, and a thousand had been employed in agriculture. The remaining two thousand, according to the president, were workers in the charqueadas, where each year 300,000 head of cattle (150 per slave) were slaughtered and meat products valued at ten to twelve thousand contos were produced—an average annual product per slave of five to six contos.[28]

The number of liberations in Rio Grande do Sul slowed in late 1884 and early 1885, as in the entire country during that period, while slaveowners waited to learn if the Dantas Bill would become law, with its provisions to free elderly slaves and to set high evaluations on slaves to be freed by the emancipation fund. Unlike the movement in Amazonas, moreover, that of Rio Grande do Sul did not achieve its declared goal of freeing all the slaves of the province by 1885.[29] Evidently the southern movement was less thorough because Rio Grande do Sul had a higher stake in slavery than Amazonas. On the other hand, the liberation movement in the southern province achieved much more than could be achieved by the movements in the coffee provinces during the same period. The level of success was obviously related to the importance of slavery in the various places.

Just before the abolition of Brazilian slavery in 1888, 8,442 slaves remained in Rio Grande do Sul—of a total of about 60,000 in 1884—most of them young and nearly all in rural areas. In mid-1887, a newspaper of the town of Pelôtas—said to have been freed of slaves—was still running advertisements for the rental of black cooks and a childless wet nurse. Even Pôrto Alegre, proclaimed free in 1884, still had fifty-eight slaves in 1888 [30] in addition to the "freedmen" who were still at work without pay to compensate their masters for their generosity.

28. *Ibid.*, September 10, October 18, 1884.
29. *Ibid.*, October 8, 1884.
30. *Relatorio do Ministerio da Agricultura*, May 14, 1888, p. 24; *Correio Mercantil*, July 5, 7, 21, 30, 1887; Cardoso, *Capitalismo e escravidão*, p. 81.

14

THE
"LIBERATION"
OF THE ELDERLY

THE DANTAS PROJECT

In June 1884, when Senator Manoel Dantas accepted the Emperor's call to head a reform ministry, Brazilian slavery was a moribund institution. Harassed, condemned, perhaps already rejected by public opinion, it was actively defended by only a small part of the population. That minority, nevertheless, was far from defeated.

Soon after Senator Dantas assumed his high office, the slavery issue was again taken up seriously in the General Assembly with the introduction of a reform bill known as the Dantas Project. The resulting debate, more furious than any that had taken place in the Brazilian parliament since passage of the Rio Branco Law, ended at last on September 28, 1885. The outcome of seventeen months of controversy was the legislation known as the Saraiva-Cotegipe Law, a complex and retrogressive act. Under severe pressure from slavocrat organizations and a powerful faction in the Assembly, the Dantas Bill had been shelved, and more conservative ministries had amended the project to produce a law offensive to genuine abolitionists. The Saraiva-Cotegipe Law, sanctioned on the fourteenth anniversary of the Rio Branco Law, was a distortion of the Dantas Project, accepted and even praised by pro-slavery spokesmen, condemned by abolitionists. Yet it was a change in the status quo and so broke the forward momentum of the liberation movement, causing it to mark time in late 1885 and early 1886 before the final rush to triumph.

The agriculturists of the south-central provinces, menaced as never before, had begun to react strongly to their abolitionist enemies even before the rise to power of Senator Dantas in June 1884. The victories of abolitionism—notably the liberation of Ceará—had caused an economic panic. Slave prices dropped. Business, industry, and credit declined. With agriculture menaced, plantation prices collapsed. In 1884 the Associação Commercial of Rio deplored the national divisions on the slavery issue, denounced the "irresponsible" abolitionists, and reported an estimated loss of crops and land values of one million contos attributable to the abolitionist agitation.[1] While the slaveholders of Rio Grande do Sul were adopting an astute solution to the abolitionist crisis, the planters of the coffee provinces were lashing out recklessly against any sign of abolitionist loyalties.

In the weeks before the rise of Dantas several planter groups of Minas Gerais and the Associação Commercial petitioned the General Assembly for strong measures. These included repression of abolitionist excesses and legislation to force former slaves to work, including the establishment of "penitentiaries" in distant parts of the country for the banishment of indigent and unemployed freedmen.[2]

After the establishment of the Dantas ministry such petitions began to reach the Assembly more often, even from northern provinces. A plea from the Bahian Institute of Agriculture and the Commercial Association of that province for strong measures to prevent the destruction of agriculture and commerce seemed to one pro-slavery writer to disprove the contention that the coffee provinces were the only ones still unconquered by abolitionism. A petition from northern planters meeting in Recife in July denounced revolutionary abolitionism, warned of plantation uprisings, and informed the government that ex-slaves flocking into cities were threatening agriculture and public morality. Hundreds of planters of Macahé, Rio de Janeiro province, asked for protection

1. For an illustration of the decline of slave prices in one município, see Stein, *Vassouras*, p. 229; for the sorry tale of a planter who tried to sell his fazenda, see *Manual do subdito fiel*, pp. 13–14; *Associação Commercial do Rio de Janeiro. Elemento servil*, p. 5; *Rio News*, July 5, 1883; *Jornal do Commercio*, June 22, 1884. For the economic pinch in São Paulo, see Morse, *From Community to Metropolis*, p. 169.
2. *Associação Commercial do Rio de Janeiro. Elemento servil*, pp. 9–10; *Annaes da Câmara* (1884), III, "Histórico," pp. 10–12; *Jornal do Commercio*, June 22, 1884.

from the threatening social paroxysm and requested a measure to compel freedmen and ingenuos "to cooperate" with their former masters in exchange for pay and a comfortable life. The agricultural associations, particularly in the coffee provinces, functioned as powerful pressure groups, directing their vitriolic petitions against the "anarchic abolitionist movement" while upholding the Rio Branco Law as the sole solution to the slavery question.[3]

Coercion and violence were a part of the reaction. Late in April 1884 a crowd of some five hundred armed men broke into a municipal jail in Rio de Janeiro province to slaughter three slaves accused of killing their masters, dragging them into a public square to mutilate their bodies in a brutal fashion as a show of force to counter abolitionism. Judges reaching decisions contrary to the interests of slaveholders had been expelled from their homes by bands of armed men. The perpetrators of crimes, protected by local authorities, allegedly went unrecognized and unpunished.[4] Several municípios in Rio de Janeiro province had created special police forces to aid planters whose security was menaced, and a representative from Minas Gerais warned the Chamber of Deputies in May that within two months all the threatened agricultural centers of the three major coffee provinces would have anti-abolitionist leagues. Notorious statutes of the Agricultural Society of São José de Além Paraíba, Rio de Janeiro province, authorized the use of that organization's funds to combat local abolitionist activities, including any outcropping of an abolitionist press.[5]

Despite growing national tension, the Emperor's Speech from the Throne of May 5, 1884, gave practically no indication that Pedro was considering the initiation of new slavery reform. The innocuous speech ignored the eradication of slavery from Ceará, a startling omission under the circumstances, while merely hinting that new measures might be forthcoming.[6] Caught between opposing forces, the Emperor had done little of an official nature to support the abolitionist cause during five years of conflict. Yet he had obviously pondered the problem and determined by mid-1884 to end the dangerous impasse. With the fall of the ministry of Lafayette Rodrigues Pereira, Pedro selected a new Council President who was to commit himself and his government to moderate reform with the full support of the Crown.[7]

3. *Diario do Brasil,* July 15, 1884; *Annaes da Câmara* (1884), III, "Histórico," pp. 10–12; *Annaes do Senado* (1884), IV, 12–15.
4. *Rio News,* May 3, July 5, 1884. Senator Otoni compared the violence to the American lynch law.
5. *Annaes da Câmara* (1884), I, 222, 234–235.
6. *Gazeta da Tarde,* May 5, 1884; *Rio News,* May 15, 1884.
7. Lyra, *Historia de Dom Pedro II,* III, 11, 19. See Pedro's penciled thoughts on the idea of liberating slaves who reached the age of sixty, AMIP, 29–1025 V.

The rise of Dantas was apparently the result of Pedro's recognition that the Brazilian government could no longer offer the nation palliatives of the kind proposed by the Lafayette ministry in August 1883. With growing social and economic disintegration, more was needed than the expansion of an ineffectual emancipation fund or a nationwide prohibition of an inter-provincial slave trade already effectively stopped by provincial action.[8] The bestowing of titles and honors on masters who freed their slaves, a stop-gap measure tried a few months before, would satisfy neither the slaveholders nor the abolitionists, though the editor of *The Rio News* admitted that if the slaveholder could be coaxed into liberating his slaves "by the cheap reward of a title or ribbon, or a resplendent gewgaw for his left breast," there was no reason why his vanity should not be satisfied so that slaves could go free.[9]

The time had come, Senator Dantas told the General Assembly in his first message as Council President, for frank and serious government intervention to achieve a progressive solution to the slavery problem. Stressing both his ministry's moderation and its determination to act, he announced his decision—apparently the Emperor's decision as well—to advance "as far as prudence permits and civilization requires, thus checking excesses and disorders which compromise the solution to the problem rather than advancing it." The government would support three basic alterations in the slavery laws, only one of which was really new: an end to the human traffic between the provinces, enlargement of the emancipation fund, and the liberation of all slaves who reached the age of sixty.[10]

The idea of emancipating elderly slaves was rejected by almost every member of the Council of State in a subsequent meeting, but the government's project nevertheless reached the Chamber of Deputies on July 15, bearing the signatures of twenty-nine representatives, all but

---

Pedro's anti-slavery sentiments and the difficulites of his personal position are suggested by the report of an interview with Henry W. Hilliard, which took place in 1880 soon after publication of the American Minister's controversial letter to Joaquim Nabuco. Hilliard writes:

"After a few general remarks he [Pedro] drew near to me and said: 'I have read your letter with great sympathy.'

"I replied: 'I am a thousand times obliged to your Majesty for saying so.'

" 'Yes,' said he, 'and I wish to say something on the subject myself.'

"I said to him: 'I shall be very happy to read what your Majesty may say.'

"He replied: 'I cannot do it here in Rio, but we shall soon go to Petrópolis. . . .' " Hilliard, *Politics and Pen Pictures,* pp. 396–397.

8. For details of the Lafayette project, which was never acted upon, see *Jornal do Commercio,* April 13, 1885.

9. *Rio News,* January 24, 1884.

10. *Organizações e programas ministeriais,* pp. 211–214.

two from provinces outside the recalcitrant coffee region.[11] The proposals contained in the new bill were almost as complex as those of the Rio Branco Law. The most important and controversial provision was the sexagenarian clause. This was intended to liberate all slaves who reached the age of sixty and to obligate masters to provide for the freedmen who chose to remain in their company in exchange for their gratuitous services. Slaves transferred from one province to another were to be free. A new nationwide registration was to take place, all slaves not registered within a year to be considered free. Maximum evaluations were to be set on all slaves to be freed by the emancipation fund:

800 milréis for slaves younger than thirty,
700 for those between thirty and thirty-nine,
600 for those between forty and forty-nine, and
400 for those older than forty-nine.

Graduated taxes would be imposed on the owners of slaves held in cities, towns, and rural areas (lowest in the latter) with the aim of concentrating slaves into the rural areas. To enlarge the emancipation fund a six-percent surtax was to be imposed upon all direct and indirect sources of government income with the exception of export duties. Heavy taxes were to be set upon the transfer of slave property by sale or inheritance. Reflecting perhaps Senator Dantas' long and continuing interest in the establishment of the small agricultural holding, the project stipulated that the freedmen and ingenuos were eventually to become owners of the land they worked.

There were illiberal provisions in the Dantas Bill among the progressive ones. Every slave emancipated by the fund was to remain regularly employed for five years in the município where he had previously lived. Violations would result in the usual punishments which Brazilian legislators were prone to impose upon shirkers, in this case fines, imprisonment, and compulsory labor on public works. Service contracts were to be legal, but limited to three years. The central government was to be authorized to create agricultural colonies for freedmen and ingenuos who did not find employment in private establishments.[12]

The reactions of the abolitionists to the Dantas Project were less than jubilant. Before its details had been made known, *The Rio News* hastily condemned the liberation of sexagenarians as the legalization of their

11. Five represented far-northern provinces (Amazonas 1 and Maranhão 4). Sixteen were from the northeast (Piauí 3, Rio Grande do Norte 1, Ceará 2, Paraíba 1, Pernambuco 1, Alagôas 3, Bahia 5). Six represented western and southern provinces, including 4 from Rio Grande do Sul and one each from Paraná and Goiás. Two others represented Minas Gerais. For the complete list, see Duque-Estrada, *A abolição*, p. 135.
12. For three original drafts of the bill, see *Obras Completas de Rui Barbosa*, Vol. XI, Tome I, pp. 275–306.

abandonment in old age. The government's proposals, said Joaquim Nabuco in the Polytheama Theater on June 22, represented very little, but no one could calculate the possible effects of even limited restrictions on the slave system. What disturbed the slaveholders, he noted, was not the government's proposals, but the frank language of Dantas. Nearly a year later, Nabuco described the project as "a slow, illogical, and insufficient solution to a problem which we would like to finish off by prompt, rapid, and effective means. . . ." Yet the bill was also "nothing less than the conversion of the Liberal Party to the national principles which the abolitionists proclaimed six years ago." [13]

The Dantas Bill, in fact, was potentially more harmful to slaveholders than its moderate provisions seemed to suggest, and therefore it was strongly resisted. Not only would it free the old and feeble without reimbursing masters, but, as frequently pointed out, it would also liberate many young and robust Africans who had been registered with false ages to avoid the consequences of the law of November 7, 1831.[14] That many slaveholders had fraudulently registered Africans, enrolling them as much older than they really were, is proved by the Census of 1872. These statistics show that where Africans were heavily concentrated (notably the provinces of Rio de Janeiro and Minas Gerais) there was a disproportionately large number of slaves whose ages were put at 51 and older—the very group that by 1884 would be eligible for freedom under the provisions of the Dantas Project (see Table 5, particularly the statistics for Rio de Janeiro, Minas Gerais, and Bahia, where most Africans illegally imported between 1831 and 1851 were settled).[15]

The threat of losing many younger slaves was, in fact, a reason for the opposition to the freeing of the sexagenarians, but one which was not easily used as an argument against the bill. Most slaveholders, Deputy Moreira de Barros had admitted in 1881, had "sought to register their slaves as having been imported before 1831 in order to avoid doubts which could arise in the future," and, as a newspaper of Pernambuco put it, it was for the purpose of maintaining the worst consequences of this "crime" that southern agricultural interests, led by such

13. *Rio News,* June 14, 1884; *Gazeta da Tarde,* April 25, 1885; Nabuco, *Conferência a 22 de Junho de 1884,* pp. 11–14.

14. *Ibid.,* pp. 13–14; *Gazeta da Tarde,* June 16, 1884.

15. Any African registered in 1873 would have had to be registered as at least 42 years of age, even presuming he had been imported in his mother's arms. Reasonably, however, any cultural African would have had to spend some of his childhood in Africa. Therefore, to have been imported legally before 1831, a cultural African would surely have been at least in his late forties by 1873. Many, of course, were younger. A ten-year-old slave imported in 1850 would have been 33 in 1873, but to be registered as a slave it would have been necessary to add some twenty years to his true age.

men as Moreira de Barros, rejected the Dantas Project.[16] As *Le Brésil,* a French-language journal of Rio de Janeiro, lamented:

The Dantas emancipation project places [many] proprietors, who have made these false declarations in order to place themselves in safety from the operation of the law of 1831, in a terrible difficulty: either the slave is in fact sixty years of age, as must be the case with regard to all Africans who were imported before the promulgation of that law, and he will be emancipated, or he is not in truth sixty years of age, yet will be enfranchised [liberated] by virtue of the . . . registration.[17]

"But it is notorious," said the London-based *South American Journal* in June 1885 in an editorial strongly sympathetic to the plight of the planters, "that the age of native-born Africans is overstated on the registers." [18]

THE OPPOSITION TO THE DANTAS PROJECT

The tone of the resistance to the project was already established at a meeting of the Council of State held on June 25, where practically every councillor rejected the concept of sexagenarian emancipation while calling for measures to impose compulsory labor upon the newly freed. Viscount Bom Retiro, who expressed the views of most of the Council members, seemed unconscious of philosophical inconsistency when he called the emancipation of sexagenarians "an arbitrary and hateful restriction upon servile property," while deeming it "altogether urgent to impose upon the freedmen the obligation to work." [19]

With the introduction of the Dantas Bill into the Chamber on July 15, 1884, the opposition grew more intense and angry. "Without attempting to decide whether the project is good or bad," wrote José do Patrocinio, "we record with pleasure the hatred of the agricultural oligarchy against it." Since the day of its presentation, he charged, the pro-slavery faction in the Chamber had tried incessantly to overthrow the Dantas cabinet in order to smother the cry of justice contained in some of its articles.[20]

The Municipal Chamber of Caconde, a coffee-producing município

16. Cited by *Jornal do Commercio,* March 30, 1885. The Pernambucans, of course, had little to lose. Of 138,560 African slaves registered in the 1872 census, 110,700 were in the coffee provinces or the Município Neutro (see Table 5), and it was principally there that slaveowners had had the need to register slaves with false ages. Only 3,084 African slaves were registered in Pernambuco, and the "elderly" therefore made up a smaller part of the province's slave population.
17. Cited by *South American Journal,* August 14, 1884.
18. *Ibid.,* June 27, 1885.
19. *Acta da conferência,* pp. 88, 90.
20. *Gazeta da Tarde,* July 19, 1884.

of northern São Paulo, sent a statement to the Chamber in July expressing the community's anxiety and displeasure with the Dantas Project:

In the afflictive and exceptional circumstances through which the country is passing [they declared], when agriculture, the sole source of income, struggles with supreme difficulties, . . . a scarcity of workers and capital, . . . a drop in the value of its products, diminished harvests and frosts which recently damaged our principal branch of cultivation; when agriculture exists in constant fear, surrounded by thousands of dangers instigated by the excesses and abuses of unbridled abolitionism—the presentation on the part of the government of an obviously unconstitutional project alarms our society, creating uncertainty and hopelessness in the hearts of the farmers who cannot depend upon the guarantee and protection of the government which so openly attempts to injure their interests and to violate their property.[21]

Liberation of slaves older than sixty was a violation of the Constitution, said the pro-slavery journal *Brazil* on the day the project appeared. Taxation of the planters for expansion of the emancipation fund was "financial madness." When slavery ceased to exist in Brazil, a self-styled "loyal subject" publicly warned the monarch a few days later, in one of a growing number of threats to the political system itself, there would no longer be any reason for the writer's humble posture before his Emperor.[22]

The opposition prevented serious consideration of the Dantas Bill. Immediately after its first reading on July 15 a dissident Liberal from São Paulo, Moreira de Barros, announced his decision to resign the office of Chamber President in protest against the bill. The Chamber accepted his resignation by a narrow margin of 55 to 52, constituting for Dantas a shaky vote of confidence. The bill, however, had lost Dantas the support of ten members of his own party, all but three from Minas Gerais and São Paulo.[23]

Even this precarious majority did not last. On July 28, by a vote of 59 to 52, the Chamber approved the motion of another Liberal dissident, João Penido of Minas Gerais, which condemned the bill and denied the confidence of the Chamber to the Dantas ministry. Seventeen Liberals, ten from the three major coffee provinces, rejected their party's ministry, while four Conservatives, all from outside the coffee region, voted for the Liberal government (see Table 24). Only ten deputies from the coffee provinces, all Liberals, supported Dantas, while twenty-eight other deputies from that region rejected him. Thus, the four coffee provinces

21. *Annaes da Câmara* (1884), IV, 84.
22. *Brazil*, July 15, 1884; *Manual do subdito fiel*, p. 132
23. *Annaes da Câmara* (1884), III, 165–171; *Obras Completas de Rui Barbosa*, Vol. XI, Tome I,, pp. 322–325.

as a group strongly rejected the reformist administration, although deputies from the other provinces supported Dantas by a broad margin. The emancipation bill had split the Liberal Party in the coffee provinces, ten deputies supporting Dantas and ten expressing loyalty to their constituents' economic interests.[24]

On the day of the vote Dantas formally asked Dom Pedro to use his constitutional power to dissolve the Chamber and to call new elections.[25] Dantas used this expedient, wrote Nabuco, as the only practical means of averting the fall of his government. Faced with a choice between the anti-Dantas Chamber and the Dantas ministry, Pedro supported the latter.[26]

The result was lionization of both Dantas and the Emperor among abolitionists. At the Chamber session of July 30 the public silently heard official explanations for the dissolution of the Chamber, then spontaneously applauded Dantas, creating an impression among those in attendance that they were witnessing the climax of an important historic event.[27] Despite Pedro's long silence on the slavery question, a forgiving abolitionist public, perhaps sensing his true feelings, was soon hailing him as one of their own,[28] and pro-slavery groups were again denouncing him circumspectly as they always did when the course of events forced Pedro out of his normally neutral position.

Before the Chamber's dissolution prior to new elections, a committee assigned to give an opinion on the Dantas Bill presented its findings to the Chamber. Written by Rui Barbosa and signed by seven other deputies, all from outside the coffee area, the report was an impressive assault upon slavery intended to explain the reformist position to the voting public.[29]

One dissident committee member, Sousa Carvalho of Paraíba, presented the views of the pro-slavery majority in the Chamber in a strongly worded separate message. Evidently reflecting the views of the 619 constituents in Paraíba who would soon re-elect him,[30] Sousa Carvalho condemned both the abolitionist movement and the government which allowed that movement to function in the streets, in schools, in public

24. *Annaes da Câmara* (1884), III, 356–363. Two Liberals of Ceará allegedly voted against Dantas because he "would not turn over the Ceará provincial government to their dictation." *Rio News,* August 5, 1884.
25. See "A Exposição de Motivos sôbre a Dissolução do Parlamento," *Obras Completas de Rui Barbosa,* Vol. XI, Tome I, pp. 351–358.
26. *Jornal do Commercio,* September 11, 1884.
27. *Ibid.,* July 31, 1884.
28. *Ibid.,* September 11, 1884; *Annaes da Câmara* (1884), IV, 98.
29. See "Emancipação dos escravos, parecer formulado pelo Deputado Ruy Barbosa como relator das Commissões reunidas de orçamento e justiça civil," *Obras Completas de Rui Barbosa,* Vol. XI, Tome I, pp. 49–235.
30. *Organizações e programas ministeriais,* p. 384.

buildings, and even in the barracks and military academies. Finding no reasons for hastening freedom other than "pure sentimentality, vain seeking after popularity, a pretext for agitation, revolution, and social subversion," Sousa Carvalho rejected the emancipation of sexagenarians as a "communist principle." The Dantas Bill was "the incarnation of the. . . new abolitionist position, created exclusively by the Crown to cause the triumph of ideas contrary to the dominant position of the Council of State, the Chamber of Deputies, the Senate, and the two great parties. . . ."[31] This, in fact, was a nearly accurate appraisal of the positions of these organizations after more than four years of abolitionist propaganda.

THE FALL OF DANTAS

Most Brazilians eligible to vote for a new Chamber of Deputies on December 1, 1884 (140,000 in a population of some 12,000,000) were not strongly sympathetic to emancipationism. Yet the election proved that even among this select few there were many persons now willing to accept a new reform, including the abolition of slavery sometime before the end of the century. After it was learned that 67 Liberals, 55 Conservatives, and 3 Republicans had been elected to the Chamber of Deputies, the *Gazeta da Tarde* claimed an abolitionist victory, announcing that 38 deputies who favored the project and 18 who opposed it had been re-elected. An analysis employing the no-confidence vote of July 28 as a standard shows, however, that Dantas supporters and opponents returned in about equal numbers. José do Patrocínio, running in a district of the capital, drew only 160 votes and went down in defeat.[32] Rui Barbosa, a leading defender of the bill, lost his seat in Bahia by a narrow margin. Joaquim Nabuco, who won a hard-fought contest in Recife, was barred from his seat, but then won a narrow victory in another district of the Pernambucan capital. Slavocrats Moreira de Barros and Antônio Prado, who were to vote consistently in opposition to the abolitionists, were victorious in São Paulo, as were their pro-slavery allies, Lacerda Werneck and Andrade Figueira in Rio de Janeiro. João Penido, author of the no-confidence measure of July 28, was returned by his constituents in the tenth electoral district of Minas Gerais.[33]

---

31. A. A. de Souza Carvalho, "Voto em separado," *Obras Completas de Rui Barbosa*, Vol. XI, Tome I, pp. 249–270. For an edited English version, see Thomas E. Skidmore, "The Death of Brazilian Slavery, 1866–88," in Frederick B. Pike (ed.), *Latin American History: Select Problems* (New York, 1969), pp. 156–157.
32. *Gazeta da Tarde*, December 5, 15, 1884.
33. Nabuco, *Cartas a amigos*, I, 138; *Organizações e programas ministeriais*, pp. 384–388.

The three victorious Republicans, Prudente de Morais and Campos Sales of São Paulo and Andrade Botelho of Minas Gerais, had run on a platform of careful neutrality, accepting the "capital ideas" of the Dantas Bill while vaguely reserving the right to support unspecified amendments to certain provisions.[34] Although they voted in general harmony with the abolitionist element in the General Assembly in 1885, in a major speech of the same year Prudente de Morais clearly revealed his opposition to rapid reform. The slavery problem, he said, restating an old Republican position, would best be settled by the provinces individually, more or less in accordance with their separate circumstances, allowing those provinces which could dispense with their slaves to do so at once without waiting for such provinces as São Paulo, Minas Gerais, and Rio de Janeiro, forced by their circumstances to delay the solution. A system of provincial responsibility, thought Prudente de Morais, would preclude the danger that a majority in the Chamber composed of representatives of emancipated provinces might impose abolition upon the entire country.[35] Although they were supporters of immigration, as Paula Beiguelman points out, the Paulista Republicans were still in no position in 1885 to advocate a rapid liberation of their province's slaves and, moreover, fully reflected the fear of their constituents that the other provinces might force a rapid solution upon them.[36]

The practical results of the election are best determined by the voting records of the winners. A study of important votes taken on matters related to the slavery question (see Table 25) indicates that most of the members of the newly elected Chamber were moderate to conservative on the slavery issue. The voting records of only 28 deputies show a consistent willingness to accept reform, whereas at least 50 others were steadfast opponents of change. Regional differences, though less clear than in 1871, were still apparent. Nearly two-thirds of the deputies in coffee provinces were resolute opponents of change, and half of the remaining sixteen were inconsistent, but in the other provinces taken together only one-third could have been classified as strong opponents of abolitionism on the basis of their voting records.

With the opening of the special session of the General Assembly in March 1885 it was evident that the Dantas Bill would be the main concern, and that debate, if it developed, would focus on the question of indemnification. The press of Rio devoted much space to the legal and philosophical questions involved in the freeing of slaves without

34. Prado Jr., *Circular,* pp. 34–39.
35. *Annaes da Câmara* (1885), I, 249–254.
36. For the theory that the two Paulista Republicans, along with the Conservative leader, Antônio Prado, represented the anti-slavery views of richer Paulista planters, see Beiguelman, *A formação do povo,* p. 61.

compensation. In late March the *Jornal do Commercio* published an article not only hostile to unrecompensed liberation of sexagenarians but even to indemnification through labor contracts, already an accepted solution in many parts of the country. Even the Rio Branco Law, the paper alleged, with its provision for indemnification through labor, had violated property rights, for masters with a permanent claim to the labor of their slaves could not be indemnified by a contract pledging services for a limited time. There was only one way to indemnify, the article concluded, and that was "to pay the money." In the same issue, ironically, "Clarkson" (the pen name of Gusmão Lobo, former deputy from Pernambuco) criticized what he regarded as timid emancipation measures in the Dantas Bill: the fixing of slave prices according to age, the progressive tax, indemnification through labor contracts, a fixed time for abolition.[37]

If there was any doubt about what provisions in the Dantas Bill most offended slaveholders, it was dispelled when debate on the project began on April 13. Moreira de Barros of São Paulo, always quick to lead the opposition, informed the Chamber that the Liberal dissidents had separated themselves from the Dantas government in 1884 because they were opposed to emancipation without indemnification. He then proposed a resolution, signed by himself and nine other Liberals (six from Minas Gerais and three from the north), to deny the support of the Chamber on the same grounds. Dantas countered this new threat to his government by suggesting that opponents frankly admit that what they wanted was monetary indemnification for the freeing of elderly slaves, a principle which his government would not accept. The vote that followed produced a tie (fifty votes for and fifty against), saving the ministry temporarily and permitting discussion to continue, but practically eliminating any hope that the Dantas Bill would ever pass the Chamber unrevised.[38]

Even this reprieve did not last more than three weeks. Another no-confidence resolution brought down the Dantas ministry on May 4 by a vote of fifty-two to fifty. The balloting generally followed party lines, only three Conservatives supporting Dantas and nine dissident Liberals voting against him—every dissident vote vital, however, and cast with the knowledge that it could topple his government.[39] As the *Jornal do Commercio* commented the following day, the Conservatives had won a parliamentary victory by merely casting their votes against the regime. The Liberal dissidents had led the opposition, drafted and signed the no-confidence resolutions, and cast the vital votes which had created the

37. *Jornal do Commercio*, March 29, 1885. For more criticism of the bill, see *Brazil*, April 12, 1885.
38. *Annaes da Câmara* (Sessão Extraordinaria) (1885), II, 313–327.
39. *Ibid.*, III, 6–11; *ibid.*, "Histórico," p. 5.

second ministerial crisis in less than a year.[40] Attempting to save his government, Dantas appealed again to Pedro to dissolve the Chamber and to call new elections. This time, however, the Emperor accepted the results of the recent elections and called upon a less committed Liberal, José Antônio Saraiva, to form a new ministry and to make the Dantas Bill more palatable to the Conservatives and dissident Liberals.[41] The first serious attempt to secure a moderate slavery reform in thirteen years had thus been stopped by a determined opposition.

THE SARAIVA CABINET

AND THE REVISED BILL

A week after the no-confidence vote, the new Council President —a strong opponent of slavery reform during his previous administration —informed the Assembly that he would press for the liberation of the slaves as quickly as possible while granting agriculture the time it needed to acquire new workers. More friendly to the planters than his predecessor, Saraiva even promised to aid the reorganization of the labor system by granting farmers "a part of the value of the slave." [42] What this meant was soon revealed. During the previous week the Dantas Project had been radically revised by the new administration and thus, when it was again presented to the Chamber on May 12, opponents of the earlier bill received the revised one with enthusiasm. Abolitionists, on the other hand, were incensed, quickly lining up against the changes and the new Liberal government. Analyzing the Saraiva Bill article by article before a crowd that jammed the Polytheama Theater, Rui Barbosa demonstrated that it departed significantly from the spirit and aims of the Dantas Bill, that while the latter was a step toward liberation, "an abolitionist transaction," the act drafted by the new ministry was "a surrender to the slavocrats." [43]

A comparison of the two bills will explain the reactions to it. The Dantas Act had proposed that slaves reaching sixty were to be *ipso facto* free, but Saraiva's bill stated that slaves so liberated were to be required, as a form of compensation to their masters, to grant them unpaid labor

40. *Jornal do Commercio,* April 14, 1885.
41. Lyra, *Historia de Dom Pedro II,* III, 21–23.
42. *Organizações e programas ministeriais,* p. 217.
43. Duque-Estrada, *A abolição,* p. 165; Rui Barbosa, *Confederação Abolicionista. Homenagem ao patriotico ministerio Dantas; Sessão publica e solemne realizada no dia 7 de Junho de 1885 no Theàtro Polytheama* (Rio de Janeiro, 1885), p. 41. The Saraiva Project was published in *Annaes da Câmara* (Sessão Extraordinaria) (1885), III, "Histórico," pp. 16–19.

for another three years (or until they reached the age of sixty-five).[44] The Saraiva Bill (and the final act sanctioned on September 28, 1885) set slave values at higher levels than did the Dantas Bill, despite a probable drop in slave prices during the months that separated the drafting of the two bills.[45] In the Saraiva Bill (as in the final act) plantation owners who agreed to rapid and total conversion to free labor were to have the right to sell all their slaves for five-percent bonds worth half the official value of their slaves. Workers thus freed were to remain in the service of their former masters for five more years in exchange for their keep and a wage of five réis per day. As Rui Barbosa pointed out, masters could receive more than 60 réis each day in interest from bonds granted to them for "liberating" their slaves, twelve times the daily stipend to be paid to "freedmen" for their labor. The interest from bonds to be received for freeing even the oldest slaves was to be more than twice the daily wage, and it was to be payable for thirty years, presumably long after the ex-slaves had died.[46]

The Dantas and Saraiva Bills (and the final law) all provided for a surtax on all forms of government revenue except export duties, but in the revised project there was a difference in how this money was to be used.[47] The original bill provided that all income from the surtax would be used to liberate slaves, but the Saraiva Bill (and the final law) divided the revenue into three equal parts. One third was to be used to free the oldest and least valuable slaves (those nearing sixty), one third to liberate slaves whose masters converted completely to free labor (in exchange for bonds and five more years of forced labor), and the last third was to be used to import colonists to work on the slaveholders' fazendas. The Dantas Bill would have imposed a surtax for the benefit primarily of slaves, but by the terms of the Saraiva Bill those who were to gain most from the surtax were the masters.

The most objectionable section of the Saraiva Bill, which Rui Barbosa compared to the American Fugitive Slave Act,[48] provided for fines of

44. The final law (see Appendix III) allowed sexagenarians to avoid this additional labor if they paid their masters 100 milréis. For the text of the law in Portuguese see *Colecção das leis do Imperio* (1885), Part I, Tome XXXII, pp. 14–19. The text in Gouveia's *Historia da escravidão* (pp. 397–401) excludes some distasteful provisions and adjusts the numbers of the articles to conform to the deletions.

45. The Saraiva Project set the highest evaluations (for slaves under 30) at 1:000$000, whereas the Dantas Project put it at 800$000. In the final act it was put at 900$000.

46. See Barbosa, *Confederação Abolicionista. Homenagem,* pp. 33–35.

47. This tax was set at six percent in the Dantas Project and at five percent in the Saraiva Bill and in the final legislation.

48. Barbosa, *Confederação Abolicionista. Homenagem,* pp. 39–40.

500 to 1,000 milréis for aiding or sheltering runaways, a provision amended in the final law to bring the crime of sheltering runaways under Article 260 of the Criminal Code. This change reduced the fine to between five and twenty percent of the value of the slave aided, but made persons who helped runaways liable to imprisonment for as long as two years.[49] Both José do Patrocinio and Rui Barbosa told abolitionist audiences that the new slave registration would permit masters to register free men as slaves, since it did not require information concerning the origins of slaves. Both men saw this change in the bill as a reason for the willingness of Andrade Figueira (Rio de Janeiro province) to accept that one part of the legislation.[50]

All three versions of the "reform" contained provisions to force exslaves to live and work for five years in the municípios where they were liberated. Freedmen who left their districts, said the final law, were to be regarded as vagabonds, arrested by the police, and put to work in agricultural colonies or on public works. A freed slave was to find work or be imprisoned for fifteen days, and incorrigible loafers were to be sent to one of several agricultural colonies administered under military discipline which the government would establish in various parts of the country.

The few provisions of the final act that abolitionists might have welcomed, if they had not been overshadowed by less acceptable provisions, included abolition of the inter-provincial slave trade (captives moved from one province to another were to be free) and a scale of descending values intended to put an end to slavery in thirteen years. The new legislation was expected, in the words of the Emperor, to bring tranquility to the nation's planters, but thousands of disgruntled abolitionists saw it as a surrender to planter interests.[51]

THE DEBATE

The Saraiva Bill created a whole new alignment in the Chamber of Deputies. Dantas had been opposed by most Conservatives, but Saraiva

49. Article 260 of the 1830 Criminal Code was contained under Title III, "Crimes against Property." It defined failure to report a discovery of lost property within fifteen days as "theft" and stated that persons found guilty of this crime were subject to the above-mentioned penalties. See *Colecção das leis do Imperio* (1830), I, 190.
50. *Gazeta da Tarde*, May 17, 1885; Barbosa, *Confederação Abolicionista. Homenagem*, p. 21; Nabuco, *Cartas a amigos*, I, 149.
51. *Annaes da Câmara* (1885), I, 10. For strong condemnations of the Saraiva Project, see Rui Barbosa, *A situação abolicionista* (Rio de Janeiro, 1885); *Rio News*, May 15, 1885

had the support of most members of the opposition party. Two small groups of Conservatives opposed Dantas. These included a few who rejected any change in the laws governing slavery—notably Andrade Figueira of Rio de Janeiro and Barros Cobra of Minas Gerais—and a somewhat larger Conservative faction, predominantly from the northern provinces, that regarded the bill as too moderate. Most of those Liberal dissenters who had opposed Dantas supported Saraiva, while Liberal abolitionists formed a new and larger anti-government faction within the Liberal Party.

So weak in fact was Saraiva after the bill passed the Chamber in mid-August, so much had the project depended for passage upon the Conservative minority that he and his ministry felt compelled to resign. Unable to find a Liberal leader who could reunite the fragmented Liberal Party, Pedro chose to stage another "imperial coup," asking a prominent Conservative, the Baron of Cotegipe, to form a minority government. To the exasperation of radical Liberals, it was under the leadership of this old pro-slavery planter-politician—who had the support of many moderate Liberals—that the bill was rushed unchanged through the Senate in time for the Emperor to endorse it on the fourteenth anniversary of the Rio Branco Law.[52]

During the long debate, Liberals in both houses bitterly and repeatedly criticized the Saraiva Bill. Joaquim Nabuco, newly returned to the Chamber after a long absence, was among the most outspoken critics, rejecting the bill because he believed that Brazil was ready for a much better act and because he foresaw an even more rapid pace of social change. The Saraiva Bill, he believed, threatened to block the more radical reform which the nation needed.[53]

Critics attacked specific provisions of the legislation. A deputy from Rio Grande do Sul noted that the surtax was difficult for a heavily taxed people to accept, particularly those citizens who had already freed their slaves and would be forced to help emancipate the slaves of less generous masters. Souza Dantas of Bahia could find no way to justify a tax which fell upon all citizens but was primarily intended to benefit a very limited number of wealthy farmers. Critics found it unjust, even absurd, that slaves under sixty could be freed by the emancipation fund while those sixty and older would work for their freedom for as long as three years. Well over sixty himself, Cristiano Otoni of Minas Gerais observed that when a slave reached that age "the obligation to serve. . . begins, while his hope for freedom through the emancipation fund disappears." [54]

52. Lyra, *Historia de Dom Pedro II*, III, 23–29; *Rio News*, August 14, 1885.
53. *Annaes da Câmara* (1885), II, 160–161, 206.
54. *Ibid.*, II, 214, 442; III, 351, 512.

Abolitionists deplored the paragraph which made it a crime to give asylum to a fugitive slave. Senator Dantas opposed the granting of subsidies—to be paid by the nation as a whole—to be used to import colonists destined to labor on agricultural properties. Opponents claimed that the freedmen's obligation to live for five years in the municípios where they were released reduced them to temporary serfdom.[55]

Drawing repeated criticism was the new table of prices for liberation of slaves through the emancipation fund. A senator from Minas Gerais complained that the project's price levels were much higher than the market price, and predicted that even the crippled would be sold at the high prices set by the legislation. Senator Otoni foresaw an end to the whole liberation movement until the government paid masters what it guaranteed. Slaveowners forced by personal circumstances to sell their captives, he predicted, would find speculators willing to pay a price below the levels set by the government, hoping for the profit which the government seemed to promise. The prices set by the bill were so high, said Nabuco, that in many places slaves would no longer be freed at current prices. Where, asked Pedro Salgado of Rio Grande do Sul, were slaves valued as high as 900$000, except in Rio de Janeiro, Minas Gerais, or São Paulo? [56] "The law will say to private persons," commented Senator Escragnolle Taunay, " 'Do not free your slaves for 200$000 or 300$000, because the state will guarantee you [an average] of 665$000.' " [57] If the slave evaluations to be established by the Saraiva Bill had existed in law in 1883, Nabuco told the Chamber, the great liberation movements of Ceará, Amazonas, and Rio Grande do Sul could not have occurred.[58]

The views of the bill's opponents were reflected in the amendments which they recommended. These included proposals to free the elderly without requiring further labor, to end corporal punishment, to free all African-born slaves over fifty-four and their children, to eliminate the fugitive-slave provision, to grant education to ingenuos, and to abolish slave sales and rentals. There were proposals to liberate slaves

55. *Ibid.,* II, 211; *Annaes do Senado* (1885), IV, 100–105.
56. *Ibid.,* IV, 43, 92; *Annaes da Câmara* (1885), III, 128, 352.
57. *Annaes do Senado* (1885), IV, 126.
58. *Annaes da Câmara* (1885), III, 123. "But what makes those prices so scandalous," wrote Nabuco to Charles H. Allen of the British and Foreign Anti-Slavery Society, "is that they amount to double, and, in many provinces, to three times more than the current prices. The Government raise so very high the value of slaves that it will be impossible for any province to do hereafter what Ceará and Amazonas did—I mean to free themselves through the falling off in slaves' values—as the slaves have now a price which will prevent people from giving them up, and will make every slave-master wait for his turn to have his slaves bought off by the State at a higher rate than he could get in the market." Cited by *South American Journal,* October 17, 1885.

used in immoral professions, to free the slaves of ministers, teachers, foreigners, and judges, to grant immediate freedom to all slaves in Brazil (with the obligation to serve their masters for five more years).[59] All these proposals were rejected, and only minor changes were allowed to temper the bill without making it more acceptable to abolitionists. In the Senate, despite incessant criticism, not a comma was changed because Cotegipe was anxious to avoid a dangerous delay. The matter rested on one point, he told the Senate in September. Either the project passed as it was, or the question would remain open "to agitate the public spirit. . . ." [60]

The speeches of the few legislators who looked upon the bill as too radical were like an echo from the Rio Branco debate, particularly when discussion turned to provisions threatening property rights. Andrade Figueira regarded the indemnification provided for in the bill as "ridiculous," the elimination of slavery through annual decreases in slave values as "a negation of indemnification," compensation through labor as no compensation at all, the concept of fixed slave prices a violation of economic law. Agriculture could not afford abolition without indemnification, warned Valadares of Minas Gerais, reminding the Chamber that both France and England indemnified.[61]

Opponents warned of the consequences of unleashing "a great mass of semi-barbarous population" upon the country, predicted that ex-slaves would migrate to the cities, that freedmen would give themselves up to vice and crime. Liberated slaves would not stay on the plantations, Andrade Figueira insisted in a personal clash with Saraiva on the Chamber floor. "Do not count on the services of the freedmen," warned Martinho Campos of Minas Gerais. "There is no way to make them work." [62]

Though more subdued than during the 1871 debate, regional differences on the slavery issue emerged in 1885 in significant ways. It was obvious, as Saraiva told the Chamber, that slavery was of no importance to Amazonas, where the few hundred blacks had already been freed and "the poor Indians" continued to labor.[63] It was obvious too that slaveowners in provinces where slave prices were high might look upon the government's table of slave values as unfair, while elsewhere the prices listed in the project might have inspired some joy. Recognizing the great variation in slave prices from province to province, Prudente de Morais favored differing price tables for the various provinces.

59. *Annaes da Câmara* (1885), II, 116, 298; III, 546–549; IV, 42; *Annaes do Senado* (1885), V, 41, 135, 188.
60. *Annaes do Senado* (1885), IV, 157–159; *Rio News,* September 15, 1885.
61. *Annaes da Câmara* (1885), I, 140, 216.
62. *Ibid.,* I, 142–143, 219, 241; *Annaes do Senado* (1885), V, Appéndice, p. 79.
63. *Annaes da Câmara* (1885), I, 243.

Paulista Delfino Cintra thought the prices for Rio de Janeiro, Minas Gerais, and São Paulo should be twenty-five percent higher than those of the table, that in the principal provinces of the north they should be the same as in the table, and that elsewhere they should be twenty-five percent less. Andrade Figueira demonstrated that in Ceará and Rio Grande do Sul the government's prices would be unfair to slaves with sufficient savings to buy their freedom at the market price, while in the coffee provinces it was the master who would be subject to loss.[64]

The most significant regional differences, however, were those which had begun to develop between São Paulo and Rio de Janeiro, the result again of economic differences between the two provinces. São Paulo, with its rich and expanding coffee industry, was already attracting some Europeans (6,500 in 1885 or 18.3 percent of the total number entering the country that year),[65] and efforts were already under way to bring in more. Richer than Rio de Janeiro province, moreover, São Paulo was better prepared to accept emancipation of slaves without compensation or even the abolition of slavery if it was imposed upon her. On the other hand, Rio de Janeiro's many insolvent planters and their representatives were in no position to compromise on the question of indemnification and were much less ready to see an end to slavery. In the debate of 1885 the representatives of both provinces were, as usual, in the forefront of the defense of the institution, but the Paulistas showed more willingness to compromise than did their allies from Rio de Janeiro. The differences came to the surface only rarely, but when they did they emerged with clarity.

Particularly significant during the four-month debate was the changing attitude of the Conservative Paulista coffee planter, Antônio Prado, one of the more famous members of a gifted family of São Paulo.[66] Prado had begun the debate as a strong opponent of reform. As a member of a Chamber committee charged with writing an opinion on the Saraiva Bill, he had dissented in May from the majority position, rejecting the bill on the basis of its failure to guarantee property rights.[67] Less than two months later, however, Prado had moved from opposition to qualified support of the bill. Indemnification was not the principal requirement of slaveowners, he told the Chamber in July. Instead, the masters were asking only that they be allowed to keep their slaves until they could replace them with new workers. A necessary complement of the Saraiva Bill, Prado thought, was a provision to aid the importation of free workers, for European immigrants could become a more powerful

64. *Ibid.,* I, 216, 250; II, 147
65. Smith, *Brazil,* p. 122.
66. For a brief outline of Prado's career as a coffee planter, banker, and Conservative politician, see Morse, *From Community to Metropolis,* p. 170.
67. *Annaes da Câmara* (Sessão Extraordinaria) (1885), III, 250.

force for the elimination of slavery than all the provisions in the bill.[68]

In August, by now a strong supporter of Saraiva and his bill, Prado declared that the planters of São Paulo no longer looked upon the Rio Branco Law as the final solution to the slavery problem. Despite the vital interests which bound his province to slavery, São Paulo, he said, possessed a practical understanding of the advantages of free labor and was taking steps toward the transformation of the labor system. The thirty or forty thousand European colonists who had already arrived in the province preferred to work as coffee pickers, and therefore Paulista planters continued to use slaves for clearing land.[69] Recently, however, with the spread of railroads into central São Paulo, planters had also begun to assign Europeans to land clearing.[70] The hardest work could be done by white men from Europe, Prado was telling his fellow legislators, and Europeans were at last arriving in meaningful numbers, at least in São Paulo. The obvious doom of slavery and the wealth of the new coffee planters had at last begun to generate "abolitionism" among the coffee planters of São Paulo. Prado's shifts to emancipationism were modest and cautious in 1885, little more than willingness to accept the very conservative provisions of the Saraiva-Cotegipe Law and to recognize the potential importance of immigration as a factor in the shift toward a free-labor system. The significance of Prado's evolving attitudes was to be more apparent by 1887, however, when under his leadership the province of São Paulo moved headlong into the abolitionist camp, dooming slavery at last to quick extinction.

68. *Annaes da Câmara* (1885), II, 86–91.
69. T. Lynn Smith's statistics show that about 26,000 immigrants had arrived in São Paulo during the eleven years from 1874 to 1884 inclusive. See *Brazil*, p. 122.
70. *Annaes da Câmara* (1885), III, 515–520.

*No one is obligated
to respect slavery. On the contrary,
it is the duty of every citizen
to fight it by every means.*

JOSÉ DO PATROCINIO
in the "Gazeta da Tarde," June 22, 1886.

15

PRELUDE
TO COLLAPSE

RESULTS OF THE SARAIVA-COTEGIPE LAW

If the sexagenarian law was intended to liberate elderly slaves, its success was partial. Official figures place the number of captives sixty and older at 90,713, but only 18,946 persons were enrolled as sexagenarians in 1886 and 1887 [1] (see Table 6). Some, of course, had died before the registration opened six months after the law was passed or before enrollment closed a year later. Some Africans who had been registered as older than they were in the 1870's to avoid the consequences of the law of November 7, 1831, might have been given ages closer to the reality in 1886 and 1887 to avoid the consequences of the law of September 28, 1885. A significant number, however, were never enrolled by their masters and were therefore legally free, and others were "liberated" in the weeks just before passage of the law with the understanding that they continue to grant their services for periods longer than those required by the Saraiva-Cotegipe Law, in some cases for terms of seven years.[2] The majority of the sexagenarians registered were located in the three major coffee provinces. Yet even in that region the number enrolled was a small minority of the persons registered as fifty-one or older during the 1870's, who, if still alive, might have benefited by the law of 1885 (compare Tables 5 and 6).

More significant than the surprisingly low enrollment of sexagenarians was the apparent failure of masters to register many younger persons in some parts of the country. The drop of more than 400,000

1. *Gazeta da Tarde*, April 13, 1885; *Correio Paulistano*, São Paulo, September 16, 1887; *Relatorio do Ministerio da Agricultura*, May 13, 1887, p. 38.
2. *O Paiz*, May 4, 1887; *Novidades*, March 21, 1887; Fonseca, *A escravidão, o clero e o abolicionismo*, pp. 581–586. This decision was reversed by Antônio Prado who, as Agriculture Minister, declared in February 1887 that any contract which violated the spirit and letter of the law of 1885 was null and void.

in the registered slave population between June 1885 and May 1887 (see Table 11) was undoubtedly the result of a high death rate, individual acts of emancipation, and, theoretically at least, the automatic elimination of the more than 90,000 slaves registered over sixty. Yet the greater decline in the slave population of the northeast during the two years (42 percent) and western and southern provinces (54.3 percent) suggests that many masters in those areas ignored the new registration and thus freed their slaves through default. In comparison, the slave population of São Paulo fell during the same period by about 30 percent, and in the coffee region as a whole, including the Município Neutro, where the loss of slave population was by far the highest in the nation, the loss was less than 34 percent. Masters in the coffee provinces registered a greater percentage of their slaves than masters elsewhere, and probably also purchased a significant part of the slave population of the Município Neutro.

NEW ABOLITIONIST GRIEVANCES

If the legislation was designed in part to silence the critics of slavery, it was only moderately successful. The law briefly "eclipsed" abolitionism, as Nabuco put it, but when the movement re-appeared it was no less impressive than before. When compared with the past, Nabuco wrote soon after passage of the law, the nation was tranquil. Provincial abolitionism, so effective in Ceará, Amazonas, and Rio Grande do Sul, had been halted and set back, perhaps a result of the maximum slave prices established by the law which the government appeared to promise, prices much higher than those paid by abolitionists in their emancipation campaigns. The abolitionist articles previously published in the *Jornal do Commercio* under such pseudonyms as Clarkson, Grey, and Garrison were no longer appearing.[3] Everywhere, wrote Nabuco, the abolitionist opinion "is being chilled by a strong glacial current" from the imperial palace. Two or three years of abolitionism, thought Nabuco, had "spent the moral reserve of the nation, its capacity to take offense." [4]

But the eclipse was partial and brief. Just after the law was passed, in fact, the anti-slavery press renewed its attack, deploring the threat to abolitionists contained in the fugitive-slave provision, denouncing the apparent alliance of the Crown with slavery interests and the ease with which masters allegedly could register slaves imported after November

3. These three "Englishmen" were Gusmão Lobo, Rui Barbosa, and Joaquim Nabuco respectively. See Nabuco, *The Life of Joaquim Nabuco,* pp. 108–110.
4. Joaquim Nabuco, *O eclypse do abolicionismo* (Rio de Janeiro, 1886), pp. 31–32.

7, 1831.[5] "The hand of Dom Pedro did not tremble when it signed this ukase," editorialized the *Gazeta da Tarde* the day after the bill became law. "There is no offense or error of the slaveholder which [the law] does not excuse and forgive," wrote Lamoureux of *The Rio News,* "while there is no possible fault of the freedman which it does not place under police supervision and judicial correction. It is to be expected, of course, that a legislature of slaveholders will make laws in their own interests, but even in this there is a limit beyond which it is not decent to go." [6]

Abolitionists soon had additional reasons to complain. Late in October it was learned that the Portuguese Havas news agency had informed the world that Brazilian slavery had been abolished. By early December the report had been widely circulated abroad, according to irate abolitionists, but the Brazilian government had allegedly done nothing to correct the error. In contrast to the information received in foreign countries, Brazilian newspapers were running advertisements threatening to prosecute persons who sheltered slaves, and the police had begun to search private homes for runaways with the authority granted by the emancipation bill.[7]

The national election of January 15, 1886 further fueled abolitionist resentment. Carried out under the regime of Cotegipe, its result was a Conservative-dominated Chamber that appeared even less sympathetic to slavery reform than its predecessor.[8] The Liberal and abolitionist reaction to this electoral travesty took the form of a rebuke of the political system itself. In a country of twelve million people, complained abolitionist editors, where fewer than two hundred thousand persons, principally slaveowners and government employees, were eligible to vote, it could not be said that the legislature represented national opinion. The nation was abolitionist, said a newspaper of the port city of Santos in proof of this charge, but slavery was supported in the Assembly. "When we see a genuine abolition measure originating from Barão de Cotegipe," said *The Rio News* in February, "we shall then believe that a good omelet can be expected from bad eggs." No new abolitionist measure could be expected either from his government or

5. *A Monarchia Brasileira se agarrando á taboa da escravidão* (Bahia, 1885), pp. 65–66; *Gazeta da Tarde,* August 14, 1884.
6. *Gazeta da Tarde,* September 29, 1885; *Rio News,* October 5, 1885.
7. *Rio News,* October 24, December 5, 1885; *Gazeta da Tarde,* October 26, 1885. According to Fonseca, *A escravidão, o clero e o abolicionismo,* p. 341, the fugitive-slave provision was first used in the city of Cachoeira, Bahia, in 1885, against the abolitionist Cesario Ribeiro Mendes.
8. Nabuco, *The Life of Joaquim Nabuco,* p. 147; *Organizações e programas ministeriais,* p. 398. The election of 1886 was a reversion to the controlled balloting normal before the electoral reform of 1881. The new Chamber was composed of 103 Conservatives and only 22 Liberals.

from the new Chamber of Deputies, the American paper predicted, "unless some powerful, popular movement forces the adoption of new progressive measures." [9] As usual, Lamoureux appeared more conscious than many Brazilians of the explosive potential of Brazilian society, though he was never in doubt about the inclinations of the ruling politicians. In fact, in less than two and one-half years this same Chamber of Deputies would be forced by greatly altered circumstances to end slavery entirely.

THE COTEGIPE MINISTRY
AND THE "BLACK REGULATION"

The pro-slavery attitude of the Cotegipe ministry—apparent in its interpretation of the new law—was perhaps the most powerful factor in the quick revival of abolitionism.[10] Under the direction of Cotegipe's Agriculture Minister, Antônio Prado, the new law was implemented with little regard for public opinion. Each decision seemed to favor the interests of the slaveholders. José do Patrocinio criticized the rules governing the new slave registration that were issued on November 4, 1885, particularly the failure to require information concerning the family origins of slaves to be enrolled. "If a mulatto slave of Mr. Antônio Prado were to die," wrote the editor of the *Gazeta da Tarde* with sardonic humor, "a slave more or less of the age of the mulatto who writes these lines, and I should have the misfortune to pass by the plantation of the illustrious minister on the day on which His Excellency takes his human cattle to the ignominious market-place of the black law, . . . I would have no means of proving that I am not the slave of that great lord." Patrocinio criticized Prado for instructions that he allegedly sent to the presidents of Amazonas and Ceará ordering them to carry out slave registrations in their provinces as provided for in the Saraiva-Cotegipe Law, an order which the abolitionist editor interpreted as an extension of the slave system into areas where it had been regarded as permanently eliminated.[11] As a result of this decision, 108 slaves were registered in Ceará during 1886 and 1887 (see Table 11), though none were found within the confines of Amazonas.

9. *Diario de Santos,* Santos, São Paulo, November 23, 1886; *Gazeta da Tarde,* January 18, 1886; *Rio News,* February 5, 24, 1886.
10. A decree of November 4, 1885, regulating the new registration, seemed to reflect the bias of its author with its repeated references to sexagenarians as "slaves." See *Relatorio do Ministerio da Agricultura,* May 4, 1886, "Annexo N," pp. 4–5.
11. *Gazeta da Tarde,* November 19, 1885; March 26, 1886.

Far more offensive, however, were the regulations of the law issued by Antônio Prado on June 12, 1886, collectively dubbed the "Black Regulation" by indignant abolitionists at huge new rallies in Rio de Janeiro. Although much of this legal directive served to underline the retrogressive character of the law, two of Prado's decisions were particulary offensive. The first of these theoretically extended the life of slavery by more than a year by directing that annual decreases of slave evaluations were to begin *with the date of the slaves' registration* instead of the date of the law.

Even more criticism was heaped upon Prado's interpretation of the ban on the inter-provincial slave trade. The slave sent from one province to another, said the Saraiva-Cotegipe Law, would become free, but, according to Prado, for the implementation of this provision the Município Neutro was to be regarded as forming part of the province of Rio de Janeiro. Thus, nearly 30,000 slaves in the Município Neutro became eligible for transfer across a provincial border into an area where the demand for new slaves persisted. "The infamous regulation . . . orders the recruitment in the Brazilian capital of victims for the plantations of the province," commented the *Gazeta da Tarde* in its usual vitriolic style. The regulation, wrote Nabuco, was "a low and sordid conspiracy against the glimmering of decency that had existed in this capital in regard to the slaves . . . ." [12] In fact, the 74.9 percent drop in the slave population of the Município Neutro from 1885 to 1887, by far the largest percentage drop for any of the twenty-one major political units of the Empire (see Table 11), was probably the result, in part at least, of the continuing slave trade between the city of Rio and the bordering province of Rio de Janeiro, and it is entirely possible that slaves transported from the Município Neutro also found their way into nearby São Paulo and Minas Gerais, though the illegality of such a movement would have prevented the compiling of statistics.

As though intended to rouse the ire of the abolitionists, the Prado decree also regulated one of the most criticized parts of the Saraiva-Cotegipe Law. Concerning the fugitive-slave provision, the directive stated that the punishment for "theft" described in Article 260 of the Penal Code (up to two years in prison) would be imposed upon anyone who knowingly concealed, employed, or took into his house or establishment a slave belonging to another person. The public had the responsibility to report runaways to the local judge or police inspector within fifteen days, and not to do so could bring imprisonment. Anyone who aided a slave who had been severely punished by his master or who fled his place of employment under a serious threat of punishment also had the duty to bring that slave to the nearest official in the shortest

12. *Ibid.*, June 22, 1886.

possible time in order that the authorities could proceed in accordance with the law.[13]

To protest against the "Black Regulation," particularly its incorporation of the capital into the province of Rio de Janeiro, more than two thousand persons assembled at the Polytheama Theater on June 29, 1886. The government was mistaken, João Clapp told this large audience, if it thought it could intimidate the abolitionist movement by a campaign of calumny and by a bush-captain police force. Brazilian slavery was a hard-dying institution, Nabuco told the same meeting. "Now a termination date is set, and then is extended; the districts are separated from one another, and then they are joined." The audience unanimously adopted a resolution protesting "full of indignation and shame against the act of the government that established the commerce in slaves between the capital of the Empire and the province of Rio, and equally against the act of the same government increasing from thirteen to fourteen and a half years the duration of slavery according to the Saraiva Law." The citizens also appealed "to the humane sentiments of the Brazilian People in order that this two-fold and infamous assault upon the national honor shall not become a consummated fact." [14]

The victory of José do Patrocinio in an aldermanic race in the capital only two days later provided more evidence that the "Black Regulation" had set the abolitionist boulder rolling once again. Patrocinio's own newspaper saw his victory as an energetic protest against the "unworthy directive that tried to turn this capital into a slave market." Celebrations were carried on during much of election day outside the headquarters of the victorious editor, who managed nonetheless to put out three editions of his paper on the same day. The *Gazeta* commented: "It would be an endless task if we were to try to publish a list of the persons of all social classes who came to embrace or congratulate our friend. Not missing among them were representatives of the army and navy, who have always looked with sympathy upon the ceaseless efforts of our director on behalf of the liberty of the slaves." Votes for Patrocinio had come from thirty-seven of the forty electoral districts of the city, a fact interpreted to mean that the idea of freedom had penetrated everywhere, "even into the emporiums of slavery, even into the houses of the masters, and perhaps into the hearts of their sons." [15]

The angry reaction to the "Black Regulation" did indeed erupt even on the most formal occasion and in the best of company. The regulation

13. For an English translation of the entire "Black Regulation," see *BFSP* (1885–1886), LXXVII, 897–909.
14. *Gazeta da Tarde,* June 30, 1886.
15. *Ibid.,* July 2, 1886.

of June 12 was a violation of the territorial autonomy of the Município Neutro, charged the president of the Municipal Chamber in the presence of the Emperor and the royal family. The directive, he said, had reopened the inter-provincial slave traffic, nullifying the efforts of the Municipal Chamber, which in one year had freed 560 slaves.[16]

Like the Cotegipe government, the Chamber of Deputies also seemed intent on arousing the indignation of the sensitive abolitionists. By a vote of sixty to twenty-seven the Conservative-dominated lower house decided in July to deny to the one popular abolitionist then included among them, José Mariano of Pernambuco, his right to his Chamber seat, setting off a new and almost unprecedented flare-up of abolitionist activity at scattered points across the country. On July 13 an overflow audience of more than eight thousand persons crowded the Polytheama Theater in Rio to protest the Chamber's action, while in the distant northern city of Recife some three thousand persons gathered outside the editorial offices of *A Provincia,* Liberal Party organ of Pernambuco. Both meetings denounced the Chamber's decision to reject the credentials of José Mariano, duly elected in the second district of the Pernambucan capital, and the fraudulent decision to grant his seat to a Conservative politician. The abolitionist activities in the two widely separated cities were bound together by telegraph. One message received in Pernambuco from the capital informed José Mariano's constituents that the man they honored was defending his cause in the national Chamber supported by a throng of sympathizers.[17]

Defeated in his attempt to retain his seat, in late July José Mariano embarked by steamship for Pernambuco, arriving three days later in Bahia, where he was met by an abolitionist crowd estimated at five thousand. Early in August the Liberal abolitionist, now a national hero, arrived in the capital of his own province to receive an extraordinary reception. "The city presented a festive appearance," reported the *Gazeta da Tarde,* "with its streets decorated with garlands and its ships adorned with flags and pendants." Met by commercial, academic, Masonic, and abolitionist organizations and a host of ladies who showered him with flowers, José Mariano was honored in a five-hour procession beginning at the city docks and ending in the heart of town. As the

16. *Ibid.,* August 4, 1886. The occasion was a meeting of the Chamber on the birthday of Princess Isabel for the liberation of slaves through the Livro de Ouro. For more on these gatherings, see *Arquivo do Distrito Federal. Revista de Documentos para a Historia da Cidade do Rio de Janeiro* (Rio de Janeiro, 1954), V, 337–338; *Emancipação pelo Livro de Ouro da Illma Câmara Municipal no dia 29 de Julho de 1885* (Rio de Janeiro, 1885); DPHAG, 6-1-15; 6-1-16; 6-1-42. A small contemporary painting of such a meeting can be seen in a hallway of the Imperial Palace in Petrópolis, a gift of the Municipal Chamber to the Emperor.
17. *Gazeta da Tarde,* July 22, 1886.

celebration took on exuberance, local garrisons went on alert. The entire business community allegedly closed down in honor of the legislator whom the city had sent to the capital of the nation and there seen rejected.[18]

Probably the most significant achievement of the revived movement in the final months of 1886 was the revocation of those parts of Brazilian laws that legalized whipping as punishment for slaves in public establishments. Inspiring this unexpected reform was an event involving the deaths of two of four slaves condemned to endure 300 lashes by a jury in Paraíba do Sul, a coffee community some forty miles from the capital. Though countless incidents of the kind had passed unnoticed before, this one was discussed by Joaquim Nabuco in *O Paiz,* and the story was carried sensationally in other papers.[19] Brought to the attention of the Senate by Dantas, the incident was warmly debated there until the Minister of Justice proposed the elimination of corporal punishment from the nation's statutes. Hastened perhaps by the complete abolition of slavery in Cuba, decreed on October 7, the bill (approved by the Senate on October 4) entered the Chamber on October 11 and was passed into law five days later.[20]

In a Chamber reputed to be almost solidly opposed to change in slavery legislation, the bill encountered remarkably little resistance, though several deputies recognized that to end the threat of physical punishment was nearly equivalent to the abolition of slavery itself. Coelho Rodrigues of Piauí colorfully informed the Chamber that a law to abolish whipping "carries abolition in its belly. . . ." Using more conventional pro-slavery rhetoric, Lacerda Werneck predicted that the abolition of the lash would bring disaster, consternation, the disorganization of labor. Agricultural establishments could not be maintained, declared this experienced planter, without "a severe regimen of punishment." Lourenço de Albuquerque of Alagôas addressed his doubts directly to the ministry: "In the event that the fears of. . . the planters are realized," he asked, "does the government possess. . . an ample public force sufficiently disciplined to guarantee their lives and property?" Foreseeing rapid emancipation resulting from the bill, the same

18. *Ibid.,* July 24, 28, August 5, 1886.
19. See Nabuco, *The Life of Joaquim Nabuco,* pp. 149–150, and *Gazeta da Tarde* for August 1886.
20. *Annaes da Câmara* (1886), V, "Histórico," p. 7.

legislator predicted: "Soon we will see who is right, I who declare this truth, or the noble deputies who would deny it." [21]

Antônio Prado, defending the bill on behalf of the government, denied that it would bring the results predicted, though he had reasons to doubt his own arguments. Degradation, exile, long prison terms, even forced labor—punishments that restrained free men—could cause little concern among slaves, whom society anyhow granted little dignity, no secure home or country, and a minimum of personal freedom. Slaves had always remained at work on their masters' lands primarily through fear of physical punishment. Without this restraint, as a few deputies explained, slavery was unworkable. Within a year, in fact, another senator from São Paulo was to tell the upper chamber that slave labor had been completely disorganized and slaves totally unmanageable since the day when corporal punishment was abolished and local jailers were no longer allowed to inflict ill-treatment upon runaways.[22] Yet the General Assembly, under pressure from abolitionists and the example of Cuba, abolished corporal punishment, the key to the slave system. With this action, as some of them had warned, they had all but ended slavery itself.

21. For the debate on the bill, see *Annaes da Câmara* (1886), V, 452–482. This was not the first time that abolition of whipping had been proposed or that it had been rejected on the grounds that other forms of punishment would not deter the slaves. In response to a proposal to end whipping discussed by the Council of State in 1868, Baron Bom Retiro argued: "With whipping abolished, there will remain galley punishment (chain gangs) and imprisonment with labor, and . . . neither of these will be effective in relation to the slave. For many of them, imprisonment with labor . . . will be an improvement of their condition, if not an incentive to crime." See Nabuco, *O Abolicionismo,* p. 131.
22. Godoy, *O elemento servil,* p. 44.

A few labourers
by entering the lock-fast slaves' quarters,
on a few estates, and telling the slaves how easily
they could get freedom, if they would revolt,
could put the whole country in a blaze . . . .
The slave does not know
how easily the thing
could be done.

A. SCOTT BLACKLAW, "SLAVERY IN BRAZIL,"
"The South American Journal," London, July 20, 1882.

Against slavery
every method is legitimate and good.
The slave who submits stands against God
and against civilization. His model,
his master, his apostle
must be Spartacus . . . .

JOSÉ DO PATROCINIO
in the "Gazeta da Tarde," June 22, 1886.

16

THE
CONVERSION OF
SÃO PAULO

ABOLITIONISM IN THE PORT OF SANTOS

Soon after passage of the law that prohibited the whipping of slaves the national conflict was indeed radicalized, and slavery itself began to crumble. Urged on by abolitionists, captives suddenly began to leave plantations in large numbers. Police units, accused of acting as paid mercenaries, were sent to recapture them and in the process came into direct and violent conflict with the runaways and their protectors. A desperate government turned toward unconstitutional processes to restrain the freedom movement and stirred up a hornet's nest of angry citizens. Equally incensed planters resorted to violence and terror, while others began to free their slaves in order to save their crops, their fortunes, and their society. Nabuco had predicted in 1883 that abolition would be achieved by an act of parliament, not through agitation in the city streets or incitement to revolt on the plantations.[1] But peaceful methods had failed to bring the results that abolitionists had anticipated. The Assembly had passed an unacceptable law, and thus the following year opponents of slavery resorted to non-legal action. A plan for simultaneous slave rebellions on Paulista plantations to begin on Christmas Eve, 1886, was thwarted, but slaves nonetheless began to leave the fazendas, and there was no force in Brazil that could stop them.[2]

The first major scene of violence during this last stage of the struggle to abolish slavery was the port city of Santos in the province of São Paulo. Though Santos and surrounding communities contained fewer than three hundred slaves in 1886, as late as October of that year the local Sociedade Emancipadora 27 de Fevereiro had failed to persuade residents to part with a significant number of their captives.[3] This tropical port on the edge of the Serra do Mar, with its economic ties to the inland plantation economy, its great coffee warehouses, its new railroad station built for the transportation of coffee, hardly seemed a likely place, in fact, for a fateful clash in the slavery struggle. Yet it was there, the urban core of a district now deprived of most of its slaves, that one of the most important local abolitionist movements developed and briefly thrived in late 1886 and early 1887, setting off a whole series of events locally, then regionally, then nationally, leading to a rapid end to slavery.

Just days after the General Assembly abolished corporal punishment, Brazil's most effective demagogue, José do Patrocinio, paid a brief visit to Santos, giving local supporters an opportunity to display their enthusiasm with speeches, fireworks, toasts, and musical entertainment.[4] Fired up by the attentions of Patrocinio and the death a week later of a leading Paulistia abolitionist, José Bonifacio de Andrada e Silva the younger,[5] the town was transformed within a week into a strategic and vital center of the abolitionist struggle.

After the departure of Patrocinio, whose presence no doubt helped to invigorate the local freedom movement as it had four years before in Ceará, abolitionists met at the Guarany Theater to pay homage to José Bonifacio and to adopt a program for the rapid liberation of Santos. Within five days all the slaves in the town had been freed, and fugitive slaves, already aware of the abolition of the lash, had begun to take refuge in the region. On November 3, in apparent response to the

1. Nabuco, *O Abolicionismo*, pp. 25–26.
2. Frank Vincent, *Around and about South America* (New York, 1890), pp. 263–264.
3. *Diario de Santos*, July 29, September 25, October 17, 1886.
4. *Ibid.*, October 21, 22, 23, 1886.
5. This was the brilliant grandson of the "Patriarch of Brazilian Independence." As a teacher at the law school in São Paulo he had helped to inspire the antislavery student movement in the late 1860's. See Chapter 5 above.

sudden appearance of a full-blown abolitionist movement in Santos, a force of twenty soldiers arrived by train from the provincial capital, and during the night patrolled the streets in the vicinity of the jail, where five captured runaways were imprisoned. The attitude of these intruders, said the abolitionist *Diario de Santos,* was "menacing, ugly, hostile." [6]

During the following weeks Santos was quickly recognized as a haven for runaways from upland plantations, and the local police began to serve as paid slave hunters. Tensions heightened until on November 20 the first blood was shed. On the previous day the police chief of São Paulo province, Dr. Lopes dos Anjos, had arrived in Santos with eighteen armed men under orders from Agriculture Minister Antônio Prado to capture runaways. Early the following morning Lopes dos Anjos, now with forty armed men, was conducting four re-captured fugitives to the railroad station for transportation to the provincial capital when his force was suddenly attacked by a crowd of abolitionists allegedly incited by the ill-treatment which the guards were meting out to the slaves. In the scuffle the police fired their weapons, wounding several people, and a slave, taking advantage of the confusion, fled to the nearby docks, leaped into the bay, and began to swim toward the opposite shore. Cheered on by spectators on the piers, the swimmer was pursued by two small boats. To the delight of the police, one of them overtook him, but instead of returning the runaway the unknown boatman pulled the swimmer aboard, turned his boat toward the opposite shore, and vigorously rowed in that direction, urged on by joyful abolitionists. Frustrated by the turn of events, powerless to recapture his prisoner, Lopes dos Anjos ordered his men to break up the crowd by force.[7]

The crisis in Santos lasted four more days. On the day after the incident on the waterfront two dozen policemen arrived from São Paulo, and three days later rumors of an impending attack upon the offices of the *Diario de Santos* (a real danger in the light of the destruction of the offices of the *Gazeta da Tarde* the year before by some fifty invading "ruffians") brought a crowd of more than a thousand persons to its defense.[8] With this show of popular determination, the crisis waned, but it had become apparent that the people of Santos were committed to abolitionism. This information quickly reached the slaves of the interior, and they were soon streaming by the hundreds into the neighborhood of the coffee port.[9]

6. *Diario de Santos,* October 31, November 5, 6, 1886.
7. *Ibid.,* November 21, 23, 1886; *Gazeta da Tarde,* November 22, 1886.
8. *Gazeta da Tarde,* January 5, 1885; *Diario de Santos,* November 23, 26, 1886.
9. Moraes, *A campanha abolicionista,* pp. 267–268.

ANTÔNIO BENTO, THE CAIPHAZES,
AND THE RUNAWAY MOVEMENT

Elsewhere in the province other abolitionists were taking direct action to put an end to slavery. At the head of these revolutionaries was Antônio Bento, leader of the provincial abolitionist movement since the death of Luiz Gama in 1882. A renegade member of the Brazilian planter class, an abolitionist zealot inspired by Christian faith, whom Nabuco and *The Rio News* compared with John Brown, Bento was an unorthodox figure with a penchant for broad-brimmed hats and flowing black capes.[10]

The activists who followed Bento were called "caiphazes," a term probably derived through a complex religious or mystical association from "Caiaphas," the high priest who delivered Jesus to Pontius Pilate. The key to Bento's use of the word is perhaps contained in John, 11: 50, in which Caiaphas, in an unconscious prophecy, claims that Jesus "should die for the people, and that the whole nation perish not." Whatever the exact significance of the term to Bento, who seems to have been haunted by the symbolism of Christ the Redeemer, he and his followers saw themselves as the instruments of Brazil's *redemption*. No longer satisfied with legal methods, with meetings, parades, and emancipation funds, by 1886 they had built an effective and widespread organization which specialized in urging slaves to abandon their masters' plantations, with an emphasis at first upon estates where slaves were notoriously mistreated.[11]

In ample rooms supplied by the black brotherhood of Nossa Senhora dos Remedios in the heart of São Paulo, Bento published a rough-hewn newspaper symbolically called *A Redempção,* a propaganda sheet in which, in the words of Evaristo de Moraes, "facts and men . . . were exposed as on a whipping post . . . ." Weak on grammar, the Paulista paper was addressed primarily to "Zé Povinho," as Bento put it, the "Joe Citizen" of Brazilian society, but the paper was soon being read in the big houses as well as in the slave huts. In São Paulo, Bento main-

10. *Ibid.,* pp. 261–262; *Rio News,* May 5, 1888. For a description of Bento by one of his followers, see Bueno de Andrada, "A abolição em São Paulo," pp. 265–266.

11. *Ibid.,* p. 266. There is evidence that by mid-1887 a decision to turn toward illegal methods had been communicated to abolitionists in more than one part of the country, perhaps by Bento or Patrocinio. "Subversive abolitionism" appeared in Paraná in June 1887 with the establishment there of a "secret anti-slavery society," significantly called Ultimatum. The members of this organization were to use pseudonyms, were to make any sacrifice, to obey every order of their leaders, and to use force if necessary to achieve the aims of the organization. See Ianni, *As metamorfoses do escravo,* pp. 228–229.

tained a lodging house for homeless blacks, marked outside by a white flag. In the sacristy of Nossa Senhora dos Remedios, headquarters of the caiphazes, he assembled a collection of instruments once used on slaves: leather whips, stocks, chains, yokes, and iron collars. In this house of religion Bento was looked upon as "a kind of Pope who heard his ministers in solemn daily audience." [12]

The men who joined Bento were drawn from all classes and every political party. They included the black members of the brotherhood of Nossa Senhora dos Remedios and the provincial intelligentsia, ex-slaves as well as former masters and the sons of masters. Enlisted in the anti-slavery cause were men who earned fame in other fields, and others who might have remained unknown, except for a brief account of their activities which an aristocratic follower of Bento, Antônio Manoel Bueno de Andrada, published some thirty years later in a newspaper of São Paulo.[13]

To his cause Bento attracted the Liberal owner of a pottery shop, a painter of altars and saints nicknamed "Chico Dourador," the cigar-makers in a shop in São Paulo and its proprietors, "a nest of caiphazes," in the words of Bueno de Andrada, always available when called upon to protect slaves sheltered in his nearby home. They included the editor of an abolitionist journal, *O Grito do Povo,* and a brilliant staff of writers. Enlisted in the movement were students from the law academy, notably the writer, Raul Pompéia, who specialized in urging shirking Republicans to live up to their alleged beliefs. Bento's followers included merchants, priests, students at the preparatory school, army officers, commercial employees, typographers, railroad conductors, and even a few members of the provincial police force.

The caiphazes were given tasks corresponding to their talents. A man whose nickname was Antônio Paciencia made a practice of working on plantations until he could find a way to start the whole crew of captives on the road to freedom. The specialty of a man named Antonico was to creep into the slave quarters during the night hours to urge the inhabitants to flee, a practice which eventually cost him his life. With branches in many parts of the province, with members in private institutions, in the government bureaucracy, and even in rural areas, the movement seemed to pervade Paulista society, yet remained secret

12. Affonso A. de Freitas, *A imprensa periodica de São Paulo desde seus primordios em 1823 até 1915* (São Paulo, 1915), pp. 315–316. (The author of this study of the press of São Paulo was a contributor to *A Redempção* and a member of Bento's secret organization, which he described.) See also *Cidade do Rio,* February 17, 1888; Moraes, *A campanha abolicionista,* p. 268; Antonio Gomes de Azevedo Sampaio, *Abolicionismo. Um paragrapho. Considerações geraes do movimento anti-esclavista e sua historia limitada a Jacarehy* (São Paulo, 1890), pp. 9–10.
13. Bueno de Andrada, "A abolição em São Paulo," pp. 261–272.

and conspiratorial. "From the church of Remedios," wrote Bueno de Andrada, "the revolutionary plot spread through many cities of the interior. From the most important rural centers Antônio Bento and the editors of *A Redempção* received information and proposals for the rescue of the slaves. In Campinas, Amparo, Casa Branca, and other places under the apparent domination of the slavists, there were groups of persons who, under great caution, plotted as true 'caiphazes'." [14]

At least one description of a meeting between runaways and abolitionists has been recorded. On a dark night in August 1887 one Antônio Sampaio found a large crowd of men milling about mysteriously on a country road, and decided that they were stealing slaves. "The crowd went toward the road, surrounding ten human creatures, women with babies at their necks and dirty, poorly dressed men with a look of hunger and misery, carrying in their hands a few bundles of clothing." Candles were lit, and Sampaio recognized most of the free men.

" 'Are you all slaves?' somebody asked.
" 'We are, yes sir,' they replied.
" 'Do you want to be free?' several men asked.
" 'Yes, sir, we do.' "

The last question convinced Sampaio that the mysterious men were not stealers of slaves, but abolitionists, "restoring the *thing* stolen to its true owner." [15]

Convincing the slaves to abandon the plantations was only the first and probably the most dangerous achievement of the caiphazes. Once the fugitives were on their way, the abolitionists escorted them to a place of refuge. The provincial capital and the port of Santos were the main goals of runaways, who traveled on foot or, aided by railroad coachmen, sped to freedom on passenger trains. Arriving at their destinations, they found shelter in private homes, warehouses, plantations, and business establishments. In Santos, where they came with little fanfare during the first five months of 1887, they constructed a shanty town, the quilombo of Jabaquara, on high, unoccupied ground between the sea and the mountains—a huge cluster of huts of wood, straw, mud, and sheets of zinc for roofing, where they were soon planting gardens and earning money as coffee carriers on the docks or through the manufacture of charcoal. [16]

14. *Ibid.*, pp. 264–270; Moraes, *A campanha abolicionista*, pp. 266–276; Freitas, *A imprensa periodica*, pp. 315–316.
15. Sampaio, *Abolicionismo*, pp. 29–31. Italics in original.
16. Moraes, *A campanha abolicionista*, pp. 263–276; Santos, *Os republicanos paulistas*, pp. 182–183; Viotti da Costa, *Da senzala à colônia*, p. 316; Morse, *From Community to Metropolis*, p. 160; Bueno de Andrada, "A abolição em São Paulo," p. 266.

Antônio Bento was as much of a showman as José do Patrocinio. To shock provincial society into supporting the growing movement, he appealed to powerful mystic tendencies that touched even the sophisticated urban life of the provincial capital. One example, related by Bueno de Andrada, suggests that the leader of the caiphazes was himself motivated by a ruthless and psychotic religiosity, which made him a particularly effective leader during the last chaotic phase of abolitionism. Having received a tortured black man from rural followers, a slave who (it was said) had been hung by the neck from an iron chain, his toes just touching the ground, his palms pierced by a knife, Bento decided to feature the victim in a religious procession, theatrically exposing the harshest aspects of slavery while identifying the fate of the tortured man and the nation's slaves with the martyrdom of Christ.

Bueno de Andrada describes the elaborately staged and fantastic procession:

Between the platforms of the saints, suspended on long staffs, appeared instruments of torture: iron collars, chains, yokes, whips, etc. In front, beneath the livid image of Christ crucified, walked the unfortunate slave, numb and tottering. Never have I attended such a sad and suggestive ceremony. The impression of the city was profound! The police did not dare to impede the march of the popular mass. The multitude followed silently. All felt deeply moved, except the unfortunate martyred black man, who was maddened by his pain.

According to the same witness, this emotional exhibition "cooled the moral force and spirit of the angriest slaveholders," and from that day forward the homes of the city were open to hordes of fugitives.[17]

SLAVES ABANDON THE
PLANTATIONS OF SÃO PAULO

The flights from the plantations began in 1886, accelerated during the first months of 1887, and by June of that year had created a full-blown crisis in the province of São Paulo. Slaveholders, seeing their labor forces reduced by mass flight, began to appeal to the provincial government, which responded with orders to local officials to guarantee the slaveholders' control over their human property. Frustrated by "blind and passionate abolitionism," in the words of Antônio Prado's newspaper, the *Correio Paulistano,* in early June the authorities of São Paulo informed the central government of the deteriorating situation and requested military aid.[18] Telegrams sent out mysteriously to individuals

17. *Ibid.,* p. 267.
18. *Correio Paulistano,* June 12, 1887.

and newspapers in an apparent attempt to justify the intervention of national forces claimed that three thousand rebellious blacks were marching toward the city of São Paulo. Newspapers of that city told of massive uprisings in Campinas and reported, with more accuracy, that two thousand fugitives had found refuge in Santos.[19]

Denials of the uprisings soon followed, but the Cotegipe government sent the requested reinforcements to São Paulo. The warship *Primeiro de Março* carrying a naval landing force of fifty men sailed from Rio for the port of Santos, and fifty-four officers and men of the Tenth Infantry Battalion were sent overland to the troubled area in São Paulo, despite the aversion of professional soldiers to the role of "bloodhound." The national forces were placed under the command of the provincial president, who was authorized to make full use of his executive powers to restore the fugitives to their masters.[20] Within hours a large force of planters and hired henchmen (*capangas*) were reportedly stopping trains in the town of Jundiaí and, with authority granted by the provincial president, Viscount Parnaíba, were making every black and mulatto passenger step down from the coaches for inspection.[21]

On June 12 the *Correio Paulistano* eased the crisis with a denial of slave rebellions, but added ominously: "There occurred simply, with greater frequency, cases of flights of slaves, who, in bands, sought refuge in the district of Santos, where they can be assured of shelter, it being difficult to discover and punish them there. . . ." [22] The *Diario de Santos* also reluctantly revealed that the people of that city had grown accustomed to the constant arrival of refugees and that large numbers of them were in fact camped nearby. The paper denied, however, that there had been a sudden uprising which might have justified the sending of a naval force to the port. The large runaway population of Santos was the result, it said, of "a slow emigration silently carried out, little by little, noiselessly and without trouble." [23]

Complaints from the press against the use of soldiers as slave hunters and an open demand for information in the Senate brought explanations of the government's action in mid-June from the new Agriculture Minister, Rodrigo da Silva. Many slave masters of São Paulo, he told the Chamber, had granted conditional freedom to their captives, but even this had not satisfied the abolitionists. The peaceful transformation of the labor system had suddenly been interrupted by a "true strike."

19. *Gazeta da Tarde,* June 13, 1887; *Rio News,* June 15, 1887.
20. *Diario de Santos,* June 14, 1887; *Correio Paulistano,* June 12, 1887.
21. *A Redempção,* São Paulo, June 14, August 4, 1887.
22. *Correio Paulistano,* June 12, 1887.
23. *Diario de Santos,* June 11, 14, 1887. Santos was probably not entirely peaceful. The *Correio Paulistano of* June 2, 1887, referring specifically to that city, told of "attacks of hordes of vagabonds driven by hunger if not by bad instincts. . . ."

"Seduced" by abolitionists, the slaves were leaving the fazendas en masse. "They flee in all directions," said the Minister, "and, transporting themselves on the railroads, they take refuge in the city of Santos, where they consider themselves immune and free from any legal compulsion from their masters." Not only was labor being disorganized, but the massing of runaways in Santos represented "a grave and imminent danger to public order and to prosperity." Having received requests for help from notable citizens of Campinas, the government had sent military and naval forces "with the exclusive purpose of maintaining public order and of tranquilizing the great agricultural and commercial interests now in a state of shock." [24]

The armed forces, however, were no longer able or willing to stop the runaways. Too many slaves were fleeing, and many soldiers and officers no longer believed in the legitimacy of slavery. Above all, captives had begun to sense that slavery was over, that they could now leave their masters and that others were leaving theirs, not only at the next plantation or the next município, but perhaps also on plantations in Pernambuco, Bahia, and Maranhão, and the other places in the north where many of them had lived. Not even the entire Brazilian army could have forced the slaves to remain on the plantations, said a member of the São Paulo Provincial Assembly months later, inspired as they were to flee in search of liberty by the "clandestine propaganda of the abolitionist agents in the centers of the greatest slave concentrations. . . ." [25]

Slaves had always run away, but as individuals or in groups of two or three, to join larger groups perhaps in the forests or in quilombos, but now, with a sudden awareness of the new state of things, whole plantation work forces, encouraged by Bento's "underground movement," were setting off for some nearby forest or distant city or entirely unknown destination. As they fled, they gained power over masters whose plans were dependent upon their labor. With their decision to flee the plantations and the inability of the soldiers and police to stop them, masters were left with no alternative but to accept a drastic change in the relationship between themselves and their slaves. It was Bento's "bold and shrewd management of this enterprise of running off the plantation slaves," claimed *The Rio News* some months later, that brought the planters of São Paulo "face to face with the alternative of providing themselves with free laborers and liberating their slaves voluntarily, or soon being left without a man." [26]

24. *Annaes da Câmara* (1887), II, 105.
25. *Annaes da Assembléa Legislativa Provincial de São Paulo. Sessão de 1888* (São Paulo, 1888), p. 433.
26. *Rio News,* May 15, 1888.

THE PLANTER-EMANCIPATIONIST
PHENOMENON IN SÃO PAULO

Thus, the abandonment of the coffee plantations of São Paulo brought a fundamental change to the labor system. Faced with the loss of their slaves and sensing that slavery would soon be abolished, some planters had already decided before the June crisis to follow the example of the masters of Rio Grande do Sul and grant provisional freedom through service contracts. In June and July there was a veritable wave of such manumissions in São Paulo. One eminent citizen who thus gave recognition to slavery's end was Manuel Campos Sales, ex-deputy, leader of the Republican Party in the seventh district of São Paulo, and later president of the Republic. Already by June 2 Campos Sales had set an example for his community with the liberation of all his slaves on condition that they serve him for four more years,[27] and dozens of other planters were soon doing much the same.

"At first sight this will appear to be a genuine case of conversion to the cause of emancipation," commented *The Rio News,* always suspecting the worst from the planters, "but when the facts are known it becomes resolved to no less an impulse than that of fear." Though the anxiety of the typical Paulista farmer had already been reduced by the arrival of many immigrant workers, "he is still in favor of getting all he can out of his slave." Nevertheless, a new movement had sprung up "among the young men in various parts of the province," continued the American paper, "which is nothing less than assisting slaves to escape. The two-thousand-odd fugitives in and about Santos are the results of their work, and hardly a day passes that they do not help others to escape." These were young men of position and influence, "not to be scared by threats or police interference. . . ." They were both numerous and well organized, and so the slaveholders had concluded that the best solution was "to purchase immunity by freeing their slaves on conditions of a short time service." São Paulo, it seemed to Lamoureux, would be a free province "before she has had time to consider the boldness of the plan which is being carried out." [28]

Fazendeiros of the coffee community of Campinas, unwilling to join the liberation movement until many of their slaves had already left them, at last held meetings in late August and early September to discuss liberation. One result of these gatherings was a published statement that urged the freeing of slaves provisionally. The problem of the extinction of slavery, it said, would best be resolved quickly by the

27. *Diario de Santos,* June 2, 1887.
28. *Rio News,* July 15, 1887.

planters themselves. *The first concern of agriculture was the stability of the labor force, which was rapidly being lured away.* Unless concessions were granted at once, slaves and freedmen would continue to leave their work since, with a changing moral climate, police could no longer stop them. Masters no longer had the support of public opinion, and people who were without slaves looked with indifference upon the flight of the captives. If slaves were to be freed on condition that they work a while longer, local officials could be relied upon to make them work. A spirit of public order would not allow intruders to lure away "free" men.

Agreeing on these principles, Campinas planters resolved on September 4 to grant their slaves conditional freedom with an obligation to serve them until the end of 1890, a period of more than three years. In addition to this, they prepared a request to the Municipal Chamber to legislate ordinances imposing prison terms of a month or two on persons who urged freedmen to forsake their labor obligations.[29]

As planters throughout the province of São Paulo continued to grant conditional emancipation and slaves persisted in grasping total freedom, major political leaders of the province were suddenly converted to abolitionism. The most spectacular change of heart was that of Antônio Prado himself, perennial target of abolitionist abuse and author of the infamous "Black Regulation," a "new Jefferson Davis" not many months before, in the words of the abolitionist *Gazeta da Tarde.*[30] Prado's plunge into the liberation movement, which according to Nabuco broke the solid resistance of the south to abolition,[31] occurred in the Senate on September 13. On that day Prado denounced a petition to the Chamber signed by the planters of Campinas asking for energetic measures to force the return of many of the community's slaves who had taken refuge in Santos. Having promised a few weeks before to free all his own slaves at the end of 1889, Prado compared the continuing plight of some Campinas fazendeiros who had been reluctant to free their slaves with the far better situation of other planters of São Paulo who had already done so and were hiring free workers, concluding that the turmoil in his province could be ended only by provisional manumission. The government itself, he warned, would eventually have to consider further slavery reform or face losing his support.[32]

The Baron of Cotegipe responded with praise for planters who granted conditional freedom, but reminded his new opponent that not all slave-

29. Godoy, *O elemento servil,* pp. 45–49; *South American Journal,* October 15, 1887.
30. *Gazeta da Tarde,* March 6, 1886.
31. Nabuco, *Minha formação,* p. 169.
32. *Annaes do Senado* (1887), V, 145–147; *South American Journal,* August 6, 1887.

holders were in the same circumstances. Four days later Senator João Alfredo Correia de Oliveira, a prominent Conservative from Pernambuco, joined Prado's defection. Any project to extinguish slavery, he announced in the Senate, *"especially if it were the last word on that subject,"* would have his sincere and dedicated support.[33]

The Conservative Party, nearly monolithic on the question of the slaves since the days of Rio Branco, had at last been severely divided— like the Liberal Party before it—by differing circumstances in the provinces. As the *Gazeta da Tarde* commented, Cotegipe could not agree with his two friends of yesterday (Prado and João Alfredo) because to do so would lose him the important support of Paulino de Souza and other political leaders of Rio de Janeiro province.[34] There was even humor in the situation. Remarking on the rapidly changing attitudes of politicians like Antônio Prado, a paper of Rio Grande do Sul predicted in late September that "one day soon we will see Mr. Andrade Figueira delivering speeches in the Polytheama at the side of Messrs. José do Patrocinio, Rui Barbosa, and Joaquim Nabuco." [35] Thus, the changed situation in São Paulo had brought Antônio Prado, formerly one of the more notorious of the pro-slavery politicians of the coffee provinces, into the ranks of the emancipationists. But Prado was not alone. The new attitudes of Paulista planters were reflected in a legislative project which another senator from that province, Floriano de Godoy, introduced into the upper chamber in late September. This "radical" bill would have abolished slavery at once throughout the Empire but obligated freedmen to work for their masters for three more years. Additional provisions were intended to enforce the labor obligation with prison sentences and stiff fines to be imposed on freedmen who failed to perform their duties and persons who encouraged them to abandon their places of employment—much the same solution decided upon by the planters of Campinas.[36]

Planter-emancipationism failed, however, to satisfy the slaves, who continued to leave the plantations in search of immediate freedom, aware that their liberation "was merely a trick to detain them in slavery" at a time when circumstances had freed them from that condition.[37] Inevitably the mass exodus brought violence, followed by even greater concessions from the planters of São Paulo, whose interest in restoring order was a most powerful consideration in the last months of 1887.

In mid-October some 150 men, women, and children, equipped with

33. Barão de Cotegipe, *Fuga de escravos em Campinas* (Rio de Janeiro, 1887), pp. 5–6; *Annaes do Senado* (1887), V, 229. Italics added.
34. *Gazeta da Tarde,* September 21, 1887.
35. *Correio Mercantil,* Pelôtas, September 23, 1887.
36. Godoy, *O elemento servil,* pp. 33–34.
37. Bastide and Fernandes, *Brancos e negros,* p. 51.

firearms, knives, and machetes, fled a plantation in the município of Capivari near the town of Itu, led by a black man named Pio. The ensuing battle with police, which brought death to one pursuer and many wounded on both sides, ended as a victory for the slaves, who overwhelmed their opponents, stripped and beat them. Frantic telegraphic reports of the incident convinced the central government of the need to send one more army unit to turbulent São Paulo, and fifty men were ordered to the beleaguered town of Itu. Before they could reach the scene, however, the band of runaways had already passed through on their way to Santos, quietly and with no offense to the frightened inhabitants. With orders to capture the fugitives dead or alive and to block their way to Santos by any means, an armed force posted itself in a position at Cubatão on the road to the port. A few days later, having lost at least one of their own, they returned to the provincial capital with thirteen runaways who had given themselves up for lack of food. Most of the others, however, "hunted like wild beasts," had been shot "without mercy" or had found refuge in nearby forests, and a telegram from Santos reported that thirty slaves from Capivari had arrived in Santos "safe and sound" and that "a great abolitionist banquet" had been held in the nearby quilombo of Jabaquara.[38] Violence also broke out in the city of São Paulo in October when police clashed with Negroes assembled for a festival at the church of São Francisco. The following day persons brandishing clubs attacked police, and blacks shouting "Death to the slavocrats!" and praising freedom stoned soldiers guarding the entrance to the government palace.[39]

The events in São Paulo caused another powerful Brazilian group to withdraw support from the slave system, a support that had only been grudgingly given. *O Paiz* reported on October 25, just days after the incident at Itu, that Marshall Deodoro da Fonseca, president of the powerful Club Militar, would present a petition to the Army Adjutant General for delivery to Princess Isabel, then acting as regent during her father's absence in Europe. The message, published that same day in *O Paiz,* asked the princess to spare the army the humiliating task of hunting down runaway slaves. Sanctioned by the members of the Club Militar, it stressed the army's willingness to maintain order in the event of slave revolts, but respectfully requested that soldiers not be ordered to capture slaves who were peacefully fleeing the horrors of servitude.[40]

The Adjutant General refused to deliver the petition to the princess

38. *Cidade do Rio,* October 19, 20, 1887; *Gazeta da Tarde,* October 20, 21, 22, 25, 1887; Bueno de Andrada, "A abolição em São Paulo," pp. 271–272.
39. Viotti da Costa, *Da senzala à colônia,* pp. 320–321.
40. *O Paiz,* October 25, 1887. For an English translation of the document, see Skidmore, "The Death of Brazilian Slavery," p. 159–161.

on technical grounds, but the position of the officers was widely publicized. Soldiers continued to be sent to places where slaves were on the loose, but were not afraid to express their unwillingness to capture fugitives. The commander of an army unit sent to a community in São Paulo early in 1888 agreed to maintain order but openly declined to capture slaves. A force sent to the town of Araras in the same province early in 1888 joined slave hunters and armed capangas who were blocking roads and stopping trains in search of runaways, but the soldiers made known their disgust with their assignment.[41] Some officers were unsympathetic to abolitionism, but the role of the slave hunter was dangerous, unpopular, inglorious, and increasingly futile, and therefore any hope that the military would vigorously prop up the slave system faded in the final months of 1887.[42]

In late November and early December unrest seemed to increase in São Paulo. Newspapers carried daily reports of slaves abandoning plantations, some of them armed. In places runaways were loitering on the roads, refusing to work. Army units sent to control them did nothing. On November 22 one Baron da Serra Negra freed more than four hundred slaves on three-year contracts, undoubtedly hoping that this would satisfy their demands and keep them peacefully at work, but three weeks later they were besieging the "big house," and the baron himself managed to escape with his life only with the help of "loyal slaves" who repulsed the rebels' attack.[43]

In response to the growing turmoil, political leaders of São Paulo began to plan a complete transformation of the plantation labor system in the last months of 1887. The intended changes included improvements in working and living conditions and the granting of salaries— all for the purpose of keeping the slaves at work. The *Correio Paulistano* took the lead on November 11, recommending that planters adjust themselves to changing conditions for their own benefit. Would it be better, Antônio Prado's paper asked, for the planters to maintain the system of unpaid labor and see their properties stripped of slaves, or to grant their workers salaries and be assured of their presence?[44] Two days after this article appeared, some twenty prominent coffee growers including representatives of all three major political parties, owners together of 2,500 slaves, agreed to establish a planter society for the

41. *Cidade do Rio,* October 30, December 1, 1887; January 23, 1888; *O Pirassinunga,* Pirassinunga, São Paulo, February 5, 1888.
42. For an analysis of the army's position in the last months of slavery, see Toplin, "The Movement," pp. 186–189. For the view that participation of former slaves in the Paraguayan War had undermined the ideology of slavery, particularly among soldiers, see Ianni, *As metamorfoses do escravo,* pp. 217–218.
43. *Correio Paulistano,* November 22, 27, 28, and December 13, 1887.
44. *Ibid.,* November 11, 1887.

specific purpose of promoting the emancipation of all slaves in the province by December 1890. Meeting in the provincial capital, they appointed a committee of five members, including Antônio Prado, to prepare the statutes of the new organization, and a public meeting was set for December 15 for the definitive establishment of "the great liberation association of the province." [45]

As the days passed, it became apparent that the planters' emancipation society intended to make significant changes in the conditions of plantation workers. On November 27 the *Correio Paulistano* proposed a course of action that included not only conditional freedom (the period of labor not to exceed three years), but also "the immediate fixing of a small salary" to be paid to those freedmen who remained peacefully at work during the entire period of additional service. Calling for a labor system compatible with the status of the free worker, the Conservative Party organ warned that reforms would have to come quickly "before the example of the successful flights can influence the spirit of the slaves of the fazendas in the neighboring districts." [46]

As scheduled, on December 15 more than 50 planters and the representatives of at least another 156—the owners of nearly 7,000 slaves—met in São Paulo. Prado's newspaper listed 199 names of persons who signed the membership book, 24 of whom owned a total of 2,755 slaves. The list included many representatives of the powerful Souza Queiroz, Prado, and Barros families.[47] One of the principal aims of the gathering was to make the public and perhaps the slaves themselves aware that the masters were meeting to discuss emancipation, and the conferences, therefore, were open to the public. The new society had two main purposes, according to the main speaker, Antônio Prado: the emancipation of every slave in São Paulo by the end of 1890 and the modification of the system of agricultural labor on the fazendas to assure that the freedmen remained at work at least during the period of transition from slavery to unconditional free labor.

The only source of conflict among the proprietors in attendance was whether emancipation was to be total and immediate or provisional. Campos Sales and a few followers favored immediate emancipation. Prado, however, argued that compelling slaves to work for an additional period was a flexible policy. If economic circumstances or other unforeseen changes demanded a shorter term or even immediate and unconditional emancipation, "our forces will converge toward that objective." One important purpose of the organization, in fact, was to

45. *Gazeta da Tarde,* November 14, 1887; *South American Journal,* December 10, 1887. The organizers included Leôncio de Carvalho (Liberal), Rafael de Barros (Republican), and Antônio Prado (Conservative).
46. *Correio Paulistano,* November 27, 1887.
47. *Ibid.,* December 17, 1887.

promote the freedom of every slave in the province through the instrument of organized propaganda.

According to Prado, keeping the freedmen on the plantations and avoiding general public disorder were the most important concerns of the planters of São Paulo and the principal goals of the new association, and he recommended ways to achieve these goals. The mere granting of freedom, conditional or absolute, did not alone resolve the planters' economic problems, said Prado. Liberation without additional concessions "does not assure the permanence of the freedman at work." The desire for the *rights* of free men, which the workers expressed by their escape, was a natural one, and reason therefore counseled the granting of those prerogatives: "rewarding his labor with a salary and modifying the labor system itself, reducing the hours of work, totally abolishing punishment, giving him better food and clothing, ceasing, finally, to consider him a mere laboring machine."

To achieve the needed economic and social reform without economic disorder and sacrifice, Prado warned, required prudence and firmness. The alternative to action was more disruption and perhaps insuperable difficulties. Under the circumstances it would be madness, he warned, for slaveholders

to stand with crossed arms and watch the sad spectacle of the abandonment of the plantations, the ruin of crops, and perhaps the destruction of properties. . . . It is to be regretted that the patriotic initiative of the planters of São Paulo and this eloquent demonstration of the power of their forces to overcome the difficulties of the situation are opposed by the disturbers of order or those who speculate upon the fate of the unhappy slaves, who, deceived, leave the work of the plantations, where in peace they could enjoy the advantages and rights of their new condition, to be abandoned on the public roads, consigned to misery and hunger, the first penalties of their black ingratitude toward their ex-masters.

A small planter faction led by Campos Sales declined to support the movement on the grounds that the only way to achieve total emancipation while keeping the freedmen at work was through immediate and unconditional liberation. Most of the planters represented at the meeting joined the association, however, setting the richest province of Brazil firmly on the side of a rapid solution to the slavery question with the cooperation of many of its most powerful and influential citizens.[48]

Immediately after the gathering many planters acted to convert their establishments to free labor. Within two days the powerful Souza Queiroz family had announced the liberation of all their slaves and

48. "Reunião dos proprietarios de escravos em S. Paulo para tratar da libertação dos mesmos em 15 de Dezembro de 1887," in Godoy, *O elemento servil*, pp. 621–632.

Campos Sales was once more reported to have done the same. Planters who had not inscribed their names in the membership book of the emancipation society hurried to fall in line. Many slaveholders of western São Paulo agreed to conform, and all the proprietors of the município of Jaú in the northwest decided at once to free all their slaves in 1889. In the days following the meeting, Rio newspapers published many telegrams from São Paulo reporting the rapid progress of the liberation movement.[49]

Though the campaign for emancipation brought criticism and even divisions within the Paulista Conservative Party, the emergency converted even diehards like Moreira de Barros to the Prado solution. As slaves persisted in leaving the fazendas, owners began to instruct their overseers to allow them to move in freedom, hoping that unrestricted workers would soon return, or that slaves from other plantations, hungry and tired of wandering, would turn up looking for paid employment. In the weeks following the meeting of December 15, trains were still being halted and searched for slaves, but in some cases it was to offer them paid employment on plantations.

Desperate for workers, planters were even willing to negotiate with Antônio Bento "for the employment of fugitives at a fair price." Bueno de Andrada described the arrangement, which was conceived after the cities of Santos and São Paulo were overflowing with unemployed runaways:

Antônio Bento then took a most original revolutionary path. He reached an agreement with some planters, by which they would accept slaves who had left other masters. Each outside worker would receive from his new patrons the salary of 400 réis per day. Without disturbing agriculture completely, the process freed crew after crew of slaves and interested many planters in the triumph of our beliefs . . . . It was a beautiful idea!

According to this participant, who himself conducted proprietors to Bento for negotiations, by the date of abolition more than a third of the plantations of São Paulo were being worked by "slaves" who had abandoned other properties.[50] For the coffee growers, of course, the arrangement was advantageous, since at 400 réis per day, probably only a temporary wage scale at that, the annual income of the newly liberated worker was about equivalent to the value of three sacks of coffee, perhaps an eighth of his productive capacity.

For some weeks in December and January there were reasons to

49. *Cidade do Rio,* December 16, 17, 1887; *Gazeta da Tarde,* December 17, 1887.
50. *Ibid.,* January 31, March 9, 1888; *Cidade do Rio,* January 5, 1888; *Gazeta do Povo,* São Paulo, January 9, 1888; *Rio News,* May 5, 1888; Bueno de Andrada, "A abolição em São Paulo," p. 267; Viotti da Costa, *De senzala à colônia,* p. 323.

doubt the success of planter-emancipationism, but by February it was apparent that it was working as intended. Many freedmen and runaways were returning to work or finding salaried employment on plantations elsewhere, and one município had allegedly made the transition to free labor without the loss of a single worker. Most proprietors had accepted the Prado solution, but some who had not done so found themselves with empty slave huts.[51]

Many landowners freed their slaves with the condition that they help only with the coming harvest, and some set no conditions at all. On a plantation in Campinas the owners freed their slaves unconditionally, offering them advantages equal to those of their new Italian workers. This, according to Patrocinio's new daily, *Cidade do Rio,* brought expressions of joy from all the freedmen, who at once declared their decision to stay on the fazenda and asked permission to adopt the surname Carvalho "as a sign of eternal gratitude toward their ex-masters." A festival followed, and the two plantation owners, Leôncio and Dr. França Carvalho, "were much applauded by the freedmen and the Italian immigrants." [52]

Despite such examples of cordiality, São Paulo was not spared violence in the final months of slavery.[53] Early in January 1888, when a group of runaway freedmen were returned to the town of Piracicaba after their removal from a train, they were snatched away at their destination by a crowd of sympathizers, and their guards were mauled in the scuffle. The following day more than a thousand blacks raced through the streets of the town provoking disorders. Shots were exchanged, and people were wounded. In Campinas abolitionists who disrupted the work of slave catchers were dispersed by the police, but then attacked the local jail, exchanging gunfire with the police until late in the night.[54]

One of the worst incidents involved two Americans, James Ox Warne and John Jackson Clink, veterans of the Confederate Army who had emigrated to Brazil like many southerners after the Civil War. In mid-February 1888 Warne and Clink urged planters of the town of Penha do Rio do Peixe to take out their wrath against a local police delegate who had refused to capture runaways, inciting them with hints of northern superiority. Brazilians had "the blood of cockroaches," Clink was later accused of telling the mob. Calling for "rivers of blood," he claimed that "in any other country" events like those occurring in

51. *Ibid.,* p. 324; *Rio News,* February 5, 1885; *Correio Paulistano,* February 21, 1888.
52. *Cidade do Rio,* February 13, 1888.
53. For an exciting account of the disturbances in São Paulo during this period, see Robert Brent Toplin, "Upheaval, Violence, and the Abolition of Slavery in Brazil," *HAHR,* XLIX (November, 1969), 639–655.
54. *Correio Paulistano,* January 12, 1888; *Cidade do Rio,* January 24, 1888.

Brazil would have brought on a revolution. Aroused by this invective, one hundred and forty planters and capangas invaded the house of the police official after dark "and killed him in cold blood." One witness later testified that Warne "seemed taken with a mad fury, . . . even jabbing him with his spurs after the victim was lifeless. . . ." [55]

Such atrocities were exceptional. Some violence accompanied the liberation of more than a hundred thousand slaves in São Paulo, but the remarkable achievement was carried out with a high degree of good will and tolerance on all sides. A major social upheaval transformed the provincial labor system in a matter of months with only a small loss of life and property, in part because of the timely arrival of Italian immigrants. Their arrival, however, was less important as a cause of planter-emancipationism than a fortunate solution to the sudden labor crisis, which had not been expected to mature for another five to ten years. Though the two events were interlocked, it was the flight of the slaves more than the arrival of the Italians that at last convinced the masters of São Paulo that the time to liberate had come. [56] The slave-owners were not yet ready to make the rapid transition to free labor, and they hesitated or granted conditional freedom while demanding help from the central government for a restoration of order and the labor system. Only when they understood—and they reached this conclusion reluctantly—that nothing but total liberation would solve their problem were they fully converted to abolitionism. This, however, was a very different kind of abolition from that envisioned by Luiz Gama, Antônio Bento, or Joaquim Nabuco. As a modern Brazilian writer has put it, the planter-emancipationism of São Paulo was not an act of generosity, but an attempt to defend threatened economic interests, an effort (and a successful one at that) to pick up the scraps of a disintegrating system. [57]

ITALIANS ON THE
FAZENDAS OF SÃO PAULO

Before Brazilian slavery was abolished nationwide, the conversion to a free-labor system had thus already occurred in São Paulo, and

---

55. *Jornal do Commercio*, February 21, 1888; *Cidade do Rio*, February 25, 1888; *O Pirassinunga* of February 19 claimed that the president of the province (later president of Brazil), Francisco de Paula Rodrigues Alves, had specifically ordered the police delegate to hunt slaves, and that his refusal to do so had brought on the attack and assassination.

56. For the view that Prado's shift to abolitionism was motivated primarily by the success of immigration, see Beiguelman, *Formação do povo*, pp. 67–68.

57. Luiz Luna, *O negro na luta contra a escravidão* (Rio de Janeiro, 1968), p. 115.

the prospects were good for the rapid recovery of an economy only slightly lamed by havoc. The planters had succumbed to the new reality in large part because of the leadership of Antônio Prado, but an older brother, Martinho Prado, a prominent Republican planter, had done much to soften the long-expected blow to agriculture through the active promotion of Italian immigration.

Already by 1884 the wealth of São Paulo had generated an over-land migration of Brazilian workers into the coffee zones, induced by opportunities that Martinho Prado hoped would also motivate Europeans.[58] Between 1885 and 1887, to prepare for the inevitable end of slavery, the older Prado had helped to organize the Sociedade Promotora de Immigração. This was a well-financed association enjoying the co-operation of the provincial president that was intended to solve the looming crisis of labor through a serious effort to promote immigration. By late 1886 Martinho Prado was preparing to publish sixty thousand copies of a booklet in Italian, German, and Portuguese intended to pro-vide prospective immigrants in Europe with a knowledge of São Paulo and its attractions, a project well subsidized by the National Treasury through an appropriation authorized by Antônio Prado.[59] Sailing for Eu-rope, Martinho Prado had there convinced the Italian government of the serious intentions of the Sociedade Promotora and personally urged Italians to make the journey to São Paulo.[60] The directors of the new immigration society used their influence to obtain a contract from the provincial government to transport immigrants to Brazil, and the Companhia Paulista de Estradas de Ferro (a railroad with which Martinho Prado was associated) agreed to give them free transportation inland to the plantation communities.[61]

In August 1886, with no facilities at the port of Santos for new arrivals, Italians were sleeping in the streets, but by June 1887 more fortunate newcomers were housed in a new government hostel, where more than a thousand immigrants had found temporary shelter during the two weeks after its opening. At about the same time the Brazilian government ordered construction of another immigrant hostel at Ribeirão Preto in the far north of the province near the terminal of the Paulista

58. Prado, Jr., *Circular*, pp. 14–15, 23–24.

59. *Diario de Santos,* August 18, 1886; *South American Journal,* August 21, November 27, 1886; Morse, *From Community to Metropolis,* pp. 161, 171. Prado also arranged to have immigrants' visas issued free of charge. *South American Journal,* May 14, 1887.

60. *Diario de Santos,* February 16, 1886; *Correio Paulistano,* June 24, 1887. The historian, Caio Prado, Jr., grandson of Martinho Prado, Jr., informed the author in 1966 that his grandfather had spoken Italian fluently and made speeches in the public plazas of Italy to promote Italian immigration to São Paulo.

61. *Jornal do Commercio,* February 14, 1887; *Correio Paulistano,* September 17, 1887; *Diario de Santos,* February 16, 1887.

line. In mid-1887, as fugitive slaves were descending from upland São Paulo to seek refuge in the shanty town of Jabaquara on the edge of Santos, Italian immigrants were departing their modern hostel to take up residence on plantations recently abandoned by black fugitives.[62]

As the crisis of slavery worsened, the number of Italian arriving to take up work on the plantations increased. To hasten their rapid absorption into the economy, in July 1887 the Sociedade Promotora began to run daily advertisements in the *Correio Paulistano* to inform coffee growers of its concession and to ask them to submit their labor requests directly to the organization, their needs to be served in the order of their receipt. These advertisements bore the names of Martinho Prado, Jr., Nicoláo de Souza Queiroz, and Raphael A. Paes de Barros, representatives of three powerful Paulista families. The highly successful Sociedade Promotora helped to raise the level of immigration into São Paulo from 6,500 in 1885 to more than 32,000 in 1887, undoubtedly making the drastic solution to the slavery problem more acceptable to coffee growers. In March 1888 the provincial assembly of São Paulo granted a fifteen-year monopoly to the National Steamship Navigation Company between Brazil and Europe (Companhia Nacional de Navegação a Vapor entre o Brasil e a Europa) to contract and transport immigrants from Europe to São Paulo. In that same year more than 90,000 Europeans entered the province, a number not far short of the 107,329 slaves who had been registered there in 1887. With this inrush of immigrants, coffee production quickly rose to former levels and then soared beyond to create a problem of overproduction.[63]

THE EXPERIMENT SUCCEEDS

By February and March 1888 São Paulo had placed itself in the forefront of abolitionism and was exuding optimism about its achievement and its economic prospects. In reply to pessimistic statements published in the pro-slavery journal *Novidades* regarding the Paulista liberation movement, the *Correio Paulistano* drew an almost idyllic picture of conditions in the province. Slavery had been eradicated in whole municípios, and in others the number of remaining captives was insignificant. Agriculture was nearly undisturbed; confidence was high.

62. *Ibid.*, August 25, 1886; *Correio Paulistano*, June 11, 18, 1887; *South American Journal*, May 14, 1887.

63. *Annaes da Assembléa Legislativa Provincial de São Paulo. Sessão de 1888*, p. 75; *Correio Paulistano*, March 14, 1888; Taunay, *Pequena historia do café*, pp. 548–549; Smith, *Brazil*, pp. 122–124; *Relatorio do Ministerio da Agricultura*, May 14, 1888, p. 24.

Freedmen were at work, and, contrary to reports, had not tramped into the cities.[64] Planters were residing on their fazendas with their families in complete security, while coffee and cereal crops grew and ripened about them. The railroads were functioning normally, and new lines were being planned. Banks were open and granting credit. Immigrants were arriving by the thousands and finding work. The task of emancipation had not halted the march of progress in São Paulo.[65]

As they watched the results of the transformation, even diehard slavocrats became propagandists for freedom. In March a once stubborn planter of São Paulo testified in a letter to a friend that, contrary to expectations, emancipation had not caused a shortage of workers on agricultural estates. The month of February had been a time of bitterness and terror in São Paulo, as four-fifths of the plantations were abandoned and "blacks sought cities or evil-minded seducers." Slowly, however, the former slaves had returned to work, and by March were "all more or less settled." Material losses would not be great, he predicted, and no labor shortage would develop.

You will remember that my grand argument as a slaveholder was that the slave body was the only force which we could count for constant and indispensable agricultural work, [continued this optimistic planter] and that if we could always rely upon free laborers, I would willingly dispense with the slaves. . . . Very well, let your friends drop this fear. Laborers are not lacking for such as know how to seek them. First we have the slaves themselves, who do not melt away, nor disappear, and who need to live and eat, and therefore to work, a feature they will comprehend in a short time. Then we have an enormous body of workers, upon which we were not counting. I do not allude to the immigrant which today is seeking us in abundance; I refer to the Brazilian, a sluggard yesterday, living upon the scraps of slave labor and on the benevolence of the rural proprietor, to whom he was attentive as an *aggregado*, a *capanga*, or in any other similar character. This Brazilian today sturdily devotes himself to labor, either because this has become more respectable through liberty, or because his former resources have failed him. . . . Many people who were living on four hills of beans and a quarter of maize, are now appearing for service in the coffee fields and on the drying grounds with pleasure, and those that I have received are lodged to their satisfaction in the old slave quarters.

His own buildings were good ones, the planter admitted, but were constructed in a quadrangle, "a repugnant feature heretofore." Nothing had been changed in the old slave quarters, "with the exception of the lock,

---

64. Most of the freedmen were at work, said *O Pirassinunga* on March 8, but others were in the cities and in the taverns, and robberies had occurred on the roads.
65. *Correio Paulistano,* February 21, 1888.

and today the quadrangle is preferred, for in it they can store their provisions without fear of damage from animals. My quadrangle is a large court, surrounded by white and clean houses, the doors of which I propose to open on the outside." The same planter was impressed with the cheapness of free labor, which was "not as dear as it appears at first. This point was to me the greatest surprise in the transformation through which we are passing." [66]

With the success of their experiment, the jubilant ruling class of São Paulo hastened to end slavery through legislative action and to urge abolition throughout the nation. On February 25, the birthday of Antônio Prado, the new hero of abolitionism, the provincial capital was declared free of slaves, and two days later a project to impose a tax of 400 milréis on every slave in the province was introduced into the provincial assembly, briefly debated, and passed on March 7, but never sanctioned by the provincial president, Rodrigues Alves. In less than a week, however, the Paulista assembly had agreed to a man to submit a petition to the General Assembly to urge it to act quickly, for social, moral, and economic reasons, to abolish slavery throughout the country.[67] The conversion of São Paulo, as dramatic and unexpected as that of the saint for whom the province was named, was complete.

A sudden and unexpected transformation had occurred in one of the richest and most influential provinces of Brazil. Strongly opposed to reform until 1887, the slaveholders of the province were suddenly faced with a massive abandonment of the plantations, promoted and aided by clever and dedicated abolitionists. Faced with the loss of their crops, economic disaster, and anarchy in the rural areas, but fortunate in possessing flexible leaders and favorable economic conditions, the planters of São Paulo made the adjustments needed and, much to their surprise, found that they succeeded easily in re-establishing control over their labor force and their economy. The abolitionists, notably Antônio Bento and the caiphazes, the thousands of slaves who fled and then returned to work for pay or a part of the crop, the planters and their leaders, notably Antônio Prado, were all therefore responsible, for different reasons, for the sudden collapse of slavery in São Paulo and thus for the rapid end of slavery in Brazil. São Paulo was late among the provinces to join the abolitionist ranks, but its sudden change of heart meant the rapid conversion of most other malingerers. The collapse then began in other provinces: in Bahia, Pernambuco, Minas Gerais, and in varying degrees in every province where slaves were still held,

66. *Rio News,* April 15, 1888.
67. *Annaes da Assembléa Legislativa Provincial de São Paulo. Sessão de 1888,* pp. 412–414, 499; *Correio Paulistano,* March 8, 1888; *Provincia de São Paulo,* March 22, 1888.

even in Rio de Janeiro. Thus, when the politicians met again in the capital on May 3, 1888 for the opening of the new legislative session, their first and most important task was to pass a bill that would confirm the de facto downfall of the slave system and restore the nation to order.

17

ABOLITION

A CRUMBLING SLAVE SYSTEM

With the end of slavery in São Paulo there were few significant obstacles to total abolition, and the forces demanding this reform were strengthened. The only substantial defenders of slavery were the Cotegipe ministry and the planters of Rio de Janeiro, abetted by a few proprietors in neighboring districts of São Paulo and Minas Gerais and laggards scattered through much of the country. The major question still open to debate in March 1888 was indemnification, certain to be demanded by many masters who had maintained their legal claim to slaves and hoped yet to retrieve something from the ruins of the system. These few problems and controversies were to be swept aside, however, in the general demand for an uncompromising solution to the slavery question.

Since the passage of the law prohibiting corporal punishment in public establishments, the Cotegipe regime had maintained a poor record on the slavery issue. Aided by the police chief of Rio de Janeiro, Dr. João Coelho Bastos, the government had carried out a campaign of repression against both fugitive slaves and the abolitionist movement.

Refusing to revoke the "Black Regulation," the government had allowed the agents of Coelho Bastos to ship runaways openly from the capital back to their masters in Rio de Janeiro province.[1] In August 1887 Minister of Agriculture Rodrigo da Silva, successor to Antônio Prado, had reached a decision regarding slave registrations that allegedly re-enslaved thirteen thousand persons in the Campos region of Rio de Janeiro province, setting off a wave of protest which brought an illegal ban on public meetings and violence in the streets and plazas of Rio.

Soon after the public learned of the government's unpopular decision, a protest meeting was held in the Polytheama Theater, but was broken up by exploding bombs and "hired ruffians" (*capoeiras*) wearing police blouses, brandishing razors and sticks, and staggering, reeling, and leaping in the traditional threatening style of the capoeira. The following day, Coelho Bastos published a police order forbidding street gatherings and meetings in public buildings at night, and threatening to break up such gatherings by force. The next day a clash occurred between aboli-tionists and police in the Campo da Acclamação, when authorities tried to prevent an abolitionist rally intended to challenge the government's order. That evening another clash occurred outside the offices of the *Gazeta da Tarde,* and acts of police brutality were reported elsewhere in the city. Though the Senate spurned the decision that had created this outburst of public indignation, the Cotegipe ministry refused to be influenced by an adverse vote, and then proceeded to get a vote of con-fidence from the compliant Chamber of Deputies.[2]

In late August some two thousand abolitionists again challenged the government's ban on public meetings with a gathering at the Polytheama Theater, where the Cotegipe regime was denounced as "an outrage to the dignity of public power and the honor of the Brazilian nation." [3] Abandoned by national sentiment and even by powerful members of its own party, the Cotegipe ministry remained defiant. The most serious abuse of public rights came in October and November in the sugar-cane region of Campos in eastern Rio de Janeiro province, where acts of violence and terror were carried out by provincial authorities with the apparent approval of the national government.

An abolitionist meeting had been broken up violently in Campos early in 1887, and, soon after, sugar-cane fields had been burned, per-haps in reprisal.[4] This was only a prelude to the violence of October and November caused by slave strikes and the massive flight of slaves to Campos, where they allegedly found refuge by the thousands.[5] To

1. *Gazeta da Tarde,* December 22, 1886.
2. *Ibid.,* August 3, 6, 8, 9, 1887; *Rio News,* August 15, 1887, January 15, 1888
3. *Gazeta da Tarde,* August 29, 1887.
4. *Ibid.,* January 31, February 1, 7, 1887; *Cidade do Rio,* October 29, 1887.
5. *O Paiz,* October 15, 1887; *Annaes da Câmara* (1888), II, 400–401.

avert strikes and the abandonment of sugar plantations, a large police force was stationed on estates of the region in mid-October to accompany captives through every step of their day.[6] Not long after—on October 25—the provincial police under the command of one Captain Fernando began a campaign of violent repression of the Campos abolitionist movement with an attack on the editorial offices of the *Vinte e Cinco de Março,* the voice of the anti-slavery movement in Campos edited by Carlos de Lacerda. Under orders from the provincial police chief, masked men overcame armed resistance, destroyed the printing press and furnishings, and threw equipment out the windows. On the same day abolitionists were arrested in their homes and imprisoned incommunicado, and Captain Fernando announced his intention of liquidating the local anti-slavery movement. Sensational telegrams from Campos published without comment in the *Gazeta da Tarde* told of marauding soldiers firing weapons and striking people with their swords. Carlos de Lacerda had gone into hiding, later turning up in Rio, but the provincial police were seeking him out with threats upon his life. On the morning of October 26 the demolished and abandoned offices of the *Vinte e Cinco de Março* were surrounded by a force of cavalrymen, policemen, and capangas who, according to a press account, intended to rip up the floor to search for the hiding place of runaway slaves.[7] On the following morning policemen appeared before the offices of the Republican *Gazeta do Povo* to taunt occupants of the building, and soon after they invaded the building to wreck its printing press. Closed down temporarily, the *Gazeta do Povo* was soon publishing with borrowed equipment, but police harassment of its staff continued into November.[8]

On the second day of that month at an early morning hour a group of some sixty slaves approached the city of Campos from the north shore of the Paraíba River with the alleged intention of crossing the bridge into town to attack the police barracks and the city jail. With telegraphic communications cut toward the north, a police patrol had been stationed at the south end of the bridge. Thus when slaves were seen crossing over an alarm was given, and most were dispersed and eight taken to jail. The new incident brought charges of abolitionist complicity in the slave raid and further arrests, and soldiers were sent out north of the city to round up runaways.[9]

Persecution continued in Campos through most of the month, but the most serious incident occurred on November 20, when police broke up a daylight abolitionist meeting and set off a bloody conflict lasting more

6. *Cidade do Rio,* October 26, 1887.
7. *Gazeta da Tarde,* October 27, 1887.
8. *Gazeta do Povo,* Campos, October 28, November 10, 11, 1887.
9. *Gazeta da Tarde,* November 8, 1887.

than a day. As a crowd began to gather at the Empyrio Theater for an abolitionist conference, a contingent of police appeared and demanded that all persons entering the theater submit to examination. In response to this harassment, the rally was transferred to the home of the scheduled speaker, Dr. Alvaro de Lacerda, who denounced police methods from a window of his home to an audience that filled the street below. While Lacerda spoke, a cavalry unit led by Captain Fernando, pistol in hand, appeared on the street. Firing weapons and cracking whips, the mounted police attacked the unprotected crowd and wounded at least three persons. A wave of revulsion spread through the city, and violence continued into the afternoon and the following day, as police picked out victims and made repeated assaults upon angry, derisive crowds. A bookkeeper with known abolitionist sentiments was severely wounded, and a black woman, shot in the street, died of her injuries.[10] Captain Fernando's police rule continued in Campos for another week with the apparent approval of the national government, until near the end of the month the hated commander and his men were at last replaced by a new but larger garrison, and peace returned to the city.[11] These and other unpopular acts, including the nearly simultaneous dispatching of military and naval units to São Paulo, had labeled the Cotegipe regime repressive and an obstacle to be swept aside as inimical to the national will.

The other major obstacle to abolition, the planters of Rio de Janeiro, led by Paulino de Souza in the Senate and Andrade Figueira in the Chamber, was the result in large part of economic difficulties. While the pro-slavery hardline had blurred and then disintegrated in São Paulo with the mass flight of slaves, resistance persisted in Rio de Janeiro until weeks before abolition. Strengthened by the comparative stability of the plantation labor system, opposition to the national crusade had begun to crack only in March when the fall of Cotegipe deprived planters of their last hope of protection. The situation in São Paulo had been modified by prosperity and a massive entry of immigrants, but that of Rio was little affected by immigration and rendered more difficult by economic decline. As late as January 1888 Paulino de Souza had promised the planters of his province another five years of slavery, and the following March planters of the Paraíba Valley community of Vassouras reacted angrily to a proposal that they liberate all their slaves prior to official emancipation to avoid a disorganization of labor.[12]

Rio de Janeiro resisted more than any other province because slaves

10. *Ibid.*, November 22, 1887; *Cidade do Rio*, November 21, 22, 1887. Reports of the Campos violence appeared in many Rio newspapers.
11. *Cidade do Rio*, December 5, 1887; *O Progressista*, São João da Barra, Rio de Janeiro, December 1, 1887.
12. Stein, *Vassouras*, pp. 253–254.

were still plentiful there and planters had grown poor. The 162,421 slaves registered in Rio de Janeiro province in 1887 (see Table 3) represented more than one-fifth of those enrolled nationwide. Their "book value" (based upon the artificial age scale in the Saraiva-Cotegipe Law) was nearly 106,000 contos (£10,600,000), almost equivalent to the financial indebtedness of the province's planters, which was estimated at 120,000 contos.[13] The nominal value of slaves, in fact, surpassed land values, and abolition therefore threatened planters, particularly those of the Paraíba Valley, with financial ruin. In defense of their pro-slavery attitudes, therefore, the Rio fazendeiros pointed out that their slaves belonged more to the banks in the capital than to themselves.[14] Even *The Rio News,* no friend of slavery, admitted that "whereas S. Paulo is in a flourishing condition [Rio de Janeiro] is loaded with debt and cannot without dishonesty free slaves that belong to its creditors. . . ."[15] Claiming to speak for the planters of that province, the *Gazeta da Tarde* stated in February that planters had a right to indemnification or an additional period of guaranteed labor from their slaves to permit them to pay their crushing debts.[16]

Though some slaveholders in almost every part of the country held onto their captives until the end, proprietors in many places were beginning to follow the example of São Paulo by early 1888. "The shocking number of Sauls," said Patrocinio's *Cidade do Rio* in January in an allusion to the sudden conversion of São Paulo, "ennobles and glorifies the Brazilian heart." [17] Planter-emancipationism, imitated by city dwellers, spread into Paraná, Santa Catarina, and northeastern provinces, and even the comparatively unaffected slave regime of Minas Gerais began to crumble early in the new year, when captives began to leave fazendas in several districts to trek peacefully toward the provincial capital of Ouro Preto.[18] By late February slaves were arriving in the old mining town each day, many urged on their way by abolitionists, and by early March fazendeiros in Minas Gerais had begun to grant unconditional freedom.[19] The planters of a Minas community, Itajuba, which bordered São Paulo, met in mid-March to declare the liberation of all their captives with the condition that they serve until Independence

13. *Relatorio apresentado á Assembléa Legislativa Provincial do Rio de Janeiro . . . em 12 de Setembro de 1887 . . .* (Rio de Janeiro, 1887); *Gazeta da Tarde,* February 21, 1888.
14. *Rio News,* November 15, 1887.
15. *Ibid.,* December 24, 1887.
16. *Gazeta da Tarde,* February 21, 1888. In August 1887 Patrocinio had relinquished the *Gazeta da Tarde* to become owner and editor of *A Cidade do Rio,* thenceforth the leading abolitionist paper.
17. *Cidade do Rio,* January 7, 1888.
18. *Ibid.,* January 13, February 15, 28, 1888.
19. *Jornal do Commercio,* March 1, 4, 1888.

Day, September 7, without pay, and from then until Christmas, the day of their total freedom, on salaries to be fixed by their ex-masters.[20]

Telegrams from cities throughout the Empire published in the *Jornal do Commercio* in March and April told of a general nationwide collapse of slavery accompanied by individual acts of defiance. Many masters were granting freedom and salaries; in contrast a few others continued to employ bush captains to hunt down their runaways, and some continued to offer rewards for the return of fugitives as late as mid-March, even in such respectable papers as the *Jornal do Commercio*. A report of March 18 from Ouro Preto exposed two conflicting attitudes regarding the slavery crisis: a master and his capangas had seized a runaway slave in broad daylight on the central plaza of the city, but the victim was soon released by abolitionists, who joyously set off rockets to celebrate their success. There was defiance, but it was a futile kind. A far greater force was the almost universal desire for an end to the crumbling institution.

On February 18 planter-emancipationism took a step forward in the northern province of Pará, when the Baron and Baroness of Guajará, "solemnizing one more anniversary of their conjugal union," restored all their slaves to freedom—their example soon followed by other provincial families.[21] From the capital of Alagôas came a report on March 26 that the ever-defiant Senator Cansanção de Sinimbú had granted unconditional freedom to the slaves on his sugar plantation in the município of São Miguel. In late March an abolitionist confederation was established in the capital of Paraná with the expressed aim of quickly freeing all the slaves of the city. The Baron of Vargem-Alegre announced his decision at the end of March to commemorate Good Friday and the birthday of his wife with the liberation of more than three hundred slaves and the granting of salaries. Early in April a telegram from Juiz de Fora, Minas Gerais, reported a slave uprising on the plantation of the Baron of Juiz de Fora and local alarm concerning its possible results. The following day in Ouro Preto fifty-eight slaves who had deserted a British mining company presented themselves to the president of the provincial assembly and were warmly welcomed.[22]

By mid-March sections even of Rio de Janeiro province had been affected. A planter-emancipationist movement had appeared suddenly in the tormented Campos region, and was soon having "magnificent results" in all the towns of the area. On March 17 leading planters began to grant unconditional freedom in São Fidelis, a coffee community in

20. *Cidade do Rio,* March 18, 1888.
21. See Ernesto Cruz, *Procissão dos seculos. Vultos e episodios da historia do Pará* (Belém, Pará, 1952), pp. 9–10.
22. *Jornal do Commercio,* March 15, 19, 26, 28, 29, 31, April 5, 6, 1888; Ianni, *As metamorfoses do escravo,* pp. 227–228.

the eastern part of the province, and the town was reported in a state of "indescribable joy." A meeting of planters for the liberation of the nearby town of Macahé, notorious as an illegal slave port just forty years before, was called on March 22. Within five days half of the 6,000 slaves of the Campos district had been freed, and a large part of northeastern Rio de Janeiro province was in open revolt against the pro-slavery leadership of Senator Paulino de Souza.[23] During March and April some 25,000 slaves were reported freed in the province, nearly one-sixth of the number registered there in 1887. As the end of slavery became inevitable, two brothers, the Count of São Clemente and the Count of Nova Friburgo, liberated all of their 1,900 slaves, constituting by this time probably about one out of every two hundred and fifty slaves in the entire country.[24]

As the date approached for the opening of the General Assembly, slavery was being abandoned in a growing list of places. In rapid succession towns and municípios were declared without slaves, including the capitals of Minas Gerais and Santa Catarina and the city of Petrópolis, where the liberation movement was carried on under the auspices of Princess Isabel.[25] Early in April a League of Redemption was established in the capital of Pará with the avowed purpose of freeing the city and province, and during April and the first days of May there was a repetition in Belém of scenes acted out four years before far up the Amazon at Manaus. As the blocks of the ancient river town were liberated one by one, citizens fixed red placards on street corners to announce that they were free of slaves and under the direction of their inhabitants.[26]

By early March the state of the nation was critical. In much of the country, both north and south, slaves were on the move toward urban centers, and, though masters everywhere were surrendering to the new demands, there was danger of open conflict. If the plantation economy of São Paulo was nearly normal, in Minas Gerais and Rio de Janeiro and parts of the north it was seriously disrupted. As Nabuco put it soon after, the abolition of slavery had already been achieved by the work of Antônio Bento in São Paulo, because what existed in Brazil just before abolition was not slavery but "a mass of runaways" pursued and unemployed, suffering greater hardships than they had as captives. For both the planters and the slaves a rapid change was essential, be-

23. *Cidade do Rio,* March 16, 18, 20, 22, 1888.
24. Gough to the Marquis of Salisbury, Rio de Janeiro, May 7, 1888, *BFSP* (1888–1889), LXXXI, 187.
25. *Jornal do Commercio,* April 16, 17, 25, 29, 1888; Rebouças, *Diário e notas,* p. 311; *Cidade do Rio,* March 26, 1888; *Gazeta Mineira,* São João d'El-Rei, Minas Gerais, April 12, 1888.
26. *Provincia do Pará,* Belém, April 4, 5, 7, 8, 13, 28; May 8, 1888.

cause continuing uncertainty regarding their relationship could mean more misery and danger for the ex-slaves and unpredictable difficulties for the planter class, even perhaps the destruction of their aristocratic way of life.[27]

A minor incident—the arrest of an unruly sailor in Rio de Janeiro early in March—brought on a conflict between the proud Brazilian armed forces and the Cotegipe cabinet, which ended in street fighting between police and sailors and nearly a week of unrest during which the army patroled the streets. After five days of inaction, the discredited Cotegipe ministry resigned, opening the way for the establishment of a government that could find a remedy to the national crisis. The man whom Isabel, the Princess Regent, chose for this task was João Alfredo Correia de Oliveira, the Conservative senator from Pernambuco who had supported Antônio Prado's break with Cotegipe the year before and at that time had called for a radical solution to the slavery problem. Without hesitation, João Alfredo called on Prado to join his government as Foreign Minister, and Prado played an active role in the conferences that led to the formation of the new cabinet on March 10.[28] In less than two months—with these leaders in power—the third session of the Twentieth Legislature was scheduled to begin, with prospects excellent for the passage of a serious abolition law. Elected under Cotegipe in January 1886 and only slightly liberalized by subsequent elections, the Chamber of Deputies had been converted by the critical circumstances into an instrument of radical action.

ABOLITION

A large and enthusiastic crowd greeted the Princess Regent when she reached the Senate building on May 3 for the opening of the General Assembly, but there were serious doubts about the kind of bill that would emerge from the new session. A project prepared by Antônio Prado, the more cautious member of the new anti-slavery alliance of the Conservative Party, had proposed the immediate liberation of all slaves, but with conditions. These included monetary compensation to masters, the obligation of ex-slaves to serve for three more months in order to assure the harvesting of a ripening coffee crop, and the further obligation of the freedmen to remain for six years in the municípios

27. For analyses of the situation just prior to abolition made in the Chamber by João Alfredo and Joaquim Nabuco, see *Annaes da Câmara* (1888), II, 400–401; *ibid.* (1889), I. 97.
28. Jarvis to Bayard, Petrópolis, March 12, 1888, *Papers Related to the Foreign Relations of the United States*, December 3, 1888, I, 57–59.

where they were emancipated and to hold paid employment.[29] Undoubt-edly reflecting these considerations, in her Speech from the Throne of May 3 Princess Isabel appealed for the elimination of slavery from the nation's laws but also recommended improvement in the legislation for the repression of vagrancy through compulsory labor. No bill could be passed at all, however, without the cooperation of the Liberal Party majority in the Senate, and on May 7 during negotiations on the project João Alfredo was informed that the Liberal majority would refuse to support any abolition project unless it proclaimed the immediate and unconditional end of slavery. Such a bill had been written by André Rebouças on March 30 and presented to João Alfredo on April 7, and thus the President of the Council had known for a full month that the abolitionists would seek an uncompromising solution.[30]

Rather than see his legislation rejected, João Alfredo opted for un-conditional abolition, and on the same day, May 7, before a packed hall, after a brief reference to his eight-month-old anti-slavery alliance with Antônio Prado, he announced his decision to propose the immedi-ate and unconditional extinction of slavery in Brazil.[31] The reference to Antônio Prado undoubtedly helped to identify the senator from São Paulo with the radical legislation, but there are reasons to doubt Prado's enthusiasm. On May 13, 1888, the day the Senate passed the bill, Prado was absent from the session without explanation.[32]

The reading of the abolitionist project on May 8 brought a prolonged acclamation both inside and outside the Chamber building and set off celebrations in the Brazilian capital that lasted for almost two weeks. The simplicity of the bill—slavery was declared extinct and all laws to the contrary were revoked—revealed the mood. The many years of delay and compromise seemed to push the government and the assem-bly headlong toward the end. The complex articles and sub-articles, regulations and directives of the Rio Branco and Saraiva-Cotegipe Laws, the work of lawyers and hesitant politicians, were all to be swept away

---

29. *South American Journal,* May 26, 1888.
30. *Annaes da Câmara* (1888), I, "Histórico," p. 4; Rebouças, *Diário e notas,* p. 311; André Rebouças, *A questão do Brasil; cunho escravocrata do attentado con-tra a familia imperial* (Lisbon [?], 1889–1890). Rebouças' abolition bill, which was only slightly modified by Antônio Ferreira Vianna, the Minister of Justice, was accompanied by a second project authored by Rebouças. This second bill, he wrote bitterly from exile in Europe less than a month after the fall of the Empire (December 13, 1889), was "a Project of Law of Rural Services, dealing a death blow to Landlordism, and preparing the advent of Brazilian Rural Democracy."
31. *Annaes da Câmara* (1888), I, "Histórico," p. 4; *Rio News,* May 3, 1888, January 14, 1889; *Organizações e programas ministeriais,* pp. 231–232; Jarvis to Bayard, March 12, 1888, *Papers Related to the Foreign Relations of the United States,* December 3, 1888, I, 58–59.
32. *Extincção da escravidão no Brasil,* p. 74.

by these brief and simple assertions. Appointed to consider the bill, a committee of five deputies including Joaquim Nabuco approved it at once, and the Chamber agreed to dispense with the customary printing to permit its consideration the following day. Only Andrade Figueira objected to these irregular proceedings.[33]

In the Chamber of Deputies opposition to the project came almost exclusively, in fact, from deputies from Rio de Janeiro, the last defiant stronghold of slavery. Led by Andrade Figueira, they denounced the bill for its failure to grant indemnification, for its lack of references to the status of ingenuous, for its lack of measures concerning the labor of freedmen and former slaves liberated on contracts compelling further labor, for its revocation of provisions contained in the laws of 1871 and 1885. Opponents of the bill were incensed by its failure to provide measures "to guarantee the society against that class of new citizens who are released upon it without even a means of gaining their subsistence." Of the nine persons who voted against the bill, eight represented Rio de Janeiro province and one was from Pernambuco.[34]

In the Senate, where the bill arrived on May 11, only the Baron of Cotegipe and Paulino de Souza delivered long speeches in opposition, and even they understood the futility of what they did. Cotegipe led the resistance with a denunciation of Antônio Prado and his policies, which had brought an end to slavery sooner than even Prado had desired. While condemning the bill, Cotegipe conceded that it recognized the country's real situation and that it would put an end to anarchy and attacks on property. Yet the law was a violation of property rights. It announced that in Brazil property no longer existed, "that everything can be destroyed by means of a law." "In a little while," Cotegipe predicted, "they will ask for division of the lands, and the state will be able to decree expropriation without indemnification. And, gentlemen," he concluded, "the property right over land is not a natural law either." [35]

At least two firm slavery supporters explained during the debate or shortly after why they voted in favor of the abolition law, undoubtedly expressing the views of other members of the Assembly that legislated the end of slavery. Lourenço de Albuquerque, a Liberal from Alagôas with a record of unbending support for slavery, declared that in casting his vote for abolition he was "rendering homage to the inevitable, submitting to fate." "I voted as I did," said Coelho e Campos, a Conservative from Sergipe, "because, as the law itself said, the question was nothing more than the acceptance of a reality practically then in existence. I voted because there was no other solution. . . , because gener-

33. *Ibid.*, pp. 7–15.
34. *Ibid.*, pp. 8–51.
35. *Ibid.*, pp. 59–73.

ally speaking the only alternative was insubordination, turmoil, the disruption of labor *and everything else,* and, as a member of the party of order, I did not have the right to refuse my vote to a law of order." [36] The law had been passed because slavery had collapsed. At the climax of nearly a decade of agitation, thousands of slaves had appropriated their own freedom and were permitted to do so by a society which no longer sincerely believed in the need for slavery. The number and "quality" of slaves had diminished to the point that the institution's small benefits no longer seemed to warrant its many dangers, humiliations, and disadvantages.

"Fortunately the people of Paraná do not need the slave worker," said a statement drawn up in the name of an anti-slavery organization which emerged in the last weeks of slavery and which could well have spoken for dozens of others like it.

The number of slaves on the plantations is small; [continued the new converts to abolitionism] we are growing accustomed to worthy labor, to the free man; thus, with the liberation of the few slaves among us, with no fear of disturbance whatever, we have only to profit from freeing ourselves from that institution which has abased our customs and our education, which makes us suspect and isolated before the nations, which so encumbers us that without its complete extinction the Brazilian people cannot attend to the serious interests that demand their attention and patriotism.[37]

THE CELEBRATIONS

The act which recognized the collapse of Brazilian slavery and declared the unencumbered freedom of hundreds of thousands of slaves and ingenuos was passed by the Senate and sanctioned by Princess Isabel on May 13, but celebrations had already begun when the bill was introduced into the Chamber on May 8 and had accompanied it every step of the way toward passage with processions, music, and public demonstrations. The final passage and Isabel's rapid sanction had brought "a burst of popular joy," as the people "dressed the city with flowers and banners. . . , filling the streets to overflowing and deluging them with a tidal wave of congratulations. . . ."

The press of Rio decided to sponsor festivities to last from May 17 to May 20, and those days were filled with unprecedented pageantry in Rio and elsewhere throughout the country. The first day's festivities in the capital featured a solemn high mass attended by the Princess Regent, her husband the Count d'Eu, the members of the cabinet, most of the diplomatic corps, and a multitude of people. On the second day

---

36. *Ibid.,* p. 46; *Annaes da Câmara* (1888), II, 461. Italics added.
37. Quoted by Ianni, *As metamorfoses do escravo,* p. 208.

there were races at the Derby Club grounds and free rides on the Dom Pedro II Railroad, and in the evening the theaters were open to all who came. The events of May 19 included processions with banners and music and in the afternoon a regatta at Botafogo Bay—once the site of illegal slave landings. On the last day, there was a grand parade in which the army, the navy, the press, and "societies of every description" were represented, "and just how long the procession was seems impossible to calculate." Its organization, however, was "a complete failure," said the exultant *Rio News,* "owing to late arrivals, a lack of marshals, and the constant breaking of the lines. . . ." After a long delay before the city fire station, the procession started at last, turning and winding through the old streets of Rio until it reached the Campo da Acclamação at about seven o'clock that night. The Princess Regent and the Count d'Eu were at the city palace that evening acknowledging the tributes of the populace.

"The victory was so sweeping and unexpected," wrote A. J. Lamoureux,

that the enthusiasm of the people overflowed all bounds, and it was sheer fatigue on the 20th more than a surfeit of rejoicing which brought it to an end. The streets have been continually crowded, business almost wholly suspended, the public departments closed for three days, the D. Pedro II railway closed to freight traffic for the same time, the post office partially closed and the mails undistributed, the demands for money incessant, over a hundred thousand people in the streets on Sunday—and during all this nothing but enthusiastic joy, good temper, and good order.[38]

THE AFTERMATH

Soon after the celebrations the country began to return to something more like its normal condition. In little more than a month the President of the Council of Ministers, João Alfredo, was telling the Chamber of Deputies that the ex-masters and former slaves had established a new relationship based upon paid labor in which the proprietors were not deprived of their dignity and the freedmen were not humiliated. Planters were again living on their estates without fear, and their colonos, as freedmen were now called, worked better than before. Ex-slaves had allegedly shown themselves astonishingly generous to their former masters, sometimes agreeing to serve them without salaries and obligingly rushing to gather coffee crops threatened by bad weather. The former slaveholder, on the other hand, had come to understand "that henceforth it would be to his benefit to provide his ex-slave with good treat-

38. *Rio News,* May 26, 1888.

ment, to conserve him as an element helping to build his fortune, no longer an element which went to make it up." [39]

Before the abolition law had restored comparative calm to rural Brazil, however, planters were already making new demands upon the central government and expressing resentment that would soon help to destroy the imperial system. As early as April 21 a pamphleteer had warned that opponents of the abolitionists now planned to propose a law for the organization of free labor, and on June 4 a bill for "the repression of idleness" was introduced into the Chamber of Deputies with the claim that "labor is a duty" and "idleness can never be a right." A similar project offered to the Chamber by the Minister of Justice on June 20, but blocked by its opponents, was intended to create penal establishments for various groups of people, including those who abandoned their employment or occupation or refused "honest labor" offered or obligated by contracts. Penalties for second offenses were to include imprisonment with hard labor for from one to three years. [40]

Planters and their representatives in communities throughout the country also demanded indemnification for their lost property, and their spokesman, Baron Cotegipe, responded to their requests with the introduction of a Senate bill on June 19 to authorize a bond issue of 200,000 contos (about £20,000,000) for the reimbursement of former slaveholders. [41] As a result, abolitionists petitioned the Chamber of Deputies through Joaquim Nabuco requesting "that the slave registration books of all the municípios of the Empire be blotted out or rendered useless, so that they will never serve as a basis of the indicated pretensions." [42] Cotegipe's bill and a similar one proposed to the Chamber were also opposed by João Alfredo, but indemnification was repeatedly discussed in the assembly in 1888, arousing the interest and resentment of former slaveholders, whose many petitions were read in the Chamber and in the Senate with suitable bitterness by their favorite representatives.

The situation in the countryside, moreover, was not as idyllic as João Alfredo had pictured it. More than a year after abolition, André Rebouças deplored the continuing existence of rural relationships much like those familiar to generations of Brazilians. Former slaves were still being locked in their huts at night, were still being whipped and placed in the stocks, and their pay was a mere 100 réis per day. The abolitionist achievement, in fact, was unfinished and threatened by "a

---

39. *Annaes da Câmara* (1888), II, 401.
40. *Ibid.*, II, 3, 311.
41. *Annaes do Senado* (1888), II, 109–111. This was about half the official value of the slaves. For an estimate of this value, see *South American Journal*, July 21, 1888.
42. *Annaes da Câmara* (1888), III, 262.

militant slavocrat reaction," he implied with a bitterness characteristic of his last years, and he gave what he thought were explanations: Slavery in the United States had been destroyed by war, but in Brazil the problem had been resolved "among flowers." Thus it had become a "Brazilian Ideal" that it would be "through propaganda, conviction, impulse, and noble enthusiasm"—through a process of evolution —that the systems of human exploitation inherited from the past would be eliminated. Such a process, he obviously believed, would be too slow and costly in human terms.[43]

To accelerate the processes of change, in fact, abolitionists were still making demands of their own, in the face of the powerful planter-Republican reaction which threatened to overwhelm their surviving organization. Abolitionist demands included, as Cotegipe had said they would, division of large landholdings, "the democratization of the soil," as Rebouças, Nabuco, and other members of the Abolitionist Confederation referred to it, the "logical consequence" of the law of May 13, 1888. Advocated by the popular Senator Dantas, a reform of the landholding system was included in the Liberal Party program of 1888 along with federation of the provinces, an extension of suffrage, and other far-reaching proposals. Just months before his fall from power, even Pedro, who was greatly under the influence of immigrationists and the proponents of Rural Democracy, notably the omnipresent André Rebouças, publicly called for expropriation of "lands bordering railroads not made use of by their proprietors . . . to serve as centers of colonization." [44]

To the abolitionists, in fact, to Nabuco, Patrocinio, Rebouças, Dantas, and others, who recognized the causes of their nation's deeply rooted ills, the abolition of slavery was only a most important first step toward the democratization of Brazil. As they had been saying for years, there was still much to be done if the nation was to shake off the effects of nearly four centuries of inequality and forced labor. The landholding and educational systems were little changed, class values and privileges almost unaffected. A host of customs and procedures had survived slavery to condemn most freedmen and their descendants to a lowly social and economic status.[45]

Slavery had been abolished by a hard and complex struggle in which

43. Verissimo, *André Rebouças*, pp. 208–211.
44. *Annaes do Senado* (1888), V, 226–227; *Annaes da Câmara* (1889), I, 16.
45. For the condition of ex-slaves and their descendants in São Paulo after abolition, see Fernandes, *The Negro*, pp. 10–13, 23, 36–40, 42, 48–50; Bastide and Fernandes, *Brancos e negros,* pp. xiii, 54–55. For a serious round-table discussion of the bitter aftermath of slavery by a group of modern Brazilian intellectuals, see *80 Anos de Abolição* (Rio de Janeiro, 1968). For the menial occupations of Africans in the city of Bahia just after abolition, see Rodrigues, *Os africanos no Brasil*, pp. 172–173.

the abolitionists seemed to be Davids fighting the Goliaths of tradition and vast economic power. Freeing the slaves, however, had been the easiest of the goals that the reformers had set for themselves, for slavery was destroyed in fact by forces that had undermined it during most of the nineteenth century. The abolitionists had hastened the collapse of slavery, but were stopped short in their pursuit of further reforms. The traditional elite maintained their power and authority and swept the democratic movement aside in the military coup d'état that overthrew the Empire of Pedro II in 1889 and established a conservative republic.

In the last years of the nineteenth century, after chaos, dictatorship, and even a senseless civil war, Brazilian society reverted to the norms that had been threatened by the brief abolitionist experience, and millions of Brazilians, particularly those whose dark skins marked them as descendants of slaves, remained much as they had been under slavery— legally free now, but unable to compete in freedom because of their class and color, with few alternatives beyond working another man's land in poverty and servility or migrating to a precarious urban environment, where opportunities were normally limited to the humblest and hardest of work. Although it was a great victory for Brazilians, though it gave them a measure of pride and a brief sense of greatness, the abolition of slavery did not create an environment in which former slaves could expect to rise up to the level of prosperous participants in national life. Nearly a century later—a hundred years in fact since the liberation of the newborn—millions of their descendants are still denied the equality of opportunity envisioned for them by anti-slavery leaders.

Appendices

APPENDIX I

The following tables are divided into five groups. These include general population counts, some data on the movement of slaves between the provinces from 1849 to 1884, statistics on the growth and decline of slave populations, on literacy and illiteracy among slaves, information on sex, marital status, and occupations among slave populations, and, finally, miscellaneous tables concerning voting on the Rio Branco and Saraiva-Cotegipe Laws, coffee production, and the earning capacity of slaves on coffee fazendas.

The accuracy of quantitative data collected by Latin American governments has often been questioned, and, therefore, the reliability of these tables and other statistics cited in this work is naturally open to doubt. Unquestionably, there are differences of varying magnitude between some of these data and the unknown quantities of people and things they represent, and this is particularly true of information recorded prior to the 1872 census, when most population statistics were based on conjecture or fragmentary evidence.[1]

For historical purposes, however, absolute accuracy is not always essential. What is normally required of statistics, certainly in a study of this kind, is that they be accurate enough to permit the investigator to draw valid conclusions.[2] One assurance of such reliability is consistency, and data are particularly convincing when they regularly reveal patterns that would not normally be expected.

An analysis of the following tables reveals significant and consistent deviations from "normal" population patterns, resulting from the abnormal conditions of slavery, and thus their general reliability would seem to be confirmed, since hopelessly inaccurate statistics would not be expected to show such patterns. Table 17, for example, indicates that less than one slave in a thousand was literate, not surprising given Brazilian conditions; but, more important, it reveals that this ratio did

1. Joaquim Norberto de Souza e Silva, *Investigações sôbre os recenseamentos da população geral do Império* (Rio de Janeiro, 1951), p. 151; Herbert S. Klein, "The Colored Freedmen in Brazilian Slave Society," *Journal of Social History*, Vol. 3 (1970), p. 31.
2. See Curtin, *The Atlantic Slave Trade*, pp. xix, 93.

not vary much from region to region, and that literate males were almost everywhere more numerous than literate females, patterns further indicating accuracy. Table 18 shows that in every province only a small minority of adult slaves were registered as married or widowed, a fact confirmed by many earlier reports on marital status. Tables 19 and 20 tell us what we would expect: that most Brazilian slaves were farm workers or servants, that women were usually preferred for domestic service, and that men were more commonly found in the fields.

The tables also reveal logical demographic trends. The rapid decline of the slave population in northern, western, and southern provinces between 1874 and 1884 (see Table 10) and the comparatively small decline of the slave population in the coffee provinces during the same period are consistent with what we know about the movements of the slave population during much of that time. Similarly, the excess of male slaves over female slaves in coffee provinces and municípios (shown in Tables 4 and 16) is reasonable on the same grounds, as are the registered gains and losses of provincial slave populations through the interprovincial slave trade reported in Table 9. Similar logical trends and peculiarities are revealed in other tables and in the larger bodies of statistics from which they were drawn, giving credence to the data and providing insights into the character of Brazilian slavery.

The sources of the statistics and the circumstances under which they were collected are of course relevant to the question of accuracy. Nearly all the population tables are based upon either the 1872 census or the subsequent reports on slave and ingenuo populations published in the annual *relatorios* of the Ministry of Agriculture. The census, begun on August 1, 1872, and completed and published in its entirety between 1873 and 1876, was a well-organized population count intended to assure frutiful results. It has since been described by authorities as a true census containing accurate information on the human composition of the entire country, both slave and free.[3] The statistics on slaves included in the census (and in later reports of the Ministry of Agriculture) were the result of the nationwide slave registrations ordered by Article VIII of the Rio Branco Law and by Article I of the Saraiva-Cotegipe Law, both of which assured reasonable accuracy by stipulating that persons not registered were to be regarded as free. A decree of December 1, 1871, moreover, ordered that changes in the status and condition of slaves and ingenuos were to be reported by local officials at regular

3. Directoria Geral da Estatistica, *Recenseamento do Brazil realizado em 1 de Setembro de 1920. Introducção* (Rio de Janeiro, 1922), I, 412–413; Giorgio Mortara, "Demographic Studies in Brazil," in Philip M. Hauser and Otis Dudley (eds.), *The Study of Population, An Inventory and Appraisal* (Chicago, 1959), pp. 235–236.

intervals,[4] and it is from this source that later ministerial reports on slave populations were derived.

As indicated at various times in this study, carelessness and fraud were as characteristic of these slave counts as diligence and good faith. Nevertheless, even the effects of dishonesty show up as demographic oddities, seeming to provide additional proof of the overall reliability of the statistics and even supporting interesting historical hypotheses. The false registration of the ages of Africans to avoid the effects of the anti-slave-trade law of 1831, for example, is clearly reflected in the slave census (see Table 5), as is the concentration of Africans in the provinces where they were mainly imported before 1852. To cite another example, Table 9 shows that the net loss of slaves through the inter-provincial slave trade reported between 1874 and 1884 by slave-exporting provinces (46,626 persons) was only a little more than half the net gain reported by slave-importing provinces (89,425 persons). The discrepancy can probably be explained in part by the failure of masters and merchants to register slaves exported to avoid paying the provincial export taxes.

Without exaggerating the accuracy of nineteenth-century statistics on Brazilian slavery, which were undoubtedly distorted by practices such as these and by other uncontrollable factors, it may be concluded that, on the whole, the data used here are historically valid and sufficiently reliable to support the conclusions contained in this study.

4. Veiga, *Livro do estado servil*, pp. 38–39.

TABLE 1

ESTIMATES OF BRAZILIAN POPULATION

	1798	*1817/18*	*1864*
White	1,010,000	1,043,000	
Free Colored	406,000	585,500	
Total Free excepting Indians	1,416,000	1,628,500	8,330,000
Indians	250,000	259,400	200,000
TOTAL FREE	1,666,000	1,887,900	8,530,000
Mulatto Slaves	221,000	202,000	
Negro Slaves	1,361,000	1,728,000	
Total Slaves	1,582,000	1,930,000	1,715,000
TOTAL POPULATION	3,248,000	3,817,900	10,245,000

SOURCE: Agostinho Marques Perdigão Malheiro, *A escravidão no Brasil* (2 vols.; 2nd ed.; São Paulo, 1944), II, 26, 197–198.

TABLE 2
FREE AND SLAVE POPULATIONS OF BRAZIL, 1874

Province	Free	Slave	Total	Approximate Percentage Enslaved
Far North				
Amazonas	56,631	1,545	58,176	2.7
Pará	232,622	31,537	264,159	11.9
Maranhão	284,101	74,598	358,699	20.8
	573,354	107,680	681,034	15.8
Northeast				
Piauí	178,427	23,434	201,861	11.6
Ceará	686,773	31,975	718,748	4.4
Rio Grande do Norte	220,959	13,634	234,593	5.5
Paraíba	341,643	25,817	367,460	7.0
Pernambuco	752,511	106,236	858,747	12.4
Alagôas	312,268	36,124	348,392	10.3
Sergipe	139,812	33,064	172,876	19.1
Bahia	1,120,846	165,403	1,286,249	12.8
	3,753,239	435,687	4,188,926	10.4
West and South				
Mato Grosso	53,750	7,054	60,804	11.6
Goiás	149,743	8,800	158,543	5.5
Paraná	116,162	11,249	127,411	8.8
Santa Catarina	144,818	15,250	160,068	9.5
Rio Grande do Sul	364,002	98,450	462,452	21.3
	828,475	140,803	969,278	14.5
South-Central				
Minas Gerais	1,642,449	311,304	1,953,753	15.9
Espírito Santo	59,478	22,297	81,775	27.6
Rio de Janeiro	456,850	301,352	758,202	39.7
Município Neutro	226,033	47,084	273,117	17.2
São Paulo	680,742	174,622	855,364	20.4
	3,065,552	856,659	3,922,211	21.8
TOTALS	8,220,620	1,540,829	9,761,449	15.8

SOURCES: Directoria Geral da Estatistica, *Relatorio e Trabalhos Estatisticos* (Rio de Janeiro, 1875), pp. 46–62; *Relatorio do Ministerio da Agricultura*, May 10, 1883, p. 10.

TABLE 3
SLAVE POPULATIONS, 1864–1887

Province	1864	1874	1884	1887
Far North				
Amazonas	1,000	1,545		
Pará	30,000	31,537	20,849	10,535
Maranhão	70,000	74,598	49,545	33,446
	101,000	107,680	70,394	43,981
Northeast				
Piauí	20,000	23,434	16,780	8,970
Ceará	36,000	31,975		108
Rio Grande do Norte	23,000	13,634	7,209	3,167
Paraíba	30,000	25,817	19,165	9,448
Pernambuco	260,000	106,236	72,709	41,122
Alagôas	50,000	36,124	26,911	15,269
Sergipe	55,000	33,064	25,874	16,875
Bahia	300,000	165,403	132,822	76,838
	774,000	435,687	301,470	171,797
West and South				
Mato Grosso	5,000	7,054	5,782	3,233
Goiás	15,000	8,800	7,710	4,955
Paraná	20,000	11,249	7,768	3,513
Santa Catarina	15,000	15,250	8,371	4,927
Rio Grande do Sul	40,000	98,450	60,136	8,442
	95,000	140,803	89,767	25,070
South-Central				
Minas Gerais	250,000	311,304	301,125	191,952
Espírito Santo	15,000	22,297	20,216	13,381
Rio de Janeiro	300,000	301,352	258,238	162,421
Município Neutro	100,000	47,084	32,103	7,488
São Paulo	80,000	174,622	167,493	107,329
	745,000	856,659	779,175	482,571
TOTALS	1,715,000	1,540,829	1,240,806	723,419

SOURCES: Perdigão Malheiro, *A escravidão*, II, 198; *Relatorio do Ministerio da Agricultura*, May 10, 1883, p. 10; *ibid.*, April 30, 1885, p. 372; *ibid.*, May 14, 1888, p. 24.

TABLE 4

SLAVE POPULATION BY SEX, 1884

Province	Male	Female	Totals
Far North			
Pará	10,130	10,719	20,849
Maranhão	21,981	27,564	49,545
	32,111	38,283	70,394
Northeast			
Piauí	8,031	8,749	16,780
Rio Grande do Norte	3,601	3,608	7,209
Paraíba	8,941	10,224	19,165
Pernambuco	36,344	36,365	72,709
Alagôas	13,119	13,792	26,911
Sergipe	12,469	13,405	25,874
Bahia	65,281	67,541	132,822
	147,786	153,684	301,470
West and South			
Mato Grosso	2,881	2,901	5,782
Goiás	4,252	3,458	7,710
Paraná	4,383	3,385	7,768
Santa Catarina	4,598	3,773	8,371
Rio Grande do Sul	30,658	29,478	60,136
	46,772	42,995	89,767
South-Central			
Minas Gerais	160,931	140,194	301,125
Espírito Santo	11,005	9,211	20,216
Rio de Janeiro	140,751	117,487	258,238
Município Neutro	15,783	16,320	32,103
São Paulo	96,737	70,756	167,493
	425,207	353,968	779,175
TOTALS	651,876	588,930	1,240,806

SOURCE: *Relatorio do Ministerio da Agricultura*, April 30, 1885, p. 372.

TABLE 5

AFRICAN-BORN SLAVES AND SLAVES REGISTERED AS 51 OR OLDER, 1872

Province	Total Slaves Registered	Slaves Registered 51 and Over	Percentage 51 and Over	Africans Registered
Far North				
Amazonas	1,545	87	5.6	13
Pará	31,537	2,362	7.5	552
Maranhão	74,598	7,786	10.4	1,741
	107,680	10,235	9.5	2,306
Northeast				
Piauí	23,434	3,885	16.6	242
Ceará	31,975	2,014	6.3	99
Rio Grande do Norte	13,634	1,614	11.8	421
Paraiba	25,817	1,367	5.3	185
Pernambuco	106,236	9,472	8.9	3,084
Alagôas	36,124	2,402	6.6	2,377
Sergipe	33,064	3,012	9.1	1,395
Bahia	165,403	24,349	14.7	10,281
	435,687	48,115	11.0	18,084
West and South				
Mato Grosso	7,054	928	13.1	360
Goiás	8,800	878	10.0	140
Paraná	11,249	830	7.4	738
Santa Catarina	15,250	1,332	8.7	1,128
Rio Grande do Sul	98,450	15,423	15.6	5,104
	140,803	19,391	13.8	7,470
South-Central				
Minas Gerais	311,304	64,401	20.7	28,148
Espírito Santo	22,297	3,109	13.9	2,262
Rio de Janeiro	301,352	66,259	22.0	56,262
Município Neutro	47,084	4,656	9.9	10,973
São Paulo	174,622	20,512	11.7	13,055
	856,659	158,937	18.6	110,700
TOTALS	1,540,829	236,678	15.4	138,560

SOURCE: Compiled from Directoria Geral da Estatistica, *Recenseamento da população, 1872, passim.*

TABLE 6

SEXAGENARIAN FREEDMEN REGISTERED IN 1886 AND 1887

Province	Freedmen	Province	Freedmen
Far North		*West and South*	
Pará	26	Mato Grosso	20
Maranhão	452	Goiás	20
	——	Paraná	10
	478	Santa Catarina	10
Northeast		Rio Grande do Sul	6
Piauí	39		——
Rio Grande do Norte	7		66
Paraíba	34	*South-Central*	
Pernambuco	259	Minas Gerais	4,121
Alagôas	202	Espírito Santo	361
Sergipe	204	Rio de Janeiro	9,496
Bahia	1,001	Município Neutro	125
	——	São Paulo	2,553
	1,746		——
			16,656
TOTAL			18,946

SOURCE: *Relatorio do Ministerio da Agricultura*, May 14, 1888, p. 27.

TABLE 7

SLAVES IMPORTED INTO RIO DE JANEIRO, 1849–1852

Year	Circumstances	Number
1849	African trade large and unrestricted	940
1850	African trade tolerated but declining	1,074
1851	African trade suppressed	3,088
1852	First three and one-half months only	1,473
	TOTAL	6,575

SOURCE: *Relatorio apresentado . . . na quarta sessão da oitava legislatura pelo Ministro e Secretario d'Estado dos Negocios da Justiça* (Rio de Janeiro, 1852), p. 9.

TABLE 8

SLAVES IMPORTED INTO RIO DE JANEIRO THROUGH INTER-PROVINCIAL TRADE, 1852–1862

Year	From North	From South	Total
1852	3,461	340	3,801
1853	2,743	658	3,401
1854	4,201	198	4,399
1855	3,156	215	3,371
1856	3,495	496	3,991
1857	3,480	619	4,099
1858	1,304	276	1,580
1859	933	183	1,116
1860	3,132	156	3,288
1861	4,502	162	4,664
To July 1862	857	101	958
TOTALS	31,264	3,404	34,668

SOURCE: Christie to Earl Russell, Rio de Janeiro, September 30, 1862 (Inclosure No. 1), *Class B. 1862*, p. 112.

TABLE 9

REGISTERED GAINS AND LOSSES OF SLAVES THROUGH INTER-PROVINCIAL
TRADE, 1874–1884

			Total for Region	
Province	*Net Gain*	*Net Loss*	*Gain*	*Loss*
Far North				
Amazonas	344			
Pará	663			
Maranhão		4,157		
	1,007	4,157		3,150
Northeast				
Piauí		2,725		
Ceará		7,104		
Rio Grande do Norte		1,876		
Paraíba		3,412		
Pernambuco		4,426		
Alagôas		2,082		
Sergipe		2,342		
Bahia		4,041		
		28,008		28,008
West and South				
Mato Grosso	311			
Goiás		360		
Paraná		212		
Santa Catarina		905		
Rio Grande do Sul		14,302		
	311	15,779		15,468
South-Central				
Minas Gerais	5,936			
Espírito Santo	3,187			
Rio de Janeiro	31,941			
Município Neutro	7,353			
São Paulo	41,008			
	89,425		89,425	
TOTALS			89,425	46,626

SOURCE: Compiled from *Relatorio do Ministerio da Agricultura*, May 7, 1884, p. 191.

TABLE 10
DECLINE OF SLAVE POPULATIONS, 1874–1884

Province	1874	1884	Percentage Decline
Far North			
Amazonas	1,545		100.0
Pará	31,537	20,849	33.5
Maranhão	74,598	49,545	33.6
	107,680	70,394	34.6
Northeast			
Piauí	23,434	16,780	28.4
Ceará	31,975		100.0
Rio Grande do Norte	13,634	7,209	47.1
Paraíba	25,817	19,165	25.8
Pernambuco	106,236	72,709	31.6
Alagôas	36,124	26,911	25.5
Sergipe	33,064	25,874	21.4
Bahia	165,403	132,822	19.7
	435,687	301,470	30.8
West and South			
Mato Grosso	7,054	5,782	16.6
Goiás	8,800	7,710	12.4
Paraná	11,249	7,768	30.9
Santa Catarina	15,250	8,371	44.9
Rio Grande do Sul	98,450	60,136	38.9
	140,803	89,767	36.2
South-Central			
Minas Gerais	311,304	301,125	3.3
Espírito Santo	22,297	20,216	9.3
Rio de Janeiro	301,352	258,238	14.3
Município Neutro	47,084	32,103	31.8
São Paulo	174,622	167,493	4.0
	856,659	779,175	9.0
TOTALS	1,540,829	1,240,806	19.5

SOURCES: *Relatorio do Ministerio da Agricultura*, May 10, 1883, p. 10; *ibid.* April 30, 1885, p. 372.

TABLE 11
DECLINE OF SLAVE POPULATIONS, JUNE 1885 TO MAY 1887

Province	June 1885	May 1887	Percentage Decline
Far North			
Pará	20,218	10,535	47.9
Maranhão	31,901	33,446	0.0
	52,119	43,981	15.6
Northeast			
Piauí	15,498	8,970	42.1
Ceará	—	108	0.0
Rio Grande do Norte	7,209	3,167	56.0
Paraíba	18,824	9,448	49.8
Pernambuco	72,370	41,122	43.1
Alagôas	25,046	15,269	39.0
Sergipe	24,325	16,875	30.2
Bahia	132,822	76,838	42.1
	296,094	171,797	42.0
West and South			
Mato Grosso	4,816	3,233	32.8
Goiás	7,788	4,955	36.4
Paraná	6,836	3,513	48.9
Santa Catarina	8,221	4,927	40.0
Rio Grande do Sul	27,242	8,442	69.0
	54,903	25,070	54.3
South-Central			
Minas Gerais	276,275	191,952	30.5
Espírito Santo	19,762	13,381	32.2
Rio de Janeiro	250,896	162,421	35.2
Município Neutro	29,909	7,488	74.9
São Paulo	153,270	107,329	29.9
	730,112	482,571	33.9
TOTALS	1,133,228	723,419	36.1

SOURCES: *Relatorio do Ministerio da Agricultura*, May 14, 1886, p. 34; *ibid.*, May 14, 1888, p. 24.

TABLE 12

REGISTERED GROWTH AND DECLINE OF SLAVE POPULATIONS
IN MINAS GERAIS, 1874–1883 (MAJOR MUNICÍPIOS)

Município	1874	1883	Growth	Decline
Coffee Municípios *(Southeastern Minas)*				
Juiz de Fora	14,368	21,808	7,440	
Leopoldina	15,253	16,001	748	
Mar de Hespanha	12,658	15,183	2,525	
Pomba	7,028	6,392		636
Rio Novo	6,957	7,336	379	
Rio Preto	6,313	6,120		193
São Paulo do Muriaí	6,938	7,775	837	
Ubá	7,149	6,020		1,129
	76,664	86,635	11,929	1,958
Coffee Municípios Net Growth			9,971	
Mining Municípios *(Central Minas)*				
Bomfim	5,824	2,919		2,905
Bom Successo	2,324	1,919		405
Caeté	2,798	1,310		1,488
Curvello	1,429	3,217	1,788	
Diamantina	2,036	7,510	5,474	
Formiga	3,625	3,352		273
Grão Mogol	3,701	2,604		1,097
Itabira	7,464	5,305		2,159
Januaria	1,115	997		118
Lavras	8,380	6,322		2,058
Mariana	8,422	6,389		2,033
Minas Novas	4,312	3,368		944
Montes Claros	4,046	3,249		797
Oliveira	7,889	5,630		2,259
Ouro Preto	5,632	2,539		3,093
Paracatú	2,638	1,638		1,000
Pitanguí	6,590	3,189		3,401
Queluz	13,998	4,322		9,676
Rio Pardo	6,722	3,667		3,055
Sabará	8,982	3,123		5,859
Santa Barbara	7,610	3,379		4,231
Santa Luzia	5,953	2,399		3,554
Santo Antônio do Monte	1,842	1,512		330
São João d'El Rei and São José d'El Rei	10,827	10,281		546
Serro	9,420	4,473		4,947
Sete Lagôas	2,295	2,527	232	
Tamanduá	4,764	2,851		1,913
	150,638	99,991	7,494	58,141
Mining Municípios Net Decline				50,647

SOURCES: *Recenseamento da população*, IX (2), 1074–1078; C. F. Van Delden Laërne, *Brazil and Java. Report on Coffee Culture in America, Asia, and Africa* (London, 1885), pp. 117–118.

TABLE 13

REGISTERED GAINS AND LOSSES OF SLAVES IN RIO DE JANEIRO PROVINCE
THROUGH INTER-MUNICIPAL TRANSFERS, 1873–1882

Município	Slave Population September 30, 1873	Net		Slave Population July 31, 1882
		Gain	Loss	
Coffee Municípios				
Barra Mansa	11,397	2,416		11,246
Cantagallo	17,562	8,251		21,621
Nova Friburgo	4,576	1,459		4,937
Paraíba do Sul	18,801	436		15,369
Piraí	13,386	506		11,360
Rezende	9,185	1,041		8,240
S. Maria Magdalena	10,003	5,122		12,891
São Fidelis	15,693	5,325		18,994
Sapucaia	—	8,145		7,377
Valença	27,099	4,454		25,344
Vassouras	21,093	1,538		18,630
	148,795	38,693		156,009
Other Municípios				
Angra dos Reis	3,807		593	2,199
Araruama	7,470		681	5,370
Barra de São João	3,534		191	2,693
Cabo Frio	6,318		706	4,383
Campos	35,668	1,222		29,387
Capivari	3,608	365		3,268
Estrella	2,613		169	1,684
Iguassú	7,350		286	5,467
Itaboraí	6,964		45	5,639
Itaguaí	5,430		622	3,511
Macahé	9,094		631	7,374
Magé	8,268		2,903	3,009
Mangaratiba	1,513		297	930
Maricá	5,775		342	4,218
Niterói	10,743	1,402		9,063
Paratí	2,025		262	1,184
Petrópolis	674	105		626
Rio Claro	2,398		456	1,544
Rio Bonito	6,621		573	4,917
S. Anna de Macacú	4,090		268	2,732
S. João da Barra	5,145		84	4,125
S. João do Principe	7,810		423	5,705
Saquarema	5,639		658	3,794
	152,557	3,094	10,190	112,822
TOTALS	301,352	41,787	10,190	268,831

SOURCE: Compiled from C. F. Van Delden Laërne, *Brazil and Java. Report on Coffee Culture in America, Asia, and Africa* (London, 1885), pp. 120–121.

TABLE 14

REGISTERED GROWTH AND DECLINE OF SLAVE POPULATIONS
IN SÃO PAULO, 1874–1883 (MAJOR COFFEE MUNICÍPIOS)

Municípios	1874	1882	Growth	Decline
North and West (Mogiana-Paulista)[a]				
Ribeirão Preto	857	1,386	529	
São Simão	777	1,194	417	
Casa Branca	2,093	3,915	1,822	
Descalvado	1,339	2,860	1,521	
Araraquara	1,626	2,247	621	
São Carlos	1,568	3,465	1,897	
Pirassinunga	1,376	3,550	2,174	
Jaú	887	1,876	989	
Brotas	1,634	1,214		420
Rio Claro	3,935	4,852	917	
Mog-mirím	5,006	3,429		1,577
Limeira	3,054	3,624	570	
Amparo	2,130	4,630	2,500	
	26,282	38,242	13,957	1,997
NET GROWTH			11,960	
Central[a]				
Campinas	13,685	15,665	1,980	
Capivari	3,189	3,612	423	
Bragança	2,522	2,157		365
Tatuí	1,059	1,110	51	
Pôrto Feliz	1,547	1,124		423
Itú	3,498	2,878		620
Jundiaí	1,852	1,631		221
Atibaia	1,066	936		130
Itapetininga	1,823	1,787		36
São Roque	1,107	650		457
	31,348	31,550	2,454	2,252
NET GROWTH			202	
East and Paraíba[a] Valley				
Mogi das Cruzes	1,496	1,048		448
Jacareí	1,574	1,478		96
S. José dos Campos	1,390	1,618	228	
Caçapava	1,602	2,609	1,007	
Taubaté	4,122	5,155	1,033	
Pindamonhangaba	3,718	4,177	459	
São Luis	2,089	2,072		17
Guaratinguetá	4,352	5,312	960	
Lorena	1,338	2,464	1,126	
Queluz	2,198	2,255	57	
Arêas	1,898	2,293	395	
Bananal	8,281	7,168		1,113
	34,058	37,649	5,265	1,674
NET GROWTH			3,591	

SOURCES: Recenseamento da população, XIX, 429–430; Van Delden Laërne, Brazil and Java, pp. 115–116.
[a] The geographical divisions used here and in Tables 15 and 16 are those in Sergio Milliet's Roteiro do café (São Paulo, 1939), pp. 10–12; and in Lowrie's "O elemento negro," pp. 14, 55–56. Their "North" is here referred to as "East and Paraíba Valley."

TABLE 15

SLAVE POPULATION OF SÃO PAULO PROVINCE (ESTIMATES)

Year	East and Paraíba Valley	Littoral	Central	North and West (Mogiana-Paulista)	Totals
1836	24,460	12,317	38,497	3,584	78,858
1854	33,823	15,445	47,574	20,143	116,985
1874	—	—	—	—	174,622
1886	43,361	4,148	53,545	67,036	168,090[a]

SOURCES: Adapted from Samuel Lowrie's "O elemento negro," p. 14, and *Relatorio do Ministerio da Agricultura*, May 10, 1883, p. 10.
[a] Includes ingenuos.

TABLE 16

SLAVE POPULATIONS BY SEX IN SÃO PAULO, 1872 (MAJOR COFFEE MUNICÍPIOS

Municípios	Male	Female	Totals
North and West			
Ribeirão Preto	566	291	857
Descalvado	784	455	1,239
São Carlos	926	642	1,568
Jaú	521	366	887
Brotas	1,024	610	1,634
Rio Claro	2,314	1,621	3,935
Mogi-mirím	2,954	2,052	5,006
Limeira	1,810	1,244	3,054
	10,899	7,281	18,180
Central			
Campinas	8,806	4,879	13,685
Capivari	1,826	1,363	3,189
Pôrto Feliz	925	622	1,547
Jundiaí	1,158	694	1,852
Indaiatuba	1,168	540	1,708
	13,883	8,098	21,981
East and Paraíba Valley			
Caçapava	966	636	1,602
Pindamonhangaba	2,147	1,571	3,718
Lorena	782	556	1,338
Queluz	1,243	955	2,198
Bananal	4,714	3,567	8,281
	9,852	7,285	17,137

SOURCE: *Recenseamento da população*, XIX, 429–430.

TABLE 17
LITERACY AND ILLITERACY AMONG SLAVES, 1872

Province	Male		Female		Totals	
	Literate	Illiterate	Literate	Illiterate	Literate	Illiterate
Far North						
Amazonas	—	487	—	492	—	979
Pará	68	13,840	21	13,529	89	27,369
Maranhão	51	36,838	21	38,029	72	74,867
	119	51,165	42	52,050	161	103,215
Northeast						
Piauí	6	11,939	—	11,850	6	23,789
Ceará	35	14,906	12	16,960	47	31,866
Rio Grande						
do Norte	4	6,567	3	6,446	7	13,013
Paraíba	26	10,655	35	10,810	61	21,465
Pernambuco	105	46,918	52	41,953	157	88,871
Alagôas	32	17,881	21	17,807	53	35,688
Sergipe	—	10,840	—	11,783	—	22,623
Bahia	49	89,045	15	78,715	64	167,760
	257	208,751	138	196,324	395	405,075
West and South						
Mato Grosso	—	3,632	—	3,035	—	6,667
Goiás	7	5,365	—	5,280	7	10,645
Paraná	6	5,500	2	5,052	8	10,552
Santa Catarina	26	8,043	20	6,895	46	14,938
Rio Grande do Sul	63	35,623	37	32,068	100	67,691
	102	58,163	59	52,330	161	110,493
South-Central						
Minas Gerais	99	199,335	46	170,979	145	370,314
Espírito Santo	1	11,858	—	10,800	1	22,658
Rio de Janeiro	79	162,315	28	130,215	107	292,530
Município Neutro	220	24,666	109	23,944	329	48,610
São Paulo	81	87,959	23	68,549	104	156,508
	480	486,133	206	404,487	686	890,620
TOTALS	958	804,212	445	705,191	1,403	1,509,403

SOURCE: *Recenseamento da população*, XIX, 2.

TABLE 18

SEX AND MARITAL STATUS OF SLAVES (SIXTEEN OR OLDER), MAY 1888

Province	Sex			Marital Status			Approximate Percentage
	Male	Female	Total	Single	Mar-ried	Wid-owed	Married or Widowed
Far North							
Pará	5,196	5,339	10,535	10,415	104	16	1.1
Maranhão	15,991	17,455	33,446	32,052	1,131	263	4.1
	21,187	22,794	43,981	42,467	1,235	279	3.4
Northeast							
Piauí	4,317	4,653	8,970	8,447	500	23	5.8
Ceará	54	54	108	81	22	5	25.0
Rio Grande do Norte	1,584	1,583	3,167	2,938	211	18	7.2
Paraíba	4,210	5,238	9,448	8,697	587	164	7.9
Pernambuco	20,531	20,591	41,122	36,734	3,480	908	10.7
Alagôas	7,449	7,820	15,269	13,700	1,322	247	10.0
Sergipe	8,147	8,728	16,875	14,541	1,872	462	13.8
Bahia	37,966	38,872	76,838	72,856	3,477	505	5.2
	84,258	87,539	171,797	157,994	11,471	2,332	8.0
West and South							
Mato Grosso	1,642	1,591	3,233	3,011	166	56	6.9
Goiás	2,430	2,525	4,955	4,582	307	66	7.6
Paraná	1,770	1,743	3,513	3,320	162	31	5.5
S. Catarina	2,769	2,158	4,927	4,875	46	6	1.1
Rio Grande do Sul	4,591	3,851	8,442	8,344	91	7	1.2
	13,202	11,868	25,070	24,132	772	166	3.7
South-Central							
Min. Ger.	104,748	87,204	191,952	158,983	27,713	5,256	17.2
Esp. Santo	7,112	6,269	13,381	12,232	953	196	8.6
Rio de Jan.	87,767	74,654	162,421	149,677	10,604	2,140	7.8
Mun. Neutro	3,653	3,835	7,488	7,432	38	18	0.8
São Paulo	62,688	44,641	107,329	79,293	24,018	4,018	26.1
	265,968	216,603	482,571	407,617	63,326	11,628	15.5
TOTALS	384,615	338,804	723,419	632,210	76,804	14,405	10.4

SOURCE: *Relatorio do Ministerio da Agricultura*, May 14, 1888, p. 24.

TABLE 19
SLAVE OCCUPATIONS, 1872

Occupations	Men	Women	Total
Artists	1,517	341	1,858
Sailors	1,788		1,788
Fishermen	1,262		1,262
Seamstresses		40,766	40,766
Miners and Quarrymen	769		769
Metal Workers	1,075		1,075
Carpenters	5,599		5,599
Textile Workers	842	12,354	13,196
Construction Workers	4,013		4,013
Leather Workers	560	3	563
Dyers	40	4	44
Clothers	1,379		1,379
Hat Makers	216	50	266
Shoemakers	2,163		2,163
Farm Workers	503,744	304,657	808,401
Servants and Day Laborers	49,195	45,293	94,488
Domestic Service	45,561	129,816	175,377
Without Profession	185,447	172,352	357,799
TOTALS	805,170	705,636	1,510,806

SOURCE: *Recenseamento da população*, XIX, 5.

TABLE 20

SLAVE OCCUPATIONS BY PROVINCE AND REGION, 1872

Province	Farm Workers	Servants and Day Laborers	Other[a]	Totals[b]
Far North				
Amazonas	223	281	475	979
Pará	10,956	5,271	11,231	27,458
Maranhão	36,694	12,390	25,855	74,939
	47,873	17,942	37,561	103,376
Northeast				
Piauí	6,264	6,631	10,900	23,795
Ceará	7,375	11,363	13,175	31,913
Rio Grande do Norte	2,353	3,057	7,610	13,020
Paraíba	9,125	5,982	6,419	21,526
Pernambuco	38,714	20,480	29,834	89,028
Alagôas	11,628	13,462	10,651	35,741
Sergipe	11,907	3,291	7,425	22,623
Bahia	82,954	33,073	51,797	167,824
	170,320	97,339	137,811	405,470
West and South				
Mato Grosso	3,907	968	1,792	6,667
Goiás	4,523	1,926	4,203	10,652
Paraná	3,167	4,693	2,700	10,560
Santa Catarina	6,231	3,598	5,155	14,984
Rio Grande do Sul	48,736	2,386	16,669	67,791
	66,564	13,571	30,519	110,654
South-Central				
Minas Gerais	278,767	30,989	60,703	370,459
Espírito Santo	12,917	3,493	6,249	22,659
Rio de Janeiro	141,575	52,806	98,256	292,637
Município Neutro	5,695	28,815	14,429	48,939
São Paulo	88,620	29,889	38,103	156,612
	527,574	145,992	217,740	891,306
TOTALS	812,331	274,844	423,631	1,510,806

SOURCE: Compiled from *Recenseamento da populaçoã, passim.*
[a] Includes slaves without occupations.
[b] Totals differ from those in Table 2 owing to incompleteness of census data.

TABLE 21

VOTES ON THE RIO BRANCO LAW

Province	Chamber		Senate	
	For	*Against*	*For*	*Against*
Far North				
Amazonas	1	1		
Pará	3		1	
Maranhão	2	2	2	
	6	3	3	0
Northeast				
Piauí	3		1	
Ceará	6	1	2	
Rio Grande do Norte	2		1	
Paraíba	3		1	
Pernambuco	8	2	5	
Alagôas	4		1	
Sergipe	3	1	1	
Bahia	10	2	3	2
	39	6	15	2
West and South				
Mato Grosso	2		1	
Goiás	1	1	1	
Paraná	1	1		
Santa Catarina	2			
Rio Grande do Sul	2	4	3	
	8	6	5	
South-Central				
Minas Gerais	6	13	5	3
Espírito Santo		2	1	1
Rio de Janeiro	1	7	3	
Município Neutro		3		
São Paulo	5	5	1	1
	12	30	10	5
TOTALS	65	45	33	7

SOURCE: *Discussão da reforma do estado servil*, II, Appéndice, pp. 128–150.

TABLE 22

THE EMANCIPATION FUND, 1878

Collected in Fiscal Years 1871/72		
to 1877/78		8,034:970$196
Expenses:		
On books, gratifications, and other	525:917$661	
Paid for Manumissions	2,880:467$001	
To Be Applied	744:728$182	4,151:112$844
Balance Subject to Liquidation		3,883:857$352

SOURCE: *Relatorio do Ministerio da Agricultura*, December 27, 1878, pp. 12–15.

TABLE 23

AVERAGE COST OF LIBERATIONS BY THE EMANCIPATION FUND, 1875–1885

Far North		*West and South*	
Amazonas	683$000	Mato Grosso	672$000
Pará	656$000	Goiás	599$000
Maranhão	608$000	Paraná	672$000
Average	655$666	Santa Catarina	479$000
		Rio Grande do Sul	631$000
Northeast		Average	610$600
Piauí	411$000		
Ceará	174$000	*South-Central*	
Rio Grande do Norte	455$000	Minas Gerais	909$000
Paraíba	430$000	Espírito Santo	709$000
Pernambuco	554$000	Rio de Janeiro	880$000
Alagôas	611$000	Município Neutro	575$000
Sergipe	557$000	São Paulo	855$000
Bahia	576$500	Average	785$600
Average	533$500		

SOURCE: *Jornal do Commercio*, July 3, 1885.

TABLE 24

ANALYSIS OF NO-CONFIDENCE VOTE AGAINST THE DANTAS REGIME, JULY 28, 1884, IN THE CHAMBER OF DEPUTIES

Provinces	Supporting Dantas			Opposing Dantas		
Coffee Provinces	*Lib.*[a]	*Cons.*[a]	*Total*	*Lib.*	*Cons.*	*Total*
Minas Gerais	3	0	3	6	6	12
Espírito Santo	2	0	2	0	0	0
Rio de Janeiro	2	0	2	1	9	10
São Paulo	3	0	3	3	3	6
Other Provinces	38	4	42	7	24	31
TOTALS			52			59

SOURCE: Compiled from *Annaes da Câmara* (1884), III, 362–363.
[a] Liberal, Conservative.

TABLE 25

VOTING RECORDS ON THE SLAVERY ISSUE, CHAMBER OF DEPUTIES, 1885

Province	Reformist	Inconsistent	Resolute Opponents
Far North			
Amazonas	2	0	0
Pará	1	0	3
Maranhão	0	6	0
	3	6	3
Northeast			
Piauí	0	3	0
Ceará	3	2	3
Rio Grande do Norte	2	0	0
Paraíba	1	1	3
Pernambuco	2	3	7
Alagôas	0	2	3
Sergipe	0	1	2
Bahia	5	4	4
	13	16	22
West and South			
Mato Grosso	0	1	0
Goiás	1	1	0
Paraná	0	1	0
Santa Catarina	0	2	0
Rio Grande do Sul	3	3	0
	4	8	0
Totals for Non-Coffee Provinces	20	30	25
South-Central			
Minas Gerais	5	5	9
Espírito Santo	0	1	1
Rio de Janeiro and Município Neutro	1	1	9
São Paulo	2	1	6
	8	8	25
TOTALS	28	38	50

SOURCE: Compiled from *Annaes da Câmara* (1885), II, 343–344; III, 66–67; III, 68; III, 163; III, 170–171.

TABLE 26

BRAZILIAN COFEE PRODUCTION, 1850/51–1890

Years	Sixty Kilo Sacks (in thousands)	Value of Total Coffee Production (in contos)	Value per Sack (in réis)	Annual Production of a Good Slave Working 2,000 Coffee Trees (in réis)
1850/51	2,485	32,604	13$120	328$000
1851/52	2,337	32,954	14$100	352$500
1852/53	2,430	33,897	13$950	348$750
1853/54	2,130	35,445	16$640	416$000
1854/55	3,190	48,491	15$201	380$025
1855/56	2,853	48,013	16$830	420$750
1856/57	3,189	54,107	16$967	424$175
1857/58	2,380	43,503	18$280	457$000
1858/59	2,735	50,138	18$332	458$300
1859/60	2,524	60,238	23$866	596$650
Decade	26,253	439,390	16$737	418$425
1860/61	3,571	79,664	22$310	557$750
1861/62	2,420	58,747	24$276	606$900
1862/63	2,136	56,575	26$486	662$150
1863/64	2,004	54,131	27$012	675$300
1864/65	2,645	64,134	24$247	606$175
1865/66	2,436	61,203	25$125	628$125
1866/67	3,157	69,743	22$092	552$300
1867/68	3,561	83,611	23$480	587$000
1868/69	3,802	90,518	23$808	595$200
1869/70	3,115	77,026	24$728	618$200
Decade	28,847	695,352	24$105	602$625
1870/71	3,827	84,504	22$081	552$025
1871/72	4,060	71,646	17$647	441$175
1872/73	3,497	115,285	32$967	824$175
1873/74	2,774	110,173	39$716	992$900
1874/75	3,853	125,812	32$653	816$325
1875/76	3,407	118,286	34$718	867$950
1876/77	3,553	111,707	31$440	786$000
1877/78	3,843	110,447	28$740	718$500
1878/79	4,904	134,029	27$331	683$275
1879/80	2,618	126,260	48$230	1:205$750
Decade	36,336	1,108,149	30$497	762$425
1880/81	3,660	126,134	34$463	861$575
1881/82	4,081	104,753	25$669	641$725
1882/83	6,687	122,643	18$341	458$525
1883/84	5,316	130,083	24$470	611$750
1884/85	6,238	152,434	24$436	610$900
1885/86	5,436	124,792	22$957	573$925
1886/87	6,075	186,925	30$770	769$250
1887	1,694	74,411	43$926	1:098$150
1888	3,444	103,205	29$967	749$175
1889	5,586	172,258	30$888	772$200
1890	5,109	189,894	37$168	929$200
Decade	53,326	1,487,532	27$895	697$375

SOURCE: Compiled from Affonso de E. Taunay, *Pequena história do café*, p. 548.

APPENDIX II

The Rio Branco Law
September 28, 1871.

The Princess Imperial, Regent, in the name of His Majesty the Emperor Senhor D. Pedro II, makes known to all the subjects of the Empire, that the General Assembly has decreed, and that she has sanctioned, the following Law:

ART. I. The children of women slaves that may be born in the Empire from the date of this Law shall be considered to be free.

§ 1. The said minors shall remain with and be under the dominion of the owners of the mother, who shall be obliged to rear and take care of them until such children have completed the age of 8 years.

On the child of the slave attaining this age, the owner of its mother shall have the option either of receiving from the State the indemnification of 600 dollars (milréis) or of making use of the services of the minor until he shall have completed the age of 21 years.

In the former event the Government will receive the minor, and will dispose of him in conformity with the provisions of the present Law.

The pecuniary indemnification above fixed shall be paid in Government bonds, bearing interest at 6 percent per annum, which will be considered extinct at the end of 30 years.

The declaration of the owner must be made within 30 days, counting from the day on which the minor shall complete the age of 8 years; and should he not do so within that time it will be understood that he embraces the option of making use of the service of the minor.

§ 2. Any one of those minors may ransom himself from the *onus* of servitude, by means of a previous pecuniary indemnification, offered by himself, or by any other person, to the owner of his mother, calculating the value of his services for the time which shall still remain unexpired to complete the period, should there be no agreement on the *quantum* of the said indemnification.

§ 3. It is also incumbent on owners to rear and bring up the children which the daughters of their female slaves may have while they are serving the same owners.

Such obligation, however, will cease as soon as the service of the mother ceases. Should the latter die within the term of servitude the children may be placed at the disposal of the Government.

§ 4. Should the female slave obtain her freedom, her children under

305

8 years of age who may be under the dominion of her owners shall, by virtue of § 1, be delivered up, unless she shall prefer leaving them with him, and he consents to their remaining.

§ 5. In case of the female slave being made over to another owner, her free children under 12 years of age shall accompany her, the new owner of the said slave being invested with the rights and obligations of his predecessor.

§ 6. The services of the children of female slaves shall cease to be rendered before the term marked in § 1, if by decision of the Criminal Judge it be known that the owner of the mothers ill-treat the children, inflicting on them severe punishments.

§ 7. The right conferred on owners by § 1 shall be transferred in cases of direct succession; the child of a slave must render his services to the person to whose share in the division of property the said slave shall belong.

ART. II. The Government may deliver over to associations which they shall have authorised, the children of the slaves that may be born from the date of this Law forward, and given up or abandoned by the owners of said slaves, or taken away from them by virtue of Article I, § 6.

§ 1. The said associations shall have a right to the gratuitous services of the minors, until they shall have completed the age of 21 years, and may hire out their services, but shall be bound—

1st. To rear and take care of the said minors.

2ndly. To save a sum for each of them, out of the amount of wages, which for this purpose is reserved in the respective statutes

3rdly. To seek to place them in a proper situation when their term of service shall be ended.

§ 2. The associations referred to in the previous paragraph shall be subject to the inspection of Judges of the Orphans' Court, in as far as affects minors.

§ 3. The disposition of this Article is applicable to foundling asylums, and to the persons whom the Judges of the Orphans' Court charge with the education of the said minors, in default of associations or houses established for that purpose.

§ 4. The Government has the free right of ordering the said minors to be taken into the public establishments, the obligations imposed by § 1 on the authorised associations being in this case transferred to the State.

ART. III. As many slaves as correspond in value to the annual disposable sum from the emancipation fund shall be freed in each province of the Empire.

§ 1. The emancipation fund arises from—

1st. The tax on slaves.

2ndly. General tax on transfer of the slaves as property.

3rdly. The proceeds of 6 lotteries per annum, free of tax, and the tenth part of those which may be granted from this time forth, to be drawn in the capital of the Empire.

4thly. The fines imposed by virtue of this Law.

5thly. The sums which may be marked in the general budget, and in those of the provinces and municipalities.

6thly. Subscriptions, endowments, and legacies for that purpose.

§ 2. The sums marked in the provincial and municipal budgets, as also the subscriptions, endowments, and legacies for the local purpose, shall be applied for the manumission of slaves in the provinces, districts, municipalities, and parishes designated.

ART. IV. The slave is permitted to form a saving fund from what may come to him through gifts, legacies, and inheritances, and from what, by consent of his owner, he may obtain by his labour and economy. The Government will see to the regulations as to the placing and security of said savings.

§ 1. By the death of the slave half of his savings shall belong to his surviving widow, if there be such, and the other half shall be transmitted to his heirs in conformity with civil law.

In default of heirs the savings shall be adjudged to the emancipation fund of which Article III treats.

§ 2. The slave who, through his savings, may obtain means to pay his value has a right to freedom.

If the indemnification be not fixed by agreement it shall be settled by arbitration. In judicial sales or inventories the price of manumission shall be that of the valuation.

§ 3. It is further permitted the slave, in furtherance of his liberty, to contract with a third party the hire of his future services, for a term not exceeding 7 years, by obtaining the consent of his master, and approval of the Judge of the Orphans' Court.

§ 4. The slave that belongs to joint proprietors, and is freed by one of them, shall have a right to his freedom by indemnifying the other owners with the share of the amount which belongs to them. This indemnification may be paid by services rendered for a term not exceeding 7 years, in conformity with the preceding paragraph.

§ 5. The manumission, with the clause of services during a certain time, shall not become annulled by want of fulfilling the said clause, but the freed man shall be compelled to fulfil, by means of labour in the public establishments, or by contracting for his services with private persons

§ 6. Manumissions, whether gratuitous or by means of *onus,* shall be exempted from all duties, emoluments, or expenses.

§ 7. In any case of alienation or transfer of slaves, the separation of husband and wife, and children under 12 years of age from father or mother, is prohibited under penalty of annulment.

§ 8. If the division of property among heirs or partners does not permit the union of a family, and none of them prefers remaining with the family by replacing the amount of the share belonging to the other interested parties, the said family shall be sold and the proceeds shall be divided among the heirs.

§ 9. The ordination, Book 4th, title 63, in the part which revokes freedom, on account of ingratitude, is set aside.

ART. V. The Emancipation Societies which are formed, and those which may for the future be formed, shall be subject to the inspection of the Judges of the Orphans' Court.

Sole paragraph. The said societies shall have the privilege of commanding the services of the slaves whom they may have liberated, to indemnify themselves for the sum spent in their purchase.

ART. VI. The following shall be declared free:

§ 1. The slaves belonging to the State, the Government giving them such employment as they may deem fit.

§ 2. The slave given in *usufruct* to the Crown.

§ 3. The slaves of unclaimed inheritances.

§ 4. The slaves who have been abandoned by their owners.

Should these have abandoned the slaves from the latter being invalids they shall be obliged to maintain them, except in case of their own penury, the maintenance being charged by the Judge of the Orphans' Court.

§ 5. In general the slaves liberated by virtue of this Law shall be under the inspection of Government during 5 years. They will be obliged to hire themselves under pain of compulsion; if they lead an idle life they shall be made to work in the public establishments.

The compulsory labour, however, shall cease so soon as the freed man shall exhibit an engagement of hire.

ART. VII. In trials in favour of freedom—

§ 1. The process shall be summary.

§ 2. There shall be appeal *ex officio* when the decisions shall be against the freedom.

ART. VIII. The Government will order the special registration of all the slaves existing in the Empire to be proceeded with, containing a declaration of name, sex, age, state, aptitude for work, and filiation of each, if such should be known.

§ 1. The date on which the registry ought to commence closing shall be announced beforehand, the longest time possible being given for preparation by means of edicts repeated, in which shall be inserted the dispositions of the following paragraph.

§ 2. The slaves who, through the fault or omission of the parties interested, shall not have been registered up to one year after the closing of the register, shall, *de facto,* be considered as free.

§ 3. For registering each slave the owner shall pay, once only, the emolument of 500 rs., if done within the term marked, and 1 milréis should that be exceeded. The produce of those emoluments shall go towards the expenses of registering, and the surplus to the emancipation fund.

§ 4. The children of a slave mother, who by this Law became free, shall also be registered in a separate book.

Those persons who have become remiss shall incur a fine of 100 to 200 milréis, repeated as many times as there may be individuals omitted: and for fraud, in the penalties of Article CLXXIX of the Criminal Code.

§ 5. The parish priests shall be obliged to have special books for the registry of births and deaths of the children of slaves born from and after the date of this Law. Each omission will subject the parish priest to a fine of 100 milréis.

ART. IX. The Government, in its regulations, can impose fines of as much as 100 milréis, and the penalty of imprisonment up to 1 month.

ART. X. All contrary dispositions are revoked.

Therefore, order all authorities to whom, &c. Given at the Palace of Rio de Janeiro, on the 28th September, 1871. 50th of the Independence and of the Empire.

PRINCESS IMPERIAL, REGENT.
THEODORO MACHADO FREIRE PEREIRA DA SILVA.

SOURCE: *British and Foreign State Papers,* LXII (1871–1872), 616–620.

The Saraiva-Cotegipe Law.
September 28, 1885.

We, Pedro II, by the grace of God and the unanimous will of the people, Constitutional Emperor and Perpetual Defender of Brazil, make known to all our subjects that the Assembly General has decreed and we have approved of the following Law:—

Of the Matriculation of Slaves.

ART. I. The new matriculation of the slaves shall be proceeded with throughout the whole Empire, declaring the name, nationality, sex, filiation, if known, occupation or service in which the slave is employed, age, and value, calculated in conformity with the Table of § 3.

§ 1. The inscription for the new matriculation shall be made on view of the statements which served as a basis for the special matriculation or entry made in virtue of the Law of the 28th September, 1871, or on view of the certificate of the said matriculation or entry, or on view of the title of ownership when the matriculation of the slave is set forth thereon.

§ 2. To the age declared in the former matriculation shall be added the time which shall have elapsed up to the day on which the declaration for the matriculation ordered by this Law shall be presented in the competent Department.

The matriculation which shall be effected in contravention of the provisions of §§ 1 and 2 shall be void, and the collector or fiscal agent who shall effect it will incur a fine of 100 to 300 milréis, without prejudice to other penalties which he may incur.

§ 3. The value to which Article 1 refers shall be declared by the master of the slave, not exceeding the maximum regulated by the age of the slave matriculating, according to the following Table:—

Slaves under 30 years	900$000
From 30 to 40 years	800 000
40 to 50 "	600 000
50 to 55 "	400 000
55 to 60 "	200 000

§ 4. The value of individuals of the female sex shall be regulated in like manner, but making a deduction of 25 percent on the above established prices.

§ 5. Slaves of 60 years of age shall not be matriculated; they shall, however, be inscribed in a special enrolment for the purposes of §§ 10 to 12 of Article 3

§ 6. The term granted for matriculation shall be one year; this will be announced by Edicts affixed in the most public places 90 days beforehand, and published by the press wherever there may be newspapers.

§ 7. Those slaves shall be considered free who shall not have been matriculated, and this clause shall be expressly and integrally declared in the Edicts and announcements in the newspapers. The slaves from 60 to 65 years of age who shall not have been enrolled shall be exempted from rendering all service.

§ 8. The persons charged with the duty of matriculating other parties' slaves, in accordance with Article 3 of the Decree of the 1st December, 1871, shall indemnify the respective masters the value of the slave who, from not having been matriculated within the due term, shall become free.

The hypothecating or distraining creditor is likewise bound to matriculate the slaves who constitute his guarantee.

The collectors and other fiscal agents shall be bound to give receipts for the documents which may be given to them for the inscription of the matriculation, and those who fail to effect the same within the lawful time shall incur the penalty of Article 154 of the Criminal Code, the right of petitioning for a new matriculation being reserved to the masters, which matriculation shall avail, with all its legal effects, as if it had been effected at the time designated.

§ 9. An emolument of 1 milréis shall be paid for the inscription or enrolment of each slave, the amount of which shall be assigned to the Emancipation Fund, after deducting therefrom the expenses of matriculation.

§ 10. As soon as the term for matriculation shall be announced, the fines incurred for the non-observance of the provisions of the Law of the 28th September, 1871, relative to the matriculation and declarations prescribed by the said Law and by its respective regulations, shall be remitted.

Any debt owed to the public Treasury for imposts in reference to the slave shall be remitted to whomsoever shall free, or shall have freed, gratuitously, any slave.

The Government, in the Regulation which they shall issue for the execution of this Law, shall designate one and the same term only for obtaining the result of the matriculation throughout the whole Empire.

ART. II. The Emancipation Fund shall be formed:

§ 1. From the taxes and revenue destined thereto by the legislation in force.

§ 2. From the tax of 5 percent additional on all the general imposts, except on those of exportation. This tax shall be collected at once, free of the expense of collecting, and inscribed annually in the estimate of receipts presented to the General Legislative Assembly by the Minister and Secretary of State for Financial Affairs.

§ 3. From bonds of the Public Debt, issued at 5 percent, with an annual cancellation of ½ percent, the interest and cancellation being paid out of the aforesaid tax of 5 percent.

(1.) The additional tax shall be collected even after the freedom (shall be accomplished) of all the slaves, and until the debt arising from the issue of the bonds authorized by law shall have become extinct.

(2.) The Emancipation Fund, of which § 1 of this Article treats, shall continue to be applied in accordance with the provision of Article 17 of the Regulation approved by the Decree of the 13th November, 1872.

The product of the additional tax shall be divided into three equal parts:

The first part shall be applied to the emancipation of the older slaves, according to what may be established in the Government Regulation.

The second part shall be applied to freeing, for half or for less than half their value, the agricultural and mining slaves whose masters desire to change into free establishments those maintained by slave labour.

The third part shall be destined to subsidize colonization by means of paying the conveyance of colonists, who shall be effectually located in agricultural establishments of any kind.

§ 4. To develop the resources employed in the transformation of the agricultural establishments worked by slaves into free ones, and to aid the development of agricultural colonization, the Government may issue the bonds treated of in § 3 of this Article.

The interest on those bonds and their cancellation may not absorb more than two-thirds of the product of the additional tax assigned in § 2 of this Article.

Of the Freedoms, and of the Freed Slaves.

ART. III. The slaves inscribed in the matriculation shall be freed by means of indemnifying their value from the Emancipation Fund, or by any other legal form.

§ 1. From the primitive value at which the slave was matriculated shall be deducted:

In the first year, 2 percent; in the second year, 3 percent; in the third year, 4 percent; in the fourth year, 5 percent; in the fifth year, 6 percent; in the sixth year, 7 percent; in the seventh year, 8 percent; in the eighth year, 9 percent; in the ninth year, 10 percent; in the tenth year, 10 percent; in the eleventh year, 12 percent; in the twelfth year, 12 percent; in the thirteenth year, 12 percent.

Any term which may have elapsed shall be reckoned in this annual deduction, whether the freedom be obtained through the Emancipation Fund or by any other legal form.

§ 2. The invalid slave, considered incapable of any service by the classifying "Junta," shall not be freed by the Emancipation Fund, but shall have recourse to the District Judge.

The slave so considered shall remain with his master.

§ 3. The slaves employed in agricultural estates shall be freed from out of the Emancipation Fund indicated in Article 2, § 4, second part, should their master purpose substituting slave labour by free labour, the following dispositions being observed:—

(*a.*) The freedom of all the slaves existing in the said establishment, and the obligation contracted not to admit others under penalty of these being declared free;

(*b.*) Indemnification by the State of half the value of the slaves so freed in bonds (bearing interest) at 5 perecnt; those masters who reduce the most the amount of the indemnification being preferred;

(*c.*) The use of the services of the freed slave for five years.

§ 4. The freed slave who is bound to serve under the conditions of the foregoing paragraph shall be fed, clothed, and treated by his master, and shall enjoy a pecuniary remuneration per diem for his labour, which shall be decided by the ex-master, with the approval of the Orphans' Judge.

§ 5. This remuneration, which shall constitute the "savings" of the freed slave, shall be divided into two parts, the one being disposable at once, and the other placed in a savings-bank or collectors' department in order to be delivered to him at the end of the term of his services to which § 3 in the last part refers.

§ 6. The freedoms obtained by these savings shall be granted on view of the certificates of the value of the slave obtained in conformity with Article 3, § 1, and of the certificate of the deposits of that amount in the fiscal stations designated by the Government.

Those certificates shall be passed gratuitously.

§ 7. Until the new matriculation be closed, the present process shall remain in force of valuing the slaves for the various means of freeing them, with the limit fixed in Article 1, § 3.

§ 8. The freedoms granted are valid, even though their value shall exceed the amount of (the inheritance of) the grantor's third part, and whether or not there be necessary heirs.

§ 9. Direct freedom granted to the slave by a third party is permitted as long as the price of the same is exhibited.

§ 10. The slave who shall have completed 60 years of age, before or after the date at which this Law shall enter into execution, shall be free, however, bound, under the title of indemnification of his freedom, to give his services to his ex-masters for the space of three years.

§ 11. Those who are over 60 and under 65 years of age, as soon as they shall attain the latter age, shall not be subject to the services alluded to, however long they may have been rendered in relation to the above term.

§ 12. The remission of the said services is permitted by payment not exceeding half the value arbitrated for the class of slaves from 55 to 60 years of age.

§ 13. All the freed slaves of more than 60 years of age, and who shall have fulfilled their term of service, of which § 3 treats, shall continue in their ex-master's service, who, on his part, shall be bound to feed, clothe, and treat them in their illness, obtaining from them in return such services as are compatible with their strength, unless they prefer obtaining elsewhere the means of subsistence, and the Orphans' Judge deems them capable of doing so.

§ 14. The domicile in the Municipality in which the slave shall have been freed, except that of the capitals, is obligatory for five years, reckoning from the date of the freedom of the slave by the Emancipation Fund.

§ 15. The freed slave who shall absent himself from his domicile shall be considered a vagrant, and shall be taken up by the police, to be employed in public works, or in the agricultural colonies.

§ 16. The Orphans' Judge may permit the removal of the freed slave in case of sickness, or for any other considerate motive, should the said freed slave conduct himself well, and declare the place to which he intends to remove his domicile.

§ 17. Any freed slave being found to have no occupation shall be bound to find employment or to contract his services for a term settled by the police.

§ 18. The term coming to an end without the freed slave showing that he has fulfilled the orders of the police, the latter shall send him to the Orphans' Judge, who shall oblige him to make a contract of location of service, under penalty of 15 days' imprisonment, with hard labour, and to be sent to some agricultural colony in case of recurrence.

§ 19. The domicile of the slave cannot be transferred to a province other than that in which he was matriculated at the time of the promulgation of this Law. The removal will amount to the obtaining of freedom, except in the following cases:—

(1.) Transfer of the slave from one to another establishment of the same master;

(2.) Should the slave have been obtained by inheritance, or by a forced adjudication in another province;

(3.) Change of domicile of the master;

(4.) Escape of the slave.

§ 20. The slave who has fled from his master's house, or from wheresoever he may be employed, cannot, while absent, be freed by the Emancipation Fund.

§ 21. The obligation of the slaves to render the services treated of by § 3 of this Article, or as a condition of freedom, shall not be in force for a longer period than that in which slavery is to be considered extinct.

General Dispositions.

ART. IV. In the Regulations which the Government shall issue for the execution of this Law, they shall determine:—

(1.) The rights and the obligations of the freed slaves, to which § 3 of Article 3 refers, towards their ex-masters, and *vice versa.*

(2.) The rights and obligations of the other freed slaves subject to render services, and of those to whom those services should be offered.

(3.) The intervention of general creditors on the part of the slave when the latter shall be bound to render services, and the attributes of the District, Municipal, and Orphans' Judge, and Justices of Peace, in the cases treated of in the present Law.

§ 1. The infraction of the obligations to which Nos. 1 and 2 of this Article refer shall be punished, according to its gravity, with a fine of 200 milréis, or imprisonment, with hard labour, for 30 days.

§ 2. The Justices of Peace of the respective districts are empowered to impose such fines, the process being that of the Decree No. 4824 of the 29th November, 1871, Article 45 and its paragraphs.

§ 3. The sheltering of slaves shall be capitulated in Article 260 of the Criminal Code.

§ 4. The right of masters of slaves to the services of the free-born children ("ingenuos") or indemnification in public bonds, according to Article 1, § 1, of the Law of the 28th September, 1871, shall cease with the extinction of slavery.

§ 5. The Government shall establish in various parts of the Empire, or in the frontier provinces, agricultural colonies, ruled by military discipline, to which shall be sent the freed slaves without employment.

§ 6. Effective occupation in agricultural labour shall constitute a legitimate exemption from military service.

§ 7. No province, not even those which enjoy the special Tariff, shall be exempted from paying the additional impost of which Article 2 treats.

§ 8. The Regulations which shall be issued by the Government shall be at once put into execution, subject to the approval of the legislative power, and all the dispositions relative to the servile element contained in the Law of the 28th September, 1871, and other unrevoked Regulations, shall be consolidated.

ART. V. All contrary dispositions are revoked.

We command, therefore, all those of our authorities who shall have knowledge of the above Law, and to whom the execution of it shall pertain, to fulfil it and cause it to be fulfilled, and to preserve it inviolate to the best of their ability.

The Secretary of State for Agriculture, Commerce, and Public Works is charged with the printing, publication, and circulation of this Law.

Given at our Palace at Rio de Janeiro, the 28th day of September, 1885, the 64th of the Independence and the Empire.

(Sign Manual of His Majesty the Emperor.)

ANTONIO DA SILVA PRADO.

SOURCE: *British and Foreign State Papers*, LXVI (1884–1885), 896–903.

Bibliography

BIBLIOGRAPHY

I. UNPUBLISHED DOCUMENTS

Arquivo do Estado de São Paulo

Caixa—Tráfico de negros.

Arquivo Histórico do Itamarati, Rio de Janeiro

235-7-19 Homens livres reduzidos a escravidão.

Arquivo do Museu Imperial, Petrópolis, Rio de Janeiro

29-1025, V.
113-5634, Carvalho, Antônio Pedro de, Projeto de lei para regular a escravidão no Brasil.
148-7179, Gomes Veloso de Albuquerque Lins, Francisco, Ensaio sôbre a emancipação do elemento servil.

Arquivo Nacional, Rio de Janeiro

I G 1-428, Mappa dos fogos, pessoas livres e escravos comprehendidos nas freguezias da cidade e provincia do Rio de Janeiro, Com^{do} das armas ao ministro da guerra e estrangeiro, 1821.
Codex 397, Termos de exames e averiguações feitas nos escravos vindos de varias localidades, 1852.
Codex 572, Oficios e outros papeis da casa imperial, 1801–1868.
Codex 622, Documentos relativos a escravatura, 1815–1880.
Codex 807, Vol. 16, Memoria sôbre a emigração chineza para o Brasil, 1855.
Codex 817, Vol. 19, Memorandum em que são expostas as vistas do Governo Imperial a respeito da colonisação e imigração para o Brasil.

Arquivo Público do Estado de Sergipe

Documents entitled "Escravos."

Biblioteca Nacional, Seção de Manuscritos, Rio de Janeiro

I-3, 17, 31. Titulo de renda anual concedido aos senhores de escravos em virtude da lei nº 2040 de 28/set./1871.
I-17, 12, 4, No. 22.
I-32, 14, 22. Sôbre a questão da escravatura (Por Thomaz Antônio da Villanova Portugal).
I-35, 32, 20. Relação das despesas com os escravos das quintas da Bôa Vista e Cajú, até Julho de 1831.
II-34, 26,26. Requerimento dos negociantes desta praça, pedindo a S.M.I. declare ser uma determinada postura da Câmara Municipal relativa apenas aos traficantes de escravos e não aos negociantes de grosso trato que, sem serem especialistas no tráfico negro, recebem escravos de outras provincias para vendê-los aqui, Rio de Janeiro, March 13, 1847.

II-34, 27, 15. Representação dos negociantes de escravos do Rio de Janeiro, pedindo a S.A.R. levantasse a proibição de desembarcarem os escravos chegados a ficar de quarantena . . . , Rio de Janeiro, s.d.

Divisão do Patrimonio Histórico e Artístico, Estado da Guanabara

6-1-1. Escravidão, 1884.
6-1-10. Avaliadores de escravos, 1777–1819.
6-1-15. Cartas de libertação de escravos, 1886.
6-1-16. Cartas de libertação de escravos, 1886–1887.
6-1-39. Escravos. Junta qualificadora para libertação, 1873–1886.
6-1-41. Documentos sobre escravos, 1881–1887.
6-1-42. Escravos, 1882–1888.
40-3-74. Capitão-do-mato, Freguesia de N.Sra. da Guia de Pacopaiba, 1823.

Instituto Histórico e Geográfico Brasileiro, Rio de Janeiro

Oficio do Conde da Ponte ao Visconde d'Anandia, Copias extrahidas do Archivo do Conselho Ultramarino, XX.

Public Record Office, London

FO 84/1244.

Secretaria de Educação e Cultura, Departamento de Difusão Cultural, Biblioteca Publica, Niterói, Rio de Janeiro

Documentos sôbre a repressão ao tráfico de africanos no litoral fluminense, No. 33 and loose unnumbered documents.

II. PUBLISHED GOVERNMENT DOCUMENTS

A. Brazilian

Acta da conferencia das secções reunidas dos negocios da fazenda, justiça e imperio do Conselho do Estado. Rio de Janeiro, 1884.
Annaes da Assembléa Legislativa Provincial de São Paulo. São Paulo, 1880, 1881, 1888.
Annaes do Parlamento Brasileiro. Câmara dos Senhores Deputados. Rio de Janeiro. Sessions of 1826, 1827, 1830, 1848–1857, 1866, 1869–1871, 1879–1889.
Annaes do Parlamento Brasileiro. Senado. Rio de Janeiro, Sessions of 1871, 1883–1885, 1888.
Annaes do Parlamento Brasileiro. Assembléa Constituinte. 1823, 6 vols. Rio de Janeiro, 1876–1884.
Arquivo do Distrito Federal. Revista de Documentos para a Historia da Cidade do Rio de Janeiro. Rio de Janeiro, 1954.
Colecção das leis do Imperio do Brasil of the years 1830, 1832, 1837, 1854, 1855, 1859, 1865, 1866, 1869, 1870, 1872, 1879, 1885.
Colecção de leis e posturas municipaes promulgadas pela Assembléa Legislativa Provincial de São Paulo no anno de 1881. São Paulo, 1881.
Directoria Geral da Estatistica. *Relatorio e Trabalhos Estatisticos apresentados ao Illm. e Exm. Sr. Conselheiro Dr. João Alfredo Correia de Oliveira Ministro e Secretario d'Estado dos Negocios do Imperio.* Rio de Janeiro, 1874.
―――, *Recenseamento do Brazil Realizado em 1 de Setembro de 1920.* Vol. I. Rio de Janeiro, 1922.
―――, *Recenseamento da população do Imperio do Brazil a que se procedeu no dia 1º de Agosto de 1872.* 21 vols. Rio de Janeiro, 1873–1876.

Discussão da reforma do estado servil na Câmara dos Deputados e no Senado. 2 vols. Rio de Janeiro, 1871.

Documentos para a história do açucar. 3 vols. Rio de Janeiro, 1954, 1956, 1963.

Emancipação pelo Livro de Ouro da Illma. Câmara Municipal no dia 29 de Julho de 1885. Rio de Janeiro, 1885.

Extincção da escravidão no Brasil. Lei n° 3353 de 13 de Maio de 1888. Discussão na Câmara dos Deputados e no Senado desde a apresentação da proposta do Governo até sua sancção. Rio de Janeiro, 1889.

Organizações e programas ministeriais. Regime parlamentar no Imperio. 2nd ed. Rio de Janeiro, 1962.

Pernambuco. Leis, decretos, etc. Pernambuco, 1854.

Recenseamento geral da Republica dos Estados Unidos do Brazil em 31 de Dezembro de 1890. Districto Federal. Rio de Janeiro, 1895.

Relatorio apresentado a Assembléa Geral Legislativa na terceira sessão da decima-quarta legislatura pelo Ministro e Secretario de Estado dos Negocios da Agricultura, Commercio e Obras Publicas Theodoro Machado Freire Pereira da Silva. Rio de Janeiro, 1871. And subsequent Agricultural Ministry Reports through 1888.

Relatorio da repartição dos negocios estrangeiros apresentados á Assembléa Geral Legislativa na terceira sessão da oitava legislatura pelo Respectivo Ministro e Secretario de Estado Paulino José Soares de Souza. Rio de Janeiro, 1851.

Relatorio apresentado á Assembléa Geral Legislativa . . . pelo Ministro e Secretario d'Estado dos Negocios da Justiça. Titles of Justice Ministry Reports vary. Volumes used are those dated 1832, 1850–1853, 1865–1867

Relatorio do Ministerio da Marinha. Rio de Janeiro, 1845.

Souza e Silva, Joaquim Norberto de. *Investigações sôbre os recenseamentos da população geral do Império.* Rio de Janeiro, 1951.

Toledo Piza, Antônio de. *Relatorio do anno de 1897 apresentado em 30 de Setembro de 1898.* São Paulo, 1899.

———. *Relatorio do anno de 1900 apresentado em 13 de Janeiro de 1902.* São Paulo, 1903.

Veiga, Luiz Francisco da. *Livro do estado servil e respectiva libertação.* Rio de Janeiro, 1876.

Reports of Provincial Presidents

Alagôas

Falla dirigida á Assembléa Legislativa da provincia das Alagôas . . . em o 1° de Marco de 1855. Recife, 1855.

Amazonas

Relatorio apresentado á Assembléa Legislativa Provincial do Amazonas . . . em 25 de Março de 1883, pelo Presidente José Lustosa da Cunha Paranaguá. In *Amazonas,* May 2, 1883.

Relatorio com que o presidente da provincia do Amazonas, Dr. José Lustosa da Cunha Paranaguá, entregou a administração da mesma provincia ao 1° vice-presidente Coronel Guilherme José Moreira em 16 de Fevereiro de 1884. Manaus, 1884.

Exposição apresentada á Assembléa Legislativa Provincial do Amazonas na abertura da primeira sessão da decima setima legislatura em 25 de Março de 1884. Manaus, 1884.

Ceará

Relatorio apresentado á Assembléa Legislativa Provincial do Ceará no dia 1º de Outubro de 1862. Fortaleza, 1862.
Annexos a Falla no dia 2 de Julho de 1877. Fortaleza, 1877.
Relatorio com que o Exm. Sr. Commendador Dr. Sancho de Barros Pimentel passou a administração da provincia do Ceará ao 2º Vice-Presidente . . . no dia 31 de Outubro de 1882. Fortaleza, 1882.
Relatorio com que o Exm. Sr. Dr. Satyro de Oliveira Dias passou a administração da provincia ao 2º Vice-Presidente Exm. Sr. Commendador Dr. Antonio Pinto Nogueira Accioly no dia 31 de Maio de 1884. Fortaleza, 1884.

Pará

Falla dirigida . . . pelo Presidente da Provincia do Gram Pará à Assembléa Provincial . . . do dia 1º de Outubro de 1849. Pará, 1849.
Discurso da abertura da sessão extraordinaria da Assembléa Legislativa Provincial do Pará. Em 7 de Abril de 1858 pelo Presidente Dr. João da Silva Carrão. Pará, 1858.

Paraíba

Exposição feita pelo Doutor Francisco Xavier Paes Barreto na qualidade de presidente da provincia da Parahyba do Norte. Em 16 de Abril de 1855. Paraíba, 1855.

Rio de Janeiro

Relatorio do presidente da provincia do Rio de Janeiro o Conselheiro Paulino José Soares de Souza . . . para o anno de 1840 a 1841. 2nd ed. Niterói, 1851.
Relatorio apresentado ao Exmo. Vice-Presidente da provincia do Rio de Janeiro o Commendador João Pedreira do Couto Ferraz . . . em 3 de Maio de 1853. Rio de Janeiro, 1853.
Relatorio apresentado á Assembléa Legislativa Provincial do Rio de Janeiro . . . em 12 de Setembro de 1887. . . . Rio de Janeiro, 1887.

São Paulo

Jaguaribe Filho, Dr. Domingo José Nogueira. *Assembléa Provincial de São Paulo. Discurso pronunciado na sessão ordinaria de 22 de Março de 1882.* São Paulo, 1882.

Sergipe.

Relatorio da presidencia da provincia de Sergipe em 1872. Aracajú, 1872.

B. British and American

British and Foreign State Papers. Vols. XLIV (1853–1854), XLV (1854–1855), XLIX (1858–1859), LIII (1862–1863), LVII (1866–1867), LVIII (1867–1868), LXXVII (1885–1886), LXXXI (1888–1889).
Class A. Correspondence with the British Commissioners Relating to the Slave Trade. London, 1827

Class B. Correspondence with Foreign Powers Relating to the Slave Trade. Volumes used include those dated 1829, 1830; From May 11 to December 31, 1840; From April 1, 1850, to March 31, 1851; From April 1, 1852, to March 31, 1853; From April 1, 1854, to March 31, 1855; From April 1, 1855, to March 31, 1856; From April 1, 1856, to March 31, 1857; From April 1, 1857, to March 31, 1858; From April 1, 1860, to December 31, 1860; 1861; 1862; 1865; 1866; 1867.

A Complete Collection of the Treaties and Conventions and Reciprocal Regulations, at Present Subsisting between Great Britain & Foreign Powers . . . so far as they relate to Commerce and Navigation, to the Repression and Abolition of the Slave Trade; and to the Privileges and Interests of the Subjects of the High Contracting Powers. 3 vols. London, 1827.

Foreign Office. *Diplomatic and Consular Reports on Trade and Commerce. Brazil. Report for the Years 1887–1888 on the Finances, Commerce, and Agriculture of the Empire of Brazil.* London, 1889.

Kennedy, Joseph C. G. *Preliminary Report on the Eighth Census, 1860.* Washington, 1862.

Manning, William R., ed. *Diplomatic Correspondence of the United States. Inter-American Affairs, 1831–1860.* Vol. II. Washington, 1932.

Message of the President of the United States to the Two Houses of Congress at the Commencement of the Third Session of the Thirty-Seventh Congress. Vol. I. Washington, 1862.

Papers Related to the Foreign Relations of the United States. Transmitted to Congress. Washington, 1885, 1889.

Report from the Select Committee of the House of Lords. Appointed to Consider the Best Means which Great Britain can adopt for the final Extinction of the African Slave Trade. . . . Session 1849. London, 1849.

III. POLEMICAL AND CRISIS LITERATURE

O abolicionismo perante a historia ou o dialogo das tres provincias. Rio de Janeiro, 1888.

Acta da sessão magna que celebrou a associação Perseverança e Porvir em 20 de Maio de 1888 pela extincção do elemento servil no Brazil. Fortaleza, 1890.

Alencar Araripe, Tristão de. *O Ceará no Rio de Janeiro, Discurso historico na grande festa da Sociedade Cearense Abolicionista no Rio de Janeiro.* Fortaleza, 1884.

———. *O elemento servil. Artigos sobre a emancipação.* Paraíba do Sul, Rio de Janeiro, 1871.

Alves, Serafim Antonio. *Relatorio apresentado na Sessão Magna da Associação Emancipadora Club Abolicionista em 21 de Agosto de 1882.* Pelôtas, 1882.

Americus. *Cartas politicas extrahidas do Padre Amaro.* 2 vols. London, 1825–1826.

Analyse e commentario da proposta do Governo Imperial ás câmaras legislativas sobre o elemento servil por um magistrado. Rio de Janeiro, 1871.

Andrada e Silva, José Bonifacio de. *Memoir Addressed to the General Constituent and Legislative Assembly of Brazil on Slavery.* London, 1826.

———. "Representação à Assembléia Geral Constituinte e Legislativa do Império do Brasil sôbre a escravatura," in Octavio Tarquinio de Sousa, ed. *O pensamento vivo de José Bonifacio.* São Paulo, 1944.

324 Bibliography

Associação Commercial do Rio de Janeiro. Elemento servil; 1ª representação da commissão especial nomeada, em assembléa geral extraordinaria de 2 de Maio de 1884. Rio de Janeiro, 1884.
Barbosa, Rui. Confederação Abolicionista. Homenagem ao patriotico ministerio Dantas: Sessão publica e solemne realizada no dia 7 de Junho de 1885 no Theatro Polytheama. Rio de Janeiro, 1885.
———. Obras Completas. Vols. I (Tome I), X, XI (Tome I). Rio de Janeiro, 1951, 1946–47, 1945.
———. Reforma do ensino primario: Parecer e projeto. Rio de Janeiro, 1883.
———. A situação abolicionista; conferencia do Conselheiro Ruy Barbosa em 2 de Agosto de 1885 no Theatro Polytheama. Rio de Janeiro, 1885.
Beaurepaire Rohan, Henrique de. O futuro da grande lavoura e da grande propriedade no Brasil; memoria apresentada ao Ministerio da Agricultura, Commercio e Obras Publicas. Rio de Janeiro, 1878.
Bocayuva, Quintino. A crise da lavoura. Rio de Janeiro, 1868.
Blacklaw, A. Scott. "Slavery in Brazil." The South American Journal, July 6, 20, 1882.
Brandão, F. A., Jr., A escravatura no Brasil. Brussels, 1865.
Brazilian Republican Address. Rio de Janeiro, 1871.
Burlamaque, Frederico L. C. Analytica acerca do commercio d'escravos e acerca dos malles da escravidão domestica. Rio de Janeiro, 1837.
Camara Leal, Luiz Francisco da, Considerações e projecto de lei para a emancipação dos escravos sem prejuizo de seus senhores, nem grande onus para o estado. Rio de Janeiro, 1866.
"Cartas de um cego." Correio Mercantil (Rio de Janeiro), May 25, 29, 1867.
O Christianismo, a civilisação e a sciencia protestando contra o captiveiro no Brasil. Bahia, 1885.
Christie, William Dougal. Notes on Brazilian Questions. London, 1865.
Clapp, João. "Relatorio do estado e das operações da Confederação Abolicionista." Gazeta da Tarde, May 29, 1884.
Congresso Agrícola, Colecção de documentos. Rio de Janeiro, 1878.
Cotegipe, Barão de. Fuga de escravos em Campinas. Rio de Janeiro, 1887.
Couty, Louis. L'esclavage au Brésil. Paris, 1881.
———. Pequena propriedade e immigração europea. Rio de Janeiro, 1887.
Demonstração das conveniencias e vantagens á lavoura no Brasil pela introducção dos trabalhadores asiaticos (Da China). Rio de Janeiro, 1887.
"The Extinction of Slavery in Brazil, From a Practical Point of View." The Anthropological Review. London, 1868.
Figueiredo, A. P. "The Need for Agrarian Reform in Brazil (1847)," in T. Lynn Smith. Agrarian Reform in Latin America. New York, 1967.
Fonseca, L. Anselmo da. A escravidão, o clero e o abolicionismo. Bahia, 1887.
Furtado, J. I. Arnizaut, Estudos sobre a libertação dos escravos no Brazil. Pelôtas, 1882.
Godoy, Joaquim Floriano de. O elemento servil e as câmaras municipaes da provincia de São Paulo. Rio de Janeiro, 1887.
Hilliard, Henry W., Politics and Pen Pictures at Home and Abroad. New York, 1892.
Lemos, Miguel. Immigração chineza. Rio de Janeiro, 1881.
———. and R. Teixeira Mendes. A liberdade espiritual e a organização do

trabalho: Considerações historico-filosoficas sobre o movimento abolicionista. 2nd ed. Rio de Janeiro, 1902.

———. *O Pozitivismo e a escravidão moderna.* 2nd ed. Rio de Janeiro, 1934.

Maciel da Costa, João Severiano. *Memoria sobre a necessidade de abolir a introdução dos escravos africanos no Brasil.* Coimbra, 1821.

Manifesto do Club Amazonia fundado em 24 de Abril de 1884. Pará, 1884.

Manifesto da Confederação Abolicionista do Rio de Janeiro. Rio de Janeiro, 1883.

Manifesto da Sociedade Cearense Libertadora ao Governo e ao Paiz. Fortaleza, September 7, 1881.

Manual do subdito fiel ou cartas de um lavrador á sua magestade o imperador sobre a questão do elemento servil. Rio de Janeiro, 1884.

Mendonça, Salvador de. *A immigração chinesa.* Rio de Janeiro, 1881.

———. *Trabalhadores asiaticos.* New York, 1879.

A Monarchia brasileira se agarrando á taboa da escravidão. Bahia, 1885.

Moniz Barreto, Domingo Alves. *Memoria sobre a abolição do commercio da escravatura.* Rio de Janeiro, 1837.

Moura, Carlos Bernardino de. *Considerações feitas pelo cidadão Carlos Bernardino de Moura na conferencia do dia 2 de Julho corrente no Theatro de S. Pedro . . . sobre o assumpto da emancipação do estado servil.* Rio de Janeiro, 1871.

Nabuco, Joaquim. *O Abolicionismo.* London, 1883.

———. *Campanha abolicionista no Recife (Eleições de 1884): Discursos de Joaquim Nabuco.* Rio de Janeiro, 1885.

———. *Cartas a amigos.* 2 vols. São Paulo, 1949.

———. *Cartas do Presidente Joaquim Nabuco e do Ministro Americano H. W. Hilliard sobre a emancipação nos Estados Unidos.* Rio de Janeiro, 1880.

———. *Conferencia a 22 de Junho de 1884 no Theatro Polytheama.* Rio de Janeiro, 1884.

———. *O eclypse do abolicionismo.* Rio de Janeiro, 1886.

———. "A escravidão." *Revista do Instituto Histórico e Geográfico Brasileiro.* Vol. 204 (1949).

———. *Henry George, Nacionalização do solo.* Rio de Janeiro, 1884.

Ouseley, William. *Notes on the Slave Trade, with Remarks on the Measures adopted for its Suppression.* London, 1850.

Peixoto de Brito. *Considerações geraes sobre a emancipação dos escravos no Imperio do Brazil e indicação dos meios para realisa-la.* Lisbon, 1870.

Perdigão Malheiro, Agostinho Marques, *A escravidão no Brasil: ensaio histórico-juridico-social.* 2 vols. 2nd ed. São Paulo, 1944.

———. *Illegitimidade da propriedade constituida sobre o escravo.* Rio de Janeiro, 1863.

Pereira da Silva, J. M. "Discurso sobre a proposta do governo acerca do elemento servil." *Discursos do Deputado J. M. Pereira da Silva.* Rio de Janeiro, 1872.

Pereira da Silva Guimaraes, Pedro. "Pedro Pereira da Silva Guimaraes (Documentos historicos)." *Revista Trimensal do Instituto do Ceará.* Vol. XX. Place and date of publication unknown.

Pessoa da Silva, José Eloy. *Memoria sobre a escravatura e projecto de colonisação dos europeus, e pretos da Africa no Imperio do Brazil.* Rio de Janeiro, 1826.

Pimenta Bueno, José Antônio, Marquês de São Vicente. *Trabalho sobre a extincção da escravatura no Brasil.* Rio de Janeiro, 1868.

Pimentel, F. L. da C. *Estatutos da Companhia Libertadora ou Reparadora dos direitos da humanidade.* Rio de Janeiro, 1858.

Pinto, Elzeario. *Reformas; emancipação dos escravos.* Salvador da Bahia, 1870.

Prado, Martinho, Jr. *Circular de Prado Junior, candidato republicano á Assembléa Geral pelo 9º districto da Provincia de S. Paulo.* São Paulo, 1884.

Rebello, Henrique Jorge. "Memoria e considerações sobre a população do Brasil." *Revista do Instituto Histórico e Geográfico Brasileiro.* Vol. 30 (1867).

Rebouças, André. "Abolição da miseria." *Revista de Engenharia.* Rio de Janeiro, November 22, 1888.

———. *Agricultura nacional. Estudos economicos. Propaganda abolicionista e democratica.* Rio de Janeiro, 1883.

———. *Diário e notas autobiograficas.* Rio de Janeiro, 1938.

———. *A questão do Brasil; cunho escravocrata do attentado contra a familia imperial.* Lisbon (?), 1889–1890.

Rebouças, Antonio Pereira. *Recordações da vida parlamentar do advogado Antonio Pereira Rebouças.* 2 vols. Rio de Janeiro, 1870.

Reflexões sobre a emancipação em relação á lavoura patria e sobre a mesma lavoura. Bahia, 1871.

Reis, Fabio Alexandrino de Carvalho. *Breves considerações sobre a nossa lavoura.* São Luiz de Maranhão, 1856.

Representação da lavoura de Sergipe aos altos poderes do estado. Rio de Janeiro, 1877.

Representation of the Brazilian Merchants Against the Insults Offered to the Portuguese Flag, and Against the Violent and Oppressive Capture of Several of Their Vessels by Some Officers Belonging to the English Navy. London, 1813.

"Reunião dos proprietarios de escravos em S. Paulo para tratar da libertação dos mesmos em 15 de Dezembro de 1887," in Joaquim Floriano de Godoy. *O elemento servil e as camaras municipaes da provincia de S. Paulo.* Rio de Janeiro, 1887.

Ribeiro da Rocha, Padre M. *Ethiope resgatado, empenhado, sustentado, corrigido, instruido e libertado.* Lisbon, 1758.

Rodrigues de Brito, João. *Cartas economico-politicas sobre a agricultura e commercio da Bahia.* Bahia, 1924.

Sampaio, Antonio Gomes de Azevedo. *Abolicionismo. Um paragrapho. Considerações geraes do movimento anti-esclavista e sua historia limitada a Jacarehy.* São Paulo, 1890.

Soares, Antonio Joaquim Macedo. *Campanha jurídica pela libertação dos escravos (1867–1888).* Rio de Janeiro, 1938.

Soares, Dr. Caetano Alberto. *Memoria para melhorar a sorte dos nossos escravos.* Rio de Janeiro, 1847.

Sociedade Brasileira contra a Escravidão. Banquete offerecido ao Exm. Sr. ministro americano Henry Washington Hilliard, a 20 de Novembro de 1880. Rio de Janeiro, 1880.

Sousa, Carvalho, A. A. "Voto em separado." *Obras Completas de Rui Barbosa.* Vol. XI (Tome I).

Tavares Bastos, A. C. *Cartas do Solitario.* 3rd ed. São Paulo, 1938.

———. *Os males do presente e as esperanças do futuro.* São Paulo, 1939.

———. *A Provincia.* 2nd ed. São Paulo, 1937.

Werneck, Luis Peixoto de Lacerda. *Idéas sobre colonisação precedidas de uma succinta exposição dos principios geraes que regem a população.* Rio de Janeiro, 1855.

Werneck, Manoel Peixoto de Lacerda. *Questão grave. Artigos a proposito do annunciado projecto do Sr. Deputado Joaquim Nabuco, fixando prazo fatal á existencia do elemento servil, publicados no Jornal do Commercio.* Rio de Janeiro, 1880.

IV. TRAVELERS' ACCOUNTS

Agassiz, Louis and Elizabeth Cary, *A Journey in Brazil.* 4th ed. Boston, 1868.

Andrews, C. C. *Brazil, Its Condition and Prospects.* New York, 1887.

Briefe über Brasilien. Frankfurt am Main, 1857.

Burton, Richard. *Explorations of the Highlands of the Brazil.* 2 vols. London, 1869.

Chamberlain, Sir Henry. *Vistas e Costumes da Cidade e arredores do Rio de Janeiro em 1819–1820.* Rio de Janeiro, n.d.

Codman, John. *Ten Months in Brazil.* Boston, 1867.

Debret, J. B. *Voyage pittoresque et historique au Brésil.* 3 vols. Paris, 1834–1839.

Dent, Charles Hastings. *A Year in Brazil.* London, 1886.

Eschwege, W. L. von. *Pluto Brasiliensis.* 2 vols. São Paulo, 1944.

Ewbank, Thomas. *Life in Brazil.* New York, 1856.

Graham, Maria. *Journal of a Voyage to Brazil and Residence There. During Part of the Years 1821, 1822, 1823.* London, 1824.

Hadfield, William. *Brazil and the River Plate 1870–76.* London, 1877.

Hesketh, Robert. "A British Consular Report on Slavery in Northern Brazil," in Lewis Hanke, ed. *History of Latin American Civilization.* Boston, 1967. Vol. II.

Kidder, Daniel P. *Sketches of Residence and Travels in Brazil.* 2 vols. Philadelphia, 1845.

——— and J. C. Fletcher. *Brazil and the Brazilians.* Philadelphia, 1857.

Koster, Henry. *Travels in Brazil.* 2 vols. 2nd ed. London, 1817.

Mawe, John. *Travels in the Interior of Brazil.* London, 1812.

Maximilian I. *Recollections of My Life.* 3 vols. London, 1868.

Nelson, Thomas. *Remarks on the Slavery and Slave Trade of the Brazils.* London, 1846.

Saint-Hilaire, Auguste de. *Viagem à Provincia de São Paulo.* 2nd ed. São Paulo, 1945.

Santa-Anna Nery, Baron de. *The Land of the Amazons.* London, 1901.

Scully, William. *Brazil: Its Provinces and Chief Cities.* London, 1868.

Smith, Herbert H. *Brazil: the Amazons and the Coast.* New York, 1879.

Tschudi, Johann Jakob von. *Reisen durch Südamerika.* Leipzig, 1866.

Van Delden Laërne, C. F. *Brazil and Java. Report on Coffee Culture.* London and The Hague, 1885.

Vincent, Frank. *Around and about South America.* New York, 1890.

Walsh, Robert. *Notices of Brazil in 1828 and 1829.* 2 vols. London, 1830.

V. CONTEMPORARY NEWSPAPERS AND PERIODICALS

O Abolicionista. Orgão da Sociedade Brazileira Contra a Escravidão. Rio de Janeiro, 1880–1881.

Amazonas. Manaus, 1883–1884.

Anglo-Brazilian Times. Rio de Janeiro, 1881.
Associação Central Emancipadora; Rio de Janeiro. Boletin. Rio de Janeiro, 1880–1881.
O Atirador Franco. Rio de Janeiro, 1881.
Brazil. Rio de Janeiro, 1884–1885.
The British and American Mail. Rio de Janeiro, 1878.
O Cearense. Fortaleza, 1878–1879.
Cidade do Rio. Rio de Janeiro, 1887–1888.
Correio Mercantil. Pelôtas, 1887.
Correio Mercantil. Rio de Janeiro, 1850–1851, 1867.
Correio Paulistano. São Paulo, 1887–1888.
O Corsario. Rio de Janeiro, 1880.
O Cruzeiro. Rio de Janeiro, 1878, 1883.
Diario do Brasil. Rio De Janeiro, 1882, 1884.
Diario de Noticias. Rio de Janeiro, 1882.
Diario Oficial. Rio de Janeiro, 1867.
Diario do Rio de Janeiro. Rio de Janeiro, 1854.
Diario de Santos. Santos, São Paulo, 1886–1887.
Gazeta Mineira. São João d'El-Rei, Minas Gerais, 1888.
Gazeta do Norte, Fortaleza, 1880–1881.
Gazeta de Noticias. Rio de Janeiro, 1880, 1885.
Gazeta do Povo. Campos, Rio de Janeiro, 1887.
Gazeta do Povo. São Paulo, 1888.
Gazeta da Tarde. Rio de Janeiro, 1880–1888.
O Grito Nacional. Rio de Janeiro, 1848–1851.
A Idéa Nova. Diamantina, Minas Gerais, 1880.
Jornal do Commercio. Rio de Janeiro, 1880, 1884–1888.
O Libertador. Fortaleza, 1881.
O Monarchista. Rio de Janeiro, 1848.
Novidades. Rio de Janeiro, 1887.
A Onda. São Paulo, 1884.
A Ordem. Baturité, Ceará, 1879.
O Paiz. Rio de Janeiro, 1887.
O Paiz. São Luiz de Maranhão, 1879–1881.
Pedro II. Fortaleza, 1878.
O Philantropo. Rio de Janeiro, 1849–1853.
O Pirassinunga. Pirassinunga, São Paulo, 1888.
O Popular. Porto das Caixas, Rio de Janeiro, 1855.
O Progressista. São João da Barra, Rio de Janeiro, 1887.
A Provincia do Pará. Belém, Pará, 1888.
A Provincia de São Paulo. São Paulo, 1880, 1887–1888.
A Redempção. São Paulo, 1887.
A Reforma: Orgão Democratica. Rio de Janeiro, 1869.
A Reforma. Porto Alegre, 1884.
The Rio News. Rio de Janeiro, 1880–1889.
The South American Journal and Brazil and River Plate Mail. London, 1881–1888.
Vinte e Cinco de Março. Campos, Rio de Janeiro, 1884.

VI. OTHER BOOKS AND ARTICLES

Alden, Dauril. "The Population of Brazil in the Late Eighteenth Century: A Preliminary Study," *Hispanic American Historical Review,* XLIII (1963), 173–205.

Amaral, Luis. *Historia geral da agricultura brasileira no tríplice aspecto politico-social-economico*. 2 vols. São Paulo, 1958.

Attila do Amaral Vieira, Roberto. *Um herói sem pedestal*. Fortaleza, 1958.

Bastide, Roger, and Florestan Fernandes. *Brancos e negros em São Paulo*. 2nd ed. São Paulo, 1959.

Beiguelman, Paula. *Formação politica do Brasil*. 2 vols. São Paulo, 1967.

————. *A formação do povo no complexo cafeeiro: aspectos politicos*. São Paulo, 1968.

Bello, José Maria. *A History of Modern Brazil, 1889–1964*. Stanford, California, 1966.

Bethell, Leslie. *The Abolition of the Brazilian Slave Trade*. Cambridge, England, 1970.

————. "The Independence of Brazil and the Abolition of the Brazilian Slave Trade: Anglo-Brazilian Relations, 1822–1826." *Journal of Latin American Studies*. I, 2 (November 1969), 115–147.

Boehrer, George C. A. *Da monarchia à republica*. Rio de Janeiro, n.d.

Borah, Woodrow, Charles Gibson, and Robert A. Potash. "Colonial Institutions and Contemporary Latin America," in Lewis Hanke, ed. *Readings in Latin American History*. New York, 1966. Vol. II.

Boxer, C. R. *The Golden Age of Brazil, 1695–1750*. Berkeley and Los Angeles, 1964.

————. *Race Relations in the Portuguese Colonial Empire, 1415–1825*. London, 1963.

Bueno de Andrada, Antônio Manoel. "A Abolição em São Paulo." *Revista do Arquivo Municipal*. LXXVII (June–July, 1941), 261–272.

Calógeras, João Pandiá. *A History of Brazil*. New York, 1963.

Cardoso, Fernando Henrique. *Capitalismo e escravidão no Brasil meridional*. São Paulo, 1962.

———— and Octavio Ianni. *Côr e mobilidade social em Florianópolis*. São Paulo, 1960.

Carneiro, Edison. *Ladinos e crioulos*. Rio de Janeiro, 1964.

Conrad, Alfred H. and John R. Meyer. "The Economics of Slavery in the Ante-Bellum South," in Robert William Fogel and Stanley L. Engerman. *The Reinterpretation of American Economic History*. New York, 1971.

Conrad, Robert. "The Brazilian Slave," in Lewis Hanke, ed. *History of Latin American Civilization*. Boston, 1967. Vol. II.

————. "The Contraband Slave Trade to Brazil, 1831–1845." *Hispanic American Historical Review*. XLIX (1969), pp. 618–638.

Corwin, Arthur F. *Spain and the Abolition of Slavery in Cuba, 1817–1886*. Austin, Texas, 1967

Cozart, Toccoa. "Henry W. Hilliard." *Transactions of the Alabama Historical Society*. IV (Montgomery, 1899–1903), 277–299.

Cruz Costa, João. *A History of Ideas in Brazil*. Berkeley and Los Angeles, 1964.

Cruz, Ernesto. *Procissão dos seculos. Vultos e episodios da historia do Pará*. Belém, Pará, 1952.

Curtin, Philip D. *The Atlantic Slave Trade, a Census*. Madison, Wisconsin, 1969.

Davis, David Brion. *The Problem of Slavery in Western Culture*. Ithaca, New York, 1966.

Dean, Warren. *The Industrialization of São Paulo, 1880–1945*. Austin, Texas, 1969.

————. "The Planter as Entrepreneur: The Case of São Paulo." *Hispanic American Historical Review.* Vol. XLVI (1966).

Degler, Carl N. *Neither Black Nor White. Slavery and Race Relations in Brazil and the United States.* New York, 1971.

Dornas Filho, João. *A escravidão no Brasil.* Rio de Janeiro, 1939.

Duque-Estrada, Osorio. *A abolição (esboço historico).* Rio de Janeiro, 1918.

Elkins, Stanley M. *Slavery, A Problem in American Institutional and Intellectual Life.* Chicago, 1959.

Ellis, Alfredo, Jr. *A evolução da economia paulista e suas causas.* São Paulo, 1937.

Fernandes, Florestan. *The Negro in Brazilian Society.* New York, 1969.

Ferreira Soares, Sebastião. *Notas estatisticas sobre a producção agrícola e carestia dos generos alimenticios no Imperio do Brasil.* Rio de Janeiro, 1860.

Fogel, Robert William, and Stanley L. Engerman. "The Economics of Slavery," in Fogel and Engerman. *The Reinterpretation of American Economic History.* New York, 1971.

Freire, Jorge. *Notas a margem da abolição.* Mossoró, Rio Grande do Norte, 1955.

Freyre, Gilberto. *O escravo nos anuncios de jornais brasileiros do seculo xix.* Recife, 1963.

————. *The Mansions and the Shanties.* New York, 1963.

————. *The Masters and the Slaves.* New York, 1946.

————. *Order and Progress.* New York, 1970.

Furtado, Celso. *The Economic Growth of Brazil.* Berkeley and Los Angeles, 1968.

Genovese, Eugene D. *The World the Slaveholders Made.* New York, 1969.

Girão, Raimundo. *A abolição no Ceará.* Fortaleza, 1956.

Gontijo de Carvalho, Antônio. "Prefacio." *Obras Completas de Rui Barbosa.* Vol. I (Tome I).

Gomes, Alfredo. "Achegas para a história do tráfico africano no Brasil—Aspectos numericos." *IV Congresso de Historia Nacional.* Rio de Janeiro, 1950. V, 29–78.

Goulart, Mauricio. *Escravidão africana no Brasil.* 2nd ed. São Paulo, n.d.

Gouveia, Maurilio de. *Historia da escravidão.* Rio de Janeiro, 1955.

Graham, Richard. "Brazilian Slavery Re-examined: A Review Article." *Journal of Social History.* 3 (1970), 431–453.

————. *Britain and the Onset of Modernization in Brazil, 1850–1914.* Cambridge, England, 1968.

————. "Causes for the Abolition of Negro Slavery in Brazil: An Interpretive Essay." *Hispanic American Historical Review.* XLVI (1966), 123–137.

————. "Landowners and the Overthrow of the Empire." *Luso-Brazilian Review.* VII (1970), 44–56.

Harris, Marvin. *Patterns of Race in the Americas.* New York, 1964.

Hollowood, Bernard. *The Story of Morro Velho.* London, 1955.

Ianni, Octavio. *As metamorfoses do escravo.* São Paulo, 1962.

Klein, Herbert S. "The Colored Freedmen in Brazilian Slave Society." *Journal of Social History.* 3 (1970), 30–52.

————. *Slavery in the Americas: A Comparative Study of Virginia and Cuba.* Chicago, 1967.

Kolinski, Charles J. *Independence or Death, The Story of the Paraguayan War.* Gainesville, Florida, 1965.
Knight, Franklin W. *Slave Society in Cuba.* Madison, Wisconsin, 1970.
Lombardi, John V. *The Decline and Abolition of Negro Slavery in Venezuela, 1820–1854.* Westport, Connecticut, 1971
Lowrie, Samuel Harman. "O elemento negro na população de São Paulo." *Revista do Arquivo Municipal.* XLVIII (São Paulo, 1938), 5–56.
Luna, Luiz. *O negro na luta contra a escravidão.* Rio de Janeiro, 1968.
Luz, Nícia Vilela. *A luta pela industrialização do Brasil.* São Paulo, 1961.
Lyra, Heitor. *Historia de Dom Pedro II.* 3 vols. São Paulo, 1938–1940.
Manchester, Alan K. *British Preëminence in Brazil, Its Rise and Decline.* Chapel Hill, North Carolina, 1933.
Marchant, Alexander. *From Barter to Slavery.* Baltimore, Maryland, 1942.
Martin, Percy Alvin. "Slavery and Abolition in Brazil." *Hispanic American Historical Review.* XIII (1933), 151–196.
Milliet, Sergio. *Roteiro do café.* São Paulo, 1939.
Mörner, Magnus. *Race Mixture in the History of Latin America.* Boston, 1967.
Moraes, Evaristo de. *A campanha abolicionista (1879–1888).* Rio de Janeiro, 1924.
———. *A escravidão africana no Brasil das origens a extinção.* São Paulo, 1933.
———. *A lei do Ventre Livre (ensaio de historia parlamentar).* Rio de Janeiro, 1917.
Morél, Edmar. *Dragão do mar—O jangadeiro da abolição.* Rio de Janeiro, 1949.
———. *Vendaval da liberdade.* Rio de Janeiro, 1967.
Morse, Richard M., ed. *The Bandeirantes.* New York, 1965.
———. *From Community to Metropolis.* Gainesville, Florida, 1958.
———. "The Negro in São Paulo, Brazil." *The Journal of Negro History.* Vol. 38 (1953).
Mortara, Giorgio. *Characteristics of the Demographic Structure of the American Countries.* Washington, 1964.
———. "Demographic Studies in Brazil," in Philip M. Hauser and Otis Dudley, eds. *The Study of Population, An Inventory and Appraisal.* Chicago, 1959.
Nabuco, Carolina. *The Life of Joaquim Nabuco.* Stanford, California, 1950.
Nabuco, Joaquim. *Um estadista do Imperio.* 4 vols. São Paulo, 1949.
———. *Minha formação.* São Paulo, 1947.
"Negro Slavery in Brazil," in Lewis Hanke, ed. *History of Latin American Civilization.* Boston, 1967. Vol. II.
Nina Rodrigues, Raimundo. *Os africanos no Brasil.* São Paulo, 1935.
80 Anos de Abolição. Rio de Janeiro, 1968.
Orico, Osvaldo. *O tigre da abolição.* Rio de Janeiro, 1956.
Osofsky, Gilbert. *Puttin' on Ole Massa.* New York, 1969.
Pereira Costa, Francisco Augusto. "A idea abolicionista em Pernambuco." *Revista do Instituto Arqueológico, Histórico e Geográfico de Pernambuco.* No. 42 (Recife, October, 1891).
Pires de Almeida, Benedicto. "Tietê, os escravos e a abolição." *Revista do Arquivo Municipal.* Vol. XCV (São Paulo, 1944).
Poppino, Rollie E. *Brazil, The Land and People.* New York, 1968.
Prado, Caio, Jr. *The Colonial Background of Modern Brazil.* Berkeley and Los Angeles, 1967.

————. *Evolução politica do Brasil e outros estudos.* 4th ed. São Paulo, 1963.

Ramos, Artur. "Castigos de escravos." *Revista do Arquivo Municipal.* Vol. XLVII (São Paulo, 1938).

Rio Branco, Barão do. *Efemérides brasileiras.* Rio de Janeiro, 1946.

Rios, José Arthur. "The Development of Interest in Agrarian Reform in Brazil," in T. Lynn Smith, ed. *Agrarian Reform in Latin America.* New York, 1967.

Rodrigues, José Honório. *Brasil e Africa: outro horizonte.* Rio de Janeiro, 1961.

————. "Brasil e extremo oriente." *Politica Externa Independente.* Ano 1, No. 2 (August 1965).

Salzano, Francisco M. and Newton Freire-Maia. *Problems in Human Biology, A Study of Brazilian Populations.* Detroit, Michigan, 1970.

Santos, José Maria dos. *Os republicanos paulistas e a abolição.* Rio de Janeiro, 1942.

Sayers, Raymond S. *The Negro in Brazilian Literature.* New York, 1956.

Segismundo, Fernando. *Imprensa brasileira, Vultos e problemas.* São Paulo, 1962.

Simonsen, Roberto. "Aspectos da história econômica do café." *Anais do Terceiro Congresso de Historia Nacional.* Rio de Janeiro, 1941. IV, 211–299.

Skidmore, Thomas E. "The Death of Brazilian Slavery, 1866–88," in Frederick B. Pike, ed. *Latin American History: Select Problems.* New York, 1969.

Smith, T. Lynn. *Agrarian Reform in Latin America.* New York, 1967.

————. *Brazil. People and Institutions.* Baton Rouge, Louisiana, 1963.

Sodré, Alcindo. "O elemento servil—A abolição," *Anais do Terceiro Congresso de Historia Nacional.* Rio de Janeiro, 1941. IV, 51–146.

Stein, Stanley J. *The Brazilian Cotton Manufacture. Textile Enterprise in an Underdeveloped Area 1850–1950.* Cambridge, Massachusetts, 1957.

————. *Vassouras: A Brazilian Coffee County, 1850–1900.* Cambridge, Massachusetts, 1957.

———— and Barbara H. Stein. *The Colonial Heritage of Latin America.* New York, 1970.

Tannenbaum, Frank. *Slave and Citizen: The Negro in the Americas.* New York, 1947

Taunay, Affonso de E. *Pequena historia do café no Brasil, 1727–1937.* Rio de Janeiro, 1945

————. "Subsidios para a história do tráfico africano no Brasil," *Anais do Museu Paulista.* X (1941), 5–311.

Taylor, A. A. "The Movement of Negroes from the East to the Gulf States from 1830 to 1850." *The Journal of Negro History.* Vol. 8 (1923).

Toplin, Robert Brent. "Upheaval, Violence, and the Abolition of Slavery in Brazil: The Case of São Paulo." *Hispanic American Historical Review.* XLIX (1969), 639–655.

Verger, Pierre. *Flux et reflux de la traite des nègres entre le golfe de Bénin et Bahia de Todos os Santos.* Paris, 1968.

Verissimo, Ignacio José. *André Rebouças através de sua auto-biografia.* Rio de Janeiro, 1939

Viotti da Costa, Emilia. *Da senzala à colônia.* São Paulo, 1966.

Wade, Richard C. *Slavery in the Cities: The South 1820–1860.* New York, 1964.

Wagley, Charles. *Amazon Town: A Study of Man in the Tropics.* New York, 1953.

Williams, Mary Wilhelmine. *Dom Pedro the Magnanimous, Second Emperor of Brazil.* Chapel Hill, North Carolina, 1937.

VII. REFERENCES AND BIBLIOGRAPHY

Freitas, Affonso A. de. *A imprensa periodica de São Paulo desde seus primordios em 1823 até 1915.* São Paulo, 1915.

Lowrie, Samuel H. "Bibliographical Sources Concerning Population Statistics in the State of São Paulo, Brazil." *Handbook of Latin American Studies* (1937). Cambridge, Massachusetts, 1938.

Sacramento Blake, Augusto Victorino. *Diccionario Bibliographico Brasileiro.* 7 vols. Rio de Janeiro, 1883–1902.

VIII. UNPUBLISHED Ph.D. DISSERTATIONS

Conrad, Robert. "The Struggle for the Abolition of the Brazilian Slave Trade: 1808–1853." Columbia University, 1967.

Evanson, Philip Norman. "The Liberal Party and Reform in Brazil, 1860–1889." University of Virginia, 1969.

Toplin, Robert Brent. "The Movement for the Abolition of Slavery in Brazil." Rutgers University, 1968.

INDEX

Abaeté, Viscount, 77
Abolicionista, O (Rio de Janeiro), 83, 142, 146 n. 46, 147, 151; establishment of, 140; denunciation of latifundia by, 161
Abolition bill. *See* Golden Law
Abolitionist Confederation. *See* Confederação Abolicionista
Abolitionist movement, 135–163, 276; slowness to develop in Brazil, xv, 17, 46; early manifestations of, 17–19, 27, 45, 68, 176; in Ceará, 56, 57, 113, 125–126, 150, 174, 176–182, 186–189; moderate phase of (1860's), 70–71, 72, 81–85, 93–94; opposition to, 77–81, 136, 142–143, 163–169, 181–182, 184, 197–198, 210–212, 216–219; in law faculties, 84, 149–150, 155, 197; in São Paulo, 84–85, 127, 128–130, 149–150, 155, 184, 197, 239–262 *passim;* in northern provinces, 56, 57, 81, 84, 92, 113, 122–126, 135 n., 146, 149, 150, 156, 174, 176–182, 186–189, 191, 199–204, 236–237; in Amazonas, 81, 125, 199–204; in Pernambuco, 81, 125, 126, 156, 190, 236–237; in Bahia, 84, 125, 135 n., 149; in Spain, 126–127 n.; in Puerto Rico, 126–127 n.; in cities, 127, 143, 146, 188, 190, 191, 192, 194–197, 202, 207–209, 244; effect of on slave prices, 131–132, 211; in General Assembly, 135–137, 138–139, 156, 193, 213–214, 219–220, 240; organizations of, 137–140, 143, 149–151, 154, 169, 176–177, 184, 186–187, 190, 193, 200–202, 207–209; weakness of, 143–146, 169, 183; in rural areas, 143, 146, 243–244; reluctance of Negroes to join, 144; in schools, 84, 146, 149–150, 155, 193–194, 196, 197, 202; weak financial support of, 146, 148, 151; leadership of, 147, 151–156, 196–197, 242–244; in Rio Grande do Sul, 149, 204–209; in Rio Grande do Norte, 149; in Minas Gerais, 149; in Maranhão, 149; and runaway movement, 155, 163, 189–190, 239–240, 242–244; goals of, 156–163, 276; nature of, 156–157; demise of, 158, 277; in-

volvement of Brazilian army in, 177, 179, 187, 193, 201–202, 218–219; in Goiás, 190–191; in Pará, 191, 269; in Piauí, 191; in Paraná, 191, 242 n., 273; in Município Neutro, 127, 148–149, 191–192, 193–197, 235–236, 264; "eclipsed" by Saraiva-Cotegipe Law, 231; in Santos, 239–241; postabolition goals of, 276
Abolitionists, 39, 41, 45, 68, 77–78, 81–85, 135–162, 176–182, 189–198, 200–203, 207–209, 242–244, 274; goals of, xviii, 156–163, 276; publications of, 81, 83–85, 94 n., 140–141, 146 n., 46, 147–153, 155–156; newspapers of, 83–84, 85, 140–141, 147–150, 156–157, 177, 184, 206, 231–232, 242–243; meetings of, 137–138, 148–156; motivation of, 145–147, 234–235; professions of, 146–147, 243; methods of, 163, 184, 186, 200–203, 239–240; defeated in elections of 1881, 144–145, 168–169
Africans: proposed colonization of in Brazil, 36–37 (see also *Bens do evento, Emancipados,* Negroes, Slave trade [international], Slaves); employment of as contract laborers, 37; illegal enslavement of, 40–44, 45, 114, 167, 215–216; in São Paulo, 13, 155; liberation of by Luiz Gama, 155; false registration of, 215–216, 230; number recorded in 1872 census, 216 n.
Agostini, Angelo, 147
Agrarian reform. *See* Land reform
Albuquerque, Lourenço de, 237–238, 272
Albuquerque Barros, José Julio de, 205, 209
Alencar, José de, 98, 99
Alencar Araripe, Tristão de, 102
Amaral, José do, 178, 181
Amazonas: abolitionism in, 81, 125, 199–204; Indians in, 199, 204; slaves in, 125, 199; rubber industry in, 199; abolitionist organizations in, 200–201; emancipation of slaves in capital of, 202–203
Andrada e Silva, José Bonifacio de (the elder), 18, 24, 136, 139, 140

335